First World War
and Army of Occupation
War Diary
France, Belgium and Germany

9 DIVISION
Divisional Troops
64 Field Company Royal Engineers
11 May 1915 - 30 September 1919

WO95/1755

The Naval & Military Press Ltd
www.nmarchive.com
Published in association with The National Archives

Published by

The Naval & Military Press Ltd

Unit 10 Ridgewood Industrial Park,

Uckfield, East Sussex,

TN22 5QE England

Tel: +44 (0) 1825 749494

www.naval-military-press.com

www.nmarchive.com

This diary has been reprinted in facsimile from the original. Any imperfections are inevitably reproduced and the quality may fall short of modern type and cartographic standards.

© **Crown Copyright**
Images reproduced by permission of The National Archives, London, England, 2015.

Contents

Document type	Place/Title	Date From	Date To
Heading	9th Division. 64th Field Coy. R.E. May 1915-1919 Sep.		
Heading	64th Field Company R.E. (9th Division). May 1915.		
Heading	9th Division 64th Field Coy. R.E. Vol 1 11-31.5.15.		
Heading	Title Page Of War Diary. Of 64th Field Co. R.E. From 11th May 1915 To 31st May 1915. (Consisting Of 5 Sheets).		
War Diary	Bordon.	11/05/1915	11/05/1915
War Diary	Southampton Dock.	11/05/1915	11/05/1915
War Diary	Havre.	12/05/1915	12/05/1915
War Diary	Southampton.	11/05/1915	11/05/1915
War Diary	Havre.	12/05/1915	13/05/1915
War Diary	Rouen.	13/05/1915	13/05/1915
War Diary	St Omer.	14/05/1915	14/05/1915
War Diary	Wiserne.	14/05/1915	14/05/1915
War Diary	Pihem.	14/05/1915	16/05/1915
War Diary	Abbaye Wostein.	16/05/1915	17/05/1915
War Diary	Le Verrier.	17/05/1915	19/05/1915
War Diary	Steenwerck	19/05/1915	19/05/1915
War Diary	L'Hallobeau.	19/05/1915	28/05/1915
War Diary	Letouquet.	28/05/1915	28/05/1915
War Diary	Pont Ballot.	28/05/1915	28/05/1915
War Diary	L'Hallobeau.	29/05/1915	31/05/1915
Miscellaneous	Billets In Pihem. 14/5/15 To.	14/05/1915	14/05/1915
Operation(al) Order(s)	27th Infantry Order No.2. App. 2.	16/05/1915	16/05/1915
Miscellaneous	March Table. Issued With 9th. Division Order No.2d/16/5/15. Ap. 3.	16/05/1915	16/05/1915
Miscellaneous	March Table. Issued With 9th. Division Order No.2. D/16/5/15.	16/05/1915	16/05/1915
Miscellaneous	64 G. Re. Billets 16.5.15. A 3a.	16/05/1915	16/05/1915
Operation(al) Order(s)	27th Inf. Bde Order No.3. Ref Map A 5. Scale 1/100,000. A. 4.	16/05/1915	16/05/1915
Miscellaneous	March Table. Issued With 9th. Division Order No.3. D/16/5/15.	16/05/1915	16/05/1915
Miscellaneous	64 Co. R.E. Billets 17.5.15. Le Verrier. A.5.	17/05/1915	17/05/1915
Diagram etc	Le Touquet Station Works. A7.		
Diagram etc	Ref:- C286 012 1/2000 Map A 8.		
Heading	64th Field Company R.E. (9th Division) June 1915.		
Heading	9th. Division. 64th 7.C.R.E. Vol: II. 1-30.6.15.		
War Diary	L'Hallobeau Ref A 1/20,000 Map. B2b.a.	01/06/1915	03/06/1915
War Diary	L'Hallobeau.	04/06/1915	07/06/1915
War Diary	Hamet Billet.	08/06/1915	25/06/1915
War Diary	Lespesses.	26/06/1915	28/06/1915
War Diary	Lilette (Chateau).	28/06/1915	29/06/1915
War Diary	En Route For Essars.	29/06/1915	29/06/1915
War Diary	Essars.	30/06/1915	30/06/1915
Diagram etc	Ref:- C 286 012 1/2000 Map App A.		
Diagram etc	Hamet Billet 64th Field Co. R.E. App B.		
Operation(al) Order(s)	27th Inf. Brigade Order No.5.	24/06/1915	24/06/1915
Miscellaneous	27th Infantry Bde. 27th I. 28th Infantry Bde.		
Operation(al) Order(s)	27th Infantry Brigade Order No.6. app D	28/06/1915	28/06/1915

Operation(al) Order(s)	27th Infantry Brigade Order No.7 App E.	29/06/1915	29/06/1915
Miscellaneous	C Form (Duplicate). Messages And Signals. App E.		
Heading	64th Field Company R.E. (9th Division) July 1915.		
Heading	9th Division. 64th 7.C.R.E. Vol: III July. 1915.		
War Diary	Essars.	01/07/1915	31/07/1915
Heading	64th Field Company R.E. (9th Division) August 1915.		
Heading	9th Division. 64th 7.C.R.E. Vol: IV August.15.		
War Diary	Le Hamel.	01/08/1915	17/08/1915
War Diary	Essars.	18/08/1915	31/08/1915
Miscellaneous	Appendix A. The Following Notes In Today Our Experience Of Placing The Village Line Is As Tate Of Defence.	21/08/1915	21/08/1915
Miscellaneous	Appendix B. Tramway Rue Del"E pinette-Indian Village.	01/09/1915	01/09/1915
Diagram etc	Rue De L'Epinette Light Railway.		
Heading	64th Field Company R.E. (9th Division) September 1915.		
Heading	9th Division 64th F.C.R.E. Vol 5. Sep 1.15.		
War Diary	Essars.	01/09/1915	04/09/1915
War Diary	Bethune.	05/09/1915	30/09/1915
Heading	64th Field Company R.E. (9th Division) October 1915.		
Heading	9th Division 64. F.C.R.E. Vol.6. Oct.15.		
War Diary	Oblinghem.	01/10/1915	01/10/1915
War Diary	Abeele.	01/10/1915	01/10/1915
War Diary	Dickebusch.	02/10/1915	31/10/1915
Heading	64th Field Company R.E. (9th Division). November 1915.		
Heading	9th Division 64th F.C.R.E. Vol: 7 Nov. 15.		
War Diary	Dickebusch	01/11/1915	30/11/1915
Heading	64th Field Company R.E. (9th Division) December 1915.		
Heading	9th Div. 64th A.C.R.E. Vol: 8.		
War Diary	Dickebusch.	01/12/1915	12/12/1915
War Diary	Caestre Sheet 27 W.3.d.2.1.	13/12/1915	16/12/1915
War Diary	Borre.	17/12/1915	17/12/1915
War Diary	Borre. Sheet 27. V. 18.d.1.6.	18/12/1915	31/12/1915
Heading	War Diary. 64th Field Company Royal Engineers. (9th Division) January 1916.		
Heading	64th. F.C.R.E. Vol: 9 Jan 16.		
War Diary	Borre Sheet 27.V.18.d.1.6.	01/01/1916	02/01/1916
War Diary	Armentieres.	03/01/1916	19/01/1916
War Diary	Plogsteert.	20/01/1916	25/01/1916
War Diary	Dou Dou Farm. Sheet 36 B5.c.76.	26/01/1916	31/01/1916
Heading	War Diary. 64th. Field Company R.E. 9th Division. February 1916.		
War Diary	Plogsteert Doudou Farm Sheet 36 B5.c.76.	01/02/1916	05/02/1916
War Diary	Plogsteert Doudou Farm Sheet 36. B.5.c. 76. 3 Leetins In Billets About Touquet Bertne.	06/02/1916	09/02/1916
War Diary	Plogsteert Doudou Farm.	10/02/1916	13/02/1916
War Diary	Plogsteert Doudou Farm 3 Sheets Advaueed Billets.	14/02/1916	18/02/1916
War Diary	Plogsteert Doudou Farm.	19/02/1916	29/02/1916
Diagram etc	64 Fd Coy. R.E. War Diary February 1916. Appendix.A.		
Diagram etc	64 Fd Coy. R.E. War Diary February 1916 Appendix 1916. Appendix B.		

Heading	War Diary. 64th. Field Company R.E. 9th Division. March 1916.		
War Diary	Ploegsteert H.Q. Dou Dou Farm 3 Sections In Advanced Billets At Plogsteert Houquet Berthe.	01/03/1916	05/03/1916
War Diary	Ploegsteert.	06/03/1916	10/03/1916
War Diary	Plogsteert Doudou Farm 3 Steets In Advd Billets.	11/03/1916	15/03/1916
War Diary	Plogsteert.	16/03/1916	31/03/1916
War Diary	War Diary. 64th. Field Company R.E. 9th. Division. April 1916.		
War Diary	Plogsteert H.Q. Doudou Farm-3 Sections In Advanced Billets In Near Touduet Poerthe.	01/04/1916	07/04/1916
War Diary	Plogsteert Doudou Fm.	08/04/1916	14/04/1916
War Diary	Plogsteert.	15/04/1916	20/04/1916
War Diary	Plogsteert Doudou Fm. 3 Sections In Advd Billets.	21/04/1916	26/04/1916
War Diary	Plogsteert.	27/04/1916	30/04/1916
Miscellaneous	C.R.E. No. 2337. O.C. 63rd Field Coy R.E. 64th Field Coy R.E. 90th Field Coy R.E. Appendix A.	15/04/1916	15/04/1916
Heading	War Diary. 64th. Field Company R.E. 9th. Division. May 1916.		
War Diary	Plogsteert H.Q Doudou Fm 3 Sections In Advd Billets Plogsteert & Touquet Bertne.	01/05/1916	07/05/1916
War Diary	Plogsteert.	08/05/1916	16/05/1916
War Diary	Outersteene Sheet 27 X.28.d.42.	17/05/1916	29/05/1916
War Diary	Sheet 36 A D.25.c.34.	30/05/1916	31/05/1916
Miscellaneous	Report On German Raid On Hampshire T. Locality. 13/5/16. 64th Field Coy. Appendix A. May 1916.	13/05/1916	13/05/1916
Miscellaneous	Report On Effects Of Bombardment On Night May 13th.	17/05/1916	17/05/1916
Heading	War Diary. 64th Field Company R.E. 9th Division. June 1916.		
War Diary	Cuhem.	01/06/1916	16/06/1916
War Diary	Bois Malars Nr. Caipilly On The Somme.	17/06/1916	26/06/1916
War Diary	Near Chipilly.	27/06/1916	30/06/1916
War Diary	Sheet B.2.d.	30/06/1916	30/06/1916
Miscellaneous	Routine Orders By Major-General W.T. Furse, C.B., D.S.O. Commanding, 9th (Scottish) Division. Sunday, 25th June 1916.		
Heading	War Diary. 64th Field Company R.E. 9th Division. July 1916.		
War Diary	Grovetown Sheet B.2.c. L 1.d Control.	01/07/1916	02/07/1916
War Diary	N,End Billon Wood Valley.	03/07/1916	04/07/1916
War Diary	Maldon St. S Of Machine Gun Wood.	05/07/1916	06/07/1916
War Diary	Maldon St.	07/07/1916	14/07/1916
War Diary	Montauban Alley.	15/07/1916	20/07/1916
War Diary	Happy Valley.	21/07/1916	26/07/1916
War Diary	Fre Villers.	27/07/1916	31/07/1916
Diagram etc	Chimney Trench 64 Field Coy R.E. July 1916 App A.		
Miscellaneous	To O.C. 60th Fd RE RE Map ?	11/07/1916	11/07/1916
Miscellaneous	Memo	14/07/1916	14/07/1916
Miscellaneous	? Order For 16/7/16	16/07/1916	16/07/1916
Miscellaneous	Messages And Signals. App E.		
Map	App E.		
Miscellaneous	O.C. 63rd Company, R.E. O.C. 64th Company, R.E. O.C. 90th Company, R.E. 64 Field Coy R.E. July 1916. App F.	20/06/1916	20/06/1916

Miscellaneous	9th Divn. No. 14/8842. Preliminary Instructions No.3 Regarding. Forthcoming Operations.	21/06/1916	21/06/1916
Miscellaneous	64 Fd Coy RE	22/06/1916	22/06/1916
Miscellaneous	Instructions No.2 Regarding Forthcoming Operations.	27/06/1916	27/06/1916
Miscellaneous	Headquarters, 1st S.A. Infantry Brigade, 30th June 1916. R.M. 47/28/13/10. Instructions No.3. Regarding Forthcoming Operations.	30/06/1916	30/06/1916
Miscellaneous	Information From 18th Division. Initial Distribution.	22/06/1916	22/06/1916
Operation(al) Order(s)	O.C. 63rd Company, R.E.	29/06/1916	29/06/1916
Miscellaneous	Para 9 Of 30th Division O.O. No.19.	30/06/1916	30/06/1916
Miscellaneous	Disposition Of R.E. And Pioneers. Appendix C.		
Miscellaneous	Affiliation. Strength etc. of Parties Place of Assembly		
Miscellaneous	Communications To Be Opened Up In Advance Of Our Present Front. Line.		
Miscellaneous	64th Field Coy. R.E.	05/07/1916	05/07/1916
Miscellaneous	Briqueterie.	02/04/1917	02/04/1917
Map			
Operation(al) Order(s)	1st South African Infantry Brigade. Operation Order No.39.	30/06/1916	30/06/1916
Operation(al) Order(s)	1st South African Infantry Brigade. Operation Order No.41.	02/07/1916	02/07/1916
Operation(al) Order(s)	1st South African Infantry Brigade. Operation Order No.42.	04/07/1916	04/07/1916
Operation(al) Order(s)	1st South African Infantry Brigade. Operation Order No.43.	06/07/1916	06/07/1916
Operation(al) Order(s)	Headquarters. 1st S.A. Infantry Brigade. Operation Order No.43.		
Operation(al) Order(s)	1st South African Infantry Brigade. Operation Order No.44.	08/07/1916	08/07/1916
Operation(al) Order(s)	1st South African Infantry Brigade Operation Order No.46.	10/07/1916	10/07/1916
Miscellaneous	Headquarters, 1st S.A. Infantry Brigade. 9	10/07/1916	10/07/1916
Map	Montauban.		
Miscellaneous	Trench Map. Montauban. 64 Field Coy Bde July 1916 Appendix K.		
Heading	64th. Field Company R.E. 9th. Division. August 1916.		
War Diary	Frevillers.	01/08/1916	11/08/1916
War Diary	Villers-Au-Bois.	12/08/1916	31/08/1916
Miscellaneous	C.R.E. No.B.101/6.	11/08/1916	11/08/1916
Miscellaneous	16-20" ?		
Miscellaneous	C.R.E. B 35/5.	11/08/1916	11/08/1916
Heading	64th. Field Company R.E. 9th. Division. September 1916.		
War Diary	Villers-Au-Bois.	01/09/1916	23/09/1916
Miscellaneous	63 Field Coy. A.	21/09/1916	21/09/1916
Miscellaneous	O.C. 63rd Coy.	22/09/1916	22/09/1916
War Diary		08/09/1916	23/09/1916
Miscellaneous	Relief Table.		
Operation(al) Order(s)	9th Divisional Engineers Operations Orders No.6.	22/09/1916	22/09/1916
Miscellaneous	March Table.		
Operation(al) Order(s)	1st South African Infantry Brigade Operation Order 59.	23/09/1916	23/09/1916
Miscellaneous	March Table To Be Substituted For One Sent Out With 1st South African Infantry Brigade Operation Order No.59.		
Heading	64th. Field Company R.E. 9th. Division. October 1916.		
War Diary	Villers Au Bois.	24/09/1916	30/09/1916

Type	Description	Start	End
War Diary	Houvin Houvigneul.	01/10/1916	05/10/1916
War Diary	Boffles.	06/10/1916	09/10/1916
War Diary	Bazentin-Le-Brand.	10/10/1916	26/10/1916
War Diary	Millencourt.	27/10/1916	31/10/1916
Heading	64th. Field Company R.E. 9th. Division. November 1916.		
Miscellaneous	Confidential 9th Division.	03/11/1916	03/11/1916
War Diary	Arras.	01/11/1916	20/11/1916
War Diary	Manquetin.	21/11/1916	26/11/1916
War Diary	Simencourt.	27/11/1916	30/11/1916
Heading	64th. Field Company R.E. 9th. Division. December 1916.		
Miscellaneous	Adjt Nr 9th Div. S.21.	01/12/1916	01/12/1916
War Diary	Simencourt.	01/12/1916	03/12/1916
War Diary	Arras.	04/12/1916	31/12/1916
Miscellaneous	63rd Field Coy R.E. 64th Field Coy R.E. 90th Field Coy R.E. B 207/1.	01/12/1916	01/12/1916
Operation(al) Order(s)	9th Divisional Engineers Operation Order No.11.	01/12/1916	01/12/1916
Miscellaneous	March & Relief Table.		
Heading	Jan-March 1917.		
War Diary	Arras.	01/01/1917	31/01/1917
Miscellaneous	Small "A" Frames-Reasons For Their Adoption.	02/01/1917	02/01/1917
War Diary	Arras.	02/02/1917	31/03/1917
Heading	9th Division. 64th Field Coy. Royal Engineers April 1917.		
War Diary	Arras.	01/04/1917	03/04/1917
War Diary	St. Nicholas	04/04/1917	11/04/1917
War Diary	Blangy.	12/04/1917	20/04/1917
War Diary	Arras.	21/04/1917	29/04/1917
War Diary	H.7.b. Cost.	30/04/1917	30/04/1917
Operation(al) Order(s)	D. 9/2. 9th Divisional Engineers Operation Order No.1. Appendix A.	08/04/1917	08/04/1917
Miscellaneous	Orders By O.C. 64th Field Coy. R.E. Appendix B.	08/04/1917	08/04/1917
Miscellaneous	O.C. 64th Field Coy R.E. Appendix C.	09/04/1917	09/04/1917
Diagram etc	Strong-Point At 1"Abbayette.		
Heading	May 1917 64 Field Co Royal Engineers.		
War Diary	H.7.B. Control.	01/05/1917	10/05/1917
War Diary	Y Huts.	11/05/1917	11/05/1917
War Diary	Moncheaux	12/05/1917	12/05/1917
War Diary	Lathieuloye.	13/05/1917	31/05/1917
Miscellaneous	A Form. Messages And Signals.		
Miscellaneous	D.107. O.C. 63rd Field Coy. R.E. O.C. 64th Field Coy. R.E. O.C. 90th Field Coy. R.E. O.C. 9th Seaforths (Pioneers). Appendix B.	06/05/1917	06/05/1917
Operation(al) Order(s)	C.R.E. Operation Order No.D.125. Appendix C.	09/05/1917	09/05/1917
Operation(al) Order(s)	26th. Brigade Operation Order No.116. Appendix D.	10/05/1917	10/05/1917
Miscellaneous	March Table For March 12th.		
Miscellaneous	9th Division R.E. Operation Order. Appendix E.	12/05/1917	12/05/1917
Miscellaneous	Programme Of Training 64th Field Coy. R.E. Appendix.F.	16/05/1917	16/05/1917
Miscellaneous	Programme Of Training 64th Field Coy. R.E. At Appendix G.	23/05/1917	23/05/1917
Heading	June 1917 64 Field Co. Royal Engineers.		
War Diary		01/06/1917	30/06/1917
Operation(al) Order(s)	9th Divisional Engineers Operation Order No.D.154. Appendix A.	28/05/1917	28/05/1917

Miscellaneous	Appendix. Issued In Connection With 9th Divl. Engineers Operation Order No.D.154.		
Miscellaneous	With Reference To 9th Divisional Engineers Operation Order D.180 Of 9/6/17. Appendix B.	09/06/1917	09/06/1917
Operation(al) Order(s)	Addendum To 9th Divisional Engineers Operation Order D.180 Of 9/6/17.	09/06/1917	09/06/1917
Miscellaneous	9th Divisional Engineers Operation Order Ref. Map: Arras, Edition 6A. 1/10,000.	09/06/1917	09/06/1917
Miscellaneous	O.C. 64th Field Coy. R.E. Appendix C.	13/06/1917	13/06/1917
Heading	July 1917.		
War Diary	St. Laurent Blangy.	01/07/1917	19/07/1917
War Diary	Fosseux.	20/07/1917	25/07/1917
War Diary	Ruyaulcourt	26/07/1917	29/07/1917
Miscellaneous	O.C. 63rd Field Coy. R.E. Appendix A.	01/07/1917	01/07/1917
Miscellaneous	Appendix B.	30/06/1917	30/06/1917
Miscellaneous	C Form. Messages And Signals. Appendix C.		
Miscellaneous	C Form. Messages And Signals.		
Miscellaneous	O.C. 90th Field Coy. R.E., Chateau Grounds, St. Laurent Blangy. Appendix D.	10/07/1917	10/07/1917
Miscellaneous	C Form. Messages And Signals.		
Miscellaneous	9th Divisional Engineers. Warning Order. D218/1. Appendix F.	21/07/1917	21/07/1917
Miscellaneous	March Table.		
Operation(al) Order(s)	26th. Infantry Brigade Operation Order No.127. Appendix G.	22/07/1917	22/07/1917
Miscellaneous	Transport March Table "A". Starting.		
Miscellaneous	Table "B" (1). Railway Moves For July 25th. Detraining Station Bapaum.		
Miscellaneous	Table "B" (2) Railway Moves For July 25th.		
Miscellaneous	March Table "C".		
Heading	August 1917.		
War Diary	Ruyaulcourt.	02/08/1917	31/08/1917
Miscellaneous	9th Divisional Engineers Operation Order No. D. 289. By Major S.W.S. Hamilton, D.S.O., R.E. A/C.R.E., 9th (Scottish) Division. Appendix A.	25/08/1917	25/08/1917
Diagram etc	Dugout In Platoon Locality. Appendix B.		
Heading	Sept 1917.		
War Diary	Gomiecourt.	01/09/1917	30/09/1917
Miscellaneous	Messages And Signals.		
Operation(al) Order(s)	9th Divisional Engineers Operation Order D.331 By Lieut-Colonel G.R. Hearn, D.S.O. R.E. C.R.E., 9th Division. Appendix B.	14/09/1917	14/09/1917
Miscellaneous	O.C. 64th Field Coy. R.E. Appendix C.	14/09/1917	14/09/1917
Miscellaneous	C.R.E. 9th Divn. Appendix D.		
Miscellaneous	C.R.E. 9th Divn. Appendix E.	15/09/1917	15/09/1917
Miscellaneous	D.350/1. Instructions For The Offensive For 9th Divisional Engineers And 9th Seaforth Highrs. (Pioneers) By Lieut-Colonel G.R. Hearn, D.S.O., R.E. C.R.E., 9th Division. Appendix F.	17/09/1917	17/09/1917
Operation(al) Order(s)	9th Divisional Engineers Operation Order No.D.372. By Lieut-Colonel G.R. Hearn, D.S.O., R.E. Appendix G.	19/09/1917	19/09/1917
Miscellaneous	A Form. Messages And Signals.		
Operation(al) Order(s)	9th Divisional Engineers Operation Order No.D.380. By Lieut-Colonel G.R. Hearn, D.S.O., R.E. C.R.E., 9th Division. Appendix J.	21/09/1917	21/09/1917

Miscellaneous	OR. 64th (Fd) Co. R.E. Appendix K.	21/09/1917	21/09/1917
Miscellaneous	O.C. 64th Fd. Co R.E. Appendix L.	23/09/1917	23/09/1917
Miscellaneous	C Form (Duplicate). Messages And Signals.		
Miscellaneous	C Form. Messages And Signals.		
Miscellaneous	Knight, Hindle, No 4 Owen, Thomas No 4		
Miscellaneous	C Form. Messages And Signals.		
Miscellaneous	25 64 Fed Coy R.E.		
Operation(al) Order(s)	9th Divisional Engineers Operation Order D.397 By Lieut-Colonel G.R. Hearn, D.S.O., R.E. C.R.E., 9th Division. Reference Maps: Sheets 19 And 27. Appendix P.	29/09/1917	29/09/1917
Heading	October 1917 64 Field Co Royal Engineers.		
War Diary	Ledringhem.	01/10/1917	31/10/1917
Miscellaneous	Urgent. O.C. 63rd Field Coy. R.E. O.C. 64th Field Coy. R.E. O.C. 90th Field Coy. R.E. Appendix A.	30/09/1917	30/09/1917
Miscellaneous		03/10/1917	03/10/1917
Miscellaneous	9th Divisional Engineers. Officers Training Course. Appendix C.	03/10/1917	03/10/1917
Operation(al) Order(s)	9th Divisional Engineers Operation Order D.411 By Lieut-Colonel G.R. Hearn, D.S.O., R.E. C.R.E. 9th Division. Reference 1/100,000 Map 5A. Appendix C.	06/10/1917	06/10/1917
Operation(al) Order(s)	9th Divisional Engineers Warning Order D.410. By Lieut-Colonel G.R. Hearn, D.S.O., R.E. C.R.E., 9th Division. Reference 1/100,000 Map 5A.	05/10/1917	05/10/1917
Miscellaneous	A Form Messages And Signals.		
Miscellaneous	A Form. Messages And Signals. Appendix G.		
Miscellaneous	O.C. 63rd Field Coy. R.E. O.C. 64th Field Coy. R.E. O.C. 90th Field Coy. R.E. Appendix H.	07/10/1917	07/10/1917
Miscellaneous	9th. Division No. QS/14. Administrative Instructions Issued In Connection With 9th. Division Operation Order No.154 Of 5th. October 1917. D 412.	06/10/1917	06/10/1917
Miscellaneous	Table Of Train Arrangements For Move Of 9th. Division. Table "A".		
Miscellaneous	26th. Infantry Brigade. Omnibus Train.-Esquebecq To Vlaeertinghe. Table. "B (1)".		
Miscellaneous	27th. Infantry Brigade. Omnibus Train.-Esquelbecq To Vlaeertinghe. Table "B (2)".		
Operation(al) Order(s)	C.R.E.'s Operation Order No.1.	28/10/1917	28/10/1917
Miscellaneous	Appendix J.		
Heading	November 1917.		
War Diary	Surrey Camp	01/11/1917	14/11/1917
War Diary	Surrey Camp Uxem.	15/11/1917	15/11/1917
War Diary	Uxem Wormhoudt.	16/11/1917	16/11/1917
War Diary	Wormhoudt Zermezeele.	17/11/1917	17/11/1917
War Diary	Zermezeele Bandringhem.	18/11/1917	18/11/1917
War Diary	Bandringhem Recquerrewck.	19/11/1917	19/11/1917
War Diary	Recquebreuck Rollez.	20/11/1917	20/11/1917
War Diary	Rollez.	21/11/1917	22/11/1917
War Diary	Rollez Planques. (Lens 11).	22/11/1917	22/11/1917
War Diary	Planques.	23/11/1917	23/11/1917
War Diary	Planques Wismes. (Hazebrouck. 5A).	24/11/1917	24/11/1917
War Diary	Wismes Coin Perdu.	25/11/1917	25/11/1917
War Diary	Coin Perdu.	25/11/1917	30/11/1917
War Diary	Heudecourt.	13/11/1917	31/11/1917
Heading	Dec 1917.		
War Diary	Coin Perdu.	01/12/1917	01/12/1917

Type	Description	Start	End
War Diary	Senlis.	02/12/1917	04/12/1917
War Diary	Heudecourt.	05/12/1917	13/12/1917
Miscellaneous	A Form. Messages And Signals.		
Miscellaneous	A Form. Messages And Signals.	30/11/1917	30/11/1917
Miscellaneous	A Form. Messages And Signals.		
Operation(al) Order(s)	9th Divisional Engineers Operation Order No.D.529 By Lieut-Colonel G.R. Hearn, D.S.O., R.E. C.R.E., 9th Division.	30/11/1917	30/11/1917
Miscellaneous	A Form. Messages And Signals.		
Operation(al) Order(s)	9th Divisional Engineers Warning Order D.537. By Lieut-Colonel G.R. Hearn, D.S.O., R.E. C.R.E. 9th Division.	04/12/1917	04/12/1917
Heading	Jan 1918.		
War Diary	Fins.	01/01/1918	29/01/1918
War Diary	Bray.	30/01/1918	31/01/1918
Operation(al) Order(s)	9th Divisional Engineers Operation Order No.E.20. By Major A.E. Bruce Fielding, R.E. A/C.R.E., 9th Division. Ref Map 57.C.	12/01/1918	12/01/1918
Operation(al) Order(s)	26th (Highland) Brigade Operation Order No.180.	28/01/1918	28/01/1918
Miscellaneous	Movement Table "A" To Accompany Operation Order No.180.		
Miscellaneous	Movement Table "B" To Accompany Operation Order No.180.		
Miscellaneous	Transport Movement Table "C" To Accompany Operation Order No.180.		
Operation(al) Order(s)	9th Divisional Engineers Operation Order No.E.65 By Lieut-Colonel G.R. Hearn, D.S.O., R.E. C.R.E., 9th Division.	27/01/1918	27/01/1918
Heading	Feb 1918.		
War Diary	Bray.	01/02/1918	12/02/1918
War Diary	Fins.	13/02/1918	21/02/1918
War Diary	Saillyle Sec.	21/02/1918	28/02/1918
Miscellaneous	O.C. 64th Field Coy. R.E. App. A.	10/02/1918	10/02/1918
Operation(al) Order(s)	39th Divisional Order No.218.	20/02/1918	20/02/1918
Miscellaneous	C.R.E. 64th Field Coy. R.E. (Through 39th Division). Transport Officer, 64th Field Coy. R.E. (C/O Town Maj. Peronne). "Q". 9th Div. Train. No. X.8/2892/38. 20th February, 1918.	20/02/1918	20/02/1918
Miscellaneous	13 To 20 Fins Waling At Corporation		
Heading	9th Div. 64th Field Company, R.E. March 1918.		
Heading	War Diary. March 1918. Of The 64 Field Coy Royal Engineers. Vol 35.		
War Diary	Bray.	01/03/1918	01/03/1918
War Diary	Moislains.	02/03/1918	03/03/1918
War Diary	Flavy.	04/03/1918	14/03/1918
War Diary	Fins.	14/03/1918	18/03/1918
War Diary	Au Goozecourt.	13/03/1918	23/03/1918
War Diary	Maricourt.	24/03/1918	24/03/1918
War Diary	Bray.	25/03/1918	26/03/1918
War Diary	Corbie.	26/03/1918	27/03/1918
War Diary	Dernancourt.	27/03/1918	31/03/1918
Heading	9th Divisional Engineers. 64th Field Company R.E. April 1918.		
Heading	War Diary April 1918. 3/ 64th F. Coy R.E. Vol 36.		
War Diary	Fieffes Candas.	01/04/1918	01/04/1918
War Diary	Abeele La Clytte.	02/04/1918	30/04/1918

Heading	9 Div.		
Heading	May 1918.		
War Diary	Reninghelst.	01/05/1918	31/05/1918
Miscellaneous	A Form. Messages And Signals.		
Operation(al) Order(s)	9th Division Order No.225. Appendix B.	21/05/1918	21/05/1918
Miscellaneous	March Table Issued With 9th Division Order No.225.		
Miscellaneous			
Miscellaneous	Details Of Moves By Bug Or Lorry.	21/05/1918	21/05/1918
Operation(al) Order(s)	9th Division Order No.226. Appendix C.	25/05/1918	25/05/1918
Operation(al) Order(s)	9th Divisional Engineers Order No.102.	28/05/1918	28/05/1918
Miscellaneous	O.C. 64th Field Coy. R.E. Appendix E.	29/05/1918	29/05/1918
Operation(al) Order(s)	C.R.E., 49th (W.R.) Division Order No.64. Appendix F.	03/05/1918	03/05/1918
Operation(al) Order(s)	O.C. 64th Field Coy R.E. Appendix F/1.	03/05/1918	03/05/1918
Heading	June-Dec 1918.		
War Diary	Hondeghem. P.36.a.22. Sheet 27 S.E.	01/06/1918	29/08/1918
War Diary	Lynde.	01/09/1918	30/09/1918
War Diary	Broodseinde.	01/10/1918	31/10/1918
War Diary	Broodseinde.	27/10/1918	27/10/1918
War Diary	29/H.4.b.7.9.	01/11/1918	03/11/1918
War Diary	Heule.	05/11/1918	08/11/1918
War Diary	Neerhof.	09/11/1918	10/11/1918
War Diary	Harlebeke.	12/11/1918	13/11/1918
War Diary	Tenhove.	15/11/1918	15/11/1918
War Diary	Quatre Vents.	18/11/1918	18/11/1918
War Diary	Trippen.	20/11/1918	20/11/1918
War Diary	30/Q.24.b.6.1.	21/11/1918	21/11/1918
War Diary	Lennick.	23/11/1918	23/11/1918
War Diary	Vlierbeek.	25/11/1918	25/11/1918
War Diary	Cocroux Biez.	27/11/1918	27/11/1918
War Diary	Genville.	28/11/1918	28/11/1918
War Diary	Bas Vinove.	29/11/1918	29/11/1918
War Diary	Flemalle Haute.	01/12/1918	01/12/1918
War Diary	Pepinster.	04/12/1918	04/12/1918
War Diary	Hahn.	06/12/1918	06/12/1918
War Diary	Mausbach.	07/12/1918	07/12/1918
War Diary	Duren.	08/12/1918	08/12/1918
War Diary	Grefrath.	09/12/1918	09/12/1918
War Diary	Nippes.	13/12/1918	13/12/1918
War Diary	Quettingham.	15/12/1918	18/12/1918
War Diary	Krahen Hohe.	23/12/1918	26/12/1918
War Diary	Krahen Hohe.	19/12/1918	28/02/1919
War Diary	Krahen Hohe.	01/02/1919	31/03/1919
War Diary	Krahenhohe Germany.	01/04/1919	30/04/1919
War Diary	Krahen Hohe Germany.	01/04/1919	27/04/1919
Heading	Confidential. War Diary of 64th. Field Company, R.E. From. 1st May 1919 To 31st May 1919. Volume.		
War Diary	Krahen Hohe Germany.	01/05/1919	31/05/1919
War Diary	Krahen Hohe Germany.	09/05/1919	31/05/1919
War Diary	Krahen Hohe Germany.	20/05/1919	20/05/1919
Heading	Confidential. War Diary. of 64th. Field Company R.E. Lowland Division. From 1st. June 1919. To 30th. June 1919. (Volume No.).		
War Diary	Kahen Hohe Germany.	03/06/1919	30/06/1919

Heading	War Diary of 64th. Field Company R.E. Lowland Division. Form 1st. July 1919. To 31st. July 1919. (Volume 5).		
Heading	Horrem Germany.	02/07/1919	31/07/1919
Heading	Confidential War Diary of 64th. Field Company R.E. From:- 1st. August 1919 To:- 31st. August 1919. Volume.		
War Diary	Horrem Germany.	01/08/1919	31/08/1919
War Diary	Horrem Germany.	06/08/1919	22/08/1919
Heading	Confidential. War Diary. of 64th Field Company R.E. From 1st Sept. To 30th Sept.1919. Vol.		
War Diary		02/09/1919	30/09/1919

9TH DIVISION

64TH FIELD COY. R.E.

MAY 1915 - ~~DEC 1918~~ 1919. SEP

64th FIELD COMPANY R.E.

(9th Division)

MAY   1915

9th Division

64th Field Coy R.E.

Vol I

11 — 31.5.15

Army Form C. 2118.

WAR DIARY
~~INTELLIGENCE SUMMARY.~~
(Erase heading not required.)

Instructions regarding War Diaries and Intelligence Summaries are contained in F.S. Regs., Part II. and the Staff Manual respectively. Title pages will be prepared in manuscript.

[Stamp: 64th FIELD COY. ROYAL ENGINEERS · 1 JUNE 1915]

TITLE PAGE

OF DIARY

WAR OF

64TH FIELD Cº R.E.

FROM

11TH MAY 1915 TO 31ST MAY 1915

(CONSISTING OF 5 SHEETS.)

WAR DIARY or INTELLIGENCE SUMMARY.

64th Field Co. R.E. Army Form C. 2118.
Sheet 1 of May 1915

Hour, Date, Place		Summary of Events and Information	Remarks and references to Appendices
11.40 a.m.	11 May 1915 BORDON	1st Train Load (X148) left BORDON, consisting of No 1 & 2 Sections complete, No 1 Pontoon, Trestle & Searchlight wagons	
12.55 a.m.	"	with part of Hd. Qrs. Section and watercart	
		1½ Train Load (X150) left consisting of No 3 & 4 Sections complete and the remainder of Hd. Qrs., No 2 Pontoon, Technical E.S. wagon & Cooks cart, & A.S.C. wagon. 1st Train Load arrived	
1.50 P.M.	SOUTHAMPTON DOCK	1½ Train Load 3 Officers & 156 all ranks embarked in	Smooth passage
2.16 P.M.	"	S.S. CONNAUGHT left SOUTHAMPTON 7.5 P.M. disembarked	
7.5 P.M.	HAVRE		
7 P.M.	12 5/15		
6.P.M.	11 5/15 SOUTHAMPTON	{1/Lt FISCHER, 20 drivers & 40 horses embarked in ANGLO-CANADIAN — 1/Lt RANKIN, 20 drivers, 41 Horses, S.S. INVENTOR Lt WOOLNER with 37 men in S.S. BELLEROPHON & all vehicles	GPA
8 P.M.	12 5/15 HAVRE	Disembarkation complete 5 p.m. Marched to Rest Camp No 2	
7.10 P.M.	12 6/15	arrived 7.10 P.M.	
5 A.M.	13 5/15	Reveille 5 a.m. Hooked in 9 a.m. Marched off 9.30 a.m. to	Wet morning
10.45 A.M.	13 5/15	Point 1 Gare des Marchandises arrived 10.45 a.m. left at	
3 P.M.	"	" the Train consisting of 47 vehicles	
6.30 P.M.	"	Arrived ROUEN. Heavy rain at ABBEVILLE. Stopped at	GPA
		8.15 P.M. till 9.15 P.M. to water & feed animals. Arrived at	
9.15 A.M.	14 5/15 STOMER	received orders & departed to WISERNE 9.40 a.m. detrained	
9.40 A.M.	" WISERNE	and cleared station 11.40 a.m. SEE PAGE II	

WAR DIARY
or
INTELLIGENCE SUMMARY.
(Erase heading not required.)

64 Field C.R.E. Army Form C. 2118.

Sheet 2 of May 15

Hour, Date, Place		Summary of Events and Information	Remarks and references to Appendices
2.50 P.M. 14/5/15	PIHEM	Arrived PIHEM - Billets - Inspection 6 P.M.	GRN
7 A.M. 15/5/15	"	Parade. Practised Outposts & duties of Sentry	Billet Plan APP. A.1
2 P.M. "	"	11'' Parade. Practised outposts & Guard mounting. Remainder evening	
7 P.M. 16/5/15	"	Parade 7am. Practised outposts & Guard mounting. Parade	1 man sick L/Cpl Kenny B 27 Field Ambulance
11.0 A.M. "	"	and proceeded by march route to ABBAYE WOSTEINE via	OPERATION ORDER No 2 APP. A.2 MARCH TABLE APP. A.3 BILLET A.B
4.55 A.M. "	ABBAYE WOSTEINE	WISERNE - ARQUES - FORT ROUGE arrived 4.55am - 10½ mile journey	1 man sick Spr Shortland to 34 Fd Ambulance GRN
6 P.M. 17/5/15	"	Parade 6am. left 6.20am by march route for LE VERRIER	
		Via COMMUNE D'RENESCURE - EBBLINGHAM - HAZEBROUCK - NODE	Wet day. Firing 2°S Augs GRN
3.30 P.M.	LE VERRIER	BOOM - arrived 3.30 P.M. - 20¾ mile march.	Heavy rain night
8 A.M. 18/5/15	"	1st Parade 8am. Inspection. Checking blankets, wagons	OPERATION ORDER A4 BILLET PLAN - 17 5
		Packing & Cycle repairs, Shoeing horses & mules, etc.	Wet morning. Rain eased
		2nd Parade 11 broken	
8 A.M. 19/5/15	"	C.O. left for duty ARMENTIERES 7 AM. 1st Parade 8am. Packed	GRN
		carts etc. 11' Parade 10 am. Marched at 10.15am to L'HALLOBEAU	Dull morning
10.15 A.M.	STEENWERCKE	via STEENWERCKE arrived L'HALLOBEAU - 12.45 P.M. 14 miles	BILLET PLAN AP.
12.45 P.	L'HALLOBEAU	March being short, saddlery repaired, Camp routine	Reconnaissance from N.E.
		Capt. FRANCIS, C.E. III Army, & C.R.E. 9th Divn to ERQUINGHEM Vicinity	Ryve & Brouchin Our Parks N.E. 9.30 P.M.
		G.H.Q lines of entrenchments	
7.30 A. 20/5/15	"	Parade 7am. The Company were employed on improving	Fine day
		G.H.Q' Line of entrenchments from R. LYS to LES TROIS TILLEULS	GRN
4 P.M. "	"	" " "	GRN

SEE PAGE III

WAR DIARY 64th Field C.E, R.E.

or

INTELLIGENCE SUMMARY.

Army Form C. 2118.

Sheet 3 of May 1915

(Erase heading not required.)

Hour, Date, Place	Summary of Events and Information	Remarks and references to Appendices
8 AM 21/5 L. HALLOBEAU	Parade 8am. Work on improvement of G.H.Q. line of entrenchments. C.O. visited from ARMENTIERES. The company returned at 4 p.m.	Line working but dull. Heavy cannonade 9 p.m. towards S.E
8 AM 22/5 "	Parade 8am. Company on work improving G.H.Q. line of entrenchments	Fine morning. GRN
9.45 am "	CAPT FRANCIS & 1st LT RANKIN left for ARMENTIERES for duty	
12 noon "	O.C. arrived with 11th LT FISCHER from tour of duty in trenches ARMENTIERES — Labor continued in improving trenches till 4pm	GRN
8 AM 23/5 "	Parade 8am. The company employed on improvement of G.H.Q line of entrenchments till 4 pm	Fine morning. GRN
8 AM 24/5 "	Parade 8am Company employed on improvement of G.H.Q. line of entrenchments. O.C. & 3 men to NIEPPE Surveying 4 & 8 S. MIDLAND DIVISION 2nd LINE Survey. They returned at 4.15pm	Line morning. Heavy Gun fire N.E. 5 to 6 am. GRN
" "	CAPT FRANCIS & 1st LT RANKIN returned from tour of duty in trenches at ARMENTIERES 4.15 P.M.	Very heavy cannonade E. 8 pm. Rec'd orders GRN
7.45 am 25/5 "	Parade 7.45 am. Company to work improving G.H. Q. line of entrenchments till 4 pm. Respirators & instructions issued. O.C. Sergt Wood, 1/Cpl Brown, 1/E Cpl Reed C. Continuing Survey of 48 S. MIDLAND DIVISION 2nd LINE also 1st LT RANKIN on same duty, they returned at 7.45 pm	Fine day, very warm. GRN

WAR DIARY or INTELLIGENCE SUMMARY

64th Field Co. R.E.

Army Form C. 2118.

Sheet 4 of May 1915

Hour, Date, Place	Summary of Events and Information	Remarks and references to Appendices
7.45 P.M. 26/5/15 L'HALLOBEAU	Parade 7.45 A.M. Company to work improving G.H.Q. Line by entrenchments. Returned at 4 p.m.	Fine day. Very warm. GRN
7.45 A.M. 27/5/15 "	Parade 7.45 A.M. Company to work improving G.H.Q. Line of entrenchments. Instructions re espionage read to troops. Lt WOOLNER & Lt Lt NAPIER CLAVERING on duty. Lt C.R.E. NIEPPE.	Dull morning cool. GRN
5.15 P.M. 27/5/15 "	7.30 P.M. O.C. — Presented F.G. Counts marked STEENWERCK 9.30 a.m. loud explosion N by N.E. ascertained at Billet of 90 C. R.E.	
7.15 P.M. " "	Lt WOOLNER R.E. I/c Supporting point at WAEMER GUIDE & LE TOUQUET STATION at work on improvements took one Company of 5/Cameronians. Returned at 2 a.m. 28/5	Skiver APP A.7 Skiver App. A.8 Moonlight (cont)
7.45 A.M. 28/5/15 "	Lt NAPIER CLAVERING O/C Supporting point PONT BALLOT FARM HOUPLINES at work with 2 Platoons of 7/Seaforths. Returned at 2 a.m 28/5. 1st Parade Company to work improving G.K.Q. Line of entrenchments. Returned at 4.15 p.m.	Dull day.
6.30 P.M. " LE TOUQUET	Lt WOOLNER R.E. Left at 6.30 p.m. for work on supporting points at LE TOUQUET STATION – 1 Co. Black Watch working Party	BRIGHT. moonlight.
" PONT BALLOT "	Lt CLAVERING Left at 6.30 p.m. for work on Supporting Point at PONT BALLOT FARM HOUPLINES – 1 Coy 4/Seaforths working Party, Sergt. wounded, Cpl. Cooper accompanied	
7.45 a.m. 29/5/15 L'HALLOBEAU	1st Parade Company to work improving G.H.Q. Line of entrenchments. Returned at 4 P.M.	Fine day. GRN
	Lt WOOLNER Left at 6.30 p.m. for work at LE TOUQUET STATION for work on Supporting Point. 1 Company Cameronians for working Party. Returned at 1.30 a.m.	Fine day cool.
	Lt CLAVERING Left at 6.30 p.m. for work at PONT BALLOT FARM for work on Supporting point. Returned at 2 a.m. – 1 Co. 7/Seaforths working Party.	GRN SEE PAGE 5

Army Form C. 2118.

64th Field C. R.E.
Sheet 5 of 7 May, 1915

WAR DIARY
or
INTELLIGENCE SUMMARY.
(Erase heading not required.)

Hour, Date, Place	Summary of Events and Information	Remarks and references to Appendices
7.45 am 30/5/15 L'HALLOBEAU	Parade at 7.45 am. Company at work on improving G.H.Q's line of support entrenchment. Returned at 4 p.m. Lt Woolner R.E. & LE TOUQUET STATION works on supporting point, working party / O. Black Watch, returned at 1.45 am.	Fine morning (cont)
	LT CLAVERING left at 6.30 p.m for PONT BALLOT FARM for work on supporting point, working party 1 - Coy Seaforth returned 2 am	6pm Fine day
9 am 31/5/15 "	Parade at 9 am. Company at work on improving G.H.Q's line of support entrenchments. Returned at 4 P.M.	
7.30 p "	No 4 Section under Clavering o/c left for PONT BALLOT FARM with tool cart to remain for work. Lt Woolner R.E. & Sgt Rickets left for work on supporting point LE TOUQUET returned at 3 am.	

E R Hearn
Major R.E.
O.C. 64th F.Coy R.E.

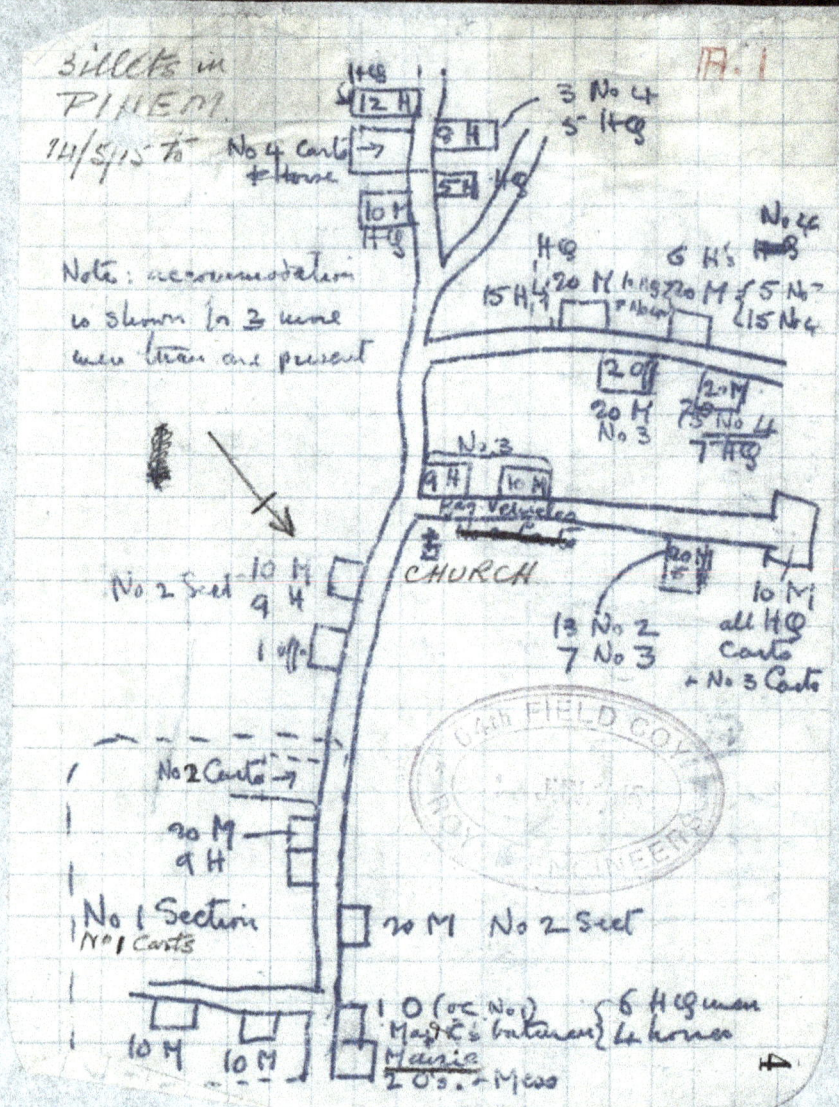

Copy No. 5
app **A.2**
16.5.15

27th Inf. Div. Order No. 2

Ref. map 1/100,000 No. 5.A.

(1) The Div. will march today, in 4 columns, and billet in area between CASSEL & the ST. OMER — HAZEBROUCK railway.

No protective detachments will be employed for this march.

(2) Owing to the scattered billets, march Table for all units have been issued by Div. HQ. One copy herewith.* In accordance therewith, units will pass the cross road just S. of the V. of WESTOVE as under:—

*Except for 27 Fd Amb Co

HQ. at Bde HQ	1. P.M. today
12 R.S.	1 " "
11 R.S.	1. 5
6 R.S.7	1. 10
10 A & S H	1. 15
64 Fd. Coy R.E.	1. 20
27 Fd Amb Co	1. 25
9" Seaforths	1. 26
Baggage Section	1. 33

Started from PIHEM 11.50 am

Started from PIHEM 11.50 am

[Stamp: 64th FIELD COY. ROYAL ENGINEERS 1 JUN 1915]

(3) Route :— HALLINES, WIZERNES, WINS, ARQUES, RENESCURE.

(4) Troops at Gd BOIS, Pt BOIS, PIHEM, BIENTQUES & CREHEM to move via NON CORNET.
Troops at WAVRANS move via ESQUERDES.

(5) Reports to head of Bde group column.

Issued at 8 AM. Rec'd 9.15 am.

Copy No. 1 to 11 RS
2 - 12 RS
3 - 6 R
4 - 10 A & SH
5 - 64 Coy. RE
6 - 27 Fd Amb Co
7 - 9/ Seaforths
8 - 106 Co. ASC
9-12 Bde HQ.

A.W. Glasfurd
Major
 B.M. 27 Inf Bde

AP 3

MARCH TABLE.

Issued with 9th. Division Order No. 2 d/15/5/15.

Column. No of march. Units in order of march.	Initial S.P.	Time	Div. S.P.	Time	Route	Remarks.
1. (Gen.Armitage) All R.A. Units except Div.A.M. Col. also baggage section.	To be arranged by Q. R. A.				50th. & 53rd. F.A. Bdes. & Heavy Battery. HELFAUT-BILQUES-HEURINGHEM-CAMPAGNE-RENESCURE. 51st. & 52nd. F.A. Bdes. REMILLY-CLETTY-HERBELLE-INGHEM-ECQUES-BELLE CROIX & roads to S.	The 2 F.A. columns will unite at road junction ½M W of EBBLINGHEM & march via WALLON CAPEL to their billeting area.
2. (Gen.Grogan) Div. H.Q. 26th. Inf. Bde. 63rd. Field Coy 28th. Fld. Amb. (less motor vehicles) Baggage Section.	Level crossing ¾ E of ARQUES Church.	1.30 pm 1.35 p.m 2.5 p.m. 2.10 pm 2.11 pm	FORT ROUGE	2 pm 2.5 pm 2.35 pm 2.40 pm 2.41 pm	FORT ROUGE-CHAU LENIEPPE-road junction ½ mile South- STAPLE.	
3. (Gen.Bruce) 27th.Inf.Bde. 54th. Fld.Coy. 27th. Fld. Amb. (less motor vehicles) 9th.Seaforths Baggage Section.	Cross roads just S of V of WESTOVE	1 pm 1.20 pm 1.25 pm 1.26 pm 1.33 pm		2.45 pm 3.13 pm 3.18 pm 3.19 pm 3.26 pm	HALLINES-WIZERNES-WINS-ARQUES-RENESCURE.	Troops at GRAND BOIS, PETIT BOIS, PIHEM, BIENTQUES & OREHEM to move via NON CORNET. Troops at WAVRANS move via ESQUERDES.

MARCH TABLE

Issued with 9th. Division Order No. 2. d/16/5/15.

No. Column. Units in order of march	A.V.S.P.	Time	Route	Remarks.
4. (Gen.Scrase Dickens) Glasgow Yeomanry 9th. Cyclists 28th.Inf.Bde. 90th.Fld.Coy. 28th.Field Amb. (less motor vehicles)	Level crossing near S of ST OMER	2 pm 2.2 pm 2.10 pm 2.30 pm 2.35 pm	CLAIRMARAIS— HAUT SCHOUBROUCK— road junction N of B SCHOUBROUCK.	Div. Am. Col. will march COIN PERDU.
Baggage Section Div. Am. Col. M.M.G.Batty		2.57 pm 2.58 pm		Follow rear of Col at any convenient distance.

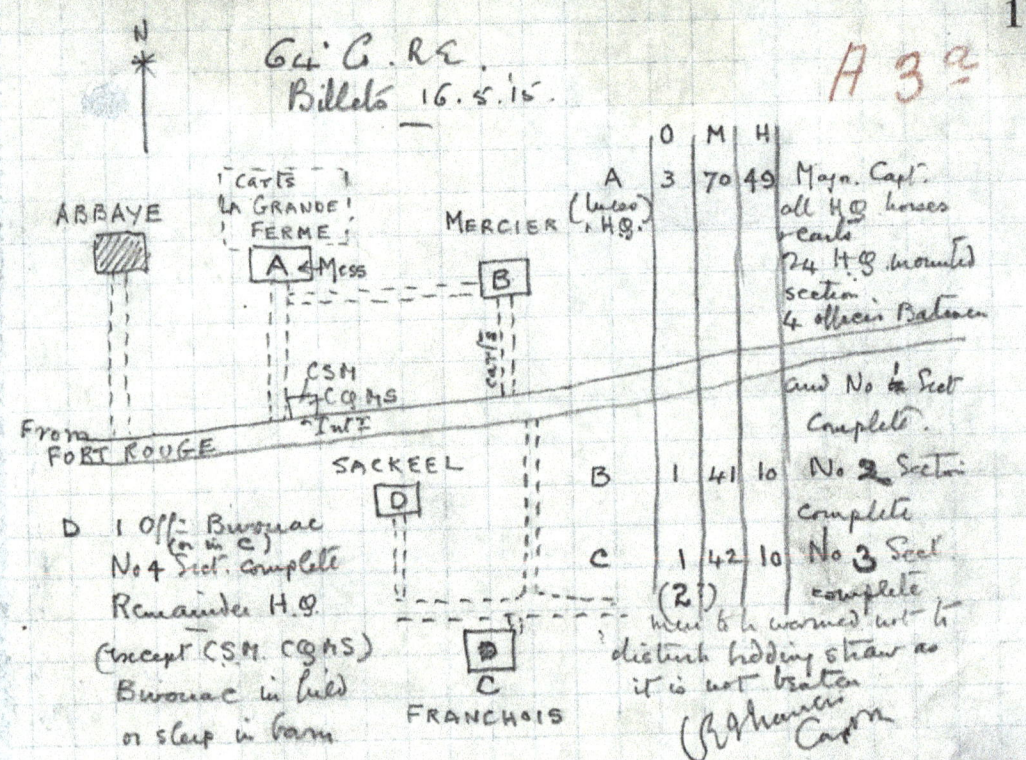

A4   Copy No. 8

27 Inf Bde Order No. 3.

16.5.15.

Ref map A5. scale 1/100,000

*Except for 27 Fd Amb&c

Received
1 am
17/5/15

(1) The Division will march tomorrow, as per march table attached for information.*

(2) Units of 27 Inf Bde area will pass the road junction, on main road, due North of the W. in WALLON CAPPEL, as under, moving to that point by the shortest road.

Head Qr unit complete	at 7 AM
6 R Sf	7
11 RS	7.5
12 RS	7.10
10 A & S.H	7.15
9. Leinsters	7.20
27" Fd Amb&c	7.25
Baggage Sect 106 Co ASC	7.28
64" Fd Coy R.E.	7.30

(3) Route:— WALLON CAPPEL, under RY on W. edge of HAZE-BROUCK, BORRE, STRAZEELE, MERRIS, OULTERSTEENE, NODLE BOOM.

(4) 64 Fd Coy RE to go into RE billetting area from NODLE BOOM; & also 27 Fd Amb&c & 106 Coy ASC, to their billetting area, about STEENWERCK

(5) Both échelons of 1st line Transport to accompany units.

(6) There will be a long halt of about 1½ hours between HAZEBROUCK and STRAZEELE.

(7) Right of way is to be given to any troops that may be crossing line of march from North to South.

(8) At point 36 just North of HAZEBROUCK, OC 6 RSf will send a mounted officer to Bde HQ for traffic control duty.

(9) Reports to head of Column.

R M Maxwell
Major
Bde 27 Inf Bde

Issued at 11.55 p.m.

Copy No.		
1	11 RS	5 to 9 Leinsters
2	12 RS	6 ... 27 Fd Amb&c
3	6 RSf	7 ... 106 Coy ASC
4	10 A&SH	8 ... 64 Coy RE
		9-12 Bde HQ.

64 Coy RE

March Table.

Issued with 9th. Division Order No. 3 d/16/5/15.

Column	Hour of start	Route	Remarks.
Maj.Macfarlane Glasgow Yeomanry 9th. Cyclists Motor M.Gun.Baty Baggage Section	6 a.m.	ST SYLVESTRE-CAESTRE-BAILLEUL-Level crossing ½ mile E of BAILLEUL Stn.-KIRLEM.	Cross roads at ST. SYLVESTRE to be passed as early as possible to avoid congestion at refilling point.
Gen.Armitage 51st.F.A.Bde. 53rd.F.A.Bde.	6.30 am	CAESTRE-BAILLEUL-RABOT-LEVEAU	
50th. F.A.Bde. 52nd. F.A.Bde. 9th. Hvy. Battery Baggage Section		Same route as mounted troops. CAESTRE-BAILLEUL-RABOT-PONT DE NIEPPE	
Gen.Grogan Div. H.Q. 26th.Inf.Bde. 29th.FieldAmb. Baggage Section	8 a.m.	LES CISEAUX- LE BREARDE-CAESTRE-BAILLEUL	
Gen. Bruce. 27th.Inf.Bde. 27th.Fld.Amb. 2th.Seaforths Baggage Section 64th. Fld. Coy.	7 a.m.	WALLON CAPPEL - under railway on W edge of HAZEBROUCK-BORRE-STRAZEELE-MERRIS-OULTERSTEENE-NODLE BOOM.	64th.Fld.Coy. will go into R.E. billetting area from NODLE BOOM
Gen.Scrase Dickens 28th.Inf.Bde. 28th.Fld.Amb. Baggage Section	8.30 a.m	Crossroads 1 Mile E of STAPLE-LE BREARDE-road junction ¼ M N of BORRE-MOOLENACHER	On no account is the BORRE-STRAZEELE road to be entered.
63rd. Fld. Coy.		To be at crossroads ¼ M N.E. of 3rd. L of WALLON CAPEL at 7.45 a.m. & follow 64th. Fld. Coy.	
90th. Fld. Coy.		To be at crossroads ¼ M N of E of WALLON CAPEL at 7.45 a.m. moving via LES SIX RUES, then follow 63rd. Field Coy.	
Div.Am.Col.	9 a.m.	STAPLE-LEBRIARD-CAESTRE-METEREN	

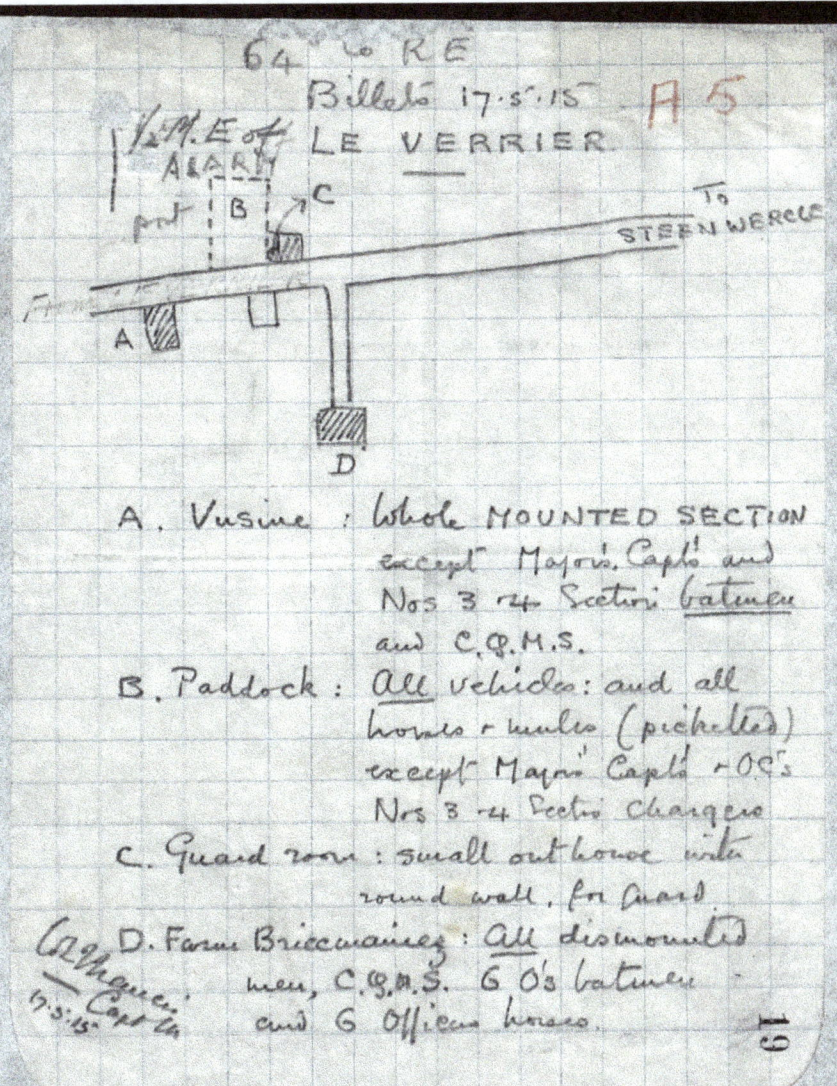

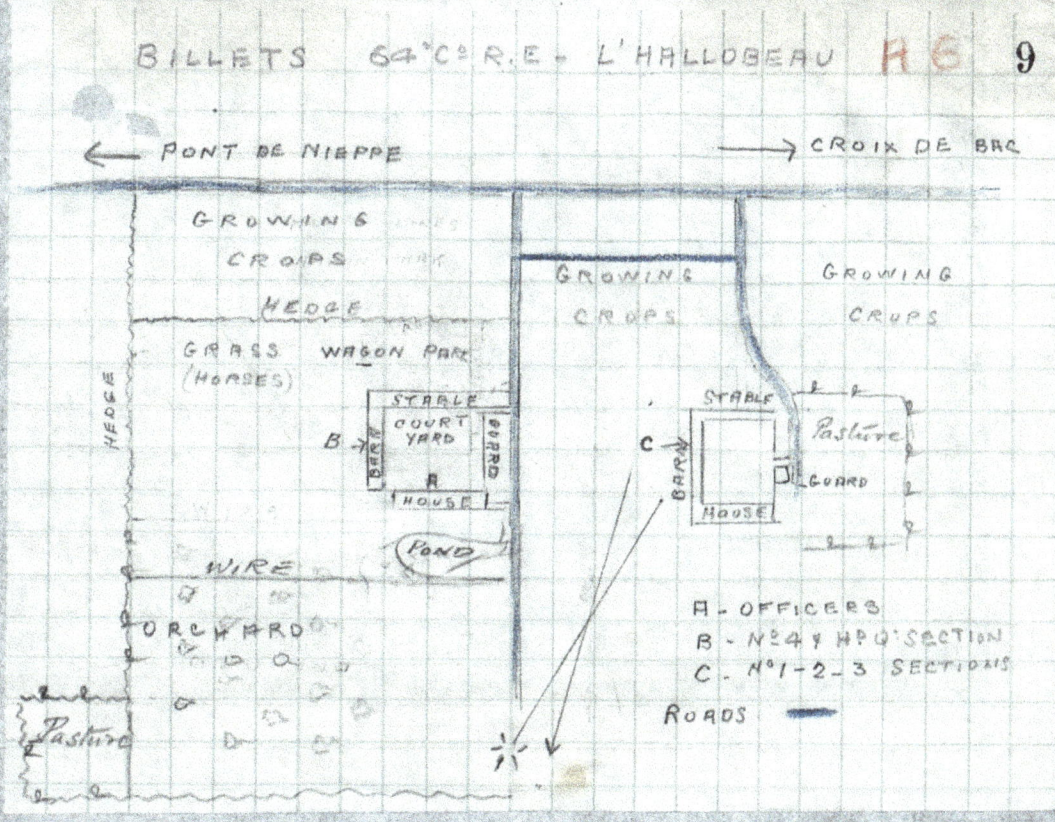

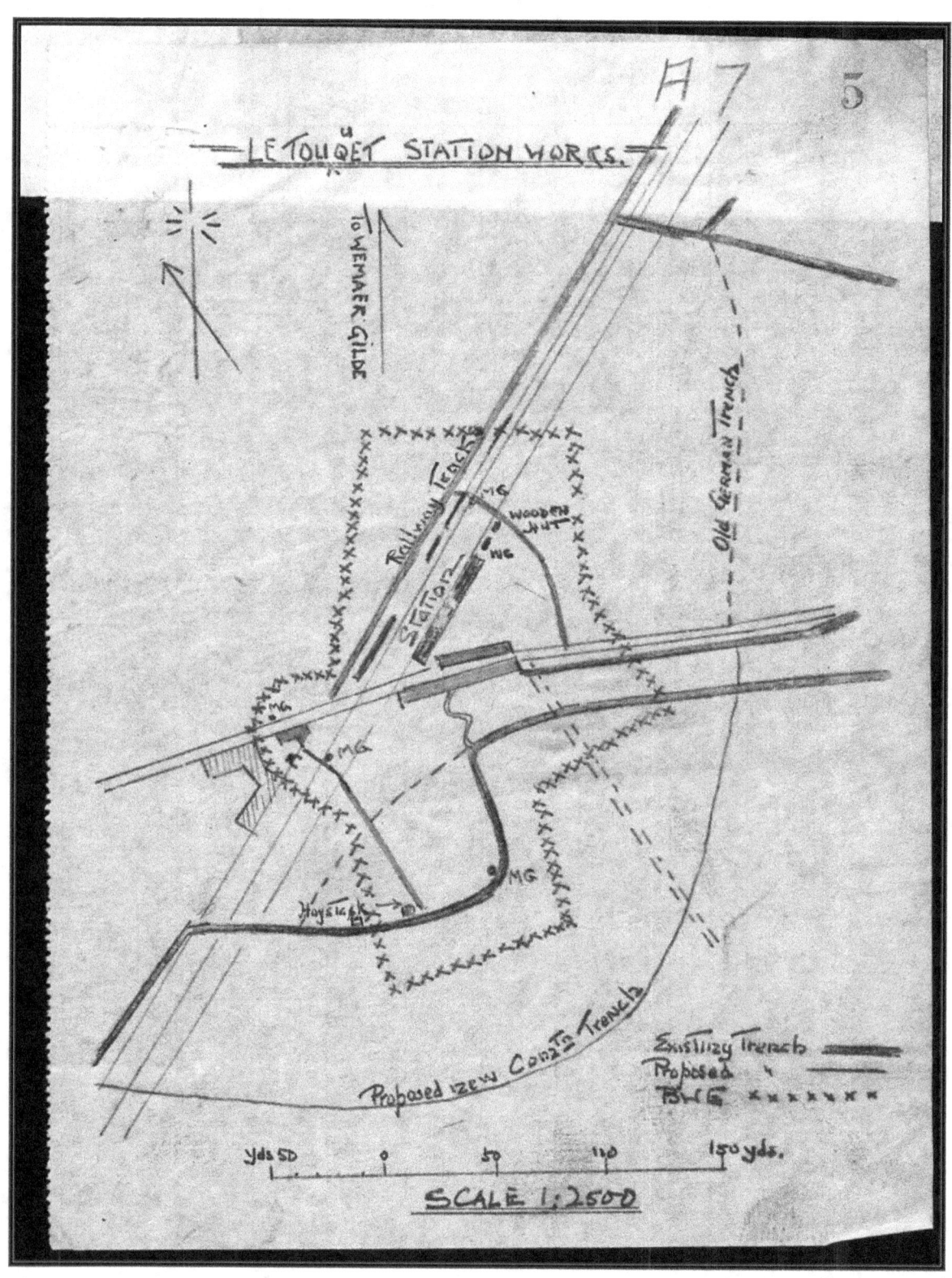

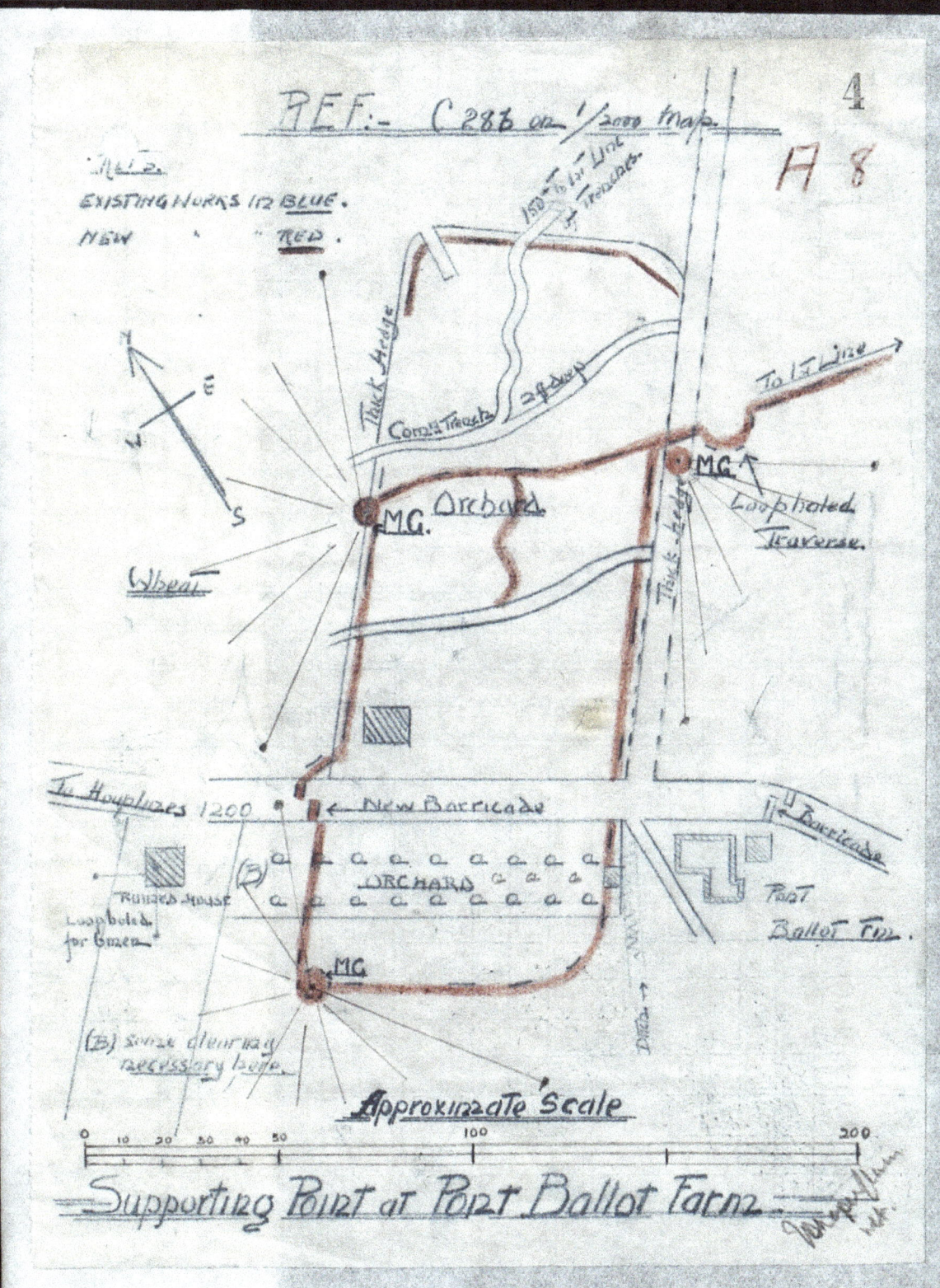

64th FIELD COMPANY R.E.

(9th Division)

June   1915

gr. Division
64.ᵗᵉ J.C.R.E.
Vol: II.
1 — 30.6.15.

187/5991

WAR DIARY or INTELLIGENCE SUMMARY

Army Form C. 2118.

6th Fld Coy C.R.E.

Sheet 1 of June 1915

Hour, Date, Place	Summary of Events and Information	Remarks and references to Appendices
1.45 AM 1/6 L'HALLOBEAU Ref to 1/20,000 map B26.a. night	Company to work – N°1 Section on Pont magazine at L'HALLOBEAU. FARM STRASEELE N°2 & 3 on G.H.Q. line of entrenchments PONT BALLOT. N°4 on detachment at LETOUQUET – Lt WOOLNER I/C of Group at LETOUQUET STATION. 1 Cpl & 1 black watch working party.	Fine clear day. Heavy firing to S.E. 2 pm to 6 pm
7.45 a.m. 2/6 night	Returned to billets. 1 Cpl & 1 BALLOT finds on 4 rifles work done. 7 cyclists support party near CROULX-BARROUILLE to 2nd line. Company to work. N°1 Section on Pont magazine at L'HALLOBEAU. RUCETIC CROUX STRASEELE N°3 on G.H.Q. line of entrenchments. Cpl Andrew & men at work at Q Signal. Hd Qn. Supp. Lt. FISCHER with interpreter orderly & escort of Hd Qn. Supp. at STEENWERCK & NIEPPE N°4 Section Lt. CLAVERING on detachment PONT BALLOT. Lt WOOLNER I/C of 3 sections at LETOUQUET STATION with 1/2 Concentration party. 1/2 Co + M.G. section.	Fine day warm. Heavy firing to S.E. 2 pm to 8 pm
7.45 a.m. 3/6 night	Company to work. N°1 Section & PRICE 3 & Wd Co. on magazine. N°2 on G.H.Q. line. Cpl Andrew & men on drainage Hd.Q. Q Signal 2/Lt Fischer + 1 Cpl & men on water supply Return to billets. Lt WOOLNER I/C LETOUQUET STATION for work on Support Point with 2 Co W/R S.MG section.	Fine day warm Heavy firing N.E. & S.E. 8 from 6 pm to 10 pm

WAR DIARY
or
INTELLIGENCE SUMMARY.

Army Form C. 2118.

64th Field Co. R.E.
Sheet 2 of June 1915

(Erase heading not required.)

Instructions regarding War Diaries and Intelligence Summaries are contained in F.S. Regs., Part II and the Staff Manual respectively. Title pages will be prepared in manuscript.

Hour, Date, Place	Summary of Events and Information	Remarks and references to Appendices
7.45 AM 4/6/15 L'HALLOBEAU	Company for work. No. 1 Section to Pont Bragan. No. 2 & No. 3 Section to LE TOUQUET STATION for work. No. 3 Section on entrenchments 7 am.	Fine day.
3.30 pm	Left at 3.30 pm for some work. Returned 4.30 am 5/6 O.C. before then visited LE TOUQUET & PONT BALLOT	Sketchg. Pont BALLOT from work Opp A.
night	Lt. MOOZNER with 2 Co. RMB cut. 1/R.S. 1IC, IO/R.S. at LE TOUQUET STATION preparing for night work. Brent bragan sleepy party & beating party. No 4 Section & Lt. Clavery returned & sketches. No. 4 Section Lt. Clavery returned	This day
7.45 AM 5/6/15 AM	from PONT BALLOT at 4 am. Billetg party 11.: Ranki Col. Osprey, 2 Cyclists & Interpreter left for Billetg area ST. VENANT at 11.30 am via CROIX d' BACN rendezvous with Staff Capt. 27 Batt 12 noon. The Company _____ approached by Brensh S. WK	This billet overcast
6/6/15	_____ to HAMEL billet & CROIX DE BAC - ESTAIRES. Cleaned billet at 7.30 pm	ST LAGORGUE MEURILLON, CALONNE ROBECQ 18½ miles
4 AM 6/6/15 AM	Arrived HAMEL billet 4 am - Billeted - HQ QRS - drove finding warm. 2 Officers at farm EMANUEL BESPREZ, No. 1 SECTION AND No 2 Section at M. BAYART N. G. at BECART MARTEL No 3 Section at LEON DESPREZ. Company _____ for inspection 3 pm.	Planfields Opp B.
7.45 am 7/6/15 am	Company parade 7.45 am _____ for bathing parade 2 pm. Pontoon drill at canal	Fine am Hot.

Army Form C. 2118.

WAR DIARY
or
INTELLIGENCE SUMMARY.

6th Field Cy. R.E.
Sheet No. 3 of June

(Erase heading not required.)

Instructions regarding War Diaries and Intelligence Summaries are contained in F.S. Regs., Part II. and the Staff Manual respectively. Title pages will be prepared in manuscript.

Hour, Date, Place	Summary of Events and Information	Remarks and references to Appendices
7.45am 8/6/15 HAMET BILLET	Company paraded from billets. No.1 Pontoon Drill. No.1 Duty & removing stores from (4 lorry loads) No. 2 & 3. on works Bomb magazine &c. Brigadier visited 8.15am Company employed removing & stacking timber on Pontoon area 4pm	Distant shelling fine & S.W. all day. 2 pm heavy rain and thunderstorm till 4p weather unsettled after.
7.45am 9/6/15 10.0	Company paraded 7.45am No.1 & 2 Pontoon drill, No.3 & 4 on works Bomb magazine &c. boots etc. 5pm	Weather dull
6am 10/6/15 "	No.1 party proceeded to [entrench?] under Lt. WOOLNER heavy fine Shmery to ROBECQ Q.M. for work on C.H.Q. Line of entrenchments they met at 1.30pm	
6.30am "	No.4 party proceeded under 2nd Lt. CLAVERING to ST. VENANT CH. for work on C.H.Q. Line of entrenchments. Returned 6pm	
7.45am "	No.2 & 3 party proceeded for work on Bomb magazine &c. Returned 6pm	11 None?
3pm "	O.C. Lectured to 30 officers 51st Inf. Brigade on Bombs & bomb throwing.	
6am 11/6/15 "	No.1 party proceeded to work on C.H.Q. Line of entrenchments	Weather dull. Fine Rain Fine later
6.30am "	No.2 party proceeded to work on C.H.Q. Line of entrenchments.	
7.45am "	Remainder of Company paraded for work on Bomb- [enlistments?] O.C. & Subaltern to officer of 152nd Inf. Brigade Officers on Bombs 2.45pm	

Army Form C. 2118.

WAR DIARY
or
INTELLIGENCE SUMMARY.
(Erase heading not required.)

64" Field Coy RE
Sheet No 4 of June

Hour, Date, Place	Summary of Events and Information	Remarks and references to Appendices
7am 12/6/15 HAMET BILLET	No 2 Section proceeded to deploy with to 7am to 6th O'Lieut ROBECQ	Fine morning Heavy Gun fire R.E. enemy
7.30am "	No 4 Section paraded & proceeded to 6th O Line at ST VINANT	
7.45a "	with 2 days rations to Cliff O Line at ST VINANT B Remainder of Company paraded for work on Road leading to Supplies 100 fuschie trucks Battalion 27th Bgde at 9/Seafth Rd	Heavy & continuous Gun fire R.E. all day Fine day fogy
7.45a 13/6/15 do	Company	
	Sames 11.45am	
8am 14/6/15 do	Company fun work on bomb throwers and also making information for mine.	Weather dull windy fine alt.
7.45a 15/6/15 do	Company for work on bombthrower. Picket for wire entanglements. G.O.M.S. visited billets 9am C.O. to Brigade Hd.Qrs for conference. Memo from G.O.C. expressing pleasure in hearing there was no fatally sent in the R.E. Company in the brazier to this Billet Read to Company on Parade. Received orders to pack Packing Carts &c	Fine morning Heavy Gun fire R.E at 2 pm onwards
6 pm 16/6/15 do	Company "Stood by" till 7.30 pm then to Billets	Fine day. Heavy Gun fire 6 D.E. 2.36 pm onwards

Army Form C. 2118.

WAR DIARY
or
INTELLIGENCE SUMMARY.
(Erase heading not required.)

Sheet N° 5 of June

Instructions regarding War Diaries and Intelligence Summaries are contained in F.S. Regs., Part II and the Staff Manual respectively. Title pages will be prepared in manuscript.

Hour, Date, Place	Summary of Events and Information	Remarks and references to Appendices
17/6/15. 9am	Part of the Company for work 1 and 4 sections route march + Instruction. Returned to Billets at 6.15pm	Weather fine
18/6/15. 8am	Work and Instruction in the use of Meldew Sentle under section Commanders.	Weather fine but cold
" 5.15pm	View of the G.O.C & Staff of R. Division for the purpose of witnessing the use of Japanalis bomb on barbed wire entanglements. A lot of Captain Eulis Lieut Milner having erected barbed wire entanglements proceeded to demonstrate how by the use of Japanalis bombs barbed wire entanglements can be destroyed.	
19/6/15. 7.45am	Section employed for work at Kem Halun, the remainder Route March to	Weather fine. Heavy firing to S.E. 10.15pm to 11pm.

Army Form C. 2118.

WAR DIARY
or
INTELLIGENCE SUMMARY.
(Erase heading not required.)

Sheet No 6 of June

Hour, Date, Place	Summary of Events and Information	Remarks and references to Appendices
20/6/15 — 8 a.m. 11·40 HAMEL BILLET.	Practice in rapid loading. Church of England parade. The amount of transport is somewhat inadequate. Although it will no doubt suit and unlikely there is sufficient, if however the unit is on the move or under orders to move at short notice is to get a wagon or cooker cart can not be unloaded and sent sufficiently quick. There is one G.L. supply wagon which is directly under the control of the A.S.C. This wagon is insufficient to carry the whole of the supplies and forage of the unit the bulk of which has made it necessary on occasion to leave some behind, which is a point to the bad. To ascertain for me hour of G.O. horses. In addition to supplies S is necessary transport for men and horses, toilet articles, mails (two to four bricks) and to call at the Ordnance Depot of the Division daily in case any materials indented for have arrived. The A.S.C. Officer does not permit the Supply wagon He used for these services and indeed	

Army Form C. 2118.

Sheet 170 of June

WAR DIARY
or
INTELLIGENCE SUMMARY.
(Erase heading not required.)

Hour, Date, Place	Summary of Events and Information	Remarks and references to Appendices
20/6/15 HAMMET BILLET.	the distance covered would be too much for the horses. One of the hairy Ordnance stores to be handed over at the refilling point at the same hour (which has not been the case) the loads would be beyond the capacity of the horses. It is suggested that a slight opening two wheeled cart and one horse should be supplied and be at the disposal of the O.C. unit for the purposes mentioned.	Weather fine and very hot.
20/6/15 4.00pm	The Coy proceeded to their Billets.	
21/6/15 7.45am to 12.30pm	Coy instrument and scheme nr INSEROUES	Fine very hot. Firing R+LE 3pm.
22/6/15 7.45am to 4pm	No 1+2 Section invited in treat BUBUFF check No 3+4 sections in loading on canal	
23/6/15 7.45am	Coy route march and pontooning. Special employed engaged in making "Rifle rest" for firing over parapet	Rain in the morning but not for any length of time. Afternoon fine but cloudy firing S.E. 3pm.
2pm	Bombs + Grenades stored from 26, 27, 28, 2 Boxes	
6-7	March Billets	

Army Form C. 2118.

Sheet 1708 of June

WAR DIARY
or
INTELLIGENCE SUMMARY.
(Erase heading not required.)

Instructions regarding War Diaries and Intelligence Summaries are contained in F.S. Regs., Part II. and the Staff Manual respectively. Title pages will be prepared in manuscript.

Hour, Date, Place	Summary of Events and Information	Remarks and references to Appendices
25.6.15		App C
3.15am	Received orders to move	Weather very wet and stormy.
9.30am	Company ready to move off. Company moved off in two columns No 1 & 2 Sections bridging echelon at 10am. No 4 and Head Qrs at 10.30 am. The route taken was via BUSHES LILLERS. ECQUEDECQUES to LESPESSES. No 3 Section remained behind Black's Guard & had parade & stores on waggons & lorries. Billets were all cleaned & inspected by Section Officers and No 3 Section filled in all latrines.	
12.30pm	No 4 Section Head Qrs arrived at their billets LESPESSES. 1 & 2 Sections already arrived.	
7.30pm	No 3 Section arrived having brought all parades and stores.	

Army Form C. 2118.

Sheet N°9 of June

WAR DIARY
or
INTELLIGENCE SUMMARY.

(Erase heading not required.)

Instructions regarding War Diaries and Intelligence Summaries are contained in F.S. Regs., Part II. and the Staff Manual respectively. Title pages will be prepared in manuscript.

Place	Hour, Date.	Summary of Events and Information	Remarks and references to Appendices
LESPESSES	26/6/15 7.45	Company for work.	Weather wet
"	27/6/15 8.15 am	Company for Services, Church Parade, and Special work until 4.0.6.	
"	28/6/15 3.45	Order to move.	Weather showery app D
"	7.45	"Stand By" awaiting orders.	Reference map No.09 Sheet
"	3 pm	Order to move received. To proceed to LILLETTE. N°s 2 & 3 Sections with Head Qrs marched off at 3.30 pm. N°1 and 4 Sections remained behind to pack stores, bombs	36 A - CHATEAU de LILLETTE Appendix
LILLETTE (CHATEAU)	5 pm	etc. 2 & 3 Sections with Headquarters arrived at the Chateau LILLETTE.	
	8 pm	N°1 Section returned from previous billet with the second load of stores	
"	29/6/15 1-15 am	Received orders to "Stand by"	Weather fine but cloudy
"	8 "	Company: Exercise mounted & dismounted. "Stand By"	

Army Form C. 2118.

Sheet N°10 of June.

WAR DIARY
or
INTELLIGENCE SUMMARY.
(Erase heading not required.)

Instructions regarding War Diaries and Intelligence Summaries are contained in F.S. Regns. Part II and the Staff Manual respectively. Title pages will be prepared in manuscript.

Hour, Date, Place	Summary of Events and Information	Remarks and references to Appendices
29/6 EN ROUTE FOR ESSARS 4.10 pm	Company marched off to new billeting area. Passed thro BOUREQ	Off E
5.35"		Rain
6-10	Passed thro LILLERS, after leaving LILLERS the weather changed from	
8.57	N° " BETHEINE. It was noticeable that at 9pm all civilians were indoors and the streets clear.	
10.30	Arrived at ESSARS having marched 15¾ miles. Troops welcome 10 minutes rest at LILLERS took a long time crossing the railway line.	
30/6 ESSARS.	The Carpenters of the Company have been working upon a somewhat novel invention which has been named the Snipers Scope. It is claimed with this that the man behind the rifle can depress his rifle over the trench without exposing himself and there is no doubt that the sight given thro the periscope is remarkably plain. The rifle is underlaid in the frame with ramrods marked "A" & "B" there is a handle which is used for re-loading the rifle when the magazine is charged, also "A" to be performed under cover. "C" also holds base at the bottom. The dotted line shows the line of sight. 8 of the SNIPERS SCOPES were sent up to Head Qrs today at 2.45 pm. It is advised essential that the periscope should be fixed in and have the eye piece in addition thus avoiding any reflection from the sun and revealing by this means showing the position of the rifle.	Fine but Cloudy

E.R. Fearn
Major
O.C. 1st/5th Batt. C.L.B.

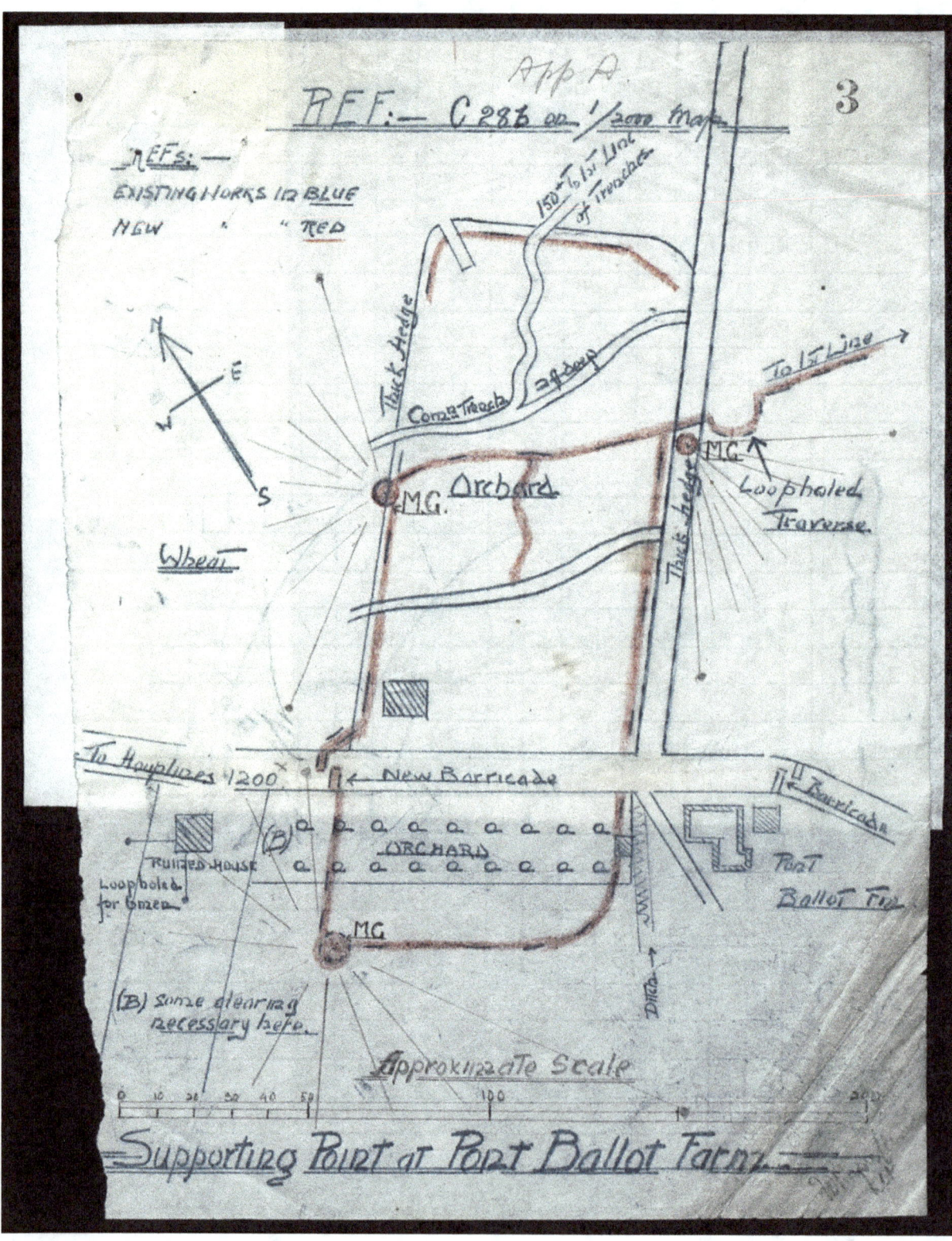

Hamel Billet
64th Field Co R.E.

28

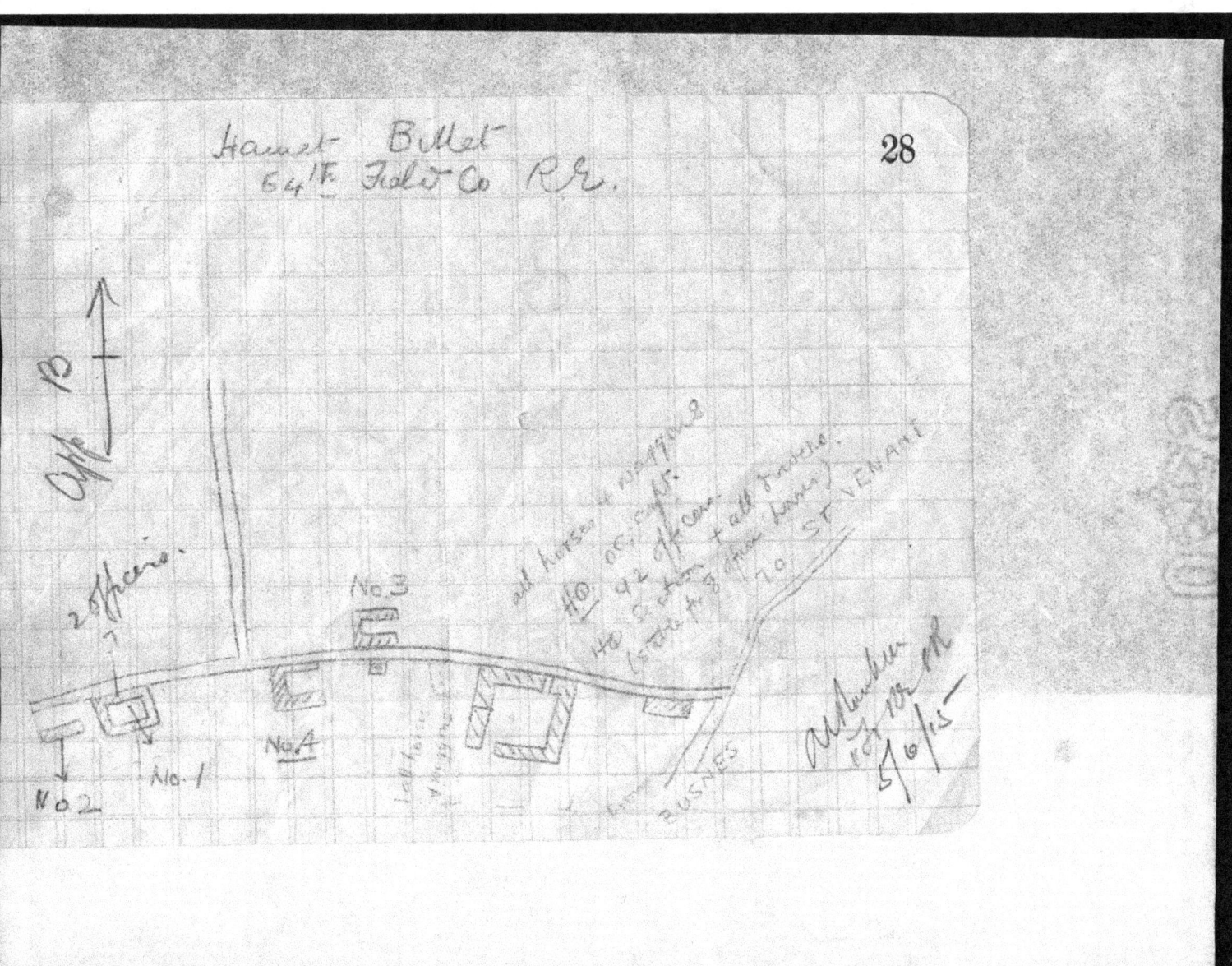

App C
Copy No 5

27th Inf: Brigade Order No 5.

24-6-15.

Ref map sheet 36A scale 1:40,000.

(1) The Brigade and attached troops will move to the ST HILAIRE billeting area tomorrow as under —

(2) Battalions will move by separate companies. ½ hour distances between each company. 64"Coy RE and 27" Field Ambce will also each move in 2 detachments, each separated by ½ an hour.

Every precaution to be taken to avoid being observed by aircraft.

Routes & times

(3) <u>12 RS</u>. via MOLINGHEM, NORRENT FONTES, ST HILAIRE, to LIERES. Leading coy to pass level crossing. Sq. O.9.d. at 9. am

<u>11 RS</u>. by same route — to ST HILAIRE. Leading coy to pass same level crossing at 11.AM.

<u>6.RS7</u> via PT CARLUY, LE CORNET BOURDOIS-LILLERS, to ECQUEDECQUES. Leading coy to cross railway, Sq: O.17. d at 8.30AM.

<u>10 A & SH</u>. via LE PONT A BALQUE, GUARBECQUE Church, then westward over GUARBECQUE river, then via LA LOTERIE, HAM-EN-ARTOIS, and S-W. to BOURECQ. Leading coy to cross canal at PONT A BALQUE at 9.30 AM.

<u>64 Coy RE</u> via main BUSNES - LILLERS road, & ECQUEDECQUES, to LESPESSES. Leading portion to leave billets at 10 AM.

<u>27.Fd Ambce</u> via LA LOTERIE, HAM EN ARTOIS, then direct to ST HILAIRE. Leading portion to pass road junction PT CARLUY at 11.30 AM.

<u>HQ 106 Coy ASC</u>. follow 27 Fd Ambce at 12 Noon.

(4) Reports up to 12 Noon to present Bde HQ: after that hour to (CHATEAU) COTTES, ST HILAIRE.

Issued 10.30 pm
Copy No 1 --- 11 Rs
2 --- 12 "
3 --- 6 RS7
4 --- 10 A&SH
5 --- 64 RE
6 --- 27 Fd Ambce
7 --- 106 ASC
8 --- Bde + Q

3-15 am
25/6/15

BM 27 Inf Bde

28th. Infantry Bde.

27th Infantry Bde.
27 K.I

27th Infantry Brigade No 6.   Order   Copy No 1
                                         App D

June 28th 1915.

Reference Sheet 36.A. Scale 1:40000.

(1) The following moves will take place to-day, consequent on changes in billeting areas.

<u>64th Field Coy: R.E.</u> From LESPESSES to LILETTE moving by road to west, thence by St HILAIRE. To start at 11.a.m.

<u>12th Royal Scots.</u> From LIERES to squares N.17c and N.29-a and b. moving by companies at ½ hour intervals, and <u>via</u> direct route. to start at 9.a,m.

<u>6th Royal Scots Fusrs;</u> From ECQUEDECQUES to NORRENT FONTES. moving by companies at ½ hour intervals, via BOURECQ and St HILAIRE to start at 11-15.a.m.

Every precaution will be taken to avoid being observed by aircraft.

Issued at 8.30 am
    Copy No 1 = 64th Coy R.E.
       do   2   12th Royal Scots.
       do   3   6th Royal Scots Fusrs.
       do   4   51st Bde R.F.A.
       do   5   27th Bde H.Q.

Major.
Brigade Major, 27th Infty Bde,

Ref Map 36A
1: 40,000.

App E.

Copy. No. 5

29-6-15.

27th Infantry Brigade Order No 7

1. The brigade will move to-day, to an area East of ROBECQ.

2. Units will march by Companies at quarter hour intervals, time of starting & route as follows:—

10th Arg & Suth Hghrs, start 1.15. P.M., route BOURECQ – LILLERS – BUSNES – after crossing canal, by Southern route to LALEAU – ROBECQ.

B'de. Head-quarters, start 2. P.M, route as for 10th A.S.H.
11th Royal Scots, start 2.30.P.M, route as for 10th A.S.H.
27 Field Ambce, start 3.35 P.M, route as for 10th A.S.H.
6th Royal Scots Fus, start 3.45 P.M, route ST. HILAIRE – BOURECQ, & thence as for 10th A.S.H.
64th Coy. R.E., start 4.45 P.M, route HAM-EN-ARTOIS – O.33 Z 8 – O.30 cb – BUSNES – thence as for 10th A+S. Hghrs.
12th Royal Scots, start 5. P.M, route as for 64 Coy R.E.
106 Coy. A.S.C, start 5.15 P.M. route as for 11th Royal Scots.

3. The usual halts will be observed.
4. Billeting parties will meet Staff Captain, at ROBECQ church at 2.30 p.m.
5. As soon as units have been allotted billets guides will be left on route to guide supply wagons.

Issued at 9-30 A.M.
Copy No 1 to 11th Royal Scots
" No 2 to 12th do
" No 3 to 6th R.S.F.
" No 4 to 10th A+S.H.
" No 5 to 64 Coy. R.E.
" No 6 to 106 Coy. A.S.C.
" No 7 to 27 Field Ambce
" Nos 8/10 to Bde H.Q.

B'HQ LOISNES X 22 C
106 Coy

Wm Teacher
Major,
Staff Capt. 27th Inf. Bde

"C" Form (Duplicate).   Army Form C. 2123.
MESSAGES AND SIGNALS.   No. of Message..........

Charges to Pay.   Office Stamp.
£   s.   d.

App E

Service Instructions.

Handed in at............ Office........m. Received........m.

TO   64 Coy R.E.

Sender's Number	Day of Month	In reply to Number	AAA
2B62	29		

Message from 9th Div begins
Please direct 64th Field Coy
to march to ESSARS X 25
moving by shortest route aaa
Please send billeting parties to
ESSARS to meet Capt YULE
at Church at 4pm aaa
acknowledge addsd 27th Inf Bde repto CRE
message ends
Please acknowledge.

Received 2.35 pm

FROM   27th Inf Bde
PLACE & TIME   2.15 pm

64th FIELD COMPANY R.E.

(9th Division)

JULY 1915

DL/6401

9th Division.

64th F.C.R.E.
Vol: III

July 1915

Army Form C. 2118.

WAR DIARY
or
INTELLIGENCE SUMMARY.
(Erase heading not required.)

Sheet No 1 of July 1915

Instructions regarding War Diaries and Intelligence Summaries are contained in F.S. Regs., Part II. and the Staff Manual respectively. Title pages will be prepared in manuscript.

Hour, Date, Place	Summary of Events and Information	Remarks and references to Appendices
8am. 1/7/15. ESSARS.	Company at work all day cleaning billets	Wet weather.
8 am 2/7/15 ESSARS. 6 pm 1/7/15 to 11-45 pm ESSARS.	Company at work all day. Lt. Beaumont + Lt. PLANT off to FESTUBERT with CRE. Received orders from C.R.E. to find a party immediately to repair bridge at B.7.A.8 (Bethune Contoured map). Work complete 3 am.	Fine weather intermittent firing all day.
5.15 pm 3rd do	Nos 1, 3 + 4 sections back on line dismissed yesterday. Young works for Infantry in series of localities. Constructing dug outs in trenches.	Fine. Thundery. Our guns fired late at night.
5.30 pm 4th do	No 1 + 2 sections and 200 Infantry continued work on dug outs dug trenches in front of LE PLANTIN South and also flanking of Communication trench. No 4 section worked on 6 dug outs for Infantry. Dug trench 3'x 1' in section at N end of locality. LE PLANTIN. Working party from 1/2 Royal Scots afterwards the at 12.30 am.	Fine.
3.30 am 5th do	sections returned to Billets.	
11-0 am do	A Taube made a very good attempt to cross over our line for observation purposes and was twice driven off	
5.30 pm do	LE PLANTIN SOUTH. The sections continued work on trenches and 5 A lines. Small engine brought away. LE PLANTIN (NORTH) One cellar completed. 3 Continued trench improved. Communication trench started. Working party 200 9/Sco. Rifles.	Working party 200 9/Sc. Rifles.

Army Form C. 2118.

WAR DIARY
or
INTELLIGENCE SUMMARY.
(Erase heading not required.)

Instructions regarding War Diaries and Intelligence Summaries are contained in F. S. Regs., Part II. and the Staff Manual respectively. Title pages will be prepared in manuscript.

The No 2 of July 1915

Hour, Date, Place	Summary of Events and Information	Remarks and references to Appendices
9.30 am 6/7 ESSARS	On our right - an observation balloon (presumably French) was today shelled. The shots at first well established short and low, but towards 11:00 am the enemy began to find the range and at mid-day the balloon descended. There (b.b) remained on the ground (and our right) two balloons which were shelled but they appeared to be out of range.	Enemy continually firing big gun fire as well as Gd Artillery. Weather hot & light wind.
5.30 pm 6/7 do	2, 3 & 4 sections to LE PLANTIN work too hot from the Colonial unit in both factory localities. Bergan moved their dug out and going to man and being often moved from LOBON Inj. 3 miles.	Rain at 9 pm mild about 11 pm. Heavy at times.
5.30 pm 7/7 do	1, 3 & 4 sections to LE PLANTIN - WILLOW ROAD - no big working party - continued work on shelters and put up revetments in readiness for duffs. - Brigades changing up - relief of trenches	High S.W. wind with showers at times all day.
5.30 pm 8/7 do	1, 2 & 4 sections to LE PLANTIN - WILLOW ROAD. Duffs from 7/Seaforth the did not come owing to their having marched back into reserve only that morning. Reconnaissances made for transfer from Rue de Bois to INDIAN VILLAGE by OC 2 & Lieut Clucking Ypres Nor section	High S.W. wind continued dropped at 8 pm.
5.30 pm 9/7 do	1, 2, & 3 to work LE PLANTIN - WILLOW ROAD no shelters preparing revetments for duffs. No working party again.	Drizzling rain & very.

Army Form C. 2118.

WAR DIARY
or
INTELLIGENCE SUMMARY.
(Erase heading not required.)

Sheet No 3 of July 1915

Hour, Date, Place	Summary of Events and Information	Remarks and references to Appendices
8 a.m. 10/7 ESSARS	No 4 section staked out line of workers tramway from BoiE du BOIS HINDIAN VILLAGE about 1517 yards, were first in with shrapnel directed probably from below.	Light breeze from SW. 3 enemy balloons up to SE and no gun near BETHUNE.
10.30 a.m. 5.30 p.m.	OC reconnoitred PETIT BOIS the platoon next section. No 2 + 3 section front of trenches with 9 platoon 10/A+S. Hd. dug'y finished informing settlers &c.	
5.30 p.m. 11/7 do	No 4 section on line of tramway making bridges and culverts and carrying up formation for leaving sleepers working party. 1 Cpl 11/H.L.I arrived at 8.30 pm in carrying up material and laying it in long grass alongside ruby. The enemy attack the exact target (not easy) and about 100 yards ventilated final forming of track which was set of story. Otherwise no casualties but no casualties. 2nd Lt Rankine with 1 Coy 10/A+S.H. continued work at LE PLANTIN North. Men were tired but progress was satisfactory sometime filling sandbags collecting bundles and making fletwork.	Dull - with rain early wind rose later, but died down towards evening. Direction SW.
8.30 p.m. do	No 4 section worked on tramway line until dark & bridges and huts - one platoon 11/HLI worked on an embankment at INDIAN VILLAGE and carried up heaps of fascines. No 1 and 2 trench at LE PLANTIN SOUTH - one Coy 10/A+S.Hm attached up front of village and in village - loopholes rifts on the housetop finished. No 5 Gunners Hd. K. practically complete.	High SW wind morning fire outside.
2 pm 8 pm 5.30 pm	No 4 section worked on tramway line - ¼ mile laid 100 11/H.L.I working party on building formation	
8 pm 13/7 8 pm	and worked lastly twice drained after 12 respn.	Calm - dull later.

WAR DIARY or INTELLIGENCE SUMMARY

Army Form C. 2118.

Thelus 4 July 1915

Hour, Date, Place	Summary of Events and Information	Remarks and references to Appendices
5.30 pm 13/7 ÉCOIVRES	Nos 1, 2 & 3 sections to LE PLANTIN NORTH & SOUTH. Continued dug outs and commenced trench — 100 lbs of A.P.'s and 100 lbs RE working parties carried up materials	Calm bright light shower
10 a.m. 14/7 do.	Wire enlisted tramway by day. OC. Broughton rail terrain impeded work (packing. Turning rail with terrain impeded work. BETHUNE for rail convoy (. 'f. no movement at Sphere about 4.30 pm.	Fine early with SW wind wind stopped aft. rain 4.30 pm becoming heavy at 9 pm. Thundery in afternoon with thick fog.
5.30 pm	Nos 2 & 3 took on wiring at LE PLANTIN NORTH. About half front main with 3 strands fence — one delayed by long grass. Very wet and to unlock most. Visit job all hit with well required and to unlock most. Visit job all hit with well	
8 a.m. 15/7 do.	Instructed party to make apron of revetment string at LE PLANTIN SOUTH. Not much completed partie — all revetment string to uninjure in trenches.	July SW wind — fine
	Starting ground about 1/4 mile of trench amongst hyperenlisted with tracks. Found about 1/2 2 men could push truck laden with tools & 3 men tools. Track rough and wheels not lubricated —	
3 pm 5.30 pm	On went round village lane park CRE until 6.45 pm Nos 1 & 3 sections to work at LE PLANTIN SOUTH & LE PLANTIN NORTH respectively — principally fulling up crater. No working parties —	S' wind fine intervals very little of each. 2 clear overcast it is every little of each
5.30 pm 16/7 do.	No 4 section continued consolidation (railway unit a 50 of KOSB up to 7.30 pm. Party who shelled intermittently. No 1 section W. Coy 8/ Gordon the worked upright wire and trenches of LE PLANTIN SOUTH wire completed along front. No 2 section worked wire along front of LE PLANTIN NORTH completed his front and wired about 300+ unknown. Interrupted for a time of firing	S' wind fine intervals supplies than L's train afternoon at 4.30 pm

Army Form C. 2118.

WAR DIARY
or
INTELLIGENCE SUMMARY.
(Erase heading not required.)

Sheet No 5-8 July 1915

Instructions regarding War Diaries and Intelligence Summaries are contained in F.S. Regs., Part II and the Staff Manual respectively. Title pages will be prepared in manuscript.

Hour, Date, Place	Summary of Events and Information	Remarks and references to Appendices
8 a.m. 17/7 ESSARS	Nos 3 & 4 sections trunk at LE PLANTIN NORTH & railway road by No 3 Coultivll with 2 platoons S/Lancs on from field fascines. Front L LLOYDS ranch and collecting planks up to MILL ON ROAD. Nos 1 completed laying & inspected trench. Railway & INDIAN VILLAGE. 8 workers with Lieutenant Knott on section S/Lancs R. Platoon LE PLANTIN SOUTH on shelter repairs. Also Col LE PLANTIN SOUTH support trench (15 feet) with huts.	Very high wind and showery.
5.30 pm 18/7 8 am	Lieut Dunn Coy's Officer 2 wnded at night right flank LE PLANTIN No 2 trench at LE PLANTIN SOUTH support repaired. No 3 works on fire wire and shelters. No 3 on shelter. No 2 on reptg orders & rev from 8 am to 4 pm up day work - No 1 on rest at	Fine but at shower until late
7.30 am 19/7 do.	night repaired. No 2 & loads carrd and upright. No 1's & 4 trench at LE PLANTIN North continued railway roads & orderly work all continued after attack to the 25 F.A. No 4 continued railway roads. Also attempting trench after Bore firing. Finished. Co inspected trenches 10.30 pm to 2.30 am. Occupied Villages 2 am - when No 4 continued work. Nos 1 & 3 on duties orders. No 2 on leading parties.	Fine, moderate S.W. wind
7.30 am 20/7 do.		Fine - dull afternoon Showers in afternoon Nos 2 on afternoon.
7.30 am 21/7 do.	Sections trunk on yesterday except that No. 2 where at PESTUBERT. Working parties & Pioneers & at RUE CAILLOUX.	Fine
7.30 am 22/7 do.	Work same as yesterday. Cap Commander & visited line Rue CAILLOUX with Lieut attack- 1 platoon 8/Black Watch under at LE PLANTIN SOUTH at night.	Dull - light SW wind rain at night
7.30 am 23/7 do.	Work same as yesterday. 1 platoon 8/Highland Lt Infantry wired at LE PLANTIN SOUTH at night. 0.25 as top right this (Pioneers) assisted at LE PLANTIN NORTH. Owing to leaflets our informing themselves after repeated warnings shelled RUE CAILLOUX with a few LYDDITE. No casualties.	Dull, heavy shower near night. Fine morn light frost.

Army Form C. 2118.

WAR DIARY
or
INTELLIGENCE SUMMARY.

(Erase heading not required.)

Sheet No 6 of July 1915

Hour, Date, Place	Summary of Events and Information	Remarks and references to Appendices
7.30am 24/7 ESSARS.	Section 2nd Fatigue in FESTUBERT & Railway respectively. 50 6/RSF + 20 Pioneers with former. 20 Pioneers to LE PLANTIN South + 20 to LE PLANTIN NORTH — No. 1 + 3 sections	Dull + showery morning. Wind - cleared up afternoon but showers again after.
4 pm.	frame of hut. 50 7/Seaforth Hrs with Lieut OC or night. Live 10 am to 8 pm. Railway completed + not visible.	
7.30am 25/7 do.	No. 1 section with 60 g/Seaforth Hrs (Pioneers) 6/7 & 20 RSF up + from worked on Keep.	Showery but wind - intervals told.
7.30am 26/7 do.	Section above as before. 20 Pioneers with each work with 7 S/F RSF in cellars. 20 Pioneers accepted at each work with 7 S/F RSF. CAILLOUX - 1 Platoon 8/Blackwatch at LE PLANTIN S. (night) 1 Platoon 8/RHY LE PLANTIN N. 100 7/RS. at FESTUBERT Div Cyclists + Glasgow Yeomanry at RUE CAILLOUX.	Fine cloudy later & wind Fine afternoon.
7.30am 27/7 do.	Sections to work as above. 20 Pioneers with each work with 7 S/F 50 6/RSF with No. 2 — House parties at RUE CAILLOUX 50 g/Blackwatch with No.	Heavy rain 8.30 am - 9 am. Light showers after & fine long.
7.30am 28/7 do.	Section to work as on 27th - No Hrs with No. 1, 50 8/Black watch with No. 5. fair to day only - 50 6/RSF 2 day with No. 2 —	Heavy shower 9 am High westerly. Fine aft.
7.30am 29/7 do.	Sections & work as before. 1 Platoon 8/Black watch LE 1 Pln with No. 1 - 1 Platoon 10/A&S Hrs with No. 2. Pioneers with No. 1, 2 + 3 as usual. Lieut Coy Company change billets to Rally Cog starting up with other half in the bt. & 20 d. + 7/136 Brig Route Force et Shell. Oct. small tent with GOC 2Bde gone at work to be done.	Light shower from am after.

Army Form C. 2118.

WAR DIARY
or
INTELLIGENCE SUMMARY.
(Erase heading not required.)

Sheet No. 7 of July 1915

Hour, Date, Place	Summary of Events and Information	Remarks and references to Appendices
1 Bn R.E. 30/7 ESSARS	Relieving troops as before —	Light W. wind.
7.30 pm do	OC 2 offrs reconnoitred trenches K.5 – 7716.	
7.30 am 31/7	Company changed billets, detrain up in farm X.20.d. 17 –	Bright W. wind – showers later. Cooler. evening.
9.30 am	OC & Sub GOC 26 Bgde about whole – afternoon & billetg.	
4.30 pm	OC to whole villages about with 1st offrs cleared Le Plantin S. & brother villages with 1st offrs cleared Le Plantin S.	
	Pools materials returned or held road by Lothian Road.	
	Forward Park —	
General	Office to works on village line – Le Plantin South is at	Bethune crowd shelt.
	A.8.a – sheet prepared. Le Hutches outpost and galated	
	from on Celland. Le Plantin North in NE corner of A.1.d.	
	Parapets are in fact – farms adapted for splinter proofs and	
	improved – enclosed country with orchards — For 1000 × 1500	
	village sunset to sheepful keep at cross roads prepared.	
	No one some in into any peripeter. Rue Cailloux 2	
	trenches S.25.b & S.19.d which contain up all round were with	
	loopholes none to splinter proofs. Wire connected up nort conne	
	Touch unth the fire and that up to forward in northern	
	orchard ½ house near Lombar Walk. Better have a	
	Bulgarian work before Hospitalople. Rue de Le Pinette	
	11.00 and S.13.d. Large wire S.B.Rue du Bois made ruled by	
	& Plantin points up wired – so-called Headquarters N of road	
	cleared up. Scheme prepared for new work not approved	
	yet.	

1/8/15

G.R. Hearne
Capt RE
OC 62 & 23 Coy R.E.

64th FIELD COMPANY R. E.

(9th Division)

AUGUST 1915

121/6743

9th Division

64th F.C.R.E.
Vol: IV

August 15

Army Form C. 2118.

WAR DIARY
or
INTELLIGENCE SUMMARY.
(Erase heading not required.)

The Month of August 1915

Instructions regarding War Diaries and Intelligence Summaries are contained in F.S. Regs., Part II. and the Staff Manual respectively. Title pages will be prepared in manuscript.

Hour, Date, Place	Summary of Events and Information	Remarks and references to Appendices
1/8. LE HAMEL	Sunday. No work - Day - orders received cancelling those of 28/7. and putting Coy into Village line again. Brigade changing in trenches - No working parties.	Fine. Variable veering to S. string at midday. Topped hill & milk.
7.30 am. 2/8. do.	Section to work No.1 LE PLANTIN S. with 20 Pnrs and No.3 LE PLANTIN NORTH with 20 Pnrs No.2. 1 Sgt.1 Pioneer with 20 Pnrs 450 1.101 A+SH's No.4. R.E. TAILLOUX & Arty Obs'n statn. BRANETTE	W. wind. medium cloudy high. S. wind straight
7.30 am. 3/8. do.	Sections to work as above. One platoon 51 Canons to work 20 Pioneers with each of No 1, 3 + 3. No 2, 3 to work also on Arty Observ. stan at or near the trenches.	Cloudy. Showers strong showery. fine later hot night.
7.30 am 4/8. do.	Sections to work as any other Day, augmented up to 2 pm only by one Platoon each of 51 Canons that. 20 Pioneers but each section as before. work continued on Arty Observ station.	Fine. Cloudy etc - S.W. wind medium temp little movement.
7.30 am. 5/8. do.	Sections to work as before on locations and Arty Observ stations. Nos 2, 1, 3, 3 each had a Platoon of 51 Canons 20 Pioneers - 1 Cpl Keeney (No 4831) was slightly wounded by a shell, on No 2 section returning from work.	Fine - Light S.W. wind
7.30 am 6/8. do.	Sections to work as yesterday. Nos 1, 2, + 3 accorded by 20 Pioneers each, a Platoon of 51 Canons each. (After nullet ruling only) Nox section sniveled by Pnrs of platoon & 51 Cadrens of Germany -	19 am light S. wind

Army Form C. 2118.

WAR DIARY
or
INTELLIGENCE SUMMARY.
(Erase heading not required.)

Sheet No 2 of August 1915

Instructions regarding War Diaries and Intelligence Summaries are contained in F. S. Regs., Part II and the Staff Manual respectively. Title pages will be prepared in manuscript.

Hour, Date, Place	Summary of Events and Information	Remarks and references to Appendices
7.30 a.m. 7/8. LE HAMEL	Sections break in marching order with tool carts. Works on localities as before (Nos 1, 2 & 3 sections) working party each of platoon Nº 4 Ars Ms	Dull; light air of wind. fine evening.
8 a.m. 8/8. do	Company paraded for muster. Baking parade at 10.30 am. Churchful Service 12.30 pm.	Dull - dull rain. fine aft. Evening. Calm.
7.30 a.m. 9/8. do	Sections broke. No 1 sect. to finish up at LE PLANTIN S. & worked half day in LE PLANTIN N. others as before. OC reconnoitred evg. for tramway to Field Ambulance in square Q33 b.	Dull. light SW air. rain evg. very close.
7.30 a.m. 10/8. do	Sections broke as yesterday. 2 sections at LE PLANTIN N. One section at FESTUBERT - each section with 2 O Pioneers + 1 platoon of Aug & A/S. No 4 section approx. GRILLOUX at Bœsinger own observation	Calm misty. fine aft. Close.
7.30 a.m. 11/8. do	Sections broke as yesterday. 1 platoon 11/RS each with No 1 & 3 sections and 2 platoons with No 2 section.	Dull. calm. fine aft & night.
6.30 p.m. 12/8. do	No 1 section on special work in front trench breaking out into near L.8. Machine Guns in each bay & returned 6.45 p.m. No 2, 3 & 4 sections same as yesterday. A section 2/1 Highld. Div. Light W. air close. R.E reported to No 3 section. The second cross rail of the fire carriage of the loop hole has been found. at the breach and two hand triggers also to the rifle. In repairing at a loop hole in trench chip. 5" x 2½" worked of 4" x 2½" were on the rifle so as not to interfere with the carrying. This trip found effective further test of Shrapnel & bullets specially of Shrapnel bem own plate - oppressive.

(73989) W4141-463. 400,000. 9/14. H.&.J. Ltd. Forms/C. 2118/10.

Army Form C. 2118.

WAR DIARY
or
INTELLIGENCE SUMMARY.
(Erase heading not required.)

Week No 30 August 1915

Hour, Date, Place		Summary of Events and Information	Remarks and references to Appendices
7.30 am	13/8 LE HAMEL	Julius trunk - No 1 & 3 at LE PLANTIN NORTH, No 2 at FESTUBERT - No 4 at RUE CAILLOUX. 10 am 2/L Highland H Coy relieved No. 2 Pireino Eer. with No 1 Plat - one Platoon 11/Rd each with No 1 & 3, 2 Platoons 11/Rd with No 2.	Fine, cloudy, light Sw and thundershower evening.
7.30 am	14/8 do	Relio trunk as yesterday, one Platoon 11/Rd with No 1 & 3 and 2 Platoons with No 2. No 4 relieved by garrison Pointe	Fine, cloudy, no wind to west.
7.30 am	15/8 do	Sunday - Relio trunk as before, one Platoon 11/Rd with each with Nos 1 & 3 - two 11/Rd with No 2.	Heavy showers - Thunder SW Wind.
8 am	16/8 do	Company referred to shift billets but did not move - own billets were not vacated.	Dull SW wind. Thunder and heavy showers in evening.
8 am	17/8 do	Company carried on arranging new ration arrangements. Billets moved to Nos. 30 a 7,8 (Béthune Cornhill Street) at 3 pm. W warenium. No 4 Coy R.E.	Cloudy, damp intervals. Thunderstorm, heavy showers - Fair aft.
9 am	18/8 ESSARS	Company Parade for drill - 2 parades at 11.15 am dismissed owing steady rain - Rest remainder of Day	Dull showers, fine aft.
7.30 am	19/8 do	Nos 1,2,3 relieving trunk at FESTUBERT and Grby Orchards Platoon on that locality - No 3 rest + drill - relieving retd from work 2 pm.	Fine early, drill by 8 am fine aft.
7.30 am	20/8 do	Nos 1,2,3 declined to work at FESTUBERT + Wg & Place Support in Form 12 LE PLANTIN NORTH - No rest + drill - relieving returned after 2 pm.	Dull, calm, misty evening.

Army Form C. 2118.

WAR DIARY
or
INTELLIGENCE SUMMARY.
(Erase heading not required.)

Sheet No. 1 of August 1915

Instructions regarding War Diaries and Intelligence Summaries are contained in F.S. Regs., Part II and the Staff Manual respectively. Title pages will be prepared in manuscript.

Hour, Date, Place		Summary of Events and Information	Remarks and references to Appendices
7.30 am	21/8 ESSARS	Sections 2 & 3 at work. No. 1 Sect. I drill. Sections worked at FESTUBERT, Rep Church & Arty Observation also at Orch. Reservation R.E. at CAILLOUX.	Dull - Snowy later moderate N.W. wind.
7.30 am	22/8 do	Sunday - Company Funk at FESTUBERT and in gardens returned at 2.30 p.m.	Fine cloudy intervals moderate N.W. wind.
7.30 am	23/8 do	No 1, 3, 4 sections at FESTUBERT - No 2 sect drill.	Dull light S.W. wind. Calm misty evening.
7.30 am	24/8 do	Company Funk FESTUBERT returned at 5 p.m. OC Capt and 2 subalterns to VERMELLES to reconnoitre defences.	Calm misty - Close - Fine afternoon Fine light air.
7.30 am	25/8 do	Company to work FESTUBERT. Sect work 9 p.m. 2/Lt Paulin & Fischer to reconnoitre VERMELLES.	Fine - $\circ E$ wind light
7.30 am	26/8 do	Company Funk FESTUBERT - O/C & R.E. at BUSNES.	Fine. N.E. wind light. Hot especially afternoon.
7.30 am	27/8 do	No 2 & 3 section stood by ready to move on orders from CRE IX. No 1 & 4 Section at FESTUBERT and Arty Obs Station see it. No 1 Sect to see trenches in 12th Divn area.	Fine calm very hot in afternoon. Thunder at night.
7.30 am	28/8 do	Nos 3 & 4 Sections prepared to move. No 1 & 2 funk at FESTUBERT round Rep Church & Arty Reinfork. Lt Clarence & 2/Lt Rankin RCE 2nd & 7th Cg Reconnoitre area & 12 Divn	
7.30 am	29/8 do	No 1 & 2 sections Funk at FESTUBERT. No 3 & 4 marched to BURNES to Square A, 19 & 4.0. in Touches and dugouts into outskirts of town. Convair Funck from HUMANITY crossroads in 12 Divn area. OC Capt Browne reconnoitred this area.	Dull calm moderate S.W. wind rising later Rain after luncheon.

Army Form C. 2118.

WAR DIARY
or
INTELLIGENCE SUMMARY.
(Erase heading not required.)

Sheet No 5 of August 1915

Hour, Date, Place	Summary of Events and Information	Remarks and references to Appendices
7.30 am 30/8 ESSARS.	No 1 + 2 to work at FESTUBERT finishing and On the 25th instant the work at FESTUBERT EAST was shelled with field gun shrapnel while O.C. was on the work, and a direct hit was made in a dugout in which 9 men were sheltering at the time. A hole was made in the roof but none of the men were killed & only no man scratched and slightly wounded. This may be attributed to the fact that the dugout had a strong roof and a brick layer on Juniter. About 12 shell were fired into the work but no further damage was done. The men living well sheltered in scattered dugouts. No 3 ep return of Detachment of CAMBRIN continued work on new communic. Handl. trench.	Fine. West wind. Fresh.
8am 31/8 do	Company rested. No 3 sent on retachment worked at night in digging under tramway for commun trench. O.C. 10th OC 81 & 91 RE 191st Div. also Village Line and Obs. Posts from RUE CAILLOUX to LE PLANTIN.	Friedrich W. wind slightly westerate
General.	Apparais obtained. Nibs or Tripmolen (?) in line of Eonidom for defence Nets on Front Tramway's RUE de l'EPINETTE-INDIAN VILLAGE Opp.13. with plan.	App R. Opp. 13.

E P Nearn
Major RE
OC 84 71 Coy R.E.

1/9/15

Appendix A.

The following notes embody our experience of placing the "Village Line" in a state of defence ~~before I was able to judge ~~~~~~

1. **Tactics.** The defended localities are intended primarily as supporting points so that if the front system of trenches has to be abandoned (it must be held at all cost but the enemy may be too strong) the garrisons of the localities may be able to hold on until a second system of trenches can be built up on the line of points of support. This may not be possible until counter attacks have driven the enemy back after they have penetrated between two or more supporting points, and the garrisons of these points may have to stand a heavy bombardment and assault. They must be designed therefore

(a) To develop frontal fire and especially to deny all roads to the enemy

(b) To sweep the intervals with machine gun fire or concentrated infantry fire from positions made as safe as possible against a bombardment while the enemy attempts to pass through the intervals, through which also the survivors of the trench system have retired

(c) To have a continuous obstacle (extending also round the gorge), the obstacle to be defended by flanking fire as much as possible and to be strongest where the flanking fire is weak.

(d) To be divided into sectors of defence suitable to one or more companies, each with its local keep, and to be designed for a step to step defence in each sector so that a lodgement in any part of a sector shall be made as difficult as possible and that occupation of any one house should not enable the enemy to fire into the next behind

(e) To have a keep for the whole locality which should defend the gorge and sweep the sectors as much as possible, all keeps to have a continuous obstacle and a garrison told off

(f) To have a sufficient number of shelters for the garrison (less guards & sentries) to live in and to be protected from the bombardment until the moment arrives for the repelling of the infantry assault.

(g) To have excellent communications, both in the houses and to the trenches, so that the garrison of the trenches may emerge quickly and man the trenches directly the bombardment ceases. Even if men remove their packs they must retain belts, pouches & bayonets and small openings will be difficult to pass. Trenches are 70ˣ in front of the houses and the enemy infantry has 200ˣ or so to traverse over open ground, so there is no time to waste.

(h) To ensure that lines of retirement of survivors in front trenches are clearly marked, so as not to embarrass the defenders of the keeps, and that provision is made for these survivors to aid the keep garrisons by manning a second line of trenches, untraversed so as to be under fire from the keep back & front. These lines of retirement may be enclosed by a wire obstacle on either side.

2. These points are now examined in detail:-

(a) Front trenches require to be narrow with a good parados not bullet proof at the top, and with traverses not more than 18 feet apart. The trace should be indented so that M.G. emplacements can be made to sweep the front of the trenches and the obstacle, and also so that ranging may be made more difficult. M.Guns should sweep the roads. M.G. emplacements should be about 5' x 4' spaced at suitable intervals but not too large; the entrance should be easy so that a killed or wounded man or the gun may be removed speedily.

(b) Trenches to a flank should have traverses not more than 9 feet apart and the traverses should be raised above parapet level. M.gun emplacements should be as secure as possible & sited well back with a large sector of fire. Positions may be prepared for the survivors of the front trench system to hold on by, but these should be outside the localities of the keeps, and sited so as not to embarrass a counter-attack.

(c) The quickest obstacle to erect is an apron fence, three lines of wire in the fence, 3 in the front apron & one along the back stays. Posts may be 9 feet apart. To widen place a post opposite centre of each bay 10 feet back and connect by wires top & bottom and crossed top to bottom. French wire may be used between aprons & posts back & front. Blockers on roads must be strong and under close fire. The obstacle should if possible be beyond bombing distance from the work.

(d) The step to step defence should be arranged so that holes may be knocked in the walls or windows cut down to floor level in the houses, & entrances to dugouts should be under fire from the house behind. The sectors should be designed to accommodate (i) garrison of front trench (ii) supports (iii) garrison of keep. The latter may accommodate more than its garrison & all access to be closed when the surplus has left to man the trenches, see 1(h) above.

(e) The garrison of the Keep requires bomb proof shelter and if loopholes can be cut in the walls of these so much the better, but if they are to develop their fire from breastworks it does not seem necessary to have traverses or parados for these unless they are likely to be exposed to rifle fire. Once the enemy infantry is in the locality or attacking the gorge, their artillery could hardly keep up the bombardment. The same argument would apply to the local Keeps.

(f) It seems impossible to construct shelters which would be proof against heavy field howitzer (or larger) shells without the expenditure of much time & labour. The main idea is to have a burster, either a wall or an upper floor or a double row of bricks on the dug out roof so that the shell may not penetrate the shelter and burst inside. A double layer of bricks ought to burst the smaller shells and ought to be on top of the roof protection unless it is visible or liable to blow about dangerously when a layer of earth should cover it. It is wrong to have the bricks immediately above the roof with a thick layer of earth into which the shell can burrow and explode with greater effect. To lessen the risk of loss not more than 8 men should be accomodated in any one shelter, the interior dimensions (free of props) being about 8' x 7'. When constructed inside a house the floors should be dug down 1½ to 2 feet to give more headroom. Ventilator shafts through the roof are good. Dugout floors may be brick on edge in cement; concrete floors are cold and liable to sweat. Shelters for commanders of garrison, sectors & keep, also for dressing station, require to be specially well protected.

(9) These remarks apply especially to narrow passages between splinter proofs and doors of the same. Directions should be painted on walls to facilitate communication.

3. It must not be forgotten that look-out posts are necessary for commanders (down to platoon commanders), and there seems to be necessity for dugouts under the parapet or in blind paradors for the guards of the front trenches. Brick in cement walls seem very suitable for these, and take up little room. The garrison commander's post may be of the conning tower type with a strong re-inforced concrete burster roof & walls and air spaces to prevent concussion. Small mesh expanded metal may be used to stop splinters entering the observing slit.

4. Water supply, ammunition & ration stores, first aid & dressing stations, & latrines are necessary accessories.

GR Hearn
Major RE
21/8 OC by Ft Cpl.

Appendix B.

Tramway RUE deL'EPINETTE - INDIAN VILLAGE

This was a wooden tramway designed for the carriage of rations, water & R.E. materials from the Rue du Bois over a distance of about 1500ˣ see plan attached. The trucks were fitted with rubber rests for 5 stretchers with wounded coming down from the trenches. Owing to a shift of Brigades northwards in the trenches, the tramway was found of little use for the first purpose (but of considerable use for the second purpose) and not so much traffic passed over it as was expected.

2. **Material.** The way consisted of wooden rails 3x2½ inches in section & about 16 feet long on the average, with wooden sleepers of ½ inch planking 8" wide, 3 feet long and spaced at about 3 feet intervals. Rails were nailed to the sleepers at 1'11½" gauge. The fishplates were wooden 12" long 2"x1½" in section, nailed to rails. Wooden chocks on the inside were found to be necessary. Each length was made up complete, rails, sleepers & a pair of fishplates & was easily portable by 2 men. By "springing" at the joints an offset of 48" was obtainable in each length for purposes of curves. The rails being of soft wood wore very considerably on curves, and sleepers were difficult to pack properly.

3. **Rolling Stock.** These were platform trucks with end railings, about 6' between rails and 4'6" wide on two pairs of wheels about 12" in diameter spaced at 3 feet centres. The wheels had small flanges and in wet weather the clay caked on them so that derailments were common. The maximum load was 2000 lbs but rails wore rapidly under such a load; experiment showed that 3 men could push 1000 lbs comfortably.

4. **Construction.** One Coy of Infantry carried up the material & hid it in the grass along the location in one night. One section R.E. with assistance from Infy completed the line in 14 days. A certain amount of shelling was experienced, but there were no casualties.

5. **Maintenance.** An A.S.C. officer was placed in charge of the line with a few Divl cyclists, but little appeared to be done. Carpenters from the 90 Fd Coy RE worked one day on repairs (the rails having been cut by shrapnel) and fitting chocks at joints

between rails. Further observation was not possible as the Compy. was employed elsewhere.

6. <u>Operation</u>. The trucks must be pushed with care round curves, one man pushing on the outside in front, so as to ease round the curves. Greasing & cleaning of wheels require attention.

1/9/15.

G R Hearn
Major RE
O C 64 Fd Coy RE

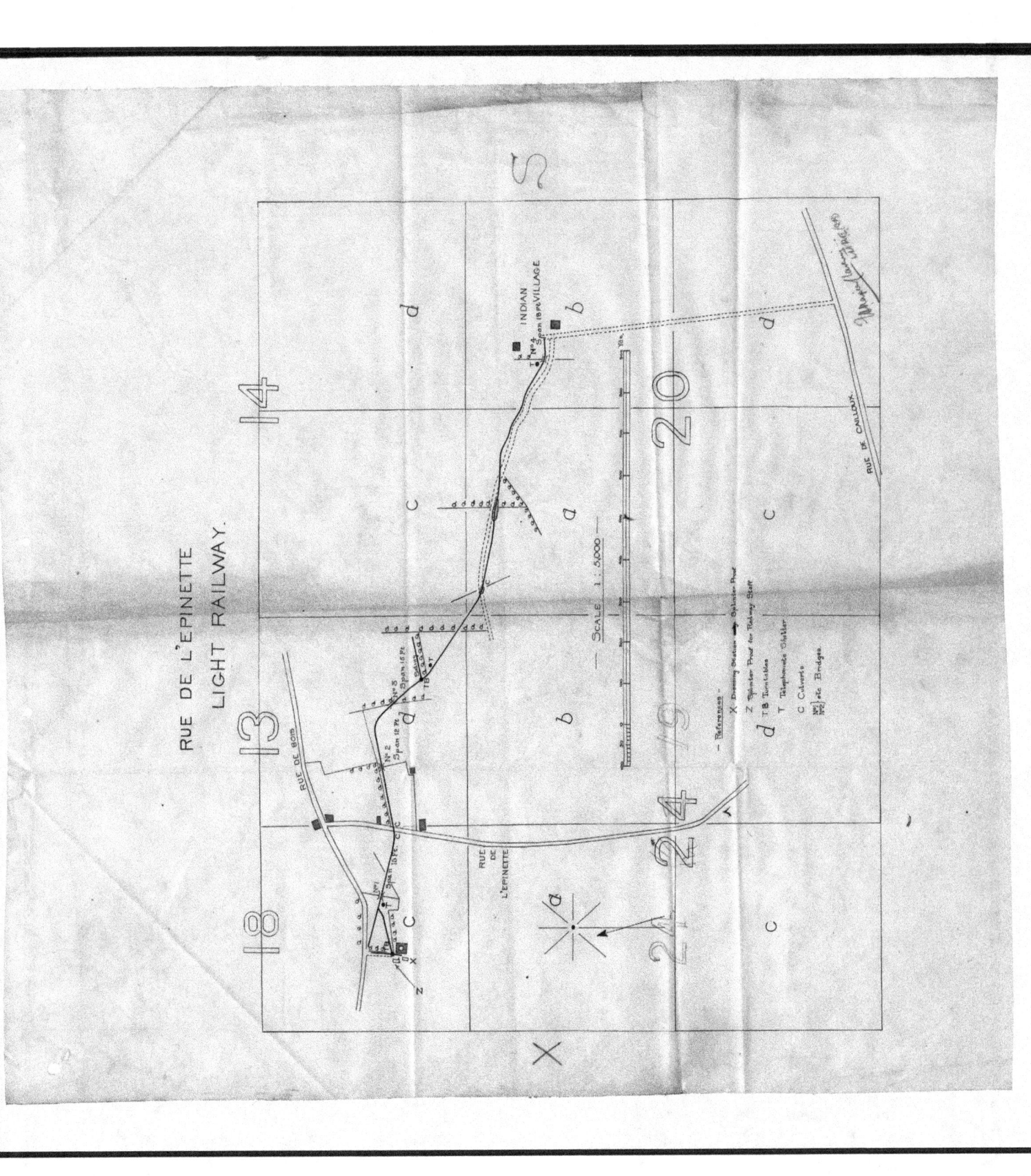

64th FIELD COMPANY R. E.

(9th Division)

SEPTEMBER   1915

121/7153

9th Hussein

64th F.C. R.E.
Vol 5
Sep 1. 15

Not very cheering reading as regards the infantry

WAR DIARY or INTELLIGENCE SUMMARY

Army Form C. 2118.

Keep Month of September 1915

(Erase heading not required.)

Hour, Date, Place		Summary of Events and Information	Remarks and references to Appendices
9 a.m.	1/9 ESSARS	1, 2, & HQ sections paraded for drill and bayonet fighting. 3rd section at CAMBRIN. D. Woollan & 2/Lt Foster moved to billets in front of CAMBRIN with entrenching area occupied by Division. 1 Coy 9/Scott Rifles continued to man trenches. 3rd echo with 1 Coy 9/Scott Rifles relieved. 2/Lt French teaching men cuts & guards from HUMANITY to PW. Q.3. called GUYS ALLEY.	Fine - cloudy intervals. Strong Sy. to S.W. wind. Showers after heavy in eng - the night. Dull, light W. wind. Showers evening & the night.
9 a.m.	2/9 do	1, 2, & HQ sections paraded for drill & bayonet fighting. 3rd section as last 5. 1 platoon "H" 1 by Day and 1 by "H"Z 1 by night continued communication trench -	
8 a.m.	3/9 do	Parade dismissed owing to rain & gale of wind. Received orders aft. but still attempt to extend the attainder defences more. No.2 section moved to SAILLY-LA-BOURSE.	Dull rain - West wind. fresh - rained all day.
7.30 a.m	4/9 do	1st and 3rd sections with all vehicles moved to BETHUNE - returning Pre Hdqrs coastways. 1 Coy 9/Scott Rifles left our from N.W. No 1 section with all vehicles marched to BETHUNE - rations Mess tarries (two in No. 4) in field attached to BOULEVARD THIERS. HQ followed later - domiciled in SKATING RINK. Officers HQ at 40 BOULEVARD THIERS. No 2 section during trips to billets, guns and erecting dugout to GOE DUG HQ at SAILLY LA BOURSE. 3rd section at SAILLY LA BOURSE. 3rd section still trench and dugouts associated by 2 platoons by day GUYS ALLEY completed. 20 ft booked by night.	Fine - left air from N.W. Cloudy later -
7.30 a.m	5/9 BETHUNE	Had section Carpenters at 6 a.m. to work on bomb store at ANNEZIN. remainder to clean up camp & - Bomb store at ANNEZIN right N.W. air. Report completed at noon. No. 2 section returned from SAILLY LA BOURSE to Hdqrs. 2 p.m.	Dull morning with rain & fine later. Cloudy at times, N.W. air. Fine, eng. calm.

WAR DIARY or INTELLIGENCE SUMMARY

Army Form C. 2118.

Sheet No. 2 of September 1915

Hour, Date, Place	Summary of Events and Information	Remarks and references to Appendices
6 a.m. 6/9. BÉTHUNE	Nos 1, 2, & HQ sections t/work at steam sawmill making trench carrying trees, trench strits, bridges, broken till 5 p.m. No 3 s.t. section on detachment at CAMBRIN making new comm. trench and shelters in railway embank near Pinhurst S.E. CAMBRIN. OE would appr reconnoitred crossings & changes	Fine – light rain – clear day
6 a.m. 7/9. do.	No 1, 2, & HQ sections as yesterday by worked up to 6.30pm on trench carrying bridges etc. Received 3 truss trees from Rimincourt. No 3 s.t. work 2 platoons W/HL1 worked on comm trench to FACTORY. con Bgde HQ undergr. 1 platoon constr. new bridges across stream. Wiring on No 2 s.t/Q on trench stores.	Fine. Typh N.W. airs.
6 a.m. 8/9 do.	No 3 s.t. at CAMBRIN w/2 plats W/HR1 widening GUIS ALLEY and making 3 bridges over stream con ry railway.	Misty. fine later. light air
6 a.m. 9/9. do.	Nos 1, 2, & HQ continued work on trench stores – No 3 s.t. completed bridges over stream. Cross entrance in trench 4 & 26 c. unknown dugn near MAISON ROUGE & VYS ALLEY near FACTORY & A26 a	Fine. warm extra misty. Calm. v. light air N.E.
6 a.m. 10/9 do.	Nos 1, 2, & HQ continued work on trench stores. No 3 s.t. on dugn Maison Rouge & shelters for 27 Bgd.a. 1 platoon W/HL.1 finished GUIS ALLEY to the FACTORY.	Fine. moderate breeze. N.E.
6 a.m. 11/9 do.	Nos 1, 2, & HQ continued work on trench stores. No 3 s.t. worked on Bgd HQ, 2 completed DP for C/53 and erected boarding for bridges over stream. We work in James Coml & Pinton very very hot night hard work at return at night. Ambulance spent carrying work wounded from right Wiltshire. Ride Pelle (?) Black ret. (?) over Ypres edge.	Fine. light N.E. breeze

WAR DIARY
or
INTELLIGENCE SUMMARY

Army Form C. 2118.

Sept No 3 September 1915

Hour, Date, Place	Summary of Events and Information	Remarks and references to Appendices
8.30 am 12/9 BETHUNE Sunday	No 1 & 2 Coy paraded for work on trench cubicles, traverses, & field workshops etc.	Fine, light breeze SE
6 am 13/9 do	No 3 Coy adjm. in attendance at CAMBRIN when General Staff Engineer name trenches, collected information regards to Coy Experiments on sandbags filled with slag. Parcel riddled & one shatter alone not proof against 6" slag at 100ft. Slag between banks if 5" thick "blist up" would not note and was mostly intact, if 6" slag + bank & sandbags an the downward most intact.	Fine light breeze SE
6 am 14/9 do	No 1 & 2 Coy work on trench steps. No 3 Coy collected material for dugouts and continued drawing ditto with so ft of dugouts near BEAM 6 by day and 100 men by night. 30 Capt reconnoitred night of Jones & brought ashine. No 1 & 2 Coy to move to trench stores. No ? came in & Rfr with several Coys officers reported. 3t night 100 Pioneers worked on GUN's ALLEY work of the FACTORY. 2nd Lt. Fisher admitted to hospital.	Louis — again Son. Fuze & Explosions etc.
6 am 15/9 do	No 1 & 2 Coy continue work on trench stores & dugouts, repairing sandbags. No 3 Coy continue work in traverse and regret. Noise marked dugouts in trenches S of FACTORY for 64 4 Coy. 50 Officers worked by GHYS ALLEY, drawing stakes and dugout for 12/RS (finished)	Dull, calm, mist. Fine later - light N airs. Fine
6 am 16/9 do	No 1 & 2 Coy continue work as before. Stores etc pegged out as noted. Coys warned of possibility of more action of kind. No 3 Coy worked on dugouts of experts in frontline - 7×2½×3' timbered, front drawing. Shank at FACTORY worked. Trench to be occupied by this Coy (?)	Dull, calm, light W breeze later - close evening
8 am 17/9 do	No 1 & 2 Coy continued work after parade in marching order. No 3 Coy continue dugouts to experts in frontline, and trench to be occupied by the Company	Dull - calm, fine later, very close

WAR DIARY or INTELLIGENCE SUMMARY.

Army Form C. 2118.

Sheet No 4 of September 1915

Hour, Date, Place	Summary of Events and Information	Remarks and references to Appendices
6 pm 18/9 BETHUNE	Nos 1, 2 & 4 HQ for work on Artillery portable bridges (new type). 2 Shee finished. 5 more frames (6"x 3", 15 checks 7½" x ½") & ribands 3"x3" in each bridge. Clear span 10'. Started with 32 Auxy limber wagons afternoon 17th for Ly. Making 79' clear water width. Left on detachment at CAMBRIN. Completed augmentation (32 wales) afternoon worked on Camp's hand.	Fine, light N.E. breeze
6 am 19/9 Sunday	Nos 1, 2 HQ to work on Bty. bridges. Completed by noon. (without ponds?) Rest of afternoon. No 3rd	Fine, light N.E. breeze heavy dew at night
6 am 20/9 8 am	Nos 1 & 4 HQ start at sawmill &c. No 2 Coy & CAMBRIN frame w. Company hutch. Transported on perambulator wagon wheel (back) broke suddenly. The front wheels (new) gave but generally weak, hats rolls being fitted. Mr &c especially to improve - bolts & nails in short supply. One greater than a GS wagon wheel & its arrangements being made to put them on a GS wagon which will reverend. Profichan? in turn. 6 & 9 & 8 for Young wheels. There are available pocket in the wagons for field & supply and lost cart lumber wagons RE, GS wagon (hand) and cart of indifferent & of spare tents and other ADC but for low wheels and young wagon wheels are apt to fall. No Bty worked on 57 Bgde RHA Negro trench LEWIS ALLEY & spare dug out near factory.	Fine - light air, late strong S.E. wind.
7 am 21/9 do	No 3rd technical Infantry HQ flag at BETHUNE = Capita.	Fine calm

Army Form C. 2118.

WAR DIARY
or
INTELLIGENCE SUMMARY.   Sheet No 5 of September 1915

(Erase heading not required.)

Instructions regarding War Diaries and Intelligence
Summaries are contained in F.S. Regs., Part II
and the Staff Manual respectively. Title pages
will be prepared in manuscript.

Hour, Date, Place	Summary of Events and Information	Remarks and references to Appendices
9 am, 22/9 BETHUNE	Coy on parade in morning: other ranks packed trucks on forage carts. Officers reconnoitred Factory Front trenches etc.	Fine - light air from S.
8 am, 23/9 do.	Coys on parade for inspection. Poured at 10 am to march: practice loaded waiting for motors after.	Fine - light air from S. Offensive after thunderstorm Heavy rain 7 pm to 10.30 pm.
8 pm.	Received operation orders from CRE. Reckon. Bridging train attached to us.	
9 am, 24/9 do.	Parade. Road wagons OCTPTTMLY to CRE	Dull: fresh late. light airs from S.
4.15 pm	No 3 Section proceeded to CENTRAL KEEP to stand by to keep in repair our kinds bridge had might to believe: arrived here 7 pm and remained	Dull: wet evening and night wind slight S.S.W.
	All wagons and animals, but Captain &c, proceeded to F19, and how --ached there.	
5.30 pm "	No 1, 2 & 4 Sections proceeded to LANCASHIRE TRENCH and remained here: OC ye: to be in Divisional room.	In readiness for action September 25th
25.9.15	No 3 Stood by in CENTRAL KEEP to repair RA bridge if required: required Coy in LANCASHIRE TRENCH at 6 pm.	Dull: very wet afternoon and evening: wind light, wind SSW.
1 pm. "	No 1, 2, re Both stood by in order to LANCASHIRE TRENCH in afternoon repaired new road up to K3 near by Artillery group. Provide Section & HQ were proceeded to ANNEQUIN, to attack group.	
11.30 am 26.9.15	No 1 & 3 Sections proceeded to Fosse 8 to support trenches if required were unable to work owing to madequiness of troops holding positions were employed as infantry holding LANCASHIRE TRENCH	Date let cine
1 pm. "	Also 2 & 4 HQ sections returned to camp LA BOURSE	
4.30 pm "	nores to operating trenches Noire SECTION	

WAR DIARY or INTELLIGENCE SUMMARY

Army Form C. 2118.

Sheet No 6, 7 Sept, 1915.

Hour, Date, Place	Summary of Events and Information	Remarks and references to Appendices
2 p.m. 26.9.15.	Nos. 1 & 3 Secs. Lt Woolner (6 servant) at HOHENZOLLERN REDOUBT and proceeded up S. FACE TRENCH (towards SLAG ALLEY): on top coming at DUMP TRENCH our infantry were seen to be retreating from the DUMP HEAP across the open. Lt Woolner arrested their retreat and took the infantry (R. Sussex Regt) [back] under him to the FOSSE where he found the re-mainder 2 the unit, which then advanced with the R.E. to the far side 2 the DUMP HEAP. No enemy in sight and infantry again retired. R.E. retreated into SLAG ALLEY & worked along two 6 FOSSE ALLEY. One Coy 2 the R. Sussex Regt was found in the trench, but so far as Cords & Sens No 3 Relief troop to the right, & no Enemy in sight. The R.E. found infantry & Lt Jones in SLAG ALLEY and returned to SLAG ALLEY where they prepared to rifle fire to the SOUTH. It was then 9 p.m. and realising that relief was un-likely, the sections returned to LANCASHIRE TRENCH. Coming the LANCASHIRE + SUSSEX Regt) letting FOSSE ALLEY and SLAG ALLEY. Reached LANCASHIRE TRENCH at 11 p.m. Nos. 2 & 4 sections O/c 2c., proceeded (6 relieve Nos 1 & 3 secs:) met Lt C.R.E. in HOHENZOLLERN REDOUBT & proceeded with him up S. FACE TRENCH where he was wounded by a shell splinter. O/c became C.R.E. & divided section to DUMP TRENCH, found the infantry had dis-organized; obtained portions 2 13th order him a wounded orderly, reform-ed 27th Bn 6 into FOSSE TRENCH. Leaving the Sappers (3 land Lds) the 27 Bn & other collected about 300 men & scattered units 2 the 27 Bn 8 2c	Quiet (no wind)
4 p.m.		

WAR DIARY
INTELLIGENCE SUMMARY

Army Form C. 2118.

Sheet 7 ? Sept 1915

Hour, Date, Place	Summary of Events and Information	Remarks and references to Appendices
26.9.15	and about 50 men 2 the Middlesex Surrey Regt in SLAG ALLEY. Trench was later manned by later. Handed over wire where this section has brought up, to the 90th C.R.E. by one of Les TROIS CABARETS. Craters were invisible but the section could do no effective work.	
1.30 p.m. 26.9.15	Section marched back to LANCASHIRE TRENCH billets by the sentries returning to 27 Brigade H.Q. Brigadier Returned to bivouac at 3 a.m. While the ACRE road.	G. Hearn Major R.E. OC 91st Coy R.E.
12.30 am 27.9.15	H.Q. & 2 mounted sections went to SAILLY-LABOURSE.	Dull: wet morning and bright light wind S.W. very wet night.
8 am. 27.9.15	Capt Raven went to LANCASHIRE TRENCH & assumed Command. 2 Gd.Co. 2 Lt Wolfe sent to take charge 1 H.Q & 2 mounted section.	
3 p.m. " "	On report 9 26th July 18th Coy. proceeded to trenches as a local reserve to infantry in front line in view of serious situation.	
10 p.m " "	Returned to LANCASHIRE TRENCH, their services here no longer required.	
6.30 p.m. 26.9.15	Coy. proceeded about from to HOHENZOLLERN REDOUBT, arriving there, with instructions to make a strong point at Pt B9, near the junction 9 BIG WILLIE TRENCH & DUMP TRENCH on the left flank 9 the 7th Divn. While 2 Corp Pioneers were sent out, to wire & make T heads in BIG WILLIE with OC Gd.Co, The sapper reserve were held in the British advanced trench under Sgt K and O.C. & Lt Clancey went forward to reconnoitre.	

Army Form C. 2118.

WAR DIARY
or
INTELLIGENCE SUMMARY.

(Erase heading not required.)

Sheet 8. 9 Sept 1915

Hour, Date, Place	Summary of Events and Information	Remarks and references to Appendices
28.9.15	At 10.15 p.m. a message was received from C.R.E. living 1st Corps orders that previous instructions were cancelled & a new attack was to be prepared. Information was received at the same time by O.C. that the enemy were in possession of FOSSE TRENCH, DUMP TRENCH, & SOUTH FACE, that new orders could not be carried out. However the 2 Coys Pioneers had already returned in receipt of the counter-order, and by the time the information as to enemy had been verified, no work could be commenced which could be any extent completed before dawn. The Coy returned to LANCASHIRE TRENCH arriving at 3 a.m.	Dull, very wet extremely and night; no wind
12.30 p.m. 29.9.15.	1, 2 & 3 Pelotons marched to ANNEQUIN billets.	Fine.
7.30 p.m.	marched to SAILLY-LA-BOURSE, picked up HQ. transports section train and marched to billets at OBLINGHEM arriving there 11.55 pm	
30.9.15.	Whole Coy rests in billets at OBLINGHEM. 1st Lt A.G. SHENSTONE Temp. Co. R.E. joined the Coy.	Fine, Sunny

(Signature) Capt R.E.
O.C. 1st Coy

1.10.15.

64th FIELD COMPANY R. E.

(9th Division)

OCTOBER 1915

121/7598

9th Division

64 I.C.R.E.
Vol. 6

Oct. 15.

Army Form C. 2118.

WAR DIARY
or
INTELLIGENCE SUMMARY.
(Erase heading not required.)

Sheet No I of Oct 7th 1915

Hour, Date, Place	Summary of Events and Information	Remarks and references to Appendices
5.45 am. 1.10.15. OBLINGHEM	Mounted section left OBLINGHEM, and Lt Lorkin R.E. to march by road to DICKEBUSCH	Fine, bright day
6.45 am " " "	Dismounted portion proceeded to FOUQUEREIL Rly STATION and entrained at 8.15 am.	
10.40 am " - ABEELE	Dismounted portion 7 Coy arrived and detrained at ABEELE, and marched to billets at H.21.b.2.4, to find on arrival three 2 R.E.(T) Coys in occupation? of his bus farm; being found room for the 6t.G. to that night and transport moved out in the following day. Farm G.C. in occupation? farm at H.21.b.2.4. The billets consist? barn, horse with usual outbuildings and 5 tents, huts erected by the R.E.(T) Coy. all men under cover and horses picketted in open lines. Guide sent to ABEELE	
2 am. 2.10.15. DICKEBUSCH	Mounted section arrived; met 6 by cyclist guide sent to ABEELE to guide them to billets.	
2.10.15 " "	No word. Coy cleaning up billets.	
7.15 am 3.10.15 " "	Two sections out to C.R.E. near RUNINGHELST to work on improving roads & making huts; returned 7 P.M. Remainder 7 Coy working in billets; improving horse lines; general cleaning up.	
4.10.15 " "	Coy working in billets. O.C. & 2 subalterns reconnoitred portion? front line which was to be occupied by 27, 2nd & 15th Batn D.L. on Oct 6 at	

WAR DIARY or INTELLIGENCE SUMMARY

Army Form C. 2118.

Sheet 2 ? October 1915

Hour, Date, Place	Summary of Events and Information	Remarks and references to Appendices
	Ladies to work — in firing trench 27 inclusion to trench 32 inclusion and position to dig-outs. Under Capt's instruction, this Co. was to be disposed as follows; 2 sections in front line, working with 2nd & 3rd Bns, 1 Section a light railway which covered from road opposite WOODCOTE HO. up to app. H.32 c 9.8, and 1 section in Support. Point I.d. and in billets. A Coy, ? Pioneers to be attached to Co., + a detachment of the Entrenching Batt.n to work in I.d.	
5.10.15 DICKEBUSCH	Coy at work in billets, preparing workshops, having to dig-outs the plan of the trenches supplied was found to be inaccurate but has to be reconsidered by 2 officers and a fresh plan made; as aeroplane photo. was available it was found very useful to prepare the new plan, but photos. were found in place. No plans of the trenches were handed over to the R.E. Coy previously, one has i.c. been in the trenches has left before this Coy took over its portion of the line.	Fine.
6 am 6.10.15 "	3 Section proceeded to CANAL BANK to make dug-outs to be 2 Section who are to work in front line returned to billets 6 pm 1 Section at work in billets.	Fine
7.30 am 7.10.15 " to 6.30 pm	Further reconnaissance of trenches by O.C. + officers. 4 section making dug-outs at CANAL BANK, and calculation of the railway. Reconnaissance of Sup. Pt. I.d. by O.C. 1 man wounded, stopped by rifle + M.S. bullet while under a railway. Used to & on line front line	

Army Form C. 2118.

WAR DIARY
or
INTELLIGENCE SUMMARY.
(Erase heading not required.)

Sheet 3) October 1915

Instructions regarding War Diaries and Intelligence Summaries are contained in F.S. Regs., Part II and the Staff Manual respectively. Title pages will be prepared in manuscript.

Hour, Date, Place	Summary of Events and Information	Remarks and references to Appendices
7.30 a.m. 8.10.15 DICKEBUSCH 6 p.m.	3 Sections continue work on CANAL BANK dug-outs in light railway. 1 Section in billets.	nil
7.30 a.m. 9.10.15 " return 6 p.m.	2 Sections continue work on CANAL BANK dug-outs into light railway.	nil
4 p.m. "	2 Sections proceed to billets dug-outs & occupy same; commence night work in front line 7 p.m.; return 4 a.m. work done by night; wiring in front 1 N. & S. CANAL POSTS; continuation of light railway; repairs to trenches.	
7.30 a.m. 10.10.15 " "	2 Sections marched from billets to improve CANAL DUG-OUTS in occupation; the other 2 sections returned to billets 4.30 p.m. Light railways continued by day; repairs to trenches & line steps. Night work: wiring in front; trenches; hence repairs light railway. Sup. Pts. I'd laid out.	nil
7.30 a.m. 11.10.15 "	2 Sections marched from billets to improve CANAL DUG-OUTS in occupation. 9 the other 2 sections returned to billets 4.30 p.m. Light railway continued by day, and by night with searchlights. Sup. Pts. I'd continued; tunnelling commenced. Platoon of pioneers. Night work on front line; wiring in front; trenches; M.S. emplacements. N & CANAL; sanitary posts in CRATER there a German mine taken has been found to be occupied by the enemy, front, line bays; repair to trenches; line steps.	nil

Army Form C. 2118.

WAR DIARY
or
INTELLIGENCE SUMMARY.
(Erase heading not required.)

Sheet 24 ? October 1915

Hour, Date, Place	Summary of Events and Information	Remarks and references to Appendices
7.30 a.m. 12.10.15 DICKEBUSCH	1 Section rode 30 men ? Entrenching Bat'n Proceeded to Sap pt. La G work in same. At 12 noon O.C. worked Sap pt. and shale; afternoon line was shelled by enemy (heavy) although at most only 6 men could have been visible — B'n each sect'n ? CANAL + 2 Officers n S. side O.C. Can. order for night work only. G.L. carried on these except tunneller which was the done by day by R.E. Entrenching C'y + ½ section marched back to billets; remainder ½ section continued to work on tunnel. 1 Section in billets. Next light Night work; entrenching C'y + ½ section on Id, 8 p.m. to 4 a.m.; light railway continued its assistance ? platoon ? proceeded thus work in bad times same as on previous night. Other night work same as on previous night.	
7.30 a.m. 13.10.15 " "	1 Section work in billets. ½ Section tunnelling at Id. Night work: ½ Section + 30 Entrenching Bat'n on Id. Other night work same as on previous night.	
7.30 a.m. 14.10.15 " "	1 Section work in billets. ½ Section tunnelling at Id. G. OC IX Div. + C.E. V Corps inspected Id and saw new lines line Sap pt. was fl cancelled all work due by G.O.C. billets in and carried – this partly carried out, on receipt ? order, by ½ Section n completed last night by ½ section + 30 Entrenching C'y. Night work as previous nights. 1 man killed, wounds in head 27	

WAR DIARY
or
INTELLIGENCE SUMMARY.

Army Form C. 2118.

Sheet 5   2 October 1915.

(Erase heading not required.)

Hour, Date, Place	Summary of Events and Information	Remarks and references to Appendices
8 am. 15.10.15 – DICKE- BUSCH	2 Sections work in billets.	Nil.
3.30 p	The 2/1st 1/5th Coy having relieved this Coy, two 2 sections in occupation 2 CANAL DUG-OUTS returned to billets to rest. One work with plans, handed over to O.C. 103 C. R.E. Whole Coy worked in the front line from 9.10.15 to 15.10.15 when various carrying parties were made & lines were wired under a Coy. Preeu ? was attacked hit-time was & station 9 nbs. Accommodation in dug-out to 1 platoon until lines made. This dug-out was. One platoon worked on light railway from 11.10.15 to 14.10.15; and 2 platoons on Communication trenches on 13.10.15 and 14.10.15.	
7 am. 16.10.15	2 Sections work in billets. 2 Section – in billets	Nil.
6 am. 17.10.15	3 Sections work on dug-outs at 14.30, assisted by C. Preeu ? in billets	Nil.
6.30 a. 18.10.15	1 Section work on dug-outs in railway bank by 15th Bdn, 6.30 – 1.30 1.30 – 6.30 p 6.30 – 11 p. Each shift with 120 wkn workers party. C. Preeu moves shift out, billets. 1 Section - in billets.	Nil.

Army Form C. 2118.

Sheet 6. October 1915

WAR DIARY
or
INTELLIGENCE SUMMARY.
(Erase heading not required.)

Hour, Date, Place	Summary of Events and Information	Remarks and references to Appendices
6:30 a.m. 19.10.15 DICKIE-BUSH	Work as on 18.10.15	ditto
6:30 a.m. 20.10.15 "	Work as on 19.10.15	ditto
" 21.10.15 "	O.C. reconnoitred trenches 33-40 and dug out by DUMP with a view to taking on from 63.c.a.relief of 9 Brigade.	ditto
22.10.15	Work as on 21.10.15	ditto
6:30 a.m. 23.10.15 "	2 Officers reconnoitred trenches 33-40, preparations to take on from 63.c. 1 Section proceeded to work on railway head dug outs, to do 2 shafts; under Lt 5.30 p.m. and handed on to 63. C.R.E. then returned to billets.	ditto
2:15 p.m.	2 Sections marched to BEDFORD HOUSE, there to be stationed, to work on front line and DUG-OUTS in rear of Hill 59: attached to 27 Bde-18th	ditto
	1 Section, work in billets.	
	O.C. reconnoitred left section of line, and DUG OUTS at HILL 59	
7:15 a.m. 24.10.15 "	1 Section marched to BEDFORD HOUSE to work on S.P. Ic, into 30 men entrenching Coy, and 100 with instruction in wiring from to with, and assistance in extension of light railway to Pioneers. 1 Section from BEDFORD HOUSE; worked in DUGOUTS at HILL 59 by day. 1 Section from BEDFORD HOUSE worked on front-line by day and night, (2 p.m. to 9 p.m.) and on dug-out RIGHT BATTN H.Q. by day.	

Army Form C. 2118.

WAR DIARY
or
INTELLIGENCE SUMMARY.
(Erase heading not required.)

Sheet 7, October 1915

Instructions regarding War Diaries and Intelligence Summaries are contained in F.S. Regs., Part II and the Staff Manual respectively. Title pages will be prepared in manuscript.

Hour, Date, Place	Summary of Events and Information	Remarks and references to Appendices
24.10.15 DICKEBUSCH 4.30 p	1 Section work in billets	Rain
25.10.15 7.15 a.m.	Section returned from work in Sup. Pt. I C. 1 Section marched to BEDFORD HOUSE to work as on 24.10.15. Subalterns Co. was did not go to work on account of bad weather. Other sections as on 24.10.15.	Very wet & strong wind
26.10.15	Work as on 25.10.15. Work in Sup. Pt. I C interrupted by enemy's aeroplanes and shelling. Major S.R. Henn M.C. assumed command of Co.	Quiet, very clear. [Sgd] Sgn in Corps re he Co.
27.10 "	Section attempts in detail 38-39 mainly on Battn HQ in woods and behind DUM Pasture dugouts are being tunnelled into the April bank with difficulty. 1 section strengthening cellars at PEPPE H.Q. 1 sect. assisting in burning at I.C Supporting Point and in laying tramway. Demolished the eight of OC Trench CRE (Lt Col Carpenter) sector of trenches.	26.10.15 Dull & rainy
28.10. "	Sections attempts as yesterday.	Rain and high wind
29.10. "	Party No 3 to as two kept in billets to continue hutting in new Horse lines afternoon - fine weather. Other works carried on as before.	
30.10. "	Works as on 29th	Cloudy - fine later.

(73989) W4141—463. 400,000. 9/14. H.&J.Ltd. Forms/C. 2118/10.

WAR DIARY or INTELLIGENCE SUMMARY

Army Form C. 2118.

Sheet No. 8 of October 1915

Hour, Date, Place	Summary of Events and Information	Remarks and references to Appendices
1.45 am 31/10/15. DICKEBUSCH	Pars 3 & 4, 2 NCOs & 11 men work on Brigade HQrs dugouts & cellars, on dugouts in H.30 putting frames & carrying out spoil, mending walls only, & superintending & instructing Infantry in revetting at supporting Point I.4, and work including frames has been straight edged dugouts near BEAUN POINT FARM with 1 platoon Pioneers. No 2 section continued mining dugouts at the DUMP and in railway cutting closed. The trolleys wagons have been giving way again and are to west of this but gifted works. Ammunition (rifle) coming up to is all being entrained.	Dull quiet, and showery at times but during foot. E.P. Hearn Major R.E. O/C 2 Coy R.E. 2/11/15

64th FIELD COMPANY R.E.

XXXTH
(9th Division)

NOVEMBER 1915

64 EZCRF.
Vol: 7

121/7693

9th Hussein

Nov. 15

Army Form C. 2118.

WAR DIARY
or
INTELLIGENCE SUMMARY.
(Erase heading not required.)

Sheet No 1 of November 1915

Hour, Date, Place	Summary of Events and Information	Remarks and references to Appendices
7.45 am. 1/11/15 DICKIE BUSCH	**Topots** No 1 & 2 section at BEDFORD HOUSE on detachment. No 1 working on dugouts in a Cy at BLAUWPOORT FARM. No 2 on Railway HQ at the Dump near railway cutting, mining into the spoil heap which is very loose made ground. No 3 HQ & FQ in billets at H.21.B.1.3. (Sheet No 28 YPRES) No 3 dulio and hutting work – hwy on various works such as Rgle HQs and dugouts for a Cy at 1.30. Accommodation in this area is bad and all mks is required.	Dull morning, wet afternoon
do. 2/11	No 3 roads preparatory to moving up. No 1, 2 & 4 employed as above. OC Proof N° 9 4 c.m.	Very wet day almost constant rain, heavy at times
7.45am 3/11	No 3 marched off below N° 2 at BEDFORD HOUSE N° 2 returned at 6 p.m. treat Ontonymous much damage to pontoon night especially wheels. Motor lorries which ride the same late but that is insufficient transport. Heavy rain not much dulio makes in progress & allow completed.	Dull morning. Some gleams of sunshine – wet from 10 am onwards –
7.45am 4/11	As 1, on at BLAUW POORT dugouts right – some shelling delayed work – No 2 ... shelling bulling. No 3 keeping Railway Depot & hut line. Many dugouts and railway.	Misty – fire after 10 am – mud rather deep.
do. 5/11	Line yesterday today – or artillery left Milne. 2 went on with HQ supplying point but no infantry arrived.	fine
do. 6/11	Artillery working parties supplied in several places, but that for T.L. arrived too late at 4pm instead of 9 am. Our lds for H.O also supplied –	Fine early – dull later.

(73989) W4141—463. 400,000. 9/14. H.&J.Ltd. Forms/C. 2118/10.

Army Form C. 2118.

WAR DIARY
or
INTELLIGENCE SUMMARY.
(Erase heading not required.)

Sheet No 2 of November 1915

Hour, Date, Place	Summary of Events and Information	Remarks and references to Appendices
7.45 a.m. 7/11 DICKEBUSCH H21 B, 1, 3.	No 1 section into dugouts to BLAUWPOORT FARM (night) 2 section hutting. 3 section acting as infy to repair firing line, 4 section dugouts at H.30 and railway. Received from Chief Engineer orders to proceed to Division entraining its left 1 Sept 2 when affording repairs to work H27.c47.	Fine - sunny, but misty.
7.45 a.m. 8/11 do.	Work as before except No 1 work on railway - O.C. and Lieut Clavering reconnoitered part of new area. No 1 section shifted dug outs to BLAUWPOORT FARM at night.	Fine.
7.45 a.m. 9/11 do.	Nos 3 & 4 sections moved from REDOUBT HOUSE and Cy HQrs respectively to dugouts in ZILLEBEKE village at night - during the day every dugout & the church with 5" H.E. guns. He returned to ZILLEBEKE that No 2 worked in hutting Camp.	Interesting hard evening.
10/11 do	No 4 & 2 in hutting Camp. O.C. reconnoitred area first line trenches with Perighley. RSM 2 Coy H. Sptr - No 3 & 4 worked in dug outs which make trenches, O.C. reconnoitred at ZILLEBEKE night.	Fine - a thunder hail in aftr - fine night.
11/11 do.	No 1 on Rue N.17, No 2 making new roadway for bombs at RESPIM P No 3 & 4 reconnoitring and No 4 Coy some sections along railway embk -	Fine noon, cloudy afts - very wet night, lightened -
12/11 do.	No 4 in P.3 Trench - filling, worked 1.3 hrs on DORMY HOUSE LANE (like the two heavy boats)	bit. wind high - S.W.
13/11 do	Nos 1 & 2 as yesterday. Proceed on PROMENADE TRENCH with hand No. 3 met on head line woods - Proceed to No Bad road in the YPRES area. French to have Canada huts big Carrols do 6 hr tick in	High N.N.W. wind - not to much rain -
	Go on 12.11.15	
	The light storing wagon broke down again and seems to be quite unsuited to the bad roads in the YPRES area. Shunts transport unable to encounter up with several times	

Army Form C. 2118.

WAR DIARY
or
INTELLIGENCE SUMMARY.
(Erase heading not required.)

Sheet No 3, November 1915

Hour, Date, Place	Summary of Events and Information	Remarks and references to Appendices
7.45 am 14/11 DICKEBUSCH	from 13.11.15 Reverting to old line — improving communic: trenches VISO & SACKVILLE STREETS. Left section: ARTILLERY RD left sector. On 14.11.15 SACKVILLE STREET & [...].	Fine, sunshine, cold frosty night. No wind.
do – do 15/11 –		Same as 14.11.15.
do – do 16.11 –	No 1 4t and Pioneer same on 14.11.15 No.3 worked till 2 p.m. and then marched to billets to rest, having relieved No.2 Section which marched at same time.	Fine but dull & frosty night. No wind.
do – do 17.11 –	Nos 2 + 4 at front line same as the GOUROCK ROAD station. 3 Section do work, trench entertainment — POPERINGHE etreen. 1 bnd in billet.	fine – no wind.
– 18.11 –	1, 2, 4 section do – 17.11.15 No. 3 work in billets – 6 hrs.	hr
19.11 –	on do 18.11.15 Tramway improved.	hr
20.11 –	On 19.11.15 OC reconnd (do) H.Q, H.Q, H.Q.	fine & fine sheet but windy.
21.11 –	No 2 4t at ZILLEBEKE JunctIon SACKVILLE ST and GOUROCK ROAD – No 3 Section with Intrenching Coy (60) on No3 supporting point. No section rest	
22.11 –	As on 21st – in addition DORMY HOUSE LANE, BORDER LANE and Tramway improved. No3 section do HQ.	Cold misty night. Frost.
23.11 –	No 1 travelled or detachment to ZILLEBEKE relieving No 4 section in left sector. No 2 section draining + repairing night sector. No 3 on guard and supporting points.	fine – thaw – mild & light rain evening.

Army Form C. 2118.

WAR DIARY
or
INTELLIGENCE SUMMARY.
(Erase heading not required.)

Sheet No 1 of November 1915

Instructions regarding War Diaries and Intelligence Summaries are contained in F.S. Regs., Part II. and the Staff Manual respectively. Title pages will be prepared in manuscript.

Hour, Date, Place	Summary of Events and Information	Remarks and references to Appendices
24.11.15. DICKEBUSCH	Nos 1 and 2 sections at ZILLEBEKE – front line – HARRINGTON AVENUE and entrance of SACKVILLE ST, SNIPERS ALLEY and GOURUCK ROAD. Floored PROMENADE. No 3 section on do. Not yet. As on 24th No 4 section worked on strutting. O/C inspected dugouts.	Dull – fine later.
25.11.15 do.	As on 24th. Not yet.	Snow shower, fine intervals. Cold wind. Hard frost night.
26.11.15 do.	As on 25th	Fine – cloudy – hard frost night.
27.11. do.	As on 26. but all available carpenters & men No 1 section worked on making pickets for revetting.	Fine – very cold.
28.11 Sunday do. I	As on 27. but No 3 worked on Ray anchorage also –	Showers of rain and snow twice today.
29.11. do	Nos 1 + 2 in front line went. No 3 + 4 respectively prepared piles for duckboards and pickets for revetting. 160 new were employed under No 1 on support trench points	Fine morning. SW wind. Dull later.
30.11. do.	No 3 section went up to ZILLEBEKE to relieve No 2 – No 1 prepared material & supervised supplying front line. Draft of 16 men arrived including 1 sadler on 29 – among the Company there are now 5 sadlers of whom 4 are paid at the rate of 2s a day – it is not probable the fully un-examined unlikely and there must have been our tackle organization in picking in many to one Company. 3 chainman is sufficient – two in the Coy are and one spare. The sadler has been asked for on AF 1823/3.	

2/12/15.

G.R. Hearn
Major R.E.
O.C., 6th Coy R.E.

64th FIELD COMPANY R. E.

(9th Division)

DECEMBER 1915

64 th ACRE.
vol: 8

Army Form C. 2118.

WAR DIARY
or
INTELLIGENCE SUMMARY.
(Erase heading not required.)

of 64 Field Coy R.E. Sheet No. 1 of December 1915

Hour, Date, Place	Summary of Events and Information	Remarks and references to Appendices
1/12/15 DICKEBUSCH	No 1 & 3 Sections in attachment at ZILLEBEKE working in trenches 278 & 279 Reserve Line — also on WARRINGTON AVENUE — Trenches to A. & against air attacks on left flank — chiefly at 27 I 73. 14, trenches A79–A12 and B1–B37 inclusive. No 2 out in billet. No 2 rested. No 4 out preparing material.	Dull — rainy morning, cleared up later — dull again after. Fine night.
2/12 do	Same as yesterday, but No 2 also preparing material	Misty — fine sunny later. dull after.
3/12 do	Same work as on 2/12	Dull all day, occasional drizzle.
4/12 do	Same work as on 3/12	Very wet morning. Wet all day.
5/12 Sunday do	No 2 rested. All others same work as on 3/12.	Evening misty.
6/12 do	No 1 & 3 at ZILLEBEKE — No 2 motoring — No 4 on support point to Hd Qrs. B3 trenches which knocked about by trench mortars yesterday. The 2 trench material officers have relieved me at ZILLEBEKE. Capt Harris took over command at 7.50 at LillCompany R.E.	dull — hard S.W.wind, fine late till evening.
7/12 do	No 1 rested. No 2 material.	Fine — S.W. wind later. dull after.
8/12 do	No 1 on work about billet and preparing material. No 3 & 4 on forward work.	Fine — sunny.
9/12 do	do as yesterday.	dull raining all day.

Army Form C. 2118.

1st Field Coy R.E.
Sheet No 2 of December 1915

WAR DIARY or INTELLIGENCE SUMMARY.
(Erase heading not required.)

Hour, Date, Place	Summary of Events and Information	Remarks and references to Appendices
10/12. DICKEBUSCH	No 1 & 2 in H.Q. billet wheeler's carpenters preparing materiel. No 3 & 4 in advanced billet at ZILLEBEKE worked respectively in trenches A7 - A12 and B1, B6, B7. Tk inclusive in each case.	Heavy rain early morning & high S.W. wind all morning — clearing up in afternoon. Dull evening.
11/12. do.	No 3 & 4 section repairing trench above at R.E. Dump. No 3 remain at company — Received instructions to move on 13th to rest area.	Heavy rain again in early morning — high S.W. wind.
12/12. do.	Prepared for move — No 3 & 4 section rejoined from ZILLEBEKE at 6 p.m.	Fine morning. Dull showers after noon.
13/12. CAESTRE. Sheet 27 W 3 d. 2.1.	March to rest area ½ mile S of CAESTRE. Mounted section & No 1 under 2/L Cashen. Dismounted section marched to PLAMBERTINGHE and on thence motor buses. Billetted in 4 different farms. R Head Coy R.E. bore over out of billet. 2 in clearing & 3 N.COs left to paint out names in No 1 section Cpl 2/L it in charge? etc — Nos 1, 2 and 3 also released wagons — Qt. reconnoitred Bath house at WOOLEN ACRE & Cy town	Dull - cold — no rain. Fine-sunny.
14/12. do		
15/12. do.	Company bombed to shirt well worth except a party for bath house.	Dull cold sunrise.
16/12. do.	Drill by sections during morning except bath house party — Haversack inspection 2 p.m.	Dull.
17/12. BORRE	Company marched at 11 am. in billets in 4 farms in square N. 18 c.&d. 27. Billets rather crowded, only 2 farms being fitted with straw & one company cold have been accommodated in not more than 2 farms in summer.	Dull scotch mist.

Army Form C. 2118.

WAR DIARY
or
INTELLIGENCE SUMMARY.
(Erase heading not required.)

64th Field Coy R.E.
Sheet No 3 of December 1915

Hour, Date, Place	Summary of Events and Information	Remarks and references to Appendices
18/12. BORRE. Huts 27 V 18 a 1.6.	Inspection of Billets & out vehicles. Party to Battalion HQ. Owing now yesterday no steel Newfoot available. Conveyed to Camp of Cluntets searchlights to be light tested, was nothing relieved to be faulty mistake to Grenade school. O.C. took over duties of CRE in addition to his own CRE proceeding on leave.	Dull, cold, no rain.
19/12 Sunday do.	Church parade. Party to noted 6H. Mess section attending internment. Party out to Batt Hmrs & 20 central. Searchlights general.	Fine - E wind - light
20/12 do.	Gas helmet drill. Reconnaissance intonation of NCO's in map reading. Battalion party.	Dull. Light E wind
21/12 do	Party to Batt Hmrs. Training suspended on account of rain.	Rain all morning.
22/12 do		Rain all day.
23/12 do.	No 2 section erecting hut at STRAZEELE STN. - Party Batt Hmrs - Remainder refilling revetments MCO's in map reading.	Showery morning. Fine till 2. Rained heavily about 4 p.m. high SW wind night.
24/12. do.	Gas helmet drill. No 1 & 2 on Batt Hmrs - No 3 at revetting. No 2 Batt Hmrs. Remainder unloading 2 lorry loads frieze. Pickets about afternoon for horse standings.	SW wind strong. cloudy - fine intervals.
25/12 do.	Church parades morning. Sent off 2 parties afternoon to MEIERIS horse mands south of BAILLEUL reported impossible owing to floods.	
26/12 do.	No 2 section unloading fric[z]e for horse standings. Wheelers and [??] artificers at work. 1 holiday for remainder - Pontoons returned as required as floods have fallen.	W wind. Fine cloudy intervals.

Army Form C. 2118.

WAR DIARY
or
INTELLIGENCE SUMMARY.
(Erase heading not required.)

64 Field Coy R.E.

Month and year December 1915

Hour, Date, Place	Summary of Events and Information	Remarks and references to Appendices
27/12/15 BORRE Sheet 27 V.18.d.1.6.	No 1 & 3 on route march. No 2 section to bathhouse. Division inspected. Coy Reserve ready to turn out at ½ hrs notice. Reconnaissance work continued. Subs & some to Inspector of Fortifications CAILLOU 01. – 1 NCO + 2 Sappers sent as instructors to 57th Inf Bde. OUTERSTEENE	Heavy rain early morning, clearing later. Light S.W. wind & fine afternoon.
28.12.15 do	No 2 to bathhouse 8 a.m. Remainder practised pontooning. Inspection of horses stores 2 p.m. – 10 reinforcements joined.	Fair. Dull later. Light W. wind.
29/12 do	Parties for uncovering munition workers 9 a.m. No 2 section to bathhouse. – Remainder Rapid loading & firing & Pontooning.	Dull. Light S.W. wind.
30/12 do	No 2 section at 8 a.m. to bathhouse. HQ section practised rapid loading & firing – at 9 a.m. No 1 & 3 + promenade in marching order. Dull parties to –	Fair, Sunny – dull aft. Light S.W. wind.
31/12 do	No 2 section at 8 a.m. to bathhouse – returned at 12 noon. Probationary 9 a.m. Remainder to bathe at 29th Inf Aust. Barths at EAST STRÉ.	Dull. Light S wind. Cloudy later.

At the end of 1915 the Company is practically up to strength with a slight excess of dismounted & slight deficit in mounted establishment. No officer casualties have occurred. 2 O.R. have been killed, 1 missing and 22 have been wounded or gassed. About 30 have gone sick and have not returned. Nominally 6 men have been killed & wounded in spite of having to pass through YPRES nightly. Thus under 25% of casualties from all causes have occurred in 7½ months inclusive of service including the action of "1005". No animals have been killed or wounded. But 3 have been destroyed. The mules have done excellent service.

E. R. Hearn
Major R.E.
OC 64 Field Coy R.E.

31/12/15

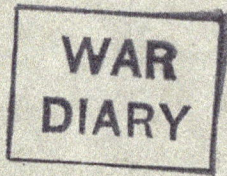

64 FIELD COMPANY

ROYAL ENGINEERS

9(Th. DIVISION

JANUARY 1916

64th F.C.R.E.
Vol: 9
Jan - 16

Army Form C. 2118.

WAR DIARY
or
INTELLIGENCE SUMMARY.
(Erase heading not required.)

64 Field Company R.E.
Sheet No 1 January 1916

Hour, Date, Place	Summary of Events and Information	Remarks and references to Appendices
1/1/16 BOERE Sheet 27 V.18.d.1.6. Saturday	Holiday for New Year's Day. 1 NCO + 30 O.R. on attachment with each battalion of 27 Infy Bgde for instruction in wiring revetting.	Wet morning – strong S.W. wind – cleared up after.
2/1/16 Sunday	Preparing for move. St. Eloi men. Stockbrokers billeting party to ARMENTIERES. No 2 section wire + musketry (rapid loading practice)	Dull stormy morning – wet afternoon – strong S.W. wind.
3/1/16 ARMENTIERES	OC attended Divl Conference at MEERIS – 10 am. Lt Clevering + 3 OR to OUTERSTEENE to attend Grenade School. Company marched off at 9 to am to ARMENTIERES (16 miles) arriving at BLUETA at ECOLE DE MUSIQUE in RUE NATIONALE. Officers mess at 93 RUE DE JULES LEBBEY, mounted section at TROIS TILLEULS (Sheet 36 B.28.b)	Fine, sunny – moderate S.W. wind. Slackened during overnight.
4/1/16 do.	OC reconnoitred LA FLENGQUE from (Sheet 36 – C.15.a.0.9.) supporting point with CRE. 21st Rautn + 2 NCOs made out list materials required. Company cleared up billets.	Dull – S.W. wind strong, misty showery afternoon. Strong wind at night.
5/1/16 do.	No 3 section + party Nos 1 to LA FLENCQUE – 2 sections to clean up. 1 section 63rd Fd Coy arrived + attached to this Coy for work.	Fine morning – cloudier over 10 am. S.W. wind.
6/1/16 do.	No 3 section to LA FLENCQUE – 2 sections knee linings – horizontal various works. Left 63rd Coy to clean up etc. knee linings – OC inspected entire firing line near GRANDE RAISERUE from (Sheet 3/b Cap C.0.2. to CALVAIRE (C.2.d.5.2) on which M.G. emplacements and new wire in salients and re-entrants.	Dull misty – strong S.W. wind – stronger at night. No rain.
7/1/ do	No 3 section at 9 am, at LA FLENCQUE – No 4 party No 2 to knee liners. No 4 sect 63rd Coy at 3 pm taking up wire + pickets to LA FLENCQUE + suitably line respectively.	Dull mostly, strong S.W. wind. Heavy rain 3.30 pm. Fine night.
8/1/ do.	No 2+3 work at LA FLENCQUE at 9 am. Frank C.E. II Corps + CRE IX Divl visited works. No party 63rd Coy work 2 pm taking up material mainly cloudy – dull after. Colder turning – frost – worked when knee liners.	Fine new strong N.W. wind.

WAR DIARY or INTELLIGENCE SUMMARY

Army Form C. 2118.

by Field Coy R.E.

Sheet No 2 of January 1916.

(Erase heading not required.)

Hour, Date, Place		Summary of Events and Information	Remarks and references to Appendices
9/1/16	ARMENTIERES	Not lecture ordnance — No 2 + 3 LA FLENCQUE farm supporting point. Party about practice moving to LA FLENCQUE at 3pm to continue wire entanglements.	Dull morn — fine aft — light N.W. wind — cold.
10/1/16	do.	Same work as yesterday, except No 2 which attacked trick at fine. LE TOUQUET station and life in tricks toutside, line by night.	Fine.
11/1/16	do.	No 2 + 3 n LA FLENCQUE — covering m.g. emplacement. No 1, 4 & sect 63rd Coy on subsiding flue — 3 shells fell in LA FLENCQUE farm morning, but enemy did not continue.	Fine morn. dull aft. moderate W wind. rain late — fine night.
12/1	do.	No 2 + 3 at LA FLENCQUE completed 2 m.g. cell and wiring man-side. No 1 + sect 63rd on subsiding line. 2/L MONTEITH posted to Company.	Fine morn. Cloudy late and thawing aft.
13/1	do.	Same work as yesterday. One m.g. cell at LA FLENCQUE concreted. Completed grays included.	Fine morn. Strong NW wind clear. Snow elect.
14/1	do.	Same work as yesterday. OC accompanied Brigadier 27 Div. recd French no 12.0 to 103 w front of PLOGSTEERT WOOD and LE GHEER to NARENNE R.	Fine. Cloudy intervals — light N.W. wind.
15/1	do.	Same work — No 2 + 3 continued M.G. cells at LA FLENCQUE — now so one in shed on west side — keeps sect 63rd worked on 2 m.g. cells to N. of LE TOUQUET Road KM1 sect worked moving by night. OC inspected GHQ 2nd line in area.	Rained early morn — light S.W. wind. Dull fair night. Some telling rest morn. little from 8 to 11 pm.
Sunday 16/1	do.	work as before.	Dull — misty — no wind.
17/1	do.	Work as before. received orders to move in relief of Field Coys 25th Division on 19/1.	Fine early — clouded over 9am. light S.E. wind.

Army Form C. 2118.

WAR DIARY
or
INTELLIGENCE SUMMARY.
(Erase heading not required.)

64 Field Company R.E.
Sheet No 3 of January 1916

Hour, Date, Place	Summary of Events and Information	Remarks and references to Appendices
18/1 ARMENTIERES	Nos 2 & 3 sections worked at LA FLENCQUE - completed concrete & second M.G. emplacement & widening roof. No 4 and Section 63rd worked on 2 M.G. emplacements in subsidiary line completing concrete roof high. No 1 section until 1730. 2 days work.	Dull morning - rained from 11 a.m. onl.
19/1 do	Marched at 10 am to DOUDOU FARM (Sheet 36 B 5 c 7 b) H.Q.Qr and No 1 section to all horse billets there KIO 1, 2 & 3 sections in PLOGSTEERT set H.Qrs near TOUQUET BERTHE (Sheet 28 U 26 a 1.1) Relieved 106th Fd Cy RE 2nd Division in relief U 28 c to U 31 b - Gas attack on 2nd Div Front at 4:30 P.m.	Fine morning light SW wind.
20/1 PLOGSTEERT	Sections working at billets making forward billets more secure. Officers reconnoitred trenches until guidance of Officers 106 Cy.	Fine morning - heavy shower afternoon. Fresh SW wind.
21/1 do.	Officers NCOs of 1, 2 & 3 sections reconnoitred trenches, many were employed in making somewhere available. New sect. of H.Q. worked on revetting frames "marriage arches" 50 made. OC handed over all work to Offr 106 Fd Cy by unexpected trenches 104 - 118.	Dull all day. Strong SW wind. No rain.
22/1 do.	No 2 section on clearing support trench 106 with wires to opening up comm alons WARNAVE to CT 105/1. No1 section revetting 117 F.T. No 3 section on 117 CT. No 4 section at HQ preparing material. OC inspected trenches 120 - 110.	Dull. Light west wind.
Sunday 23/1 do.	Work continued as yesterday - No1 section placed 5 frames. No 3 revetted entrance. section 17 frames - No 2 revetted entrance	Calm - night - fine cold light SW wind - misty evg.
24/1 do	No1 section placed 11 frames - No 2 revetted & try cleared 3 more, also made shutters for 6 loopholes in 111. No 3 section placed 12 frames + cont on OC inspected trenches 102 - 118 and drainage with GOC 75th Bde	Dull, hazy. Light SW wind.

WAR DIARY
or
INTELLIGENCE SUMMARY.
(Erase heading not required.)

Army Form C. 2118.

Sheet No 9 of January 1916
171 Field Co. R.E.

Hour, Date, Place	Summary of Events and Information	Remarks and references to Appendices
25/1. PLOEGSTEERT. Dv Dov FARM. Hut 36 P.S. C.76.	No 1 section worked on Trenches 116 (placed 18 frames 4'x3' - above L.G.H.F.F.R. C.T. revetting - No 2 section revetting 106 ST. No 3 placed 13 frames in 117 C.T. 16 infy parties for working or carrying. No 2 section placed 11 frames 116, No 2, 13 frames in 106 ST, No 3, 20 frames & end run in 117 C.T. No 4 on materials.	First entry morning fine Light S.W. air.
26/1.	No 1 placed 5 frames & revetted 4.5' in 116 - continued L.G.H.E.F.R. C.T. front. one drain 16' long. No 2 contd 106 S.T. 6 frames, drain up. cleaning - No 3 on 117 C.T. morning: relieved by No 4 section afternoon. No infy parties for carrying or materials.	Dull. light air from W.
27/1.	No 1 placed 2 frames 116 & contd L.E.G.H.E.F.R. C.T. front. No 2 placed 11 frames in 106 S.T. 'B' Coy Trenches morning. No 2 placed 11 frames in 106 S.T. 'B' Coy Pioneers assisted in 10-ST. C.T. carried up materials - fried at with shrapnel after 4-2 Sappers wounded. No 4 placed 16 frames in C.T. 117. No 3 on manufacturing frames.	Dull - hazy - lightrain.
28/1.	No 1 section fires ups in F.T. 116 & 2 frames in L.E.G.H.E.F.R C.T. only 12 infy - No 2 frames revetted in tray in ST 106 - no infantry. No 4 section 8 frames in C.T. 117 + making loopholes in 'C' Coy cupboard. No 3 section with 36 G/R.F. & 20 11/R.S. (nos. 6 frames + 36' fire steps in North C.T. 114, 115 F.T. (infantry Half Day only) No 2 section with 50 G/R.S.F. & 30 half Day only) placed 10 frames revetted 2 traverses. No 4 section (no infy working party arrived) continued frames in 117 C.T. + placed and set the fires etc. Supplement in position. Staffd by French Foreman.	Dull haze, light E wind evening 80.
Sunday 30/1.	No 1 section with 20 11/R.S placed 5 frames trenchd 30ft F.T. 115 also with 40 11/R.S continued sandbag L.G.H.E.F.R. C.T. No 2 section with 80 G/R.S.F. placed 11 frames erected 2 traverses in 106 S.T. also made screen for inadeping along the French.	Very misty. Calm. light NW wind aftn.
31/1.		Dull misty colder - light N.E. wind.

Army Form C. 2118.

WAR DIARY
or
INTELLIGENCE SUMMARY
(Erase heading not required.)

6th Field Coy RE
Sheet No 51 Jan 1916

Hour, Date, Place	Summary of Events and Information	Remarks and references to Appendices
3/1 cont'd	No 4 section placed 8 frames in 117 C.T. — No framing party — No 3 section making retrinds at H.Q.	
General	On January 24th detachments returned from being attached to Infy Battalions. Those 2 yth Byle & 9 Durhams instructing them in revetting, rivetting & tho Enlyt R.E. say definitely that the duty of the C.O's is fixed by the instruction authorizing their work. CO's of Inf Btns — 6/R.8.F. expressed appreciation of the work. The HC's Letter no attached & same. It has been decided to replace the hind wheels of pontoon wagons which have dust caps with the type fitted wheel used on G.S. wagons — The hind wheels are the same although the pontoon wagon carries a heavier load, but it is indistinct [?] to have the dust caps as the grease cap much longer. What is really required is a stronger wheel with dust caps. The change is not for the better.	

E.C Heanug
Major
OC 6th Field Coy RE

1/2/16.

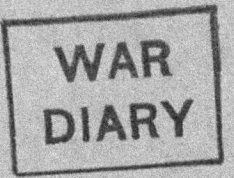

64th. FIELD COMPANY R. E.

9th DIVISION

FEBRUARY 1916

Army Form C. 2118.

WAR DIARY
or
INTELLIGENCE SUMMARY.
(Erase heading not required.)

64 Field Coy R.E.
Sheet No 1 of Feby 1916.

Instructions regarding War Diaries and Intelligence Summaries are contained in F.S. Regs., Part II. and the Staff Manual respectively. Title pages will be prepared in manuscript.

Hour, Date, Place	Summary of Events and Information	Remarks and references to Appendices
1/2/16. PLUGSTEERT DOUVE FARM Sheet 36 13 S 6.76.	No. 1, 2 & 4 sections in advanced billets PLUGSTEERT-PLOTOUR VIET BAT. No 3 section in reserve BIZRTMS. No 1 section on making materials. No 2 sect placed 5 frames revetted Ft 0/16 - cont LE G HEER CT. No 2 sect retaining wall revetting 106 S.T. placed 10 frames. No 4 sect put in 117 CT placed 5 frames 35 ft line drain & 25 ft floor. 40 I/RS worked with No 4 sect. 27 ft bgds. 28/8 bgds arrived.	Dull - misty - fine at noon - cold.
2/2/16. do	No. 1 section in FT 116 placed me gun emplacement. Revet 20 ft. Lafayette. Placed 9 frames revetted LE-G-HEER CT. No 2 sect. SD 7/Seaforths placed 20 frames in frames 106 CT. 3 men drew 20 to make head from MINDEN MANOR to road. No 4 sect. completed rivetting 117 CT. 8/FORT WALTER started flooring frames. Brigr Stopford inspd. party arrived - OC ac'd Brigadier Brittain inspected rivetting line with a view to flanking line with new loops, repelling drainlets to exit line. 50 7/Seaforths worked on G N Rs. drainlets raplet nvright.	Misty fine wea. light S.W. wind.
3/2/16. do	No 1 section work 30 OR ft by day & 40 by night on LE G HEER CT. 8/Humberts CT & cleaning - also m.g. cell in F.T 1114, cut'd in 3 gun emplacements and draining FT 112. No 2 work SD dug trench and continued 106 S.T. No 4 section amcd. work 30 OR ft by day + 3 OR by night. enclosed CT 117 FORT WALTER & drainage. Havensbury party arrived for french tramway.	Fine - sharp S.W. wind. Cloudy later. Fine night. Cold.
4/2/16. do	No 1 section work 45 OR by day + 40 by night on LE G HEER CT. 8/Humbertson CT 16 frames rivetting - also m.g. cell PICKET HSIE. + draining - No 2 section work. SD OD/Gordons + 20/6 C.S.T. on 106 S.T & 110/1 CT. 17/Sambs + 3 bays worked). Cellars in content. No 4 sect continued work in 117 CT. S/FORT WALTER traverses and intermediat PARK VILLA. also dugouts at Left Bn. HQ. 50/7 Cameronians worked well on french tramway.	Strong S.W. wind. occasional showers - no rain later until evening. wind dropped suddy. fine night.
5/2/16.	No 1 section work 28 OR ft by day + 60 by night worked on LE G HEER CT and placed 2 gun emplacements + 113 F.T. No 2 section work 100 ft (100 OR ft) worked on 106 S.T. and 110/1 CT placed 11 frames. No 4 section worked on 118 CT FORT WALTER + undergnds. PARK VILLA. also shelter post in any of 80 OR ft filled sandbags SD OR ft worked on drain FREADING POST. CT I/Lancelots and 12 of CT No 3 sect. relieved on french tramway. 45/12 RES worked on G N R french tramway.	Fine. sunny. cloudy internals moderate S.W. wind.

(73989) W.4141-463. 400,000. 9/14. H.& J. Ltd. Forms/C. 2118/10.

WAR DIARY / INTELLIGENCE SUMMARY

Army Form C. 2118.

64 Field Coy R.E.
Sheet No 2 of February 1916.

Hour, Date, Place	Summary of Events and Information	Remarks and references to Appendices
6/2/16 Sunday PLOEGSTEERT BOWDON FARM Sheet 36. 13.50.76. 3 sections in billets about TOUQUET BERTHE	No 4 section with 80 R&F continued LE GHEER CT placing 12 frames further in. 2 gas cups in 113 FT and worked on drainage. No 3 section with 106 ST (with 30 Black Watch) filled 1000 bags. 119/1 CT (with 20 R&F) placed 22 frames – 30 R&F worked on cleaning new CT. on left bank HARNAVIE, to Returned to FT. No 1 section CT 118 to FORT WALTERE in 119 CT placed 14 frames, also fixed pump in PARK VILLA. 30 7/Seaforths filled 800 bags for CT 120/1. 30 8/Gordons on 119 CT. "no progress" reported. 36 8/Gordons on drain to sump at READING POST. RE sump fixed – Loopholes put. OPs 3 FT RE continued – No 2 section filled 49 8/Gordons on Railway.	Dull - light SW wind, cold, drizzle evening
7/2 do.	No 4 placed 2 gas cups in 113 FT clearing drain 6 FT. ST Commenced entire revetment in LE GHEER CT with 50 R&F. No 2 materials and repairment Loopholes in PLOEG. ST SENT work under OC. No 3 with 4 OC and 119/1 CT placed 12 frames revetments. 100 6/R&F worked at night sandbagging 106 ST. Placed 17 frames in FORT section FT WALTERE and drain at KEMPER CT POST to sump. 50 R&F by day R50 by night filled sandbags for 120/1 and 117 CT respectively.	Fine - hazy through intervals, fine afternoon, light SW wind. 26 8/R&F relieve 27th B/R&E
8/2 do.	No 4 section with 20 R&F by day placed 2 gas cups (5 + dug drain) with 100 R&F by night placed 10 frames in LE GHEER CT sandbagged do & cleaned drain along road - No 3 dealt with No 4 duty by day + 20 by night and 119/1 CT placed 12 frames 50 R&F sandbags 106 ST by day. R50 by night - No 1 section on FT WALTERE cellar in PARK VILLA pump dugout + drain to READING POST - 30 R&F filled sandbags for 119 CT and 30 placed sandbag 120/1 CT. 46 8/R&F cleaning tramways of railway wiggling roadmains.	Fine cold. mod. SW wind. Rain after 8pm cleav.
9/2 do.	No 4 section with 80 R&F placed 2 gas cups in 113 FT. Placed 8 frames in LE GHEER CT and worked at LONDON SUPPORT FM & frames 27 Bde HQ. No 3 with 40 R&F worked on 119/1 CT + CONVENT 50 R&F filled sandbags by day. R50 R&F placed thru by night in 106 ST. No 4 section worked on FORT WALTERE + cellar in PARK VILLA + with 30 R&F on dugout + pump at READING POST. 6 8/R&F filled sandbags for 119/1 CT. 30 8/R&F worked down drain - 80 R&F filled sandbags for 120/1 CT. 30 6/R&F on Northern Trench Tramway.	Fine - cloudy intervals - fine apt night, light went with threats to N. the E night cold.

WAR DIARY

INTELLIGENCE SUMMARY

Army Form C. 2118.

6th Field Coy R.E.
Sheet No 3 February 1916

Hour, Date, Place	Summary of Events and Information	Remarks and references to Appendices
10/2 PLOEGSTEERT BOW BOW FARM.	No 1 section with 20 dfts placed 4 Gro emps b. with 30 dfts worked on LONDON SUPPORT FARM (2) Repeated as with 100 dfts Continued LE GHEER C.T. placed 15 frames. No 3 section with 20 dfts on 106 placed 8 frames, 16 dfts sandbag fatigue. 50 dfts by day 20 by night worked on 106 S.T. section also repairing m.g. emp. near LANCASHIRE SUPPORT FARM & on CONVENT - NAMUR section with 30 dfts built pump dugout at READING POST YPT pump with position by night. 30 dfts worked on 129f CT and 30 dfts on 117 CT. 50 dfts worked on Nunthorpe French tramway.	Fair - dull later - cold. Light N.W. wind. Fine night.
11/2 do.	No 1 section with 65 dfts placed 19 frames in LE-GHEER CT + built earth cubicle - with 30 dfts (filing Salvage) worked on LONDON SUPPORT FARM. 1 with 8 dfts gtmg 6 emps b in FT 114. No 2 section on 106 ST. with 20 dfts placed 11 frames in CT 110/1, materials & by day. No 3 section with 20 dfts placed FT & GLOUC. ST. ST. FORT + worked on CONVENT cellars m.b. emp. in front. C.T. cellar in PLOG STREET. host section with 8 dfts on FT WATER 4 with 30 dfts Continued dugout for pump READING POST - 30 dfts filled sandbags for 129f CT.	Stormy - rain & sleet - cleared during. Sunk all day. Cold.
12/2 do.	No 1 section with 60 dfts placed 18 frames revetted LEGHEERE C.T. with 30 dfts worked on LONDON SUPPORT FARM. No 2 section with 20 dfts on 106 S.T. & small works as yesterday. 50 dfts filled sandbags for 106 S.T. by day. No 4 section placed 16 frames in WATER, with 30 dfts Continued Pump dugout. 50 dfts filled sandbags for 129f by day but partly unwind thorn by night. Lot 6 killed (1 R.E. Corpl.) & 10 wounded M/RD by Salient Em.R. — Sundial READING POST unmanned.	Dull - Fair evening. Later mg. N. wind veering light N.W. in eng.
13/2 Sunday. do.	No 1 section with 30 dfts on LONDON SUPPORT FARM - with 60 dfts Completed frames in LE-GHEER CT. down to tramway, service & tilting of pumps. No 3 section on 106 CT. CONVENT cellars. 50 dfts sandbagging. 106 S.T. No 4 section unlining pump - 40 dfts trickand pumping CT 119f 2nd end. OC wrote Perigueux Revetlamdon.	Full mrg. sun. wind Frederick W.

(73989) W4141—463. 400,000. 9/14. H.&J.Ltd. Forms/C. 2118/10.

WAR DIARY
INTELLIGENCE SUMMARY

(Erase heading not required.)

1/4 Fd Coy R.E.
Sheet No 4 of Feby 1916.

Hour, Date, Place	Summary of Events and Information	Remarks and references to Appendices
14/2. PLOEGSTEERT. Bois FARM. Work advanced trenches.	Part section returned by No 2 after operation after O.C. involved duty course about stores returned not granted. KYS GHEER & fin boundaries breastwork left trenches. No 3 section placed 3 gas emptys with 60 dfys sawbags LEGHEER C.T. No 3 section placed 18mm 110ft C.T. 50 dfys filled also CONVENT cellars. No reports arrived for 106 S.T. night. Part section built WATER on dugout for pumping station READING POST with 30 dfys - 40 dfys filled earth above C.T. 117. 50 men on trench tramway.	Cloudy, Strong SW wind fine night.
15/2. do.	No 2 section with 30 dfys in LONDON SUPPORT FARM. 60 dfys sandbags LEGHEER C.T. No section placed 25 frames 110ft C.T. 50 dfys sandbags CONVENT cellars drainage cont'd in running sand. 50 dfys sandbags parapet 106 S.T. No section with 30 dfys pumping station - 30 dfys sandbags 117 C.T.	SW gale, Rain early. Lulling later, cloudy intervals.
16/2. a.	No 2 section on LONDON ST FARM with 30 dfys 60 dfys sandbag LEGHEER C.T. No 3 Places 15 frames in 110ft C.T. 50 dfys sandbagging. - 50 dfys sandbagging parade 106 S.T. CONVENT cellars continued. No 4 section on 117 C.T. with 40 dfys - with 30 dfys pump station & front row for 10 hrs. everything after heavy rain. 30 dfys on tramway.	Very high SW gale & heavy showers morning & noon/rain aftn.
17/2. d.	No 2 section continued LONDON SUPPORT FARM, groups and Offrs dugout in 113 F.T. with 60 dfys sandbags LEGHEER C.T. No 3 with 50 dfys by day & 50 by night on 110ft C.T. (9 frames fixed) & working CONVENT cellars. No 4 section working from DUMP to O.P. for R.A. also with 40 dfys on 118 C.T. (left) & 30 dfys on 120/1 C.T. 40 dfys worked tramway.	Strong W. wind. dull some sunshine after, wind dropped.
18/2. do.	Shower in morning - No dfys parties straight being night before. light relief. No 2 with 30 dfys sandbagging L.S.F. No 3 working L.GHEER C.T. blown in by shells No 4 1101/125 C.T. 4 on CONVENT Cellars. No 4 advanced O.P.s	Strong S wind - dull rain evening - cloudy night.

E.T. de COMMERCE

WAR DIARY or INTELLIGENCE SUMMARY

64 Field Coy R.E.
Sheet No 5 of Feby 1916.

(Erase heading not required.)

Place	Date	Hour	Summary of Events and Information	Remarks and references to Appendices
PLUG STREET DOW FARM	19/2/16	—	2nd Coy relieved by 1st Coy R.E. No 2 section on LONDON SUPPORT FARM making it sleeping for Bde H.Q. No 3 section rold — 50 dr/ft sandbagged 110/1 CT. Not any dam along S side wood Byde HR. No 2 section rold — 50 dr/ft sandbagged 110/1 CT. Not any dam along S side wood continued O.P. R.A. 40 dr/ft sandbagged 118 CT (left) + 30 dr/ft sandbagged 120/1 CT.	Cloudy light N Wind. Cleaner.
do	20/2/16	—	No 1 section (relieved No 1 section) with 30 dr/ft sandbagging 120/1 CT with 30 dr/ft on 118 left FT. No 3 section with 80 dr/ft in CT 110/1, with 20 dr/ft on drainage log S.T. No 2 section with 110 dr/ft on 8 houses in LEGHEER CT. (12 houses) with 20 dr/ft 5 yds cmft in FTs 114, 115 — with 50 dr/ft on LONDON SUPPORT FARM.	Fair day light air N.W. Cold.
do	21/2/16	—	No 1 section with 30 dr/ft sandbagging 118 FT left with 30 dr/ft sandbagging 120/1 CT rocky. This misty making splinterproofs TOUQUET BERTHE and drainage. No 2 section LONDON SUPPORT F. light E wind with 32 dr/ft on faceworkft (© portion) FTs 114, 115, and on O.P.s 15 GHEER. with 40 dr/ft on draining L to HEER road, with 60 dr/ft on LEGHEER CT. No 3 section with 80 dr/ft on 110/1 CT, with 15 dr/ft on right flank CONVENT LOCALITY (106-110 inclusive) 3 frames placed. 20 dr/ft on drainage of 109-110 S.T.	Veered to NW eveng colder.
do	22/2/16	—	No 1 section 450 dr/ft in 118 left, 50 dr/ft on 109/1 CT remainder drainage. No 2 section L.S. Farm, gas cmft (1) in 115 F.T. with 80 dr/ft LEGHEER CT. No 3 placed 7 frames 106 R Flank to 80 dr/ft sandbagged No 1 with 20 dr/ft on 110/109 S.T. 20 dr/ft opening out NORFOLK AVE. Concreted.	Dull, constant W wind light, fine night.

WAR DIARY
or
INTELLIGENCE SUMMARY.

(Erase heading not required.)

64 Field Coy.
Sheet No 6 9 Sept 1916.

Instructions regarding War Diaries and Intelligence Summaries are contained in F. S. Regs., Part II. and the Staff Manual respectively. Title pages will be prepared in manuscript.

Place	Date	Hour	Summary of Events and Information	Remarks and references to Appendices
POTIJZE STREET DUGOUT F.M.	23/7/16		No 1 section with 50 drft on 118 F.T. Left with 36 drft 126/1 C.T. with 36 dry drain wg & shelter attemp. No 2 section No op's for RA ESTAMINET & Coy MESS & AID G.HOUSE with 20 RFA with left. 70 drft on LE GHEER C.T. with 50 drft on LONDON SUPPORT FARM, with 16 drft refce emplt. No 3 section with 50 drft on 106/1 Right flank, with 80 drft on 110/1 C.T. with 20 drft on LIVERPOOL BORDER AVENUE. 20 drft drain wg 109 S.T.	Snow. very cold. E wind light. fine night. hard frost.
	24/7/16		No 1 section clearing drain 116 C.T ESTAMINET & first aid post RIFLE HOUSE & No 2 section on same works to day. No 3 section on same works & 110 S.T. No drft working parties.	Fine misty. sun later.
	25/7/16		Ammunition parties - Ryke Relief. No 1 section on 116 C.T. and first aid post. No 2 section on right flank 106/1 (7 frames) on 110 S.T. relaying duckboards & new Cmd BORDER AVENUE. Drawing slabwork to be formed with 113 S.T. revolvashooting dugouts on 113 F.T. No 3 section with no drft drawing HAMPSHIRE S.T. locally 416 C.T. with 80 drft on 126/1 C.T.	Dull. unsettled NE wind. drizzle evening
	26/7/16		No 1 section on first aid post. No 2 section on London Support Farm, OP & Estaminet de Commerce near S.T. 113 also 70 drft emplt FT 115. 70 drft on LE GHEER C.T. duckbd gd. No 3 section on 108/1 (9 frames) night with 100 drft on 110/1 C.T. continued duckboarding Liverpool BORDER AVENUE	Cold. light E wind - Warm at 11 fine night.
	27/7/16		No 1 section on same works, 110 drft on 126/1 C.T. started wire along HUNTERS AVENUE line of posts with 36 drft. No 2 section on same works - 70 drft on LE GHEER C.T.	SE wind, warm fine night.

WAR DIARY or INTELLIGENCE SUMMARY

171st Coy R.E.
Sheet No 7 Feby 1916

Place	Date	Hour	Summary of Events and Information	Remarks and references to Appendices
PETITE STEENE & ROI FARM	28/2/16		Commenced drainage R 113 St. in PICKET Ho locality. No 3 section on Rt flank.	Dull, light SE wind. Rain in aftn.
			100 dfts on 110/1 C.T.	
			No 1 section revetting + draining 116 C.T. + 3 dfts commenced shelter trenches off 116 C.T.	
			30 dfts on digging drain alongside PARK VILLA - ESTAMINET de COMM. E.P.C.E. 60 dfts on 110/1 C.T.	
			No 2 section on LONDON SUPPORT FARM & O.P. R.A. EST. de COMM. E.P.C.E. also on group of FT. 114 - 115	
			70 dfts on LE-GHEER C.T. No drainage 113 St. & at LE-GHEER St. No 3 Section with 50 dfts	
			No 6 Rt flank – 50 dfts improving earth protection 110/1 C.T.	
	29/2/16		No 1 section on 116 C.T. + 30 of C.T. 36 dfts digging shelter trenches off 116 C.T. + drain at back	Fine, cloudy. Later rain. SE wind egg. lightened.
			60 dfts on 110/1 C.T. No dfts mining along HUNTERS AVENUE. No 2 section & done work as yesterday, 100 dfts on LE-GHEER C.T. No 3 section with 50 dfts on No 6 Rt flank (with 3 delayed by arty firing) No dfts on 110/1 C.T. as yesterday.	
General			In reclamation trenches and revetting generally. The A frames shown in drawing the A frames chown in drawing received great approval. The fire step frame also has proved very efficient. The corner frames are placed at the four corners of traverse – sharpening of the ordinary and firestep frames is about 3'6" centre to centre with corrugated iron or rough cover	Apps A+B

T2134. Wt. W708—776. 500000. 4/15. Sir J. C. & S.

INTELLIGENCE SUMMARY.
(Erase heading not required.)

6th Fd Coy RE
Sheet No 8 of Feby 1916.

Place	Date	Hour	Summary of Events and Information	Remarks and references to Appendices

Planking & everything material & fundamental has been used but the twin new supplied has been found very weak & generally faulty. The much been in carried without upper cross piece leaving a strain between upper & lower cross pieces — Shellfire has not damaged the frames much, repairs are easy, the whole trench is so strong that the revetting is not likely blown in. As many as 85 of these frames have been turned out by a section at H.Q. in one day using a circular saw worked by an inferior portable engine.

Trench at LONDON SUPPORT FARM used for Bn/de HQ 27 Pople - walls on the river entered therefore were sandbagged on the inside - a 9ft wall was built 5ft outside the frame wall + sandbagged on inside thus providing a double bunker & air space to protect the staff. The floors were well shuttered with pit props & over the floor are 2 layers sandbags, two sandbag walls 3 sandbags high in compartments 5'×3' with corr iron sheets over + 2 layers of thick sandbag over on top as well. Quarters was taken of gable walls in checking sites for office dug outs (trench cupola type) for staff - the SW of tunnel (a Gunner) is of opinion that all this is proof against 4.2" HE shell.

E R Hearn Major RE
OC 6th Fd Coy RE
27/2/16.

64 Fd Coy R.E.
Harmary February 1916.

Appendix A.

C.T. FRAME

- 3'
- 5'7"
- 4"x3" or 4½"x3"
- 3"x3"
- 3"x3"
- 1'6"
- 1'2"
- 1'
- Notch 1" deep
- Hoop iron
- Halved joint

CORNER FRAME

- 4'3"
- 5'7"
- 4"x3" or 4½"x3"
- 3"x3"
- 3"x3"
- 2'4"
- 1'
- Notch 1" deep
- Hoop iron
- Halved joint

Scale 1/15

Appendix B.

by Ft Coy R.E.
War Diary February 1916.

FIRING-STEP FRAME.

Scale 1/15

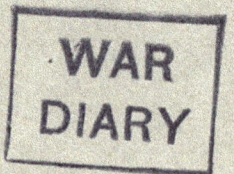

64th. FIELD COMPANY R. E.

9 ~~SCOTTISH~~ DIVISION

MARCH 1916

Army Form C. 2118.

WAR DIARY
or
INTELLIGENCE SUMMARY.
(Erase heading not required.)

64th L.g. R.E.
The Month of March 1916

Place	Date	Hour	Summary of Events and Information	Remarks and references to Appendices
PLOEGSTEERT Ha. DOUDOU FARM. Section in advance billets at PLOEGSTEERT HOUPLET BERTHE	1/3/16		No 1 section in CT 116 and erecting hutment to FORT WALTER, also altering revetment CT 120/1 - 40 dfys wiring HUNTERS AVENUE. No 2 section on LONDON SUPPORT FARM d.O.P. at ROZENBEEK, with 19 dfys shuttering FT 113 + 115. Sunk 16 dfys draining ST 113. No 4 section on 106 Rt flank CONVENT locality sump 110/1.	Dull. misty S.W. wind fine aft.
	2/3/16		26 Brigade relieved 27 Bgde. Section rested.	Fine cloudy later clear air cold
	3/3/16		No 3 section relieved No 2 section aft. No 4 section with 55 dfys on draining relief to 116 CT with 60 dfys revetting sandbagging 120/1 CT, 30 dfys wiring HUNTERS AVENUE. No 2 section placed 11 frames in ST 113, put up on O.P. EST DE COMMERCE, 120 dfys sandbagging LE GHEER CT. No 4 section with 85 dfys placed 12 frames + sandbagged Rt flank CONVENT locality, with 25 dfys on sump in 110/3 CT. Continued BORDER LANE	Dull. N.E.wind shifting to N. heavy rain aft + heavy snow.
	4/3/16		No 3 section with 55 dfys 116 CT (6 frames, draining to lits) with 60 dfys on 120/1 CT and Trans. N.E. 30 dfys wiring HUNTERS AVENUE. No 3 section with 128 dfys 113 ST (12 frames) Avg H.E.E.R. O.P. tree frame to founds, with 120 dfys sandbagging LE GHEER CT. No 4 section with 40 dfys 106 Rt flank (15 frames + sandbagging) also sump in 110/1 CT	wind clean aft.
	5/3/16		No 1 section with 55 dfys 116 CT (18 frames + clearing slurry) with 60 dfys CT 120 ft revetting also sump N wind light N wind sandbagging. 30 dfys wiring HUNTERS AVENUE. No 3 section on 113 ST (9 frames placed + best timber later. unsettled)	fine sunny

T2134. Wt. W708-776. 500000. 4/15. Sir J. C. & E.

Army Form C. 2118.

WAR DIARY or INTELLIGENCE SUMMARY.

(Erase heading not required.)

64 Field Coy R.E.
Sheet No 2 of March 1916

Place	Date	Hour	Summary of Events and Information	Remarks and references to Appendices
PLOEG STEERT			No 1 R.A at EST DE COMMERCE & No 4. G.HEER CT.	
PLOEG G HEER CT			No 2 R.C.A at EST DE COMMERCE & No G.HEER work 50 dr/fs repairing + sandbagging L.E	
	6/3/16		No 1 section +55 dr/fs on 116 C.T. (36 frames in) with 60 dr/fs sandbagging 120/1 C.T. 30 dr/fs sandbagging Hunters Avenue. No 3 section on 113 S.T (12 frames) on OP's R.A (short caves) erected at A4 G.HEER, with 90 dr/fs sandbagging L.E G.HEER C.T. No 4 section with 90 dr/fs sandbagging 106 R. flank firesteps & on various jobs.	Fine but snow showers calm.
	7/3/16		No working parties from drfs being day before relief. Section on snow work as yesterday & in addition hut had erected on O.P R.A MOUNTAIN GUN FARM. 27 Byde relieved 26 Byde 2pm.	Snow light. west wind. measured 4" last night
	8/3/16		No 2 section relieved No 1 section afternoon. No 1 placed 15 frames in C.T 116 - No 3 with 42 dr/fs placed 17 frames in S.T 113 + sandbagged. 50 dr/f sandbagged L.E G.HEER C.T. No 4 section on Right flank, L.E G.HEER C.T. +120/1 C.T. They are given 4 day tasks on sandbagging 106 R. flank, 106 + 109 J.T. + CONFT dr/fs from reserve battalions were to work as then please provided the tasks are finished during period out of the line.	Fine snowy snow 2" in wind
	9/3/16			Dull grey humid light.
	10/3/16		No 2 section with 55 dr/f placed 25 frames & sandbagged 116 C.T. No 3 section + 30 dr/f placed 12 frames + sandbagged S.T. 113. No 4 section placed 10 frames in 110 S.T. + revised work.	Dull cold light E wind.

Army Form C. 2118.

WAR DIARY
or
INTELLIGENCE SUMMARY.
(Erase heading not required.)

by Field Cay RE
Week No 39 March 1916

Place	Date	Hour	Summary of Events and Information	Remarks and references to Appendices
Ont. Street Gordon Farm Ideas in and billets	11/3/16		No 2 section with 55 infy placed 23 frames & sandbagged C.T.M.B. 8/3/ Argyll watch 120 C.T. No 3 section with 142 infy placed 32 frames & sandbagged 113 S.T. & 18/B.W. whose LE GHEER C.T.M.B. say in tasker & sandbagging C.T. No 4 section with 26 infy placed 20 frames in 106 Rt plank & relieved. Then 8/Gordons on line sandbagging this trench. 8/Bn. wires in HUNTERS AVENUE.	Dull misty light E wind.
	12/3/16		No 2 section with 40 infy placed 18 frames C.T.116. No 3 & 4 dfs continued S.T 113 (34 frames completed). No 4 & 29 infy on R/Plank 106 (8 frames 1 August). Made centerings for M.G. empt. CHESHIRE light & on AVENUE & 20 infy carried aggregate up. dfy tack-work continued except B.W. established in 3 days.	Mostly fine sun later.
	13/3/16		No 2 section & 50 infys placed 20 frames in "Elie" & 116 C.T. sandbagged. No 3 section & 2 infys placed 40 frames in S.T 113 sandbagged. No 4 section & 20 infys placed 8 frames & dugout in Trench 106 R/flank. No working or carrying parties from infy - day of for relief.	Mostly fine sunny warm.
	14/3/16		26 Brigade relieved 27 Brigade 7:30 am. 1 section 20 to 66 except Noy which with 25 infys got in frames 7 M.G. empt. CHESHIRE AVENUE.	Fine sunny calm.
	15/3/16		No 1 section relieved No 4 section afternoon. No 2 section & 40 infys placed 6 frames & sandbagged 116 C.T. 11/R.S. 1 Coy on light sandbagging trench to Ft WALTER. 1 Coy o/120 C.T. 1 Coy LE GHEER C.T. Others det for 4 days. No 2 section 4 & 2 dfs placed 5 frames & sandbagged S.T. 113. G men concreted cupola or MED. Cover AVG HEER O.P. (bs cliff) front	Dull showing mod SE wind.

Army Form C. 2118.

WAR DIARY
or
INTELLIGENCE SUMMARY.
(Erase heading not required.)

64 Field Coy RE
Sheet No 4 of March 1916

Place	Date	Hour	Summary of Events and Information	Remarks and references to Appendices
PLUG STREET	16/3/16		No 1 section with 20 Infy placed 17 frames & sandbagged R.H. flank 106. Put up centering of M.G. emplacement CHESHIRE AVENUE. No 2 section RSS Infy placed 16 frames & sandbagged LOOP. 116 C.T. Infy in trenches sandbagging 116 CT + 112 CT. No 3 section 142 Infy placed 16 frames and sandbagged 113 ST. also repaired damage by shellfire in LE GHEER CT. Infy in back sandbagging 116 CT.	Fine lightning N to SE wind.
	17/3/16		No 1 section maintenance also fixed 8 frames 109 ST. No 2 maintenance also dug a new S.T. 116 to HICKS HOUSE from 116 CT. No 3 on same work (10 frames fixed)	Dull light W wind.
	18/3/16		No 1 section 420 Infy on R.H. flank 106 (8 frames) and 2 mins dust bags completing 106 S.T. also dustbags completing M.G. cell CHESHIRE AV. No 2 section 420 Infy 30 Infy carrying materials for trench. Placed 6 frames in ST 109. No 3 section 142 Infy & 18 frames in SLIT. also sandbagging LOOP. No 3 section 153 Infy 12 frames in 116 CT & 18 frames in SLIT also sandbagging in AU GHEER O.P. for R.A. Snow sheeting in day interrupted work or same work as yesterday also in AU GHEER O.P. for R.A.	Calm dull & frosty dull light showers etc.
	19/3/16		No 1 section same work (15 frames in R.H. flank 106 & 11 frames in 109 ST.) fires guts re my cell. No 2 section placed 14 frames in 116 CT & 4 + 2 lit frames. No 3 section on same work but principally SE work in AU GHEER O.P.	Fair cloudy later light calm.
	20/3/16		Brigade Relief. 27 Bgde relieved 28 at 6.30 am. Sections rested	Dull, mist fine, later calm.

Army Form C. 2118.

WAR DIARY
or
INTELLIGENCE SUMMARY.
(Erase heading not required.)

61st Field Coy RE
Sheet No. 5 8 March 1916

Instructions regarding War Diaries and Intelligence Summaries are contained in F. S. Regs., Part II. and the Staff Manual respectively. Title pages will be prepared in manuscript.

Place	Date	Hour	Summary of Events and Information	Remarks and references to Appendices
PLOEGSTEERT	21/3/16		No.1 Sec. continued concrete M.G. cell. No.2 Sec completed dugouts nr 116 S.T. & put in 32 frames in 116 C.T. No.4 Sec. relieved No.3.	
	22/3/16		No.1 Sec. twilight, put in 11 frames & built up parapet on right flank of CONVERT LOCALITY. Started from CHESHIRE AVE. Hark lurks. Continued M.G. cell. No.2 Sec. started frames 116 S.T. continued reclaiming 116 CT. No.4 Sec. putty in firestep in 113 S.T., 15 frames in —	
	23/3/16		No.1 Sec. putty, indents on right flank of locality. 18 frames in CHESHIRE AVE. Continued M.G. cell. No.2 Sec. put in 16 frames in 116 CT. and 116 S.T. Infantry wiring completed making HUNTER'S AVE. No.4 Sec. 24 frames & duckboards firestep in 113 S.T. Continued work on AU SHEER O.P. Replaced chimney at LONDON FARM by wooden dummy.	
	24/3/16		No.1 Sec. put in 2 dugouts on right flank of locality. 20 frames in CHESHIRE AVE. Continued M.G. cell. Fine. No.2 Sec. 11 frames in 116 C.T. No.4 Sec. 31 frames & 1 dugout in 113 S.T.	W. wind
	25/3/16		No.1 Sec. 1 dugout 106 S.T. 20 frames CHESHIRE AVE. No.2 Sec. 18 frames 116 C.T. 9 frames 116 S.T. No.4 Sec. 4 dugouts & duckboarding 113 S.T.	
	26/3/16		Sections nothing. Working parties cancelled. Brigade Relief.	
	27/3/16		No.1 Sec. 18 frames CHESHIRE AVE. Nothing in dugouts 106 S.T. Began work on S.T. north of CONVENT. No.2 Sec. half day 4 frames in 116 S.T. No.4 Sec. 113 S.T. 3 dugouts + 11 frames. No.3 Sec. relieved No.2 Sec.	pouring rain

Army Form C. 2118.

WAR DIARY
or
INTELLIGENCE SUMMARY.
(Erase heading not required.)

64th Field Company R.E.
Sheet No. 6 b. of March 1916

Place	Date	Hour	Summary of Events and Information	Remarks and references to Appendices
PLOEGSTEERT	28/3/16		No. 1 Sec. 106 CT 3 frames, 1 dugout. Spring frames fitted. St. Nat. & Concert St. Nat. & Concert 7 frames.	New arclight. SW wind.
			CT from convert to old BEDFORD AVE. 11 frames at eastern end. CHESHIRE AVE 26 frames.	
			No. 3 Sec. CT 116 & ST 116. 10 frames & digging traverses in LOOP. No. 4 Sec 113 ST. 7 frames. Fresh up.	
			113 CT. 10 frames. 2 cupola dugouts in fire trench.	
	29/3/16		No. 1 Sec CHESHIRE AVE 26 frames sandbagging beyond infantry. 106 CT. 3 frames. ST. M. & Concert	
			7 frames. No. 3 Sec. 116 CT. 3 frames. LOOP 18 frames (traverses) No. 4 Sec 113 ST. 2 dugouts 113 CT	
			leaving through sandbagging. Take at Target Butts raised to Eff. ground (3mm) & (196 cyrs)	
	30/3/16		No. 1 Sec. 106 CT. 3 dugouts. Lewis gun loophole began. CHESHIRE AVE. 28 frames. Duckboards.	Fine and no wind. Cloudy after
			St. M. & Concert 10 frames. No. 3 Sec. MG. dugout M. EVEREST. Preparing frames. 116 ST. 15 frames	
			LOOP 16 frames. No. 4 Sec 113 ST. 1 dugout 10 frames.	
	31/3/16		Mat section in CHESHIRE AVENUE (22 frames) and S.T. 109 (6 frames) No 3 section on 116 CT.	Misty morn- ing but light winds.
			116 ST & LOOP (20 frames in all) No 4 section on ST 113 & CT 113 (17 frames)	

E. Mears
Major R.E.
OC 64th Field Coy R.E.

4/4/16.

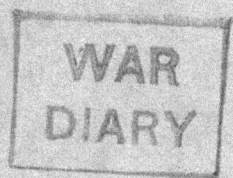

64 th. FIELD COMPANY R. E.

9 th. DIVISION

APRIL   1916

Army Form C. 2118.

WAR DIARY
or
INTELLIGENCE SUMMARY.
(Erase heading not required.)

IX

1st Field Coy R.E.
Sheet No 1, April 1916.

Vol 12

Place	Date	Hour	Summary of Events and Information	Remarks and references to Appendices
ROCLINCOURT HQ Dugout Farm – 3 Section in	1/4/16		No 2 section on right flank CONVENT LOCALITY (Sewing loopholes ST 109 (7 frames) and CHESHIRE AVENUE renewed covering of concrete M.G. cell. No 3 section on CT 116 & ST 116 (13 frames) No 4 section in ST 113 & CT 113 squaring up frames. Infantry on listening posts wire snapping. Wire trenches also 120 /1 CT & loop.	Fine sunny morning E. wind
Advanced Billets in + near TOUQUET	2/4/16		Section in same tasks.	Fine hazy light E wind rift
	3/4/16		27 Ryl. Rs. relieved 20 Ryle. Section reld. OC and Brigadier inspecting trenches. Infantry allotted tasks in Cent of last tour tasks.	Fine hazy calm. mor.
BERTHE	4/4/16		No 2 section relieved Nov afternoon. No 1 fixed 26 frames ST 109 Rendered M.G. cell CHESHIRE AVENUE. No 3 placed 13 frames in 116 ST. No 4 placed 10 frames in 116 ST.	Dull haze cold Light N.W. wind
	5/4/16		No 2 section placed 24 frames in 109 ST. No 3 placed 20 frames in 116 CT & 116 ST. No 4 placed 9 frames in 113 ST.	Fine hazy light N.E. wind
	6/4/16		No 2 section placed 8 frames in 109 ST. & 13 in CHESHIRE AVENUE. No 3 placed 16 frames in CT 116 & ST 116 reg frames in CT 118. No 4 placed 12 frames & 1 dugout in ST 113.	Dull hazy light N wind
	7/4/16		No 2 section on 109 ST (13 frames) & CHESHIRE AV. (13 frames) keeping revetment up + dugouts. No 3 on 116 CT (13 frames) & 117 CT (11 frames) keeping revetment up + dugouts – part on 113 ST (14 frames) revetment 2 dugouts.	Rain early. Cloudy rft N.W. wind

Army Form C. 2118.

WAR DIARY
or
INTELLIGENCE SUMMARY.
(Erase heading not required.)

64 Field Co[y] R.E.
Sheet No 2 April 1916.

Place	Date	Hour	Summary of Events and Information	Remarks and references to Appendices
PLOEGSTEERT DOCKOU FM	8/4/16		No 2 section on 109&110 ST (10 frames) & CHESHIRE AV. (12 frames 1 dugout) Keepers superior locality. 5 other works. No 3 on 116 CT + 117 CT (37 frames) No 4 ST 113 + 2 full flank PICKET H2 locality + 30 other works.	Fine. Some high cirrus clouds. Fresh N.E. wind
	9/4/16		26 Bgde relieved 27 Bgde - section noted.	Dull misty. WtyNW wind
	10/4/16		No 1 section relieved half afternoon. No 2 section on ST 109 & 110 (11 frames) & CHESHIRE AV. (9 frames) superviring 3 buft works. No 3 on 116 CT working & overhauling - also superviring 3 works. No 4 on ST 113 & R[t] flank. superviring 2 works.	Fine during light N wind
	11/4/16		No 1 section on "ABERFELDY" is Right Flank PICKET Ho locality opening out + preparing for tunnel to work. Superviring 2 works. No 2 on CHESHIRE AVENUE (2 dugouts) 110 ST (9 frames) + 2 Dft works. No 3 on 116 CT + 14 works.	Rain - light
	12/4/16		No 1 on ABERFELDY (22 frames) + 1 work - no night parties owing [to] rain. No 2 on CHESHIRE AVENUE (21 frames) & 110 ST (12 frames) + 4 Dft works. No 3 on CT 116 + 3 Dft works.	S.W. gale + rain.
	13/4/16		No 1 ABERFELDY (10 frames) + 113 ST (15 frames) + 2 works. No 2 CHESHIRE AV. (23 frames) + 2 dugouts + 110 ST (4 frames) + 3 Dft works. No 3 on CT 116 + 3 Dft works.	Changeable high SW wind
	14/4/16		No 1 ABERFELDY (16 frames) & 113 ST (5 frames) No 2 CHESHIRE AV. (23 frames) + 110 ST (1 frames) High SW wind. + 2 Dft works. No 3 116 ST (2 dugouts)	High wind showers

T2134. Wt. W708—776. 500000. 4/15. Sir J.C.&E.

WAR DIARY
or
INTELLIGENCE SUMMARY.
(Erase heading not required.)

Army Form C. 2118.

by Field Coy RE
The sheet No 3 for April 1916

Place	Date	Hour	Summary of Events and Information	Remarks and references to Appendices
PLOEGSTEERT	15/4/16		27 Bgr relieved 28 Bgde – sections ready.	W. gale. hail.
	16/4/16		No 4 section relieved No 3 aft. – No 1 on ABERFELDY.	Fine light W. wind. Fair phases with rain at night.
			No 2 M 110 ST (15 frames) CHESHIRE AV. (21 frames) No 3 on 116 ST + 3 Infy tasks.	
	17/4/16		No 1 section ABERFELDY (25 frames) revetting 3 loops (16 frames) No 2 section	Rain. high W. wind.
			110 ST (9 frames) CHESHIRE AV. (2 frames) Infy returning GORDON AV on account of	
			wet + having handed in gumboots. No 4 section rounding off corners of 116 ST for stretchers	
			supervising 4 Infy tasks + doing 2 odd jobs. O Coy Pioneers attached for work.	
	18/4/16		No 1 section ABERFELDY (25 frames) revetting 2 loops (2 frames) – No 2 section 110 ST	W. gale
			+ CHESHIRE AV. (28 frames in the way) + 2 Infy tasks. No 4 section 2 dugouts + corners in ST	heavy showers
			116 + CT 116 respectively + 3 Infy tasks.	
	19/4/16		No 1 section ABERFELDY (30 frames) superintending 113 CT (13 frames) No 2 section 110 ST (14	strong W wind
			frames) squaring up CHESHIRE AV. superintending 4 Infy tasks. No 4 section 1 dugout ST 116	showers
			+ 2 other jobs at OP's also supervising 3 Infy tasks.	
	20/4/16		No 1 section ABERFELDY (20 frames) + 1 Infy task. No 2 section 110 ST (17 frames 1 dugout)	Fine mod.
			CHESHIRE AV (24 frames 1 dugout) supervising 3 tasks. No 4 section on ST 118 (6 frames)	W. wind.
			ST 116 (1 dugout) OP's + 3 Infy tasks.	

Army Form C. 2118.

WAR DIARY
or
INTELLIGENCE SUMMARY.
(Erase heading not required.)

Ln Field Eng RE
Sheet No 4 of April 1916.

Place	Date	Hour	Summary of Events and Information	Remarks and references to Appendices
PLOEGSTEERT Bn Pay HQ Section and Reliefs	21/4/16		2 B Byde relieved 27 Byde. de Chow Rooted. B. Coy Pioneers on FUSILIER TERRACES & LANCS SUP. FARM. D Coy Pioneers on Breastwork & dugouts KEEPERS HUT & Cheshire of Oxy new work St Eloi to fort N. part of PLOEGSTEERT. Byg billets.	Dull light S.W. wind. rain eve. heavy though
	22/4/16		Working parties cancelled aftn & night on account of rain — No 1 section ABERFELDY (16 frames) No 2 squaring up 110 ST and CHESHIRE AV. No 4 on S.I. 117 (9 frames) S.I. 116 (dugouts) + 2 small gfts — No 3 section relieved No 2 section.	Dull light. Enroute from quarry all day.
	23/4/16		Easter Sunday. Church parade 9 am. No 1 ABERFELDY (21 frames) & 4 dug'y traks. No 3 section on S.I. 110 & CHES. AV. supervising wire across to RESERVE FARM from last trench. No 4 on S.I. 117 (9 frames) CT 116 repaird 8 frames damaged by shell, & small gfts supervised 3 dug'y traks.	Fine. Some clouds. light W. wind
	24/4/16		No 1 section ABERFELDY (28 frames) replaced 7 frames in IOTHIAN ROAD & 4 dug'y traks— No 3 on CHESHIRE AV. & S.I. 109 & 110 (42 frames together) + 2 dug'y traks. No 4 section on S.I. 117 (5 frames) + S.I. 116 & 2 dug'y traks.	Fine. light W. wind. Showy aftn
	25/4/16		No 1 ABERFELDY (24 frames) & 3 dug'y traks. No 3 CHESHIRE AV. & S.I. 110 (25 frames together) No 4 on 117 ST. (9 frames) and 2 dug outs in 116 ST.	Fine. hazy light E air
	26/4/16		Supervision Parties. No 4 on 117 ST. (9 frames) work interrupted by trench mortars. No 3 CHESHIRE At. (20 frames & dugouts) No 1 ABERFELDY (38 frames) work interrupted by trench mortars. No 4 on 117 ST (8 frames) and 2 dugouts in S.I. 116. gas alarm night and S.I. 109 & 110 (17 frames)	Fine light W wind Fine. light E wind

Army Form C. 2118.

WAR DIARY
or
INTELLIGENCE SUMMARY.
(Erase heading not required.)

6 N Field Coy R.E.
Sheet No. 3 for April 1916.

Place	Date	Hour	Summary of Events and Information	Remarks and references to Appendices
PLOEGSTEERT	27/4/16		27 Rgfs. relieved 26 Bgde. section, relief except that placed 24 frames in ABERFELDY	Fine, light E. Stars, warm.
	28/4/16		No 2 section relieved No 1 afternoon – no work after to-morrow on account of trench mortar operations at 12.30 p.m. No 3 in S.I. 109, 110 (11 frames) CHESHIRE AVE. and 9 R.E. tasks	Fine, hot light E. wind.
			Men on various works – 2 frames in 117 ST, work delayed by shellfire.	
	29/4/16		No 2 ABERFELDY (12 frames) + 2 Infn tasks. No 3 CHESHIRE AVE (11 frames 2 dugouts) S.I. 109, 110 (17 frames 1 dugout) interrupted by shellfire. + 4 Infy tasks. Men on various jobs – guardtents on 24 Div nightwork.	Fine, hot and SE wind – calm. night.
	30/4/16		No 2 ABERFELDY (15 frames) + 6 Infy tasks. No 3 CHESHIRE AVE. (14 frames) Infy. hot. Left S.I. 109+110 (13 frames) + 6 Infy tasks. New 117 ST (10 frames) + 2 Bgft. tasks.	Enrich.

General.
On 15/4/16 a commendatory order was issued by the GOC on improving the satisfaction of II Corps Commander himself of the work done by the RE II Div. He believed that the framing of the trenches by this Coy was very well carried out on – In 3 months time 3000 frames have been put in, representing some 2500 ft frames reclaimed, much of which could not have been done without frames. The drainage has been much improved. Comparatively few frames, perhaps 100 knocked to be replaced, repair damage by shellfire + much of the damage was done where trenches had not been completed + backed up. Dugouts have not been able to keep pace with the R.E. who can place frames much faster than Infy can sandbag + back up.

WAR DIARY
or
INTELLIGENCE SUMMARY.
(Erase heading not required.)

Army Form C. 2118.

by Field Coy RE
Sheet No 6 of April 1916

Place	Date	Hour	Summary of Events and Information	Remarks and references to Appendices
			Attention is drawn to the great expenditure in noseboys, done of which are of poor quality. Noses from the boys of tear them. Binding with leather has not proved a complete success. It is suggested that cellophane tin discs which could be fitted as wanted or put in the ground would save much money. These could be made on the principle of cellophane camp lanterns. Out of 8 boxes of RICKFORD FUSE examined 6 were perished (after one year) the fuse burnt very badly either without cracking or cracked or gapes. It is noticed probably because damp gets in under the tin tear-off strip which is not properly closed.	
	3/5/16.			

G.R. Hearn
Major R.E.
O.C. 64 Field Coy R.E.

Appendix A

C.R.E.No.2337.

O.C. 63rd Field Coy R.E.
    64th Field Coy R.E.
    90th Field Coy R.E.

        The G.O.C.Division has asked me to inform you that the Corps Commander has expressed his admiration for and appreciation of both the quantity and the quality of the work done by the Field Coys R.E.

        It is hardly necessary to add that the Divisional Commander has the same high opinion of the work, and has frequently expressed his satisfaction with the manner in which the R.E. of the Division are carrying out their duties.

        Will you please convey this to the Officers, N.C.Os and Men of your Company.

Lieutenant-Colonel, R.E.,

15/4/16.   C.R.E. 9th (Scottish) Division.

WAR DIARY

64 th. FIELD COMPANY R. E.

9 th. DIVISION

~~SHANKEEQUEEXX~~

MAY 1916

WAR DIARY
or
INTELLIGENCE SUMMARY

Army Form C. 2118.

64 Field Coy R.E.
Sheet No 7 May 1916.

Place	Date	Hour	Summary of Events and Information	Remarks and references to Appendices
PLOG STREET	1/5/16		No 2 section ABERFELDY (39 frames) repairing 5 frames damaged by shell fire LOWNDES LANE + 2 dugout trks. No 3 on S.I.110 (10 frames) 1 cupola dugout, CHESHIRE AVE (11 frames) 1 dugout + 66 dug trks. 10 Ams.	Fine, cloudy later - light E ams.
HQ DOUBON			No 4 S.I.117 (10 frames) + 3 dug trks.	
P.m 3 section				
in what hills	2/5/16		No 2 section ABERFELDY (17 frames dugout) 113 C.T. (4 frames) PLOG reconstruction 1 post (6 frames)	Cloudy. Kinda shelter light W.aid.
PLOG STREET +			HQ Both + 1 post (8 frames) + 30 ft stores. No 3 S.I.110 (16 frames) CHESHIRE AVE (14 frames) + 6 ft.	
TOURQUET BERTHE			trks. No 4 on S.I. 117 + S.I.116 + 2 dug trks	
	3/5/16		26 Bgde relieved 27 Bgde. Bgde. section noting	Dull. Lighter wind
	4/5/16		No 2 section ABERFELDY (10 frames 1 dugout). 113 C.T. (10 frames) PICKET No bombing post (5 frames)	Fine close
			116 Bombing post (8 frames) + 3 dug trks. No 3. S.I.110 (12 frames) CHESHIRE AVE. (11 frames) + 4 dug trks (3 shrapnel	due at 7 min S. Shrapnel
			trks. No 4 on S.I.116 + S.I.117 + 2 dug trks. No 4 section relieved No 4.	
	5/5/16		No 1 on C.T. 116 (3 frames) S.I.117 (12 frames) + 3 ft tanks. No 2. ABERFELDY (8 frames) + 2 dug	Dull, close. Dust. light
			trks. No 3 CHESHIRE AVE (14 frames) S.I.110 (6 frames) one + dug trks. Gas alarm 8.10 p.m.	missile sire.
	6/5/16		No 1 on S.I.117 (33 frames) + 5 dug trks. No 2 ABERFELDY (18 frames) dugout) bombing trk.	Fine, showers
			in C.T. 113 + F.T.116 + 2 dug trks. No 3 CHESHIRE AVE (14 frames) S.I.110 completed framing + 4 trks.	Mortar wind
	7/5/16		No 1 on S.I.117 (46 frames) started revetting. in FT 1117 + 2 dug trks No 2 ABERFELDY and	Showery. Dull mod SW wind
			bombing post, PICKET No 6 FT 116 + 2 dug trks. No 3 CHESHIRE AVE (10 frames) M.G.dugout completed	
			framing. S.I.109 S.I.110 44 dug trks.	

WAR DIARY
or
INTELLIGENCE SUMMARY
(Erase heading not required.)

Army Form C. 2118.

6n Field Cy RE
Sheet No 2 ? May 1916

Place	Date	Hour	Summary of Events and Information	Remarks and references to Appendices
	8/5/16			Showery. chy SW wind.
Ploeg STEERT	9/5/16		27 Bgde relieved 26 Bgde sections relating. No 1 section on 117 (12 frames) dugouts in 116 CT dugouts in 117 FT + 3 dugs tasks. No 2 ASERFELDT, sounding post PICKET. No 4 right flank HAMPSHIRE T. 1 dug task - No 3 CHESHIRE SW. wind.	Cloudy + dull SW wind.
	10/5/16		Av. M.G. dugout, cleaning up. 4 dug tasks completed wire in front 1 CHESHIRE AV. to south. No retieros No 3. No 1 m 117 S1 (12 A frames) finished dugouts 116 CT. OC 10th R OC 237 Coy round line + OC 237 Coy round line.	Cloudy fine interests & light W. wind.
			Started covering dug by box on 117 FT. + 3 dug tasks. No 2 sounding post + 2 dug tasks.	
	11/5/16		Most Hq. August CHESHIRE AVE. & 3 dug tasks. No 2 OC 237 round line again. No 1 on dug by box 117 FT. + various small jobs. No 2 OC 10th R OC 237 put another picketed & passes track as SO.	Cloudy, light SW air.
	12/5/16		Most MG dugout on 117 FT. No 2 on bombing Fair dull the Most MG dugout to Brig taster. rain off + light as yesterday also put up taster for OP. LANCASHIRE COTTAGE. No 1 continued sentry box in 117 FT. No 2 on bombing SW air. Sections on various jobs cleaning up. No 1 continued cleaning up. Sunken night of 16.	Fair dull that rain after light SW air.
	13/5/16		Sections on same work as yesterday. From 6.30 pm to 8.30 pm. Bombardment of trenches 113 - 120 and comm'n trenches (report of damage attached) at letter time raid on FT 116 & 117 which failed. At midnight order received by advanced echelon to repair damage. Mg proceeded in 10 minutes line under 2/L Clavering & Fischer and others on FT 113 (No 2) on 116 117 (No 4) + on 16 CT (No 1) until 5 am. Sandbag screens thrown up across nearly every gap in front parapet & CT. cleared out.	Rain, light W air. App A.

Army Form C. 2118.

WAR DIARY
or
INTELLIGENCE SUMMARY.
(Erase heading not required.)

64 Field Coy RE
Sheet No 3 of May 1916.

Place	Date	Hour	Summary of Events and Information	Remarks and references to Appendices
NIEUSTEKET	14/5/16		2 Bgde relieved 27 Bgde normally except that Coy in 113 kept below via CONVENT locality. Section relied until evg. OC inspected trenches afternoon. GOC IV Divison commended Coy for good trenches made & rapidity of repair. Advanced section (No1) worked at night on PICKET 40 retrenchment (No 2) on reclaiming one bay of HAMPSHIRE T.ao bombing post & new OPs 117 & 116 (Nos 3) Bldg Pioneers on ST 114, 118 & 119.	Dull light wind.
	15/5/16		Section relied and preparing for move on 16th	Dull warm lightish wind
	16/5/16		Nos 1, 2 & 4 sections left advanced billets at 9.15 am. & No 3 with HQ left Gravier Fm at 9.55 am. Marched to rest billets at crossroads between BAILLEUL & OUTERSTEENE arrived at 1.30 pm. All Munitn & 3 NCOs left to make at 237 stay.	Fine light wind, warm
OUTERSTEENE	17/5/16		Company muster, Inspection of arms equipment etc.	Fine hazy warm lightish wind
Sheet 27 X 28 d 4 2	18/5/16		Physical drill 7.30 am - 8 - Section practised in battn at Rifle exercises, section drill, musketry & bombing.	Fine light E wind hot.
	19/5/16		Physical drill 7.30 am - 8 - training same as yesterday. Staff Coy inoculated	Fine light SE wind hot.
	20/5/16		Physical drill, extended order, trenching, rapid firing, musketry for those not inoculated	Fine warm
	21/5/16		Sunday - Inspection of Billets, bayonets and boots.	Fine warm lightish rain.
	22/5/16		Pontooning, knotting, lashing, rapid firing bayonet fighting - Staff Coy inoculated	Fine calm hot aircraft.

Army Form C. 2118.

WAR DIARY
or
INTELLIGENCE SUMMARY
(Erase heading not required.)

6th Leicesters
Shipton & May 1916

Place	Date	Hour	Summary of Events and Information	Remarks and references to Appendices
OUDERSTEENE X28 d 4.2 Sht 27	23/5/16		Physical drill, extended order, bombing, rapid firing musketry from men not inoculated.	Windy calm
	24/5/16		Company to Baths at 4.45am. at STEENWERCK & back at 10.30 am march 12 miles	Fine light E wind
	25/5/16		Physical drill, Kaiths & Lewis & bombing (2 hours)	Showers Changeable Light & SE wind
	26/5/16		Training same as yesterday.	Cloudy light SW wind
	27/5/16	7 am	Coy proceeded on route march. Nos 1 & 2 via VIEUX BERQUIN & canal 1 mile N. of LA MOTTE, reconnaissance on spreading. Nos 3 & 4 to LA MOTTE for bombing in canal. Nos 1 & 2 joined them later & their bombing - arrived back at billets 4.15pm. much 14-15 miles	Cloudy cool Light Breeze above fine fine
	28/5/16		Clothing & gasshelmet inspection.	Fine light SW wind
	29/5/16		Whole Coy exercised at live grenade throwing - Pay - picked up ready to move.	Fine light N wind Enough
Sht 36 a D 25 C 34	30/5/16	8.45 am	Marched via VIEUX BERQUIN and LA MOTTE to billets near STEENBECQUE about 11½ miles - arrived 1.15 pm.	Rain Am & Pm mod N. Wind
	31/5/16		Halted	Fine hazy calm

3/6/16.

J.R. Hearn
Major
O.C. 6th Leicesters R.E.

CRE. B31
64th Field Co.
No: X4/13*2.
Appendix A.
May 1916.

Secret

Report on German Raid on HAMPSHIRE T. Locality.
13/5/16.

At 3.30 p.m. on the 13th inst. the enemy began an intensive bombardment of our line, extending from the centre of PICQUET HOUSE Locality to the left of T.120.

It was most violent against HAMPSHIRE T. Locality and consisted of 15, 10.5 and 7.7. c.m. shells, trench mortars and rifle grenades.

Very large craters were made in certain places, which may have been caused by either 21 c.m. or heavy trench mortars, but this point has not yet been definitely settled.

There was also a considerable amount of machine gun fire which was directed principally against our front line.

At 7.40 p.m. the bombardment ceased.

It was found impossible to clear the trenches and movement was out of the question.

The moment the bombardment ceased, all men, who were able to stand, lined the parapet ready to resist a raid, though this was considered unlikely, as the hostile wire had been examined just previous to the bombardment, and any existing gaps had been made by our own guns in the course of the afternoon.

The situation was well in hand.

The second bombardment commenced at about 7.50 p.m. and continued with unabated violence till 8.45 p.m.

It was even more intense than the first bombardment and it was noticed that a much greater proportion of the fire was directed against our support lines and communication trenches, though the front line received a good share of it.

The left and centre groups retaliated vigorously. This retaliation was spasmodic until 7 p.m., when it developed into a steady rate of fire, 18 pounders being directed on the hostile trenches and the Howitzers on the support trenches.

The 60-pdrs., 6" guns and the Howitzers of the Right Group assisted in this retaliation and the flanking section of the right Division enfiladed the enemy's trenches.

The raiders seem to have been in 3 parties of about 20 each.

The objective of one party was the junction of T.117 with C.T.117, the objective of the second party being about 30 yards further South; the third party lay out in front of their own wire.

The raiding parties must have reached our parapet about 8.40 p.m.

The first party encountered about 5 men, while the second encountered Lieut. Henry, 11th Royal Scots and 1 man.

Surprise in each case seems to have been mutual, as the fire had barely lifted when Lieut. Henry saw the Germans on the parapet.

P.T.O.

To use Lieut. Henry's own words "I shot them down like rats, and none got in", but a few men apparently gained a footing at the junction of T.117 and C.T.117.

The remainder bolted back to their own trenches as fast as they could, assisted by our rifle fire.

The Lewis gun did not take part, and has since been found lying buried in the arms of a Lewis gunner.

The enemy left 10 of their dead behind them, who belonged to the 104th Regiment, 40th Division.

Among those killed are 2 Lance-corporals, 2 corporals, and 1 sergeant.

Two of them wore the Iron Cross ribbon.

The buttons, fastening the shoulder strap bore the numbers 1, 4, 11 and 12. This does not, however, indicate that men of these four companies took part in the raid. It is now an understood thing that the numbers on these buttons do not necessarily represent the company to which a man belongs.

The raiders threw bombs and some carried rifles and revolvers.

All identification marks had been removed and each man had a strip of white cotton about 1½" wide sown on the collar.

The enemy brought over notice boards with them, which they stuck in the parapet.

It is worthy of note that our men, who were south of the junction of T.116 with C.T.116 had no idea that a raid had taken place, as they were cut off by a bad block in the trench and there was too much noise going on to distinguish rifle shots.

All ranks behaved splendidly and worked magnificently throughout the night and succeeded in repairing a considerable amount of the damage, which had been done to our trenches by the enemy's bombardment.

General Staff, 9th (Scottish) Division.
15th May, 1916.

SECRET

REPORT ON EFFECTS OF BOMBARDMENT ON NIGHT MAY 13th.

Accounts differ as to duration of the bombardment, but it appears to have lasted about 2 hours with a pause of 10 minutes in the middle. A raid followed at about 8-30 p.m. The leaders carried a sort of notice board, a frame covered with canvas, and started to plant them on the parapet but were shot in doing so; it is supposed that these frames were to act as guiding marks. The raiding party are said to have appeared almost immediately the bombardment lifted, and perhaps came out to cut the wire during the 10 minutes pause.

2. The extent of line bombarded was from Trench 113 (inclusive) to about 100 yards North of PICKET HOUSE, Trenches 116 and 117, C.T.116 (several shells dotted down this) Sq 116 and the LOOP, C.T.117 near PALK VILLA, Trenches 118, 119 and 120. Also along GLENCORSE AVENUE and the front end of LOWNDES LANE behind the EST.DU COMMERCE. No damage is noticeable in Gap F or the CONVENT locality or in most of Gap G.

3. The extent of the damage was on the whole much less than I expected to find. In several places the front parapet has been breached, but on the afternoon of the 14th it was quite possible to pass along the whole front to the top of C.T.117, the holes in the parapet having been closed by sandbag screens erected between midnight and 5 a.m. by 3 sections of this Coy under Lts Clavering and Fischer. C.Ts 116 and 117 were both open throughout except the front end of the latter, where communication was open to 116 F.T. along an improvised control trench. Practically the whole of 117 F.T. was destroyed, however, except one bay on each side of the top of C.T.117, and a temporary block had been made at the end of this bay. Where the next bay to the north had been was one big crater probably made by a heavy Minenwerfer bomb. Some heavy shells or bombs had been thrown into PICKET HOUSE and just to the north of it and the wisdom of abandoning this was amply demonstrated. Yet the screen of sandbags E. and S. of PICKET HOUSE still stood and only a little clearance had been necessary to make a safe passage into Gap G.

4. C.T.118 between the M.G.Emplacement at PALK VILLA and the right of F.T.118 was intact and defensible, but F.T.118 was blown in at many points. F.T.119 suffered somewhat, but many shells appear to have just gone over and the duckboard path leading to F.T.119 was almost completely destroyed. F.T.120 was slightly damaged, C.T.120 not at all. It surprised me to find that S1 117 was not damaged as the enemy have shelled this somewhat frequently of late. There was one shell-hole at LONDON BRIDGE.

5. Relief was carried out normally on the morning of the 14th, except that the Coys in PICKET HOUSE locality relieved via the CONVENT. This was because the screen wall just behind the EST DU COMMERCE was knocked down and it was thought inadvisable to take bodies of men past this point, but individuals could pass up and down, proceeding via LOTHIAN ROAD, S 113 and C.T.113. This duplicating of communications in PICKET HOUSE and HAMPSHIRE T. localities has been thoroughly justified.

6. The following points were noticeable:-
(1) The A frames were broken where shells had burst outside the trenches but very seldom were more than 3 frames broken at any one point, and the lower parts held up the lower parts of the trench so that clearing was easy, while a little sandbagging would have given cover had this been necessary. In some cases one of the legs of the frame came over a little but the frame was practically effective. The importance of packing well

down at the cross-piece and below is very great.

(2) A few dugouts collapsed wholly or partially because the explosion of shells at the rear, which was insufficiently protected, blew the frames forward. In one case, I think in the LOOP, the frames were specially strong ones of 5" X 4" timber the centre post strutted on both sides with a tie sloping upwards from back to front. The importance of an earth slope at the back to resist the blast was shown. Some of our dugouts which have control trenches close behind, are likely to collapse similarly, if a shell lands in the control trench.

(3) A half cupola section dugout (25th Div. type) in Fort WALTER was quite undamaged, although a shell landed within a few inches of the back (towards the enemy)

(4) The concrete sentry box in F.T.117 was damaged but was only half finished. The concrete was "green" but had been to some extent protected by sandbags. The unprotected reinforcement was not shifted much, but no lesson can be drawn from this.

(5) One thing which I noticed particularly was that the cut-off corners in C.T.116 were weak and although not always blown in completely were bulged in. Communication trenches adopted for stretchers should have the wide frames and not narrow frames with cut-off corners.

(6) Lieut.Colonel Croft, Commanding 11th R.S. was impressed with the support given to front line parapet by the overhead strutted frames ("marriage arches") of 3" X 3" timber, put up by the 25th Div. I found a good many of these broken, while Lieut. Fischer informs me that the A frames in F.T.119 were intact, although the parapet was bulged in.

(Sd) G.R.Hearn,
Major, R.E.,
O.C.64th Field Coy R.E.

17/5/16.

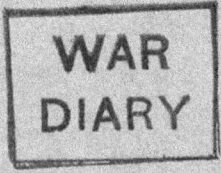

64th Field Company R.E.

9th Division.

June 1916.

Army Form C. 2118.

WAR DIARY
or
INTELLIGENCE SUMMARY.

(Erase heading not required.)

6th K.Shly. R.E.
Shed No. 1 8 June 1916

Instructions regarding War Diaries and Intelligence Summaries are contained in F. S. Regs., Part II. and the Staff Manual respectively. Title pages will be prepared in manuscript.

Place	Date	Hour	Summary of Events and Information	Remarks and references to Appendices
	1/6/16	8am	Left Hill of STEENBECQUE and marched via AIRE & WITTERNESSE. Arrived 11am. about 8 miles	Fine, light wind. Cool.
	2/6/16	9.30 am	Left Witternesse and marched to CUHEM about 5 miles. arrived 10.30 am.	Cloudy wind W. to N.
CUHEM.	3/6/16	8am	Started training - one hour Company drill. Men by section musketry - rapid aiming & charging not retained distance, rapid loading & firing, bayonet fighting and lecture on demolitions.	
	4/6/16	8am	Company drill one hour, musketry aiming & firing discipline, bayonet fighting & rapid loading & firing in turns by sections.	Fine, stronger wind showers afs.
	5/6/16	8am	Company drill one hour. Pspection extended order & bayonet fighting. 2 hrs each.	Strong SW wind showers
	6/6/16	8am	Company drill - lectures on map reading, consolidation of trenches &c.	Heavy rain showers SW wind cool aft
	7/6/16	8am	Company drill - consolidation of trenches & strong point, blowing in of trench & form attack extended order & bayonet fighting - Demonstration of Lewis gun & practice afternoon.	Cloudy not cool. SW wind fine intervals.
	8/6/16	9am	Company drill - 9.30 route march about 9 miles & map reading for N.C.O.s.	Cloudy no. S.W.
	9/6/16	8am	Company drill. Consolidation of trenches - defence of village - cutting brushwood & musketry practice afternoon.	Cloudy in afternoon, rather cool night & cool
	10/6/16	8am	Musketry practice & bayonet fighting. O.C. attended conference S.A. Bgde in preparation for Brigade manoeuvres.	Cloudy, light SW wind - thunder aft

WAR DIARY or INTELLIGENCE SUMMARY

Army Form C. 2118.

64 Field Coy R.E.
Sheet No 2 of June 1916.

Place	Date	Hour	Summary of Events and Information	Remarks and references to Appendices
CHEM.	11/6/16	8 am	Brigade manoeuvres. Section attached to battalions for consolidation of strong supporting points. 2 phases - advance over open country and assault from aft. & flatter trenches - section returned 2 p.m.	Dull S.W. wind. Thunder storm aftn.
	12/6/16	9 am	Section on gas helmets - gas helmet drill & bayonet fighting - musketry practice 30 yards range for bad shots aftn.	Dull gloomy morn. W. wind.
	13/6/16		Company went to FLECHINELLE mine for baths, and performed 6 more.	Heavy rain thunderstorm. Dull mod W. wind.
	14/6/16		Orders received to move overnight 14/15. Completed preparations	Dull showery morn. W. wind.
	15/6/16		Left CHEM. 3.30 am. and marched via WESTREHEM & ST. HILAIRE to LILLERS about 10½ miles. arrived 7.20 am. entrained - shoed train with 9th Signal Coy accommodation for vehicles inadequate. Loaded 69 carts on vehicles meant for 42. Had to leave 3 carts behind which came by next train. d/p LILLERS 10.50 - arrived LONGUEAU 7.10 pm. AMIENS. Detrained at 8 pm. received orders to march to CORBIE about 8 miles - arrived 12.30 am. having halted ½ hour for water fed the horses - no long halt on railway journey.	Dull showery morn to wind. This evening bright.
	16/6/16		Left CORBIE 5 pm. and marched to camp near BOIS MAJOR S. arrived 7.10 pm attached to XXX Division received orders for work on 17/6	Cloudy light N. wind.

WAR DIARY or INTELLIGENCE SUMMARY

Army Form C. 2118.

1st Field Coy RE
Sheet No 3 of June 1916

Place	Date	Hour	Summary of Events and Information	Remarks and references to Appendices
BOIS MALPAS	17/6/16	6.45 a.m.	All 4 sections marched to point N. of CRANE PORAY road. N.E. of camp. Embarked in motor lorries	Fine, strong N.E. wind
nr CHIPILLY			lorries taken to BRONFAY Fm. S. of CARNOY. Worked on dressing stations in 4 different	N E wind
on the SOMME			places. Returned at 5.30 pm. And reached camp at 6.30 p.m.	
	18/6/16	7.15	Sections (except No 3) embarked in lorries near camp & proceeded to same works	Dull, early & later fine from N wind
			No 3 Section at 4 p.m. to work on dressing station near TALUS BOISÉ.	
	19/6/16	7.15	Sections 1,2 & 4 to same works. No 3 section at 4 p.m.	Dull, calm, N.E. moderate
	20/6/16	7	Gas helmet worn when inspecting sections & work as yesterday.	Fine dull wind to E. light SW wind
	21/6/16	7.15	1,2 & 4 for morning work. No 3 section night work as before.	fine N. light fine N wind.
	22/6/16	7.15	Same work as yesterday. No 3 section & men on M. Duty at 3.45 p.m.	Fine hot day light heavy hot
	23/6/16	7.25	1,2 & 4 sections to same work. No 3 section at 4 p.m. This was battery of light S.22
			work for 30th Division. Subsequently an order was published in Divn orders arranging	
			appreciation of work done by Company received from G.O.C. 30th Divn	
	24/6/16	9.	Sections practised in entwined wire & spinning obstacles	Rain, S.W. wind
	25/6/16	10.	Inspection of Coy preparatory to going into action & completing deficiencies	Cloudy, dry light air
	26/6/16	8.	Inspection by lighter water. Sections practised in intended order. O.C. visited	Cloudy light SW wind
			1st? Brigade. Drew up scheme for work of consolidation after attack	raining

T2134. Wt. W708—776. 500000. 4/15. Sir J. C. & S.

Army Form C. 2118.

WAR DIARY
or
INTELLIGENCE SUMMARY

(Erase heading not required.)

by Field Coy R.E.
Shutment of June 1916

Instructions regarding War Diaries and Intelligence Summaries are contained in F. S. Regs., Part II. and the Staff Manual respectively. Title pages will be prepared in manuscript.

Place	Date	Hour	Summary of Events and Information	Remarks and references to Appendices
near CHIPILLY	26/6		A summary of casualties in the Coy for a period of 13 months gives 7 killed, 1 missing, wounded 7 gassed and 62 evacuated sick. Of these 1 killed & wounded were in the mounted section.	
	27/6/16	9.	Inspection in fighting order. OC attended Conference of COs 3rd S.A. Brigade afternoon.	Cloudy, showers N.W. wind
	28/6/16	9.	Check parade. Preparing to move. Received order afternoon informing move at 4.8 hours. Conference of Officers evening.	Dull, misty showers. Calm.
	29/6/16	9	Physical drill and baths afternoon. OC till conference with Brigadier 1st R.B. Sqn afternoon.	Cloudy, strong S.W. wind.
Shutbred	30/6/16	10	Check parade. Conference of officers afternoon. Marched at 10 p.m. to GROVETOWN L.i.d central arrived 12.50 a.m.	Cloudy, strong S.W. wind. Sunshine fine afternoon.

E.P. Hearne
Major
O Co, 9 Field Co R.E.

3/7/16

ROUTINE ORDERS BY MAJOR-GENERAL W.T.FURSE, C.B.,D.S.O.
COMMANDING, 9th (SCOTTISH) DIVISION.
Sunday, 25th June 1916.

PART 1.

Nil.

P.A.V.Stewart, Lieut.Colonel,
General Staff.

PART 2.

444. The Major-General Commanding 9th Division has much pleasure in publishing the following letter received from Major-General J.S.M.SHEA, C.B.,D.S.O. Commanding 60th Division:-

"I am writing to express my most sincere thanks to you for the good work done for me by your 63rd and 64th Companies R.E., 9th Seaforth Highlanders, 6th K.O.S.Bs., Royal Scots and the 2nd & 3rd S.African Battalions. They came and helped us at a time when we were really hard put to it to get finished in time and had they been working for their own Division they could not possibly have done more. They put such good heart into their work that the results were excellent.

Will you please tell them how very much I appreciate all they did.

Good luck to you and them".

---

445. LEAVE

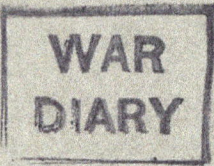

64th Field Company R.E.

9th Division.

July 1916.

Army Form C. 2118.

WAR DIARY
or
INTELLIGENCE SUMMARY.
(Erase heading not required.)

64 Field Coy RE
Sheet no 8 July 1916

VOL 15

Place	Date	Hour	Summary of Events and Information	Remarks and references to Appendices
Gotentown Sheet 62C L1 d central copy	1/7	6.25 am	Offr preliminary intensive bombardment started at 7.30am Attack commenced. Division being in Support and 1/2 SA Brigade at GROVETOWN this Company took no part in attack. Stood by all day	Fine light Seraï cloudy very
	2/7	11am	no orders received up to this hour. OC received by Brigadier 1st SA Bgde went to Bgde HQ at A24986 Sheet 62C & reconnoitered OC 200 & 7 July to DUBLIN TRENCH via MONTAUBAN road. Beyond town DAWES REDOUBT crossing NOMANS LAND by MARICOURT MONTAUBAN road Beyond town BRIQUETERIE occupied. Went to GLATZ REDOUBT down SILESIA ALLEY via TRANS BORSE to BILLON WOOD VALLEY returned to GROVETOWN about 4pm received orders to move. Left camp at 9.45pm arrived in BILLON WOOD VALLEY at 11.45pm.	Fine light mo Airo
Billon Valley Wood VALLEY	3/7	11am	OC Via 1/7 Sgd Pipe NR with GOC SA Bgde – stood by. no further orders.	Dull calm light 25 mi
	4/7	10.30am	Battalion Conference received orders to move – at 2.30pm proceeded take over from Officer field Coy in MARICOURT. REDUMP A16a 2.5 Trenches nursed up at 5pm No 3 wkS NAPIERS KEEP MARICOURT. No 1 2 4 left trenches between S. of MACHINE GUN WOOD – & later mch up for night work – Nos 2 & 4 prd NE of BRIQUETERIE at E end CHIMNEY TRENCH wth Infy working parties (2) on a Cov trail from TRAM	Dull close Sai Sanderston Heavy rain 3pm.

T2134. Wt. W708—776. 500000. 4/15. Sir J. C. & S.

Army Form C. 2118.

WAR DIARY
or
INTELLIGENCE SUMMARY.
(Erase heading not required.)

1/1 Field Coy R.E.
(or Intelligence Summary)
Sheet No 2 July 1916

Place	Date	Hour	Summary of Events and Information	Remarks and references to Appendices
MALTZ HORN ST.			ALLEY to NORD ALLEY about in centre of CHIMNEY trench (6) strong point A3 d 58. Owing to	MONTAUBAN SHEET
S.P. MACHINE GUN WOOD.			extensive shellfire little was done - hostile bombing attack in GLATZ REDOUBT (mainly on IDENNERWERK to Germans) Parties from 1/SA1 on adjoining GLATZ REDOUBT aid	
			in strong point at A3 d 63 & A10 a 37 - front party did a good front - remember hampered by enemies fire. No 2 section in strong point about A3 C 28 - working parties of 1/3/SA1 did not arrive. No 3 section could write in sufficient numbers	A C28 - working A pp. A
	5/7		Section front No 3 at 9am in strong point about A4 b 29. 3 M.G. emplacements No 2 at 2pm. up my C.T. from A4 c 39 to A4 d 39. strong point at A4 c 28. North bombing step to GLATZ REDOUBT & strong point A10 a 37 made defensible by working party (Fry) hostile improved strong point A4 b 65. Night high pressure parties improved dug line from S.E. BERNAFAY WOOD to A4 b 65, old German trench A4 b 84 to A4 b 52, new trench Trench b A4 d 10 & trench to A4 d 32.	Sull mid Winns mid aft Irusberg See Sketch Opp. A
	6/7		Most of front was taken from A4 d 32 to A4 b 49 including CHIMNEY TRENCH. No 4 to make SP opened at A10 a 5/10. That C.omm trench. No 1 section completed 3 m.g. emplacements at BRIQUETERIE - making position 1/SA1 coys on junction of CHIMNEY TRENCH and NORD ALLEY also on Comm. Trench to TRAM ALLEY. No 2 section with 1 platoon 3/SA1 coys on	Bull. wd Cloudy. mid to warm.

T2134. Wt. W708—776. 500000. 4/15. Sir J. C. & E.

WAR DIARY or INTELLIGENCE SUMMARY

Army Form C. 2118.

By Field Coy R.E.

Sheet No 3 of July 1916.

Place	Date	Hour	Summary of Events and Information	Remarks and references to Appendices
MALTON ST.				MONTAUBAN SHEET
	7/7		Strong point A.10.d.27. No 4 section on strong point A+D 50 and dugouts for M.G. GLATZ REDOUBT. No 3 section improved strong point junction NORD ALLEY & CHIMNEY TRENCH. No 2 section unit 2	Dull md.
			Platoons 2/SAI continued yesterdays work. No 4 section completed strong point A+D 50 except for some wiring. Continued Mch dugouts GLATZ REDOUBT & commenced deep dugouts A+D 32 Q	S.W. wind
			Working party H/SAI dug comm trench 100 ft road near this point from DUBLIN TRENCH & CREMENT TRENCH av depth 3'6".	Rain
	8/7	2pm	No 1 section proceeded to BERNAFAY WOOD to reconnoitre for entrance of troops preceding through wood	Dull md.
			to attack LONGUEVAL (this operation was abandoned) About 200 were cut under heavy shell fire, section having 5 casualties. The platoon of 2/Inf party with it losing 10. Remaining section did not work.	N.W. wind
	9/7	9am	No 2 section attempted work on strong points A.11.a.49 & A.11.b.29 but owing to continuous & heavy shelling little work was done except 150' of wiring. No 1 & 2 sections straight improved strong points GLATZ REDOUBT. No 4 section on S.P. A+D 50. No 3/4 [working] party on wire.	Fine md. W. wind.
	10/7	1.16pm	No 2 unit ½ Coy 1/SAI on GLATZ REDOUBT deepening DORHAM TRENCH. No 3 unit 1 Coy 1/SAI & ½ Coy Pioneers on progress in new ct from NORD ALLEY to TRAIN ALLEY & new tinch deepening CHIMNEY TRENCH & across shelled area to Sw corner BERNAFAY WOOD - good progress.	Cloudy & just a W. wind

WAR DIARY or INTELLIGENCE SUMMARY

Army Form C. 2118.

64 Field Coy R.E.
Sheet north of July 1916

Place	Date	Hour	Summary of Events and Information	Remarks and references to Appendices
	10/7		No 1 section with 1/Coy 1/SA I on SP DUBLIN TRENCH, NE of Bois Augut & deepened CT west of road DUBLIN TRENCH & CASEMENT TRENCH. No 2 Upper Clearing accompanied 4/SA I to advise in improvement of strong post in LONGUEVAL ALLEY S 23 d 43 C 2. There is no trifurcation as shown in map - aeroplane also show none. A captured plan gives certain German trenches which may be useful for identification.	Appendix B
	11/7	10pm	No 3 section continued revetting CT NORD ALLEY & TRAIN ALLEY - 1 Coy 4/SA I improved new trench from NORD ALLEY towards BERNAFAY WOOD & Bay. Pincers completed this trench. Before all one having been destroyed by 8" shell. No 1 section worked on new approach trench out from direction of DELVILLE WOOD. No 2 section improved wire and trench from GLATZ REDOUBT. No 4 section made a T-head on DUBLIN ALLEY to cover approach from north - wired SP A and S O.	cloudy lightning wind
	12/7	6.30pm	No 2 section completed cutting side started on 9th is BERNAFAY WOOD. Pits were made to rail. Work through enemy barrage SW of wood. Under instructions from CRE No 3 + 4 section + 2 Coys 2/SA I sent to dig new trench east of LONGUEVAL ALLEY & to wire round the latter - delayed by heavy bombardment. Did not move up til 11pm. Unable to work as enemy patrols were close & lit of wire & very lights were being sent up constantly from TRONES WOOD 4/SA I had improved the trenching post but unable to wire under heavy fire.	Cloudy. not SW wind. Appx E

WAR DIARY or INTELLIGENCE SUMMARY

Army Form C. 2118.

Field in Rear Trenches 5th July 1916.

Place	Date	Hour	Summary of Events and Information	Remarks and references to Appendices
	13/7		No work today - preparing for operation tomorrow.	Cloudy, fine later, dull flash SW wind.
	14/7	3 am	Coy assembled in MALDEN ST. Horses & Ltd carts & ambulances loaded with materials at NAPIER REDOUBT MARICOURT. arrived at 3.25 am. SA Pigle in reserve. Coy in Batt reserve.	Dull showers no Sat wind.
		7.50 am	Rec'd instructions from ORG ¾ to chr RE + B.Sy. Pioneers moved off at 9.5 am to construct a CT from S17 C86 to about S17 C32 on Southeast. Work was completed at 8.15 pm. At 2 pm heard advance of A Pigle applied to accompany + this was afterwards - prepared memo for defence DELVILLE WOOD. 3.45 pm accompanied Brigadier to MONTAUBAN - attack deferred + Coy bivouacs MONTAUBAN ALLEY for night. Heavy beating machine gun shelling all evening.	U. Fischer wounded 11.30 am. Appendix C.
MONTAUBAN ALLEY	15/7	5.25 am	Attack by SA Pigle on DELVILLE WOOD - No. 1+3 sections accompanied 2nd + 3/SA1 respectively. 2nd Lt Deller at S22 d 09 in reserve. 11 am went up to ward. No. 4 section moved up. Found these in new trench BUCHANAN ST under rifle & shell fire. Later section deepened this trench. 2nd Lt Mortalit killed while No. 1 section on protective duties near Chateau of LONGUEVAL. Sections were withdrawn between 4+6 pm. At 7.30 pm No 2 went up to improve + wire BUCHANAN St trench but owing to heavy fire did not do much.	No. 143 cabin has fire + WI rounds later.
	16/7	10 am	Owing to enemy being still in N part of LONGUEVAL + NW corner of wood SA Pigle ordered stay to gain in attack. No. 1+3 sections sent up to consolidate but attack was unsuccessful & after pause at night.	Fine, clouds they rouen.

WAR DIARY
or
INTELLIGENCE SUMMARY.
(Erase heading not required.)

Army Form C. 2118.

by Field Coy R.E.
Sheet No 6 of July 1916.

Hour, Date, Place	Summary of Events and Information	Remarks and references to Appendices
16/7 cont.	sustaining several casualties. They went withdrawn by me about 4pm. O/Cy 6m materials went safely to wire edge of wood from PRINCES ST South but unable to get through the barrage. 2 Platoons B Cy manage to get up two Lewis wire N.of PRINCES ST about 2.30 a.m. on 17/7.	misty – fine rain. Appendix II
17/7.	No 173 section got up to BUCHANAN ST, made 2 Lewis gun emplacements one to right of Bn H.Q. redoubled hence trench PRINCES ST towards Strong point S.18.a.06 held by 5/Cameron. Inside wood team work including abatis fence NW being made by B Cy Pioneers about S.18.a.38. Gave directions for strong point at S.18.a.67 which was commenced at 7.30 pm. by No 2 section going up at 1pm. at 7.30 pm. respectively. S.P. was which no 2 worked also on their emplacement & 3 S.P. for emmas near S.12 & S.2. B Cy dug 140' French mentioned in 3 shifts of 8 one platoon at a time. One platoon wired 200' N. of PRINCES ST & along edge of wood – Dly Pioneers attacked white wood our 3.30 of edge of wood – worked up the & cleared old German trench in S.17.d. to B wood – also carried up running material – Heavy bombardment with small for shells 10.15 pm for several hours –	Rain morning, windy NE air.
18/7.	Work deferred on account of rain – CRE (Lt Col Romersal (?) R.E.) was wounded on previous night in DELVILLE WOOD & Major Henry left at 3pm. to take over at our H.Q. At 11 am. position being rather critical owing to counter-attack. Cy orders to dig a fire trench S.17.c.74– make forming blocks in LONGUEVAL ALLEY & new CT. S.17.c.74– B Cy & Dly Pioneers cooperated. Trench completed by 10 am. Average 4'6 deep.	Rain from 11pm. Point TRONES WOOD.

G R Hear Major R.E.

Army Form C. 2118.

WAR DIARY
or
INTELLIGENCE SUMMARY.
(Erase heading not required.)

Intelligence
Sheet No 7 of July 1916

Instructions regarding War Diaries and Intelligence Summaries are contained in F. S. Regs., Part II. and the Staff Manual respectively. Title pages will be prepared in manuscript.

Hour, Date, Place	Summary of Events and Information	Remarks and references to Appendices
19/7 7.0 pm	S.A. Bde relieved last night by 53rd Bde to which the Company was attached. Situation uncertain all day. 2nd Lts C.T. ALLEN and G. PARKER (both T.C.) arrived as reinforcements. Lt Ac. Rawson wounded and evacuated. 11th & 14.3 Secs sent up to make a supporting point in DELVILLE WOOD south of PRINCES ST. and east of BUCHANAN ST. B Coy Premises sent up to attempt to move the Northwards and Westwards from the SE corner of the wood. Both parties ran into a German attack and some nimble work was done hurling 40 odd mills to get Lab No 4 Sec were sent up to complete block & strand widing last night. Trench shelled and no work done.	Appendix F Contains Instructions (13 pages) Appendix G Contains Information from OKE Division XIII Corps (8 pages) Appendix H Contains Operation Orders (9 pages)
20/7	No work all day. 9th Div relieved by 3rd Div Company relieved by Cheshire Field Company R.E. (T.F.) Marched out 10.30 pm and returned to have huts at GROVETOWN	Appendix J is a sheet showing MONTAUBAN and written undertaken by S.A. Bde enlarged by 23rd Btn RF & R Co 2 Engls (with 1 by fr 2 Engls)
21/7 HAPPY VALLEY	Joined S.A. Bde in bivouac in HAPPY VALLEY. Resting all day	Appendix K - ment Army work done by SA Bde
22/7	Transport under Lt Clearing marched out for rest area 11.15 am and bivouaced for the night at ALLONVILLE. Reinforcements arrived namely 2nd Lt H.S. BESANT R.E.(SR) and 2nd Lt H.CAWTHRA R.S. (T.C.) and 13 men OR's. Sitting Parade. Check parade for clothing deficiencies of Ret. Marched out with S.A. Bde 8.30 am arrived MERICOURT L'ABBE station 11.30 am entrained in S.P. train timed to leave	
23/7	No news on train with SABde Arrived at billets at L'ETOILE 5.30 pm, left at 10.30 pm Transport arrived at billets at L'ETOILE 6.30 am Resting all day at about 5.0 am	
24/7 L'ETOILE	Detrained HANGEST 4.30 am arrived L'ETOILE 6.30 am Resting all day.	

Army Form C. 2118.

WAR DIARY
or
INTELLIGENCE SUMMARY.
(Erase heading not required.)

by Field Coy RE
Sheet No 8 of July 1916.

Instructions regarding War Diaries and Intelligence Summaries are contained in F. S. Regs., Part II. and the Staff Manual respectively. Title pages will be prepared in manuscript.

Hour, Date, Place	Summary of Events and Information	Remarks and references to Appendices
25/7	Billeting party left LONGPRÉ by train 7.0 am. Bathing parade in R.SOMME 10.30 am. Completed checking deficiencies.	
26/7	Marched to LONGPRÉ station, entrained and left 4.30 pm. Arrived BRIAS 10.0 pm. Detrained, marched to DIEVAL, arriving 1.30 am.	
27/7	Resting in billets. Made a hot-house in the village and gave all the men a hot bath. Arranged with S.A.B. Co. for billets in FRÉVILLERS.	
28/7	Marched at 10.0 am. arrived FRÉVILLERS 12.0 noon. Checking tools in afternoon.	
29/7	7.0–7.30 Physical drill. 9.0 marching orders. Owing to shortage of own 2 mules every available man entrained in morning for unloading horses & washing carts. 2.30 pm unloading and checking indging equipment.	
30/7	7.30–8.0 Physical drill. 9.30 Parade Service. Collects on the whole in afternoon. No work.	
31/7	7.0–7.30 Physical drill. 9.0–12.30 Coy drill, Bayonet fighting and saluting. No work in heat of the day. Parade 5.0 pm. Trestle drill, Packing & unpacking wagon, musketry.	

LW Woolway Lt R.E.
OC 64th Coy R.E.

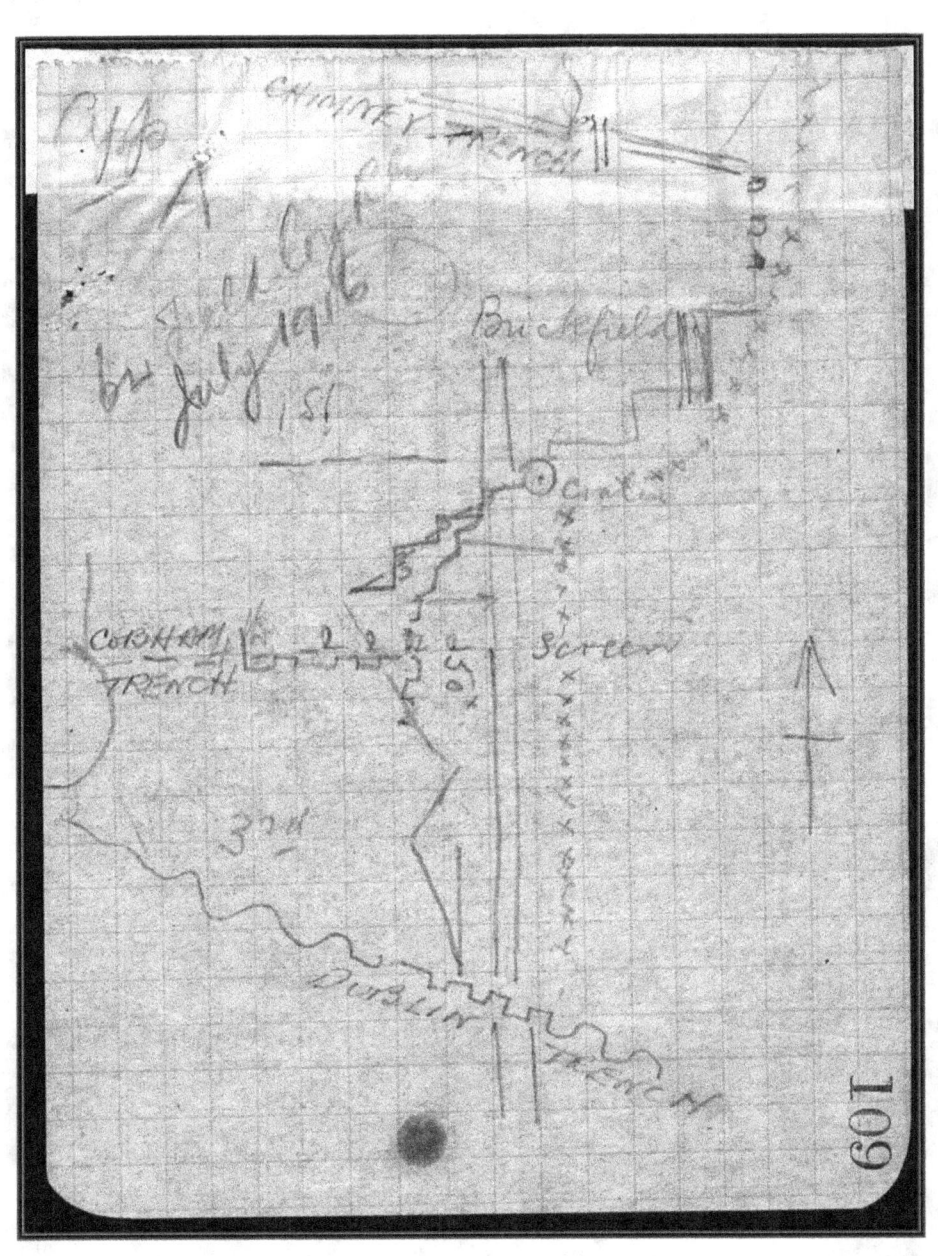

No 1 — wire Boring T Kench — S.P.
Bomb stop opp Kilonaway
Blocked sunken road
M.G. Bombing post above
STOP. CT A — B.
2. H S.P.

4. I
wire Dublin
NewCT. CASEMENT — DUBLIN
informs KorT

? M infants in KorT

See stores

To OC 60th Fd. Coy R.E. B
R.E. Map is handed herewith

Gun = REDOUBT is marked KÖNIG
LUDWIG HÖHE = King Ludwigs Height —

To EAST, that the chimney of the
Briquetteer is marked — almost
undecipherable but probably ZYL -
short for ZYLINDER — (cylinder)
                                                (light railway)
The Railway is marked KLEINBAHN
- RWDE — I'm not clear of the "R"
but it is evidently only a title
short for M Mulde
They apparently call GERMANS WOOD
SCHONQUELL WALD = Beautiful well
wood!
Machine Gun Wood is BIRKENWALD
= Birch Wood
AVIERE WOOD = BAYERNWALD
= Bavarian Wood
                                        W.E. Murray
                                        Capt
11.7.16

Memo.   C

The defence of DERVILLE
Wood against Counter attack
requires that the valley about
S12 c 5 8 towards FLERS shall
be well commanded.

To do this small works should be
constructed about
S 12 c 1 6
S 12 c 2 7
S 12 c 9 5
each containing a machine gun
& 2 sections infantry.

Other works may be made about
S 12 d 3 .
S 18 b 6 9.
S 18 d 9 5 commanding the C.T.

Second line supporting points
at S 18 b 5 7 & S 18 a 5 4
with bombing posts covering the
rides at S 18 a 7 7 & S 18 a 6 4

The posts round the wood

C

should be constructed as much visible as possible but must have a good view & the M.g. must have a good field of fire. Branches to be heaped in front of the works as an obstacle with or without wire all round.

The work to be started as a series of pits deep & narrow

say 75ˣ

which can be joined up by traverses afterwards.

Bombs should be plentiful.

14/7

G R Hearn
Major RE
OC 61st Coy

Company Orders for 16/7/16

1. 1st S.A. Infantry will cooperate with 11/R.S. to capture position still held by enemy in North of LONGUEVAL village.

2. This operation will take place at or after 10 am.

3. Nos 1 & 3 sections under the command of Lt Rankin will move & consolidate the position when gained especially a strong point about S11 d 4 5 to command the ELERS Rd and bring a crossfire with a work to be constructed by 90 Fd Coy at S11 d 3 4 — The work on the right will be improved if possible.

4. Lt Rankin will report to OC 1/S.A.I at LONGUEVAL at

9 a.m. and arrange to accomodate the sections in the trench during the operations. The H.Q. trench at S.18 a central should be used so as to be close up.

5. Lt Clavering with Nos 2 & 4 sections will go up at 2 p.m. & will consolidate the strong points on the perimeter of the STRAND. If unable to work on these a supporting point on the right will be made about S.18 d central. Bloy pioneers will be sent up to assist.

16/7/16.

G R Hearn
Major R.E.
O.C. 171 Coy

"A" Form.
MESSAGES AND SIGNALS.
Army Form C. 2121.

| TO | O.C. 64th Fd. Cy. R.E. | | |

| Sender's Number | Day of Month | In reply to Number | |
| 2653 | 12 | | AAA |

Herewith a tracing of BERNAFAY and TRÔNES WOODS showing in red a proposed new trench running from S.23.d.2.7 on LONGUEVAL TRENCH to where the latter crosses the valley at the bottom of the valley at S.23.c.7½.1½.

2. The G.O.C. Div. wishes this trench to be constructed tonight.

3. The suggested general alignment is as shown on the tracing, so that ~~the trench~~ fire can be brought to bear to the east and to the south.

4. A continuous fire trench is not required. The trench should be dug as narrow as possible with say 12ft fire bays at 12ft intervals. These bays to be traversed from one another

Continued page 2

"A" Form.
MESSAGES AND SIGNALS.

Army Form C. 2121.

Recd. at *Page* m.
Date 2

by leaving them thus :— ⎍⎍
or thus :— ⌐⌐   ↓ ↘ FIRE BAYS
as found most suitable.

(4) Possibly this trench may be continued to the south as shown by dotted red line.

(5) There are, I understand, certain posts held along the east and south edges of BERNAFAY WOOD. The G.O.C. wishes these posts to be made easy of access to facilitate re-inforcing. If tracks through the wood up to these posts have not already been cleared, this should be done as early as possible. Please inform me how the matter stands.

E V Sawer Lieut
Lt. Col. R.E.
12/7/16   C.R.E. 9th Div.

From 11 hs.
Place
Time   Continued page 3

"A" Form. Army Form C. 2121.
MESSAGES AND SIGNALS.

Date: Page 3

P.S.
The trench referred to above (para 1 (4))
must be wired with low wire
entanglement of some sort, even if
only one trip wire can be put out.
A quantity of German wood and
short corkscrew pickets, barbed wire &c
is available in MONTAUBAN at S 27. b 70.15

MESSAGES AND SIGNALS.

TO: O C 64th Fld Cy R.E.

Sender's Number: 2653/1
Day of Month: 12/7/16
AAA

In continuation of my N° 2653 of date.

(2) In addition to the work therein detailed the following is to be carried out tonight:—

(a) wiring on north side of LONGUEVAL TRENCH

(b) strengthening to utmost extent the line of defence on east side of BERNAFAY WOOD as far south as junction with 30th Div.

(c) the construction of a key redoubt at some suitable point about the centre of BERNAFAY WOOD

(d) completion of communication trench up to S.W. corner of BERNAFAY WOOD if not already done.

From: C R E 9th Div.
Time: 12 15 hrs

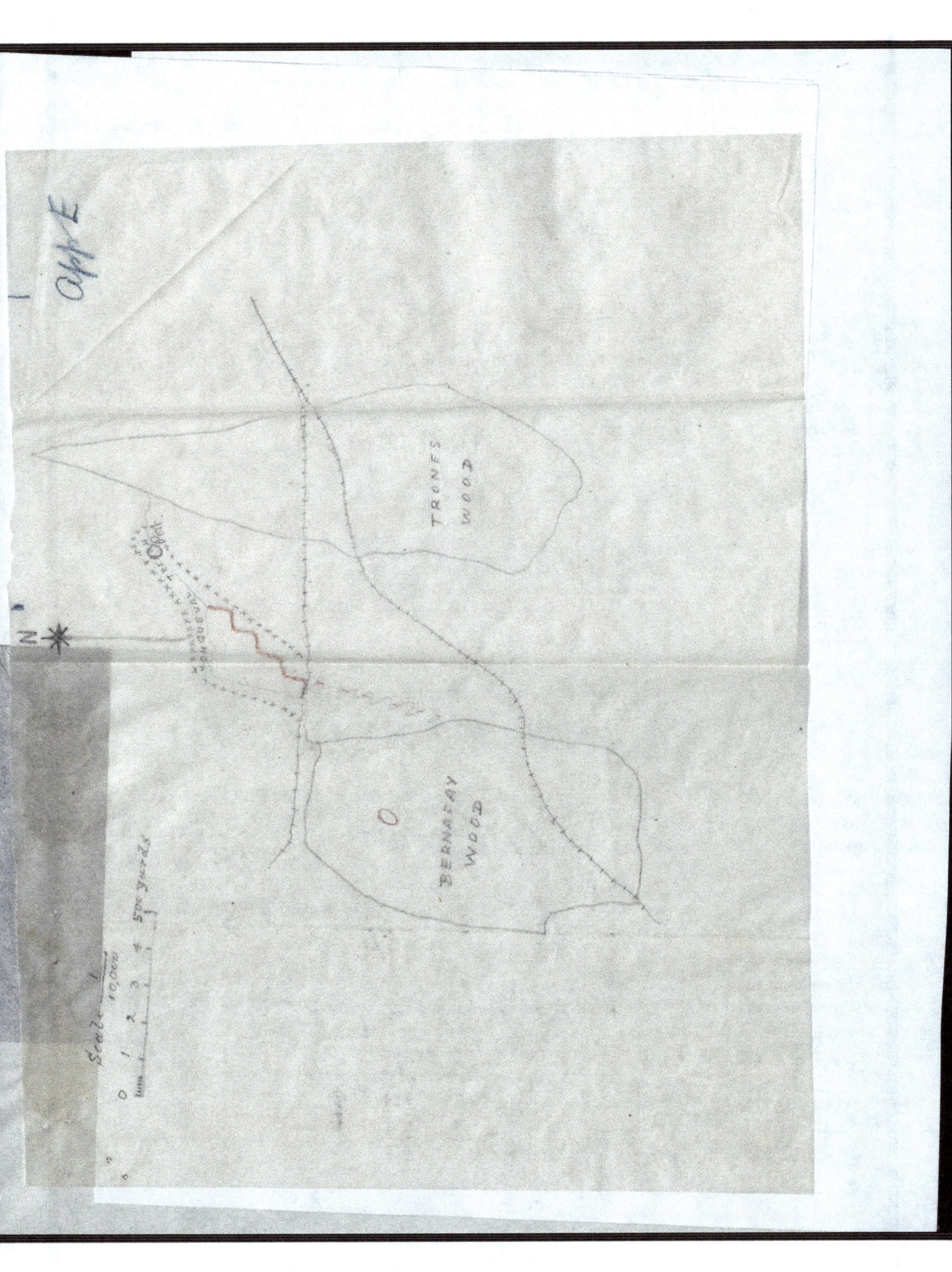

64 Field Coy RE App F.
July 1916.

SECRET.

C.R.E.No.B.52/5.

O.C. 63rd Company, R.E.
O.C. 64th Company, R.E.
O.C. 90th Company, R.E.

Battle Headquarters are as follows:-

30th Division.		L.16.b.5.2.
89th Inf.Bde.	(right Bde)	A.21.b.3.2.
21st " "	(left Bde)	Copse B (A.21a.3.5)
90th " "	(supporting Bde)	Copse B (A.21.a.3.5)

18th Division.		L.16.b.3.7.
55th Inf.Bde.	(right Bde)	A.25.d.6.5.
53rd " "	(centre ")	A.25.b.4.8.
54th " "	(left ")	F.24.c.5.5.

9th Division.	GROVETOWN.
27th Inf.Bde.	BILLON WOOD VALLEY.
1st S.A.I.Bde.	GROVETOWN.
26th Inf.Bde.	BOIS des CELESTINS.

These will be taken up as follows:-

    Leading Divisions   'T' day.
    9th Division.   'X' day.

Headquarters of the 9th Division from the morning of 'U' day will be at ETINEHEM.
'A' office of the 9th Division will be at ETINEHEM when the Division takes up its battle Headquarters.
Headquarters of the left Brigade of the French 39th Division will be at "Round-Po" "ROUND POINT", MARICOURT.

Please acknowledge receipt.

W.K.Wood

20/6/16.   Adjutant, 9th Divisional Engineers.

Lieut.R.E.

SECRET
9th Divn. No. 19/8842.

PRELIMINARY INSTRUCTIONS No 3 REGARDING
FORTHCOMING OPERATIONS.

DUMPS.

1. Positions of Forward Dumps of 18th & 30th Divisions for:-

    3" T.M. Ammunition
    Grenades.
    Reserve Rations.
    S.A.A.
    Water Tins
    R.E. Stores.

will be notified later.

9th Division are forming:-

(a) Main dump East end of GROVETOWN valley.
(b) Forward dump about F.24.c.8.2 (BILLON FARM)

(a) & (b) will contain some of all above items also Very Pistol Ammunition.

9th Division will in addition endeavour to establish dumps of R.E. Stores as follows:-

(c) A forward dump in TALUS BOISE.
(d) A forward dump in MARICOURT CHATEAU.

A Reserve of Smoke Helmets will be at (a).

PACKS AND
PRIVATE EFFECTS

2. Facilities will be given to store private effects of intrinsic value at CORBIE, in charge of one man per battalion. Packs may also be stored there. Greatcoats will be carried at discretion of Brigadiers but if dumped must be dumped in an organised manner and 2 men per battalion left in charge. — Position of dumps to be reported to Divisional Headquarters.

RATIONS. 3. An extra ration of cheese will be issued on Y day for consumption on Z day. — an additional biscuit and meat ration will also be made available.

The soldier at noon on Z day would thus have
- Unexpired portion,
- Extra cheese,
- Extra preserved ration,
- Iron Ration.

Troops are warned against eating any food found in enemy's lines.

N.B. 1st Line of 30th Division at present takes supplies to A.21.a.2.10 S.W. of MARICOURT.

AMMUNITION ? R.E. 4. Each man will carry 170 pounds S.A.A. — the extra 50 lb be drawn from 1st Line.

GRENADES 5. The hand and rifle grenades to be carried will be drawn by 26th & South African Bgdes at GROVETOWN dump, and by 27th Bgde at BILLON FARM dump.

SANDBAGS 6. Each man to carry 2 sandbags. to be drawn beforehand under arrangements of C.R.E. 27th Bgde from (BILLON WOOD) — 26th & S.A. Bgde from GROVETOWN.

WATER 7. Accurate positions of "Water Points" will be circulated. Forward "Water Points" are at
  (a) CARNOY (limited)
  (b) TALUS BOISE (about A.9.c.3.2.)
  (c) 4 WILLOW TREES A.15.b.10.5. (if completed by Corps)
  (d) MARICOURT CHATEAU.
Other "Water Points" are.
? (e) BILLON WOOD S.W. end.

3

WATER (cont'd)
(f) CONTOUR WOOD
(g) A.22.a.7.4.
? (h) GROVETOWN.

Filled water tins will be at BILLON FARM dump. Steps will be taken by Brigadiers to ensure that all troops moving N. of BILLON WOOD do so with full water bottles.

Troops are warned against drinking water from shallow wells or ponds within enemy lines. This does not apply to Artesian wells.

TRENCH TRAMWAYS
8. Officer i/c Tram Lines is 2/Lieut Whiting 10th Essex, BRONFAY FARM. For use of trams apply to that officer. Trams chiefly serve 18th Division front.

TOOLS
9. Tools to be carried by battalions will be drawn from GROVETOWN and BILLON FARM dumps.

PUBLIC CASH
10. Officers will not carry sums of public money into action. If for any reason this is unavoidable in some special case a record to be kept in the Orderly Room showing sum carried and by whom.

LUGGAGE WAGONS
11. All baggage wagons packed with there normal loads will be withdrawn to Train Companies on Y day.

SURPLUS OFFICERS and MEN - REINFORCEMENTS
12. Surplus Officers & men will be in first instance with 1st Line Transport. Reinforcements arriving will also be directed there. Brigadiers will issue instructions to ensure that reinforcements are not sent up until:-
(a) The distinguishing marks of Companies have been sown on their shoulders.

12. (contd)
(b) The yellow patch fastened on there haversack
(c) They have been fitted out with Smoke Helmets and taught how to use them.
(d) Taught to use bombs as far as time permits.

Reinforcements must only then be sent forward in organised parties under officers.

Surplus officers will be utilised to supervise the above details.

MEDICAL ARRANGEMENTS

13. 9 Regimental Aid Posts, and Advanced Dressing Stations are established in the present Trench system – (MARICOURT – CARNOY)

From Advanced Dressing Stations wounded are evacuated to Corps Dressing Station at DIVES CORPSE (CORBIE–BRAY road).

Corps collecting station for walking wounded at L.13.d.2.2.

Each Bgde on entering the forward area will be accompanied by bearer division of its affiliated Field Ambulance which will collect all sick and wounded as casualties occur and evacuate to Advanced Dressing Stations.

VERMOREL SPRAYERS

14. Vermorel Sprayers as available will be issued to Battalions and R.A. by D.A.D.O.S. 9th Division

VETERINARY ARRANGEMENTS

15. Mobile Veterinary Section at SAILLY LAURETTE. Advanced collecting post at K.34.b.3.6.

BATTLE STOPS

16. The line of "Battle Stops" is from L.4.a central to BRONFAY FARM then S.E. to the N.E. of TRIGGER WOOD and southwards along the Western edge of CEYLON WOOD. – Bgdes are responsible for there own police arrangements N & E of this line

4

PRISONERS OF WAR

17. Divisional Collecting Stations for prisoners of war as follows:-

18th Division BILLON FARM
30th Division DONES REDOUBT. (A.15.d)

From these places they will be sent to the main joint Divisional Collecting Station at L.14.c.8.8. GROVETOWN and handed over to A.P.M., 9th Division there.

Corps Collecting Depot is at BOIS-DE-TAILLES K.17.c.8.1.

Prisoners will be searched if practicable before arrival at Joint Collecting Station. At any rate on arrival there. All papers and effects to be handed over to A.P.M. 9th Division.

Escorts from Bgdes which should be in the proportion of 15% to 20% will proceed as far as the Joint Collecting Station. Returning thence to their Bgdes.

SALVAGE AND CLEARING BATTLEFIELD

18. Parties for Clearing Battlefield will be organised under Divnl. H.Q. from the surplus personnel with 1st Line Transport, the Salvage Company and the Divnl. Band

REPORTING CASUALTIES

19. Commanders are reminded that failure to follow routine for reporting casualties delays the arrival of reinforcements and may ultimately impair the efficiency of their commands.

(a) <u>Estimated</u> Casualties to be reported without delay once they have attained 100 or over. Names of officers known to be casualties should also be reported.

(b) <u>Accurate</u> Casualties including names of officers follow in the usual daily wires.

20th June 1916

(Sd) Turner
LIEUT COLONEL
A.A. & Q.M.G.
9th (SCOTTISH) DIVISION

DRO 438 – Interpreters to remain with 1st divn Transport until further notice   21/6/16.

C.R.E.
9th (Scottish) Division.
No. 260
Date 22/6/16

5

REINFORCEMENTS.   9th Divn No.14/8891.

TO,- 64th Coy R.E.

1.   Railhead for Reinforcements - HEILLY.   S W of MERICOURT
                                             N E of CORBIE

2.   An Officer detailed by Divisional Headquarters will meet
     all reinforcements at the Station and arrange for their
     disposal.

3.   Following will be normal method of disposal -

     (a) March from Station to Headquarters, 9th Divl.Train
         at SAILLY LAURETTE.

     (b) Proceed from SAILLY LAURETTE with Train Supply Wagons
         of their Units to 1st Line Transport of their Unit.

     (c) Remain with 1st Line Transport until required when
         they will go up with their 1st Line Transport and
         join their unit.

4.   In the event of Railhead being changed the above method
     of disposal will take place.

                                                    Major,
                                                    D.A.A.& Q.M.G.
22/6/1916.   9th (Scottish) Division.

SECRET.

INSTRUCTIONS No. 2
Regarding Forthcoming Operations.

PERSONNEL.

1. **Reinforcements.** The senior surplus officer of each unit with the First Line Transport will be resopnsible that reinforsements are not sent up until

    (a) The distinguishing marks of companies have been sewn on their shoulders.
    (b) The yellow patch fastened on their haversacks.
    (c) They have been fitted out with smoke helmets and taught how to use them.
    (d) Taught to use bombs as far as time permits.
    (e) They are in possession of an iron ration and have waterbottles filled.

   They will also ensure that reinforcements are only then sent forward in organised parties under officers.

2. **Company Commanders.** Company Commanders will NOT go on patrols or wiring parties.

2a. **C.Q.M.S's.** These will be left with the 1st Line Transport.

WORKING PARTIES, CARRIERS, etc.,

3. **R.E. Working Parties and Carriers for same.** The Os.C. 1st, (1½ Co) 2nd and 4th S.A. Infantry will each detail a Company (approximately 200 all ranks) as a R.E. party (working and carrying).

   In addition to these Companies the Commanding Officers mentioned will detail the following parties for work on Corps strong points at points stated, namely,

   (Map reference - MONTAUBAN sheet).

1st Regt.	2 Platoons at A.3.d.5.8.	(Train Alley).
2nd Regt.	2 Platoons at A.10.d.3.7.	(Faviere Support).
4th Regt.	2 Platoons at A.3.d.6.2.	(Five-trench Junction).
4th Regt.	2 Platoons at A.10.a.3.7.	(Junction of Casement and Gatz Alley).

   These Companies and Platoons will parade for checking by a Staff Officer at 3 p.m. on the 28th inst., in the open ground at K.33.d.8.5. (Sheet 62d N.E.).

   As all members of these Companies and Platoons will carry tools, stores, etc., issued by R.E. they will carry in addition thereto only the normal fighting outfit as per Appendix "B" of "Instructions for the Organisation and Training of Formations and Units of the 9th Division for the Attack", plus two Mills' Grenades in their pockets.

   The bombs, tools, etc., necessary to organise these Working Parties and Carriers into fighting sections at a later stage in the operations will be arranged for regimentally as and when required.

4. **Ammunition, Stores, etc., and Water Carriers.** Each O.C. Inf. Units will detail the following Carriers -

   For M.G. ammunition,   1 N.C.O. (not below the rank of full Corpl.) and 15 men.
   For Brigade Dump (Stores, etc.)   do   do   do
   For Brigade Dump (Water)   do   do   do

(2)

These 45 Carriers per Battalion will be attached to Brigade Headquarters for rations from the 30th inst.,

All Carriers will parade alongside Working Parties at 3 p.m. to-morrow - vide para 3.

All Carriers will wear a distinguishing badge, which will be issued by Brigade.

5. **Brigade Police.**
Os.C. Infantry units will each detail 3 O.R. as Brigade Police. These will bring with them "M.P." armlets, and will parade alongside Working Parties and Carriers to-morrow afternoon at 3 p.m. They will be attached to Brigade H.Q. for rations from 30th inst.,

6. **Advance Detachments.**
The following Advance Parties will be detailed, to report to Lieut. Broadwood, Brigade H.Q. Staff, at 1 p.m. 28th inst., at point K.33.d.8.2. to proceed to GROVETOWN ahead of the Brigade:-

From each Infantry unit,	1 Off.	5 O.R.
M.G. Coy.	1 Off.	2 O.R.
L.T.M. Battery,	1 Off.	2 O.R.
Bearer Section,	-	1 O.R.
64th Field Coy. R.E.	1 Off.	2 O.R.

7. **Trained Bombers for Detonating Bombs.**
Two trained Bombers for detonating Bombs at the Brigade Dump will be detailed by each O.C. Infantry Battalion. They will parade alongside Working Parties and Carriers at 3 p.m. to-morrow. They will be attached to Brigade H.Q. for rations from the 30th inst.,

REGIMENTAL RUNNERS, POLICE, and WATER SENTRIES.

8. **Runners.**
All regimental runners should be shown the Brigade Dump before moving forward with their units, in order that they may know exactly where to go if sent back with indents. These runners should wear the same badge as Brigade H.Q. runners, namely, a strip of white cloth up the outer side of the left cuff of the tunic. This badge will be their passport through police posts en route to the Brigade Dump.

9. **Police Posts.**
Os.C. units will establish Police Posts at suitable points between the area held by their units and Brigade H.Q. These should be, as far as possible, placed so that anyone proceeding to the back lines from the regimental area must pass them.

10. **Water Sentries.**
Os.C. units will place sentries over all water standpipes and tanks from which water is drawn within the area occupied by the unit under their command.

They will also place sentries over water standpipes and tanks which may be in the vicinity of a halt made by their regiments. Special attention is to be paid to this on "Z" day.

11. **Vermorel Sprayers.**
These are carried under regimental arrangements (vide Appendix "D" of "Instructions for the Organisation of a Fighting Section"). Os.C. units will send Carriers to the Brigade Dump for the necessary solution. One jar of solution will be supplied at a time for each Sprayer. These jars must be kept labelled in such a manner as will prevent any mistake arising as regards their contents.

(3)

ARTILLERY.

12. **Barrage.**

If any portion of the line is held up in the advance, and calls for the Artillery barrage to be brought back to assist it, the bombardment of the spot to which the barrage has been brought back will continue for 30 minutes, the last 5 minutes of which will be as intense as possible. Infantry Commanders must carefully note the comencement of the re-bombardment, and check the time in order that they may be ready to seize the opportunity immediately the barrage lifts again.

INFANTRY.

13. **Flags, Flares and Mirrors.**

The primary object of these is to enable the Artillery to note where our front line is.

Flags.

The greatest care must be exercised to ensure the red and yellow flags being waved only when fixed points have been reached, or when the held up. They will be waved to mark the forward line of the Infantry, and the bearer of the flag must be within 50 yards of our firing line.

Flares.

These will be used in the same way as flags, and will be carried by Officers, N.C.O's and selected men. They will only be sent up by order of a Company Commander.

STOKES' GUNS.

14. **To be used defensively.**

L.T.M.Batteries are to be used defensively, i.e., the guns will be placed in defensive positions behind the front line, with definite zones of fire allotted to each gun or pair of guns to deal with the enemy should he penetrate our front line.

If guns are temporarily moved up to the front line for any special operation they should be withdrawn to their defensive emplacements as soon as the operation is over.

15. **Ammunition.**

The O.C. L.T.M. Battery will arrange for 500 rounds Stokes' Gun ammunition being carried with the guns by Battery, relief and reserve personnel under his command.

The reserve and relief personnel will, as soon as they have dumped the ammunition at a spot to be selected by the O.C. L.T.M. Battery near the defensive position of the guns, return to the Brigade Dump and obtain a further supply of ammunition. They will wear the same distinguishing badge as other Carriers - to be issued by Brigade.

The supply of Stokes' Gun ammunition with the guns will be built up in this manner under the orders of the O.C. L.T.M. Battery to the extent desired by him. He will notify Brigade H.Q. if these means should prove insufficient.

O.C. L.T.M. Battery will ensure that all relief and reserve personnel of his Battery should know the position of the Brigade Dump in order that they can find their way back from the front line.

REPORTS AND MESSAGES.

16. Addressing and Despatch of.
All messages and reports sent by hand to Brigade H.Q. by units, and vice versa, will be addressed with the name of the unit. The registered address will not be used in such cases. In telephone messages registered addresses must invariably be used.

Although in principle it is the duty of the Brigade Signal Section to keep communication between Brigade H.Q. and H.Q. of Battalions, Os.C. units will use all means in their power to ensure important messages being despatched to Brigade H.Q. without delay. Should it be necessary to despatch such a message by runner, and a Brigade H.Q. runner is not available, they will send it by regimental runner.

17. Hourly Reports.
Os.C. Infantry units will report the situation to Brigade H.Q. every hour - to be despatched from Battalion H.Q. every clock half hour. If nothing to report a 'Nil' return must be sent.

In addition to these hourly reports all events of importance will be reported to Brigade H.Q. at once.

Care must be taken to see that the time of despatch is given on all messages and returns.

Reports and messages from M.G. coy. and L.T.M. Battery Officers for Brigade H.Q. will be sent if desired from the nearest Battalion H.Q.

18. Priority of Messages over 'Phone.
Signalling Officers will ensure messages being sent over the 'phone in order of priority.

Important messages sent over the 'phone will be confirmed in writing as soon as possible. All orders must be acknow- -ledged at once, and must be carefully kept for future reference

ORDERS, INSTRUCTIONS and MAPS.

19. Not to be carried by Officers going into action.
Copies of orders and instructions, and map containing information which may prove of value to the enemy if captured are not to be carried by Officers and other ranks when going into action. The greatest care must be exercised to ensure this order being carried out.

RATIONS.

20. Procedure re drawing of.
The ordinary trench procedure will be followed. Os.C. units will send their representatives to the rendezvous notified to them. The Brigade Transport Officer (Captain Ward) is responsible for getting rations and stores up to the rendezvous.

If it should be impossible to get transport up to the rendezvous the Brigade Transport Officer will send forward and advise units' representatives accordingly, and they must then proceed to where the transport is.

21. Reserve Rations.
The reserve rations dumped in the forward trenches are not to be touched without permission from Brigade H.Q.

BOMBS, AMMUNITION, STORES, etc.,

22. Procedure re obtaining.

Regimental dumps will be established under regimental arrangements, and will be replenished from Brigade dumps.

Os.C. units will send a runner to the Brigade Dump with a written request for such bombs, ammunition, stores, etc., as are required. These will be sent forward by the Officer i/c of the Brigade dump by the Carriers at his disposal.

The orderly who brings the indent will lead the carrying party to his regimental dump.

23. Tools.

In addition to picks and shovels a few jumpers and hammers should be carried regimentally. These will be obtainable from Brigade dump.

24. Handcarts.

All handcarts used by units of the Brigade will be returned to the Brigade dump as soon as the work for which they are used is completed.

IDENTIFICATION OF ENEMY UNITS.

25. Officers Commanding units will report with the least possible delay to Brigade H.Q. any German units encountered which have been identified.

If units are encountered which cannot be identified, but regarding which particulars can be given which may enable higher commands to identify them, these particulars must be furnished at once to Brigade H.Q.

The necessity for making these reports must be impressed on all leaders down to the Platoons Commanders.

Care must be taken to report Company and Battalion as well as the Regiment of all prisoners Captured.

Companies, squadrons, batteries, are indicated by their number on the shoulder buttons. In Infantry the Companies are numbered throughout their Regiments, an M.G. COY. is No.13.

Reports regarding enemy units encountered must be sent by special runner to Brigade H.Q. and not by the Officer or N.C.O. in charge of the escort with prisoners.

Reports to reach Divisional H.Q. long before any prisoners who may have been taken; and unit commanders will issue special instructions as will ensure this being the case.

NOMINAL ROLLS.

26. The Officer or N.C.O. i/c of a Carrying Party will be in possession of a nominal roll of all members of the party. A copy of that roll must be kept for reference at regimental H.Q.

ARMY TIME.

27. Unit Commanders will arrange for the Army Time being obtained from Brigade H.Q. daily, and all Officers are to take special care that their watches always show the correct Army Time.

CLEARING THE BATTLEFIELD.

28. To facilitate arrangements for clearing the battlefield the Commander of every unit, however small, will do all in his power to collect arms, equipment, etc., into dumps ready for removal. The Divisional Commander lays stress on the fact that the speedy tidying up of the field acts as a valuable incentive to discipline.

Please acknowledge.

Major.
Brigade Major.

Officer Commanding,
    1st S. A. Infantry.
    2nd   do   do
    3rd   do   do
    4th   do   do
    S.A. Bde. L.T.M. Battery.
    28th Coy. MG Corps.
    64th Field Co. R.E.
    Bearer Section S.A.F.A.
    107th Coy. A.S.C.
    51st Brigade R.F.A.
    Brigade Signal Section.
    Brigade Transport Officer.

B.M.47/26/13/9. 27th June, 1916.

HEADQUARTERS,
    1st S. A. INFANTRY BRIGADE.

* * * * * * * * * * * * * * * * * * * *

S E C R E T.

HEADQUARTERS,
1st S.A.Infantry Brigade,
20th June 1916.
S.S. 47/22/12/10.

INSTRUCTIONS No. 3.

Regarding forthcoming operations.

1. **BOUNDARIES.** The dividing line between the XIII Corps and the French XX Corps is the MARICOURT-BRIQUETERIE road (inclusive to the French) as far as A.10.d.2.6., thence to A.10.b.75.80.

   That between the XIII Corps and the XV Corps is Trench F.12/5 (inclusive to XIII Corps — junction of Trenches F.12.a.5.8. (inclusive to XIII Corps) F.6.a.84.10 (inclusive to XV Corps.) F.6.a.8.9. - thence the track running N.N.E. through S.25.d. and b. as far as junction of tracks at S.25.d.4.9. thence to point S.25.b.37.85.

   The boundary between Divisions is the TALUS BOISE Tramline as far as A.3.c.2.6., thence the road due north to MONTAUBAN, thence northwards to the trench running from S.27.c.2.8. to S.27.a.7.8. (inclusive to 30th Division).

2. **DISPOSITIONS FOR HOLDING CAPTURED ENEMY TRENCHES.** Trenches should be held as lightly as possible consistent with being in a sufficient state of preparedness to repel any counter-attacks. The fact that the crowding of trenches with men merely increases the losses without giving any corresponding security to the defence against attacks preceded by a heavy bombardment must be kept in mind. Small local counter attacks must be delivered immediately should the enemy succeed in gaining a footing in our trenches.

   A map (MONTAUBAN sheet) is enclosed showing the areas which it is proposed the Battalions of the S.A.Brigade should hold in the event of the Brigade taking over that portion of the enemy's trench area between MONTAUBAN and the left of the trench. An explanatory statement is attached to the map.

   It must be clearly understood that the proposed dispositions are based on what must necessarily be meagre information. Battalion Commanders may alter these dispositions if they find that by doing so they will reduce the number of casualties. In making any alterations, however, Battalion Commanders must bear in mind that although it is their duty to keep down casualties as far as possible, they are responsible for holding the trench areas allotted to them in the statement and shown on the map.

   Whatever dispositions are decided upon they must be in depth, and must not encroach on the areas allotted to other Battalions.

3. **BARBED WIRE OBSTACLES ON REAR SIDE OF ENEMY TRENCHES TO BE DESTROYED.**

   Any barbed wire obstacle on the near side of a trench which has been captured from the enemy, which might prove an obstacle to our own troops in a counter-attack, should the enemy succeed in recapturing the trench, must be destroyed.

4. **ARRANGEMENTS FOR PASSAGE OF TROOPS THROUGH OUR OWN WIRE.** The 18th and 30th Divisions will cut gaps in our wire north of a line joining COPSE "A" and (BRONFAY) FARM.

   These gaps will be 20 yards wide, and will be cut so as to facilitate the movement of reserves up to and across the PERONNE road by the existing crossings over the latter in the event of reserves being ordered forward over the open.

(4 contd.)
The sides of these gaps will be marked by poles standing about 5 feet above the ground, with a small piece of yellow cloth or straw tied round the top.

5. **ARTILLERY SUPPORT DURING THE ATTACK.** In the event of the Brigade being ordered forward to take part in the attack, Battalion Commanders will receive from Brigade Major a map (MONTAUBAN sheet) showing the lines of our artillery barrage and the times at which the Heavy Artillery will lift from each of these lines.

6. **BATTALION HEADQUARTERS.** Battalion Commanders must notify Brigade Headquarters as soon as possible where they have established their Headquarters.

ATTENTION IS AGAIN DIRECTED TO THE FOLLOWING POINTS.

7. **WATER** All troops moving north of BILLON WOOD, must do so with full water-bottles.

No drinking water should be drawn from shallow pools or ponds within the enemy's lines. This does NOT apply to artesian wells.

8. **CORPS COLLECTING STATIONS FOR WALKING WOUNDED.** The position of the Corps Collecting Station for walking wounded, i.e., L.13.d.2.2. (sheet 62a N.E.) must be clearly indicated to all ranks.

Major,
Brigade Major.

Officers Commanding,
    1st S. A. Infantry.
    2nd   -do-
    3rd   -do-
    4th   -do-
    S.A.Bde.,L.T.M.Battery.
    28th Coy, M.G.Corps.
    64th Field Coy, R.E.
    Bearer Section, S.A.F.A.
    107th Coy, A.S.C.
    22nd Bde. R.F.A.
    Bde Signal Section.
    Bde. Transport Officer.

SECRET

64th Field Coy
July 1916.
22/6/16
Appendix G

CRL. B52/12

9th DIVISION No.14/8869.

INFORMATION FROM 18th DIVISION.

INITIAL DISTRIBUTION.

GRENADES.

```
* BILLON FARM................  3544.
* BILLON WOOD................   870.
  A1 Sector Right Coy.Res.....   400
          Centre Coy.  ......   215.
          Left Coy.    ......   300.
          Battn. Res.  ......   885.
  A2.Sector    "       "  ....  1908.
* CARNOY LODGE  ............   1440.
* DEANSGATE STORE  ..........    342.
```

* Divisional Reserve.

ADDITIONAL DUMPS -
     in Front Line trenches   17,000.
     in 3 Bde. Dumps CARNOY.   8,000.

S.A.A.

CARNOY Dump .... 40,000 rounds.
In CARNOY VALLEY 3 Bde. Dumps Total ... 300,000   "
Divisional Dump in CARNOY Valley 144,000   "

PRESERVED RATIONS.

Divisional Reserve in CARNOY .... 42,730 rations.

WATER

C.R.E., 18th Division is arranging for water tanks or barrels to be erected on trollies which will be pushed forward as soon as the line to MONTAUBAN is opened. These will be filled from the Stand pipes in CARNOY.
                              or TALUS BOISE.

R.E. STORES.

The R.E. Dump at Sapper Corner L.9.d.5.2.

SMOKE HELMETS.

CARNOY.............. 3000.
BRONFAY FARM .... 5000.

                                    Lieut.Colonel,
                                    A.A. & Q.M.G.
                                    9th DIVISION.

21/6/16.

COPIES TO:-
   Inf.Bdes., 9th Seaforths. R.E., R.A.

SECRET.

C.R.E.No.B.52/27.

O.C. 63rd Company, R.E.
O.C. 64th Company, R.E.
O.C. 90th Company, R.E.

Extract from Operation Order No.1 of C.R.E. 18th Division, forwarded for your information.

ORDERS TO TROOPS.

3. (a) FIELD COMPANIES.

Field Companies (less 2 sections) will be under the orders of the Brigadiers to whom they are attached, for the consolidation of captured positions.
The remaining sections will be employed as follows:-
79th Field Company. One section for repairing CARNOY-MONTAUBAN Road. To begin work one hour after 'ZERO' time.
80th Field Company. One section for maintenance of SUZANNE - CARNOY Water supply.
92nd Field Company. One section for repairs to CARNOY-MONTAUBAN Railway. To begin work two hours after 'ZERO' time.
One section of each Field Company will be held in Divisional Reserve and will move into CARNOY 3 hours after 'ZERO' time.

(b) PIONEERS.
The O.C., 8th Royal Sussex Pioneers will make the following dispositions:-
   (i) Two platoons per Brigade to work with the R.E. sections under the orders of Brigadiers.
   (ii) One Platoon to work on the CARNOY - MONTAUBAN Road with the 79th Company. To begin work one hour after 'ZERO' time.
   (iii) One company to open up Nos. 1, 2, 5 & 6 saps in NO MAN'S LAND. To begin work one hour after 'ZERO' time, and to take over the remaining saps Nos. 3, 4, 7 & 8 from the O.C. 183rd Tunnelling Company at 9 p.m. on "Z" day.
   (iv) The remaining 5 platoons to be held in Divisional Reserve and to move into CARNOY 3 hours after 'ZERO' time.

(c) Army Troops Company.
The 238th Army Troops Company, R.E. (less two sections) will be employed on the CARNOY - MONTAUBAN ROAD between CARNOY and our front line.
They should reach CARNOY one hour after 'ZERO' time.
This Company will bivouac in CARNOY on "Z" night and after

29/6/16.

Lieut.R.E.
Adjutant, 9th Divisional Engineers.

Para 9 of 30th Division O.O. No. 19.

Technical troops.

9. The C.R.E. will tell off 1 section Fd.Coy. R.E. and 1 platoon of Pioneers which, with 2 platoons to be detailed by 89th Bde. will make the "Strong point party" to follow the 89th Bde. He will also tell off 1 section Fd.Coy. R.E. to assist in the BRIQUETERIE Operation.

He will tell off another section Fd.Coy. R.E. and 1 platoon of Pioneers which, with 1 platoon to be detailed by 21st Bde. will make the "Strong point party" to follow the 21st Bde.

These "Strong point parties" will be under command of the Brigadiers whose Brigades they are to follow. Their first duty is to construct Nos. 1 and 2 Strong Points 89th Bde. area and No.1 Strong Point in 21st Bde. area, vide para 3 (i) and attached plan - after which they will be available to assist in the completion of the other "Strong Points" as ordered in that paragraph.

The C.R.E. will arrange for the maintenance of communication trenches within our own lines, the digging of new ones where necessary, and the repair for use as communication trenches of certain German trenches (vide G.405 of 11th June).

He is also responsible for (i) preparation for use of the MARICOURT - MONTAUBAN road (ii) formation of R.E. dumps other than the forward dumps which are under the Brigadiers (iii) issue of R.E. stores as necessary to the Brigades.

The scheme for employment of technical troops is set forth in Appendix 'G'.

O.C. 6th Fd.Coy RE

Copy to you for your information.

Mitchell Baker
Major

B/Major
30. 6. 16

APPENDIX 5.

DISPOSITION OF R.E. AND PIONEERS.

Affiliation	Strength, etc. of Parties	Place of Assembly	Objective	Remarks.
1. STRONG POINT PARTIES:				
89th I.Bde.	(a) 1 Sec. 208th Fld.Coy.RE	Trenches in HARICOURT (N) (East face and part of South face of CHATEAU KEEP - 140' of trench)	To prepare "Strong Points" at A.10.d.1/5 and A.10.a.4.5.	To assemble & move under orders from 89th Bde.
	1 Platoon Pioneers			
	2 Platoons Infantry.			
21st I.Bde.	(b) 1 Sec. 202nd Fld.Coy.RE	Assembly Trench X X	To prepare "Strong Points" at A.3.d.5/2.	To assemble & move under orders from 21st Bde.
	1 platoon Pioneers			
	1 platoon Infantry.			
90th Inf.Bde	(c) 201st Fld.Coy. R.E.	COPSE VALLEY.	Defence of MONTAUBAN Village.	To assemble with 201 Fd.Coy. by 8 p.m. 'Y' day and move under orders from 90th Bde.
	2 platoons Infantry			
2. COMMUNICATION TRENCH PARTIES:				
Divan.	(a) ½ Coy. Pioneers	Trenches in HARICOURT (E. face of NAPIER'S REDOUBT - 300' of trench)	To open communication trench from Sap A.P.5. to GERMAN'S WOOD. (STANLEY AVENUE).	To move as detailed in separate instructions.
	(b) 1 Coy. Pioneers.	---do---	To open communication trench from Sap A.P.4. to enemy's trenches and onwards. (HARICOURT AVENUE).	
	(c) ½ Coy. Pioneers.	"Y" Works North of PERONNE Road.	To open communication trench from Sap No.6 (A.9/8) (SUPPER AVENUE) to enemy's trenches and onwards.	

2.

Affiliation	Strength etc. of parties	Place of Assembly	Objective	Remarks
	(a) ½ Coy. Pioneers.	"U" Works North of PERONNE Road.	To open communication trench from Sap No.5 (A.9/4) (WASP AVENUE) to enemy's trenches and onwards.	} To move as detailed in separate instructions App. O.2.
Division.	3. ROAD PARTIES.			
	(a) 1 Sec. 216th Fld.Coy.RE } 1 platoon Infantry. }	MARICOURT trenches. (South face of NAPIERS Redoubt - 200ᶠ of trench)	Roads and bridges North of PERONNE Road.	Infantry to assemble by 8 p.m. 'Y' day.
	(b) Headquarters & Sec. A.T.Coy.R.E. }			
	4. TRENCH MAINTENANCE PARTIES.			
	(a) 1 platoon Pioneers.	STANLEY & MARICOURT AVENUES.	Maintenance STANLEY and MARICOURT AVENUES.	} Appendix O.3.
	(b) 1 platoon Pioneers	SUPPORT & WEST AVENUES.	Maintenance SUPPORT and WEST AVENUES.	
	5. DIVISIONAL RESERVE.			
	200th Fd.Coy. (less 2 Secs)	COPSE VALLEY.	} Divisional reserve.	
	222nd Fd.Coy. (less 1 Sec.)	TALUS BOISÉ VALLEY.		
	2 platoons Pioneers	CAFTS VALLEY		

SECRET.

Communications to be opened up in advance of our present front line.

1. ROADS.
30th Division area.   HARDECOURT - MONTAUBAN.
18th Division area.   CARNOY MONTAUBAN.

2. TRACKS.
30th Division area.   Nil.
18th Division area.
(a) On west of tramway line from CARNOY to MONTAUBAN.
(b) CARNOY MARICTZ road as far as bank running N.E. between points F.12.c.4.4 and A.7.d.9.9 and thence along depression under bank to MARICTZ-MONTAUBAN road east of POMMERS redoubt.

3. SAPS AND C.Ts.
30th Division area

(a) Up Trench.
Continuation of STANLEY avenue to the north on the west side of MARICOURT BRIQUETERIE road up to FAVIER support trench where it crosses to east side of road and continues north to Casement trench.
(b) Down trench.
Via WESTERN AVENUE and THE BEND to point A 185 on MARICOURT MONTAUBAN road thence north passing GERMAN WOOD on west side up to GLATZ redoubt.
(c) Up Trench
Continuation of SUPPORT AVENUE northwards from A 65 via SILESIA ALLEY and junction of SPAIN ALLEY and road to MONTAUBAN.
(d) Down trench.
Continuation northwards of WEST avenue via BRICK POINT BRICK LANE, thence N.W. to TRAIN ALLEY IN TALUS BOISE, following latter to A.3.b.4.0 thence north to MONTAUBAN

18th Division area.
(a) Up trench
No.1 Sap (open) from trench A 9/8 at A.9.c.3.5.
(b) Down trench
No.2 Sap open from trench A 9/8 at A.9.c.3.1.5
(c) Up trench.
No. 3 Sap (covered) from trench A 8/4 at A.9.c.3.1.
(d) No.4 Sap (covered) UP TRENCH. from trench A.8/4 A.9.a.9.1.
(e) Down trench.
No 5 Sap (open) from trench A 8/8 at A.8.c.1.8.
(f) Up trench.
No.6 Sap (open) from Trench A.7/8 at A.7.d.8.9.
(g) Up trench.
No.7 Sap (covered) from Trench F.12/8 at F.12.c.7.0.
(h) Up trench.
No.8 Sap (covered) from Trench F.12/8 at F.12.c.4.9.

Down traffic for Left Brigade should go over the open in the valley between MAY and CASINO POINTS, A.7.c.v.8.
In 18th Divisional Area communications through the enemy trenches are at present being left to the respective Brigadiers.

4. TRAMWAYS.   18th Division Area.   Tramway from CARNOY to outskirts of MONTAUBAN will be repaired.

64th Field Coy R.E.

Notes by C.R.E.
20th Divn herewith
for your information

W L Wood
Lt R.E.
ADJUTANT 9th DIVISIONAL ENGINEERS

5/7/16

2632
Date 5/7/16

BRIQUETERIE.

Two Strong Points (marked 1 & 4 on map) are being made — each for 1 Platoon & one or two machine guns (as may be available)

"A" is not very well sited — it commands the Valley to the West, but to the East it has no field of fire — It would have been better sited at (2) and another strong point made at (3).

(1) was not inspected but O.C. 200th Inf. Coy states it is on a good site —

Work on 1 is very slow as it is constantly shelled —

"A" about 3/4 wired & fire trench in progress. This S. Point is defensible —

Wire has been erected as shewn on map. Two Platoons could hold 1. 2. & 3, alternative machine gun emplacements being made in each — "A" could be connected to 2 by a short trench & could be held if necessary —

Communication from 2 & "A" to 3 should be overhead provided —

JB
4/7

S E C R E T.   Copy No....... 7

[handwritten: 64 Field Coy RE, July 1916, app H.]

1st SOUTH AFRICAN INFANTRY BRIGADE.

Map reference-   OPERATION ORDER No. 39.   In the Field,
57d N.E.   30th June, 1916.

1. **MOVE.**   The 1st S. A. Infantry Brigade, 64th Field Coy. R.E.,
                    28th Bde. M.G. Coy., and Bearer Section, S.A.F. Ambulance will
                    move to GROVETOWN to-night by "X" Route.

2. **STARTING POINT.**   Starting Point will be at K.34.b.9.7.

3. **ORDER OF MARCH & TIMES OF PASSING STARTING POINT.**   Units will march
                                                            in the following
   order, passing the Starting Point at the times stated:-

Brigade Headquarters,	9.50 p.m.
1st S. A. Infantry,	10.00 p.m.
4th do do	10.10 p.m.
2nd do do	10.20 p.m.
3rd do do	10.30 p.m.
64th Field Coy. R.E.	10.40 p.m.
28th Brigade M.G. Coy.	10.50 p.m.
Trench Mortar Battery,	10.55 p.m.
Bearer Section,	11.00 p.m.
Transport, under Brigade T'port Officer, (to march in same order as units)	11.15 p.m.

4. **ADVANCE PARTIES & GUIDES.**   Units, on reaching GROVETOWN, will be led
                                    to their camping sites by a member of
   their Advance Party which visited GROVETOWN on 29th inst.,
   Advance Parties, as follows, will be detailed by Officers
   Commanding units to proceed to GROVETOWN at 7 p.m. this evening
   by other than "X" Route. These Advance Parties will proceed
   from GROVETOWN to TRIGGER WOOD, etc., to-night with the units of
   the 27th Inf. Brigade, whose camping sites in TRIGGER WOOD, etc.,
   will be taken over by the units to which the respective Advance
   Parties belong:-

Infantry Battalions,	1 officer		5 Other Ranks.	
64th Field Coy. R.E.	1 do		2 do	do
28th Brigade M.G. Coy.	1 do		2 do	do
Trench Mortar Battery,	1 do		2 do	do
Bearer Section,	-		1 do	do

   These Advance Parties will rejoin their units in GROVETOWN VALLEY
   on the morning of the 1st July, not later than 9 a.m., marching
   by "X" Route so as not to miss their units should they be on
   the march by that hour.

5. **MACHINE GUNS.**   The Officer Commanding, 28th Bde. M.G. Coy. will
                        detail, to accompany each of the 1st, 2nd and 4th
   S. A. Infantry when they leave GROVETOWN, two Machine Guns with
   their teams, under an Officer. These Machine Guns will not,
   for the present, be attached to the units which they accompany,
   but they will march immediately in rear of them from GROVETOWN.

6. **WORKING PARTIES & CARRIERS.**   The Working Parties and Carriers detailed
                                      in Brigade Instructions No.2, para 5,
   (dated 27th inst.,) will march with their units, but after the
   Brigade leaves GROVETOWN those parties will be at the disposal
   of the O.C. 64th Field Coy. R.E., who will advise Battalion
   Commanders where and when he wishes them to report to him or his
   representative.

7. **BRIGADE HEADQUARTERS.**   Brigade Headquarters in GROVETOWN VALLEY will
                                be about L.8.c.2.9.

   Please acknowledge.

                                                        [signature]
                                                              Major.
                                                        Brigade Major.

1st SOUTH AFRICAN INFANTRY BRIGADE.

OPERATION ORDER No.41.   2nd July, 1916.

Starting hour is at 8.30 p.m. to-night.

Major.
Brigade Major.

S E C R E T.

Copy No..5....

1st SOUTH AFRICAN INFANTRY BRIGADE.

OPERATION ORDERS No. 41.

In the Field,
2nd July, 1916.

1. **MOVE.** The South African Brigade, 64th Field Company, R.E., and "B" Company, 9th Seaforths, will move by "X" Route to BILLON WOOD VALLEY, TRIGGER WOOD VALLEY and COPSE VALLEY this afternoon [today] in relief of the 27th Brigade. Time of move will be notified later.

2. **ORDER OF MARCH.** The Brigade will march by Companies or similar formations in the following order:-

   1st S. A. Infantry.
   2nd do do
   4th do do
   3rd do do
   28th Bde. M.G. Company.
   S. A. Bde. L.T.M. Battery.
   64th Field Company, R.E.
   "B" Company, 9th Seaforths.
   Bearer Section, S.A.F.A.

3. **STARTING POINT.** The starting point will be at L.8.d.8.0.

4. **INTERVAL.** The leading Company of the 1st S. A. Infantry will pass the starting point at the starting hour, and each succeeding Company will follow its preceding Company at five minutes' interval. This interval will be maintained throughout the march.

5. **TRANSPORT.** Transport will march by ~~sections (to be decided by the Brigade Transport Officer)~~ in rear of the ~~Brigade, in the same order as~~ units.

   Such First Line Transport as Commanding Officers desire to take may be taken as far as to BILLON WOOD, but all must be sent back to GROVETOWN VALLEY as soon as off-loaded, excepting cookers and water carts. The animals for the cookers will also be returned to GROVETOWN VALLEY, the only animals remaining at BILLON WOOD, being the animals for water carts.

6. **CAMPING SITES.** Units will occupy the camping sites taken over by their advance parties.

7. **BRIGADE HEADQUARTERS.** Brigade Headquarters will be in BILLON WOOD VALLEY at A.25.d.4.5.

Please acknowledge.

J Mitchell Baker
Major.
Brigade Major.

Copy No.1 to 1st S. A. Inf.	Copy No.10 to 107th Company, A.S.C.
2 2nd do	11 O.C. Bearer Section.
3 3rd do	12 9th Division.
4 4th do	13 50nd Brigade, R.F.A.
5 64th Field Coy. R.E.	14 G. O. C.
6 O.C. "B" Coy, 9th Sea. Hrs.	15 Brigade Major.
7 O.C. 28th M.G. Coy.	16 Staff Captain.
8 O.C. L.T.M. Battery.	17 Office Copy.
9 O.C. Bde. Signal Sect.	18 War Diary.

Issued by Orderly at..................

SECRET.

Copy No. 5 ~~4~~

1st SOUTH AFRICAN INFANTRY BRIGADE.

OPERATION ORDERS No. 42.

In the Field,
4th July, 1916.

---

1. **MOVE.** The 1st S. A. Infantry Brigade will relieve the 21st and 89th Brigades to-day, as follows:-

   2nd S. A. Infantry will relieve the 21st Brigade in the Trench Area in the vicinity of TALUS BOISE. This Battalion will move by platoons under regimental arrangements, but must be clear of BILLON VALLEY by 6 p.m.. An officer detailed by the 21st Brigade will meet the O.C. 2nd S. A. Infantry at the North West corner of CAMBRIDGE COPSE at 5 p.m. An officer will be detailed by the O.C. 2nd S.A. Infantry to report to the Headquarters of the 21st Brigade in COPSE "B" at 4 p.m. to take over stores, etc.,

   3rd S. A. Infantry will relieve that portion of the 89th Brigade at present quartered in MARICOURT. This Battalion will move by platoons under regimental arrangements, but must be clear of COPSE VALLEY by 5.30 p.m.

   Billeting party from 3rd S. A. Infantry will be met by and officer of the 89th Brigade at the entrance to MARICOURT (22.a.1.5.) at 3.30 p.m.

   1st and 4th S. A. Infantry will relieve to-night the units of the 89th Brigade in the line.

   These Battalions will move by platoons under regimental arrangements, but must not cross the PERONNE ROAD before 9.30 p.m. They must be clear of their present billeting areas by 10.30 p.m.

   The 64th Field Coy, R.E., "B" Coy, 9th Seaforths, 28th Brigade M.G. Coy, Brigade L.T.M. Battery and Bearer Section, S.A.F.A. will each move under the orders of its Commanding Officer, and, with the exception of the Bearer Section, will move into portions of the line. They will send an officer to Brigade Headquarters to receive information regarding these portions.

   The Bearer Section will be accommodated in MARICOURT, and an officer will report at Brigade Headquarters for instructions.

2. **TRANSPORT.** The Brigade Transport Officer will arrange for regimental transport to be sent to each unit this afternoon. The Officers Commanding 2nd and 3rd S. A. Infantry will arrange for guides to meet their transport on the BRONFAY FARM - MARICOURT Road at point 20.b.7.7. at 7.30 this evening.

   The Officers Commanding 1st and 4th S. A. Infantry and the O.C. L.T.M. Battery will arrange for the necessary Carriers to meet their transport on the MONTAUBAN Road, North of MARICOURT, at 16.a. centre, at 11 p.m.

   The transport of the 64th Field Coy. R.E., and 28th Bde. M.G. Coy. will move under orders of the Officers Commanding these units, but must not proceed beyond MARICOURT before dark.

   Cookers, water carts, mess cart and Maltese cart of the 2nd and 3rd S. A. Infantry will be sent to their respective units.

(2)

The cookers and water carts of the 1st and 4th S. A. Infantry will be sent to 16.a.centre, North of MARICOURT, where Carriers from these units will be provided to carry forward the dixies from the cookers - the water carts being retained at the Bde. Forward Dump.

3. BRIGADE DUMP. The Brigade Dump will be North of MARICOURT at 16.a.4.8.

4. TOOLS. The regimental tools (mobilisation stores) at present in the Brigade Dump will be sent up to the 2nd and 3rd S. A. Inf. under Brigade arrangements. These tools will be off-loaded and the wagons sent back to the First Line Transport.

The regimental tools (mobilisation stores) of the 1st and 4th S. A. Infantry will be taken under Brigade arrangements to the *rendezvous* North of MARICOURT at 16.a.centre, where the tools will be taken over by regiments.

5. BRIGADE HEADQUARTERS. Brigade Headquarters will be North of COPSE "C", approximately 21.b.1.4.

6. COMPLETION OF RELIEF & UNIT HEADQUARTERS. Officers Commanding units will report without delay when they have taken over, and where they have taken up their Headquarters.

7. COMMAND. On completion of relief, the command of the portion of the line at present held by the 89th Brigade and of the Trench Area at present occupied by the 21st Brigade will pass to the G.O.C., South African Brigade.

8. DIVISIONAL RESERVE. The 3rd S. A. Infantry will be in Divisional Reserve.

9. BATTALIONS IN RESERVE. The Officers Commanding 2nd and 3rd S. A. Inf. will reconnoitre routes to the front line held by both the 1st and 4th S. A. Infantry, so as to be able to lead their commands to reinforce any part of the line.

Please acknowledge.

Major.
Brigade Major.

```
Copy No. 1 to 1st S. A. Inf.         Copy No.10 to 107th Coy. A.S.C.
        2    2nd    do                       11    O.C. Bearer Sect. Fd. Amb
        3    3rd    do                       12    9th Division.
        4    4th    do                       13    52nd Brigade, R.F.A.
    X   5    64th Field Coy. R.E.            14    G. O. C.
        6    O.C. "B" Coy. 9th S.H.          15    Brigade Major.
        7    O.C. 26th Bde. M.G. Coy.        16    Staff Captain.
        8    O.C. Bde. L.T.M. Batty.         17    Office Copy.
        9    O.C. Bde. Signal Sect.,         18    War Diary.
                                             19    21st Inf. Brigade.
                                             20    89th Inf. Brigade.
                                             21    26th Inf. Brigade.
```

Issued by Orderly at.....................

SECRET

Copy No...... 5

1ST SOUTH AFRICAN INFANTRY BRIGADE.

OPERATION ORDER No. 43.

In the Field,
6th July 1916.

1. **RELIEF.** The 1st S.A.Infantry will come out of the front line tonight - with the exception of the strong points in the area at present occupied by that unit - to make room for other troops.

    The relief of the 1st portions of the S.A.Infantry in the BRIQUETERIE will take place at 8.pm. On coming out of the front line the 1st S.A.Infantry will be accommodated in the portions of the British original front line trenches.

    (X) the remainder of the relief will take place at 10 pm

2. **OFFICERS TO TAKE OVER NEW TRENCH AREA.** The Officer Commanding 1st S.A.Infantry will send whatever number of officers he considers necessary to report to the Staff Captain at the Headquarters of the 2nd S.A.Infantry (CAMBRIDGE COPSE) this afternoon at 5.pm.in order that they may be shewn the trenches to be occupied by their unit to-night. These Officers will return to their unit to lead it to its new quarters.

3. **STRONG POINTS TO REMAIN GARRISONED.** The Officer Commanding 1st S.A. Infantry will leave a garrison of 1 platoon in each of the strong points within the area now occupied by him.

    Machine guns at present in these strong points will also be left there.

4. **NEW FRONT LINE OF S. A. BRIGADE.** On the withdrawal from the front line of the 1st S.A.Infantry, the South African Brigade will hold the line from the point on the BRIQUETERIE - MONTAUBAN Road, where there is a screen. This point is at the end of the hedge running, roughly, east and west, and from the other end of which a communication trench runs back to GLATZ REDOUBT, as shewn in sketch plan attached.

    The 4th S.A.Infantry will hold the line from that point (inclusive of the communication trench from the hedge to GLATZ REDOUBT) to the left of the French.

5. **COMPLETION OF RELIEF.** The Officer Commanding 1st S.A.Infantry will report to Brigade Headquarters :-
    (1) Completion of relief,
    (2) When his unit has arrived at its new quarters, stating where he has taken up his Headquarters.

6. **TOOLS.** All tools belonging to the Brigade now on charge to the 1st S.A.Infantry will be brought out of the trenches, excepting such as may be required to be left in the strong points. Tools which were drawn from the Brigade will be collected and dumped at A.4.c.1.9. by 8.pm., and a guard placed over them. This point is where the MONTAUBAN-MARICOURT Road cuts GLATZ REDOUBT. They will be removed from there to the Brigade Dump by the Brigade Transport Officer.

7. **STORES.** Receipts for Stores, etc., handed over will be obtained in duplicate in the usual way.

8. **RATION RENDEZ-VOUS.** The rendez-vous for Rations for the 1st S.A.

(2)

...... Infantry to-night will be at FOUR WILLOWS, east of MACHINE GUN WOOD.

9. <u>BRIGADE HEADQUARTERS.</u> Brigade Headquarters is now in "B" COPSE south of PERONNE Road.

Please acknowledge.

Major.
Brigade Major.

```
Copy No 1 to  1st S.A.Infantry            Copy No.11 to O.C.Bearer Section
         2    2nd      -do-                        12    9th Division
         3    3rd      -do-                        13    52nd Bde. R.F.A.,
         4    4th      -do-                        14    G.O.C.,
         5    64th Field Co R.E.,                  15    Brigade Major
         6    O.C. "B" Co 9th Seaforths            16    Staff Captain
         7    O.C. 28th Bde M.G.Co.,               17    Office Copy
         8    O.C.Bde. L.T.M.Battery               18    War Diary
         9    O.C.Bde. Signal Section              19    21st Infantry Bde.
        10    107th Co A.S.C..                     20    27th Infantry Bde.
```

Issued by Orderly at ....

HEADQUARTERS.
1st S.A. INFANTRY BRIGADE.

OPERATION ORDER No.45.

With reference to above, the whole arrangements are postponed for 24 hours.

The Order will come into force to-morrow, 7th inst., and will be carried out without further orders, unless further postponement is advised.

Major.
Brigade Major.

1st Field Coy. RE

9

S E C R E T.

Copy No. 5

1st SOUTH AFRICAN INFANTRY BRIGADE.
OPERATION ORDER No.44.

In the Field,
8th July 1916.

1. **RELIEF.** The Headquarters and two Companies of the 2nd S.A. Infantry, with two Machine Guns with teams to be detailed by the O.C., 26th Brigade M.G.Company, will relieve portions of the 12th Royal Scots and 6th K.O.S.Borderers this afternoon in BERNAFAY WOOD.

2. **GUIDES.** The 27th Infantry Brigade will arrange for guides to be at the junction of CHIMNEY TRENCH and NORD ALLEY at 3.pm. to lead above units to positions.

3. **REPORTS.** Situation reports will be sent to Brigade Headquarters every clock half hour after position is taken over.
Completion of relief to be reported to Brigade Headquarters, at the same time giving map reference of Battalion Headquarters.

4. **BATTALION HEADQUARTERS.** The Headquarters of the 2nd S.A.Infantry will take over the Headquarters of the 12th Royal Scots.

Please acknowledge.

Major.
Brigade Major.

Copy No. 1 to	1st S.A.Inf.	Copy No. 11 to	Bearer Coy. S.A.F.A.
2	2nd -do-	12	9th Division
3	3rd -do-	13	52nd Brigade R.F.A.
4	4th -do-	14	G.O.C.
5	64th Field Co.R.E.,	15	Brigade Major
6	"B" Co. 9th Seaforths	16	Staff Captain
7	26th Bde.M.G.Coy.	17	Office Copy
8	Bde. L.T.M.Battery	18	War Diary
9	Brigade Signal Section	19	27th Inf.Brigade
10	107th Co. A.S.C.,	20	

Issued by Orderly at 2.15 pm

SECRET   Copy No........ 5.

1st SOUTH AFRICAN INFANTRY BRIGADE

MAP.   OPERATION ORDER No.46
MONTAUBAN
SHEET.
                                                            In the Field,
                                                             10th July 1916.

1. RELIEF.   The O.C. 4th S.A.I., will detail two Companies to relieve the 2nd S.A.I., to-night in BERNAFAY WOOD. Relief to commence at 10.pm.

                Headquarters 4th S.A.I., to take over from Headquarters, 2nd S.A.I.

                O.C. 28th M.G.Company will detail two machine guns with their teams and two fresh teams to replace those in BERNAFAY WOOD to report to the O.C., 4th S.A.I., at Headquarters of the 4th S.A.I., GLATZ REDOUBT at 9.pm.

                These four machine guns will be disposed as ordered by the O.C. 4th S.A.I.

                Separate orders will be issued to the O.C., 4th S.A.I., regarding his dispositions in BERNAFAY WOOD and the holding of LONGUEVAL ALLEY.

                The 2nd and 4th S.A.I., will move to and from BERNAFAY WOOD via MONTAUBAN - MARICOURT Road and CHIMNEY TRENCH VALLEY to avoid clashing with the reliefs which are taking place of troops of the 30th Division.

                The 2nd S.A.I., will return to their original CAMPING SITE in the vicinity of CAMBRIDGE COPSE.

2. MOVES.   Those portions of the S.A.Brigade which are at present outside the S.A.Brigade area will move into that area tonight.

                The remainder of the 4th S.A.I., will occupy that portion of the S.A.Brigade area within NORD and TRAIN ALLEYS (both inclusive)

                The O.C. 4th S.A.I., will leave one Company in DUBLIN ALLEY and down DUBLIN TRENCH connecting with the left of the French until relieved by 30th Division troops. This relief will probably take place about midnight.

                The O.C., 3rd S.A.I., will detail a garrison for GLATZ REDOUBT and will take over from the O.C., 1st S.A.I., the strong points within the S.A.Brigade area.

                Four guides from the 1st S.A.I., will report to the O.C., 3rd S.A.I., at 9 o'clock to-night where the MONTAUBAN - MARICOURT Road cuts the GLATZ REDOUBT.

                                                         Major.
                                                       Brigade Major.

```
Copy No. 1 to 1st S. A. Infantry.
      2     2nd    do    do
      3     3rd    do    do
      4     4th    do    do
    ✗ 5     64th Field Co., R.E.
      6     "B" Coy, 9th S. H..,
      7     28th de. M.G. Coy.
      8     Brigade L.T.M. Battery.
      9     Brigade Signal Section.
     10.    107th Coy. A.S.C.
     11     Bearer Section, S.A.F.A.
     12     9th Division.
     13     Right Group, R.F.A. 9th Div.
     14     G. O. C.
     15     Brigade Major.
     16     Staff Captain.
     17     Office Copy.
     18     War Diary.
     19     Captain Ward.
```

Issued by Orderly at...................

HEADQUARTERS,
1st S. A. INFANTRY BRIGADE.

Officer Commanding,
4th S. A. Infantry.

B.M.X31/106.   10th July, 1916.

The following orders are issued in connection with the relief being carried out by you to-night:-

1. The front of BERNAFAY WOOD to be taken over by you will be held as lightly as possible, the usual distribution in depth being arranged for in so far as that is possible.

2. Men must be well dug in in deep, narrow trenches.

3. LONGUEVAL ALLEY (which is the trench running from the N.E. corner of BERNAFAY WOOD up to the Northerern point of TRONES WOOD) is to be held by posts distributed throughout its length. The post at present held by the 2nd S. A. Infantry at S.23.b.5.0. is to be consolidated inconspicuously. That post is to be held to the last.

4. Every precaution is to be taken to prevent the enemy being aware of this position, and aggressive action will be withheld until our forces move Northwards through TRONES WOOD. Every advantage will then be taken of the surprise effect which our occupation of the post should render possible.

5. The garrison of this post will be a platoon with two Lewis Guns, with their teams. Suitable positions for the Lewis Guns will be selected.

6. A sniping post should be put out at about S.23.centre. At about S.23.a.9.6. there is an enemy observation post from which patrols periodically visit TRONES WOOD. A post should be put out as indicated to snipe such patrols with the object of preventing the post in the trench being discovered.

7. At two points in LONGUEVAL ALLEY, between the forward post and BERNAFAY WOOD, Lewis Guns should be placed.

8. Special arrangements must be made for water, rations, wire, tools and bombs to be taken up to this post, and (with the exception of wire) also to the connecting posts.

9. An Engineer officer is being sent up to advise regarding the method of consolidating the main post. This consolidation must be inconspicuous.

10. Every endeavour must be made to keep the enemy in ignorance of the fact that we hold this post, and no aggressive action is to be taken except in conjunction with our forces pushing forward through TRONES WOOD, or unless the post is attacked.

11. The Commander of the post will send reports at least every hour, and you will keep Brigade Headquarters fully notified. These messages should be sent back by a system of relays from one post to the other back to your Headquarters. It is of the utmost importance that constant communication with the forward post should be kept up by you, and between you and Brigade Headquarters.

The Brigadier-General directs me to say that he feels it is unnecessary for him to point out that the holding of LONGUEVAL ALLEY, with the forward post, is all important at the present time.

Major.
Brigade Major.

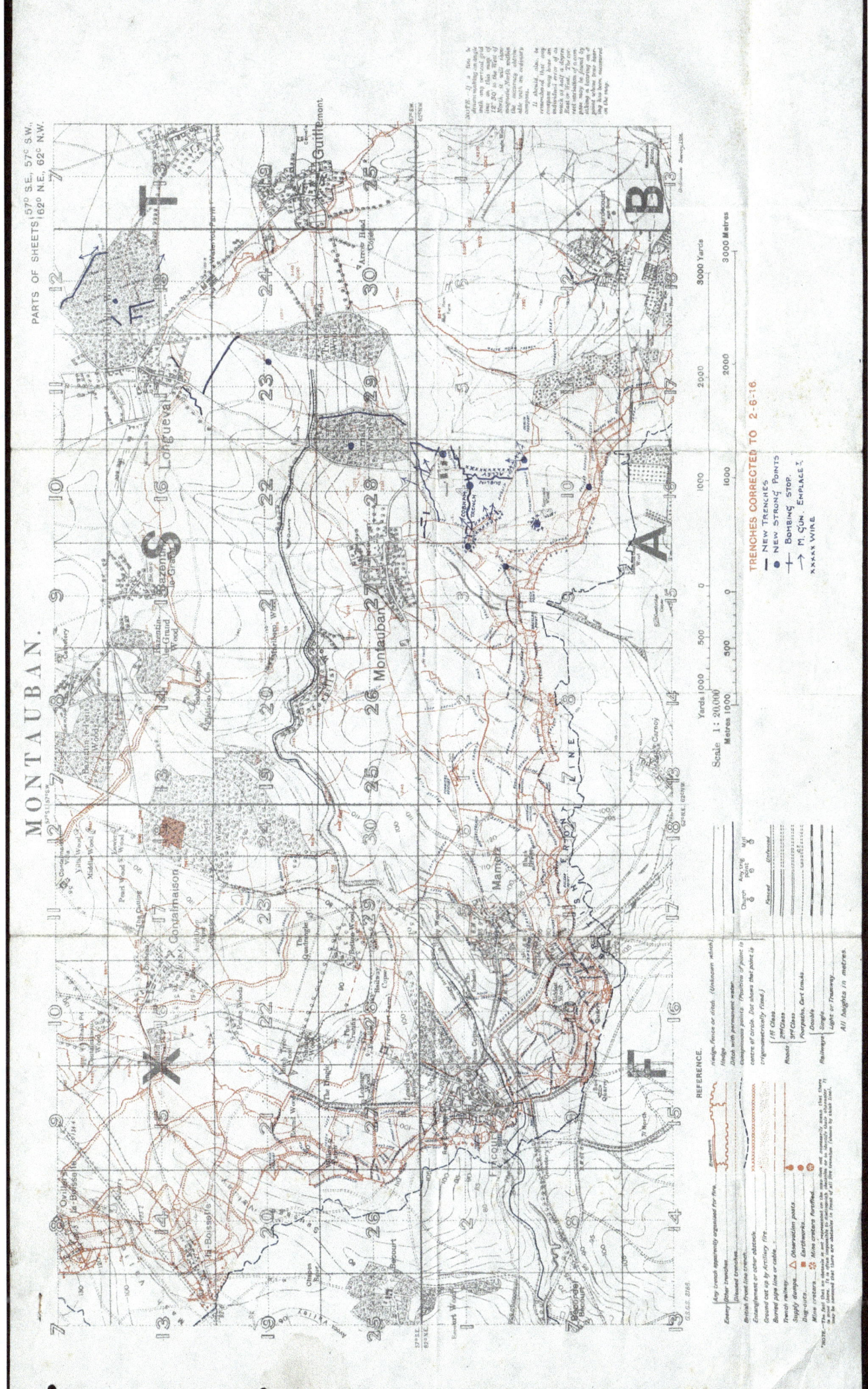

TRENCH MAP.

MONTAUBAN.

Scale 1:20,000.

64 th. FIELD COMPANY R. E.

9 th. DIVISION.

AUGUST 1916

WAR DIARY or INTELLIGENCE SUMMARY

Army Form C. 2118.

5th Field Coy. R.E. Vol 16

Hour, Date, Place	Summary of Events and Information	Remarks and references to Appendices
FRENVILLERS 1/8	7.0–7.30 Physical drill. 9.0 Route march to TIRQUES and back. Sergts & NCOs on Scheme - Defence of Village and woods. Arranged with CRE for supply of material to Battalions for instructional purposes. Lecture on lessons to be learnt from our part in the 2.0 pm offensive with special regard to consolidation.	
2/8	7.0–7.30 Physical drill. 9.0 Coy drill. 10.30 Drafts digging, remainder marching bayonet fighting, bombing message. Some more NCOs on scheme. 5.0–6.0 Trestle drill, bridge, pontoon & musketry.	
3/8	7.0–7.30 Physical drill. 9.0 Saluting Misc. bayonet fighting. 1 NCO, 12 men left to be attached to each Battn for instructional 2.0 pm purpose. Mazleno on wagons to Indra in quarry at BOUGIN Ptn. Sec to lay cable at NAGNICOURT. 9.30 pm Parade with pickets, shovels, axes and for night scheme. Subject – setting on the Sgt (a) in open country (1) in a woods. Successfully carried through. Returned to trenches 12.0 m	
4/8	10.0 Harehrig 9 a.m. bayonet fighting. Rode round Battalions to see how instructors were settling down. Some were jumping in once or two instances. 3 men wanting training. 5.0–6.0 Trestles, large pontoon, required in one or two instances. Direct Battns at PRESNICOURT 8.0 Joint concert with 16th S.A. Haut. Searchlights, musketry. Successful up to limelight.	
5/8	7.30–8.0 Physical drill. 9.0 Trestle drill, unloading pontoons Saluting. 2 Offrs out to reconnoitre approaches to BERTHOPPVAL	

WAR DIARY
or
INTELLIGENCE SUMMARY.
(Erase heading not required.)

Army Form C. 2118.

Instructions regarding War Diaries and Intelligence Summaries are contained in F.S. Regs., Part II. and the Staff Manual respectively. Title pages will be prepared in manuscript.

Hour, Date, Place	Summary of Events and Information	Remarks and references to Appendices
5/8 (cont)	2nd CARENCY section 5.0 pm Lecture by O.C. on Reporting	
6/8	Roll up with remaining two sections Officers and reconnoitred approaches to CARENCY & BETHONVAL Section. Day very different to view from VIMY RIDGE and about 1/2 hour walk is necessary. Parade service in the morning. Company was then marched to SJARNY at BOUGIN to bathe in the afternoon.	
7/8	7.0–7.30 Physical drill. 7.0 Parade for chocolate, clothing, equipment and necessaries. 10.15 Parade with Lewis buckets tube rifle. Draft's baths cleaning & Lewis Guns platoons S.D. 6.10 Transfer, M.O.'s parties musketry	
8/8	7.0–7.30 Physical drill. 9.0 Bath march to BOUGIN attack with a Coy in the SJARNY to meet and granted passes till 7 pm to visit their friends. the neighbouring villages	
9/8	7.0–7.30 Physical drill 10 Section with section officer B Coy Route March field to the parade in running dress to follow march Record SAISEL HQ. ec. shot of this moving with Clear and attached. Return at 2.7 Bn Hd. on Moving by Controller Service O.C. Army	
10/8	7.0–7 30 Physical drill 9.0 up to tunnels with O.C. 65 Coy RE. Scheme under section officer Consult at 1.30 Section SAR/Bde Contraction dull	
11/8	7.30–8.0 Physical drill. 7.30–10.30 HM Ra Ring mines the village all trustees attacks on Controll in Ancillary. Since then rest train moved to Ardon own	

WAR DIARY or INTELLIGENCE SUMMARY

Army Form C. 2118.

(Erase heading not required.)

Hour, Date, Place	Summary of Events and Information	Remarks and references to Appendices
VILLERS-AU-BOIS 12/8	Taken over from 152nd Field Coy at VILLERS-AU-BOIS. Lt. G.ALLEN Company marched at 7.0am arriving VILLERS 10.30am. Proceeded to 1st Army School for a course of instruction. Horse lines one at GOUY-SERVINS. No. 3 & 4 Sections marched up to RUGBY (on SOUCHEZ-ARRAS road) to live in dugouts there for work in front line. No. 2 Section marched up to dugouts in front of BERTHONVAL WOOD to work with R.F.A. Both these were took the place of the tanks. No. 1 Sec. remains at H.Q. for work in shops at advanced sections cleaning dugouts, taking stock of dumps and learning the way about the trenches. Bn Inf. on excavating new light railway from BIRMINGHAM to LIVERPOOL.	Appendix A Distribution of Company. Appendix B Orders for work.
13/8	Levels of Railway checked and corrected. 24th Inf excavating Work on others Shafts Scheme in ZOUAVE VALLEY dugout for Stokes gunners near VINCENT, emplacement for Heavy Trench Mortar near TOTTENHAM ROAD and shelter for Gunners. No. 2 Sec. on R.F.A. B.H.Q. and one O.P. on ARRAS road.	
14/8	237 Inf in Railway 200 x nails for laying track. Others working continued. Orders received to hand over R.F.A. work to 153 Co R.E. No 2 Sec. orders to move up to join Stokes at RUGBY where they will make themselves dugouts. This will continue work on O.P.s only and also front line work made. B Coy Pioneers deepening CENTRAL AVENUE.	
15/8		
16/8	260 Inf on railway. 12 Pl. on improving deep dugout in front line for M.G. Other works continued.	

Army Form C. 2118.

WAR DIARY
or
INTELLIGENCE SUMMARY.
(Erase heading not required.)

Instructions regarding War Diaries and Intelligence Summaries are contained in F. S. Regs., Part II. and the Staff Manual respectively. Title pages will be prepared in manuscript.

Hour, Date, Place	Summary of Events and Information	Remarks and references to Appendices
17/8	130 Infantry on railway excavating and collecting rails from disused railway which runs parallel to new one. 10 gas drums fixed. Other works continued. B Coy Pioneers transferred from CENTRAL AVENUE to TOTTENHAM ROAD.	Wet.
18/8	1½ Secs & 100 Inf on gas boxes. 33 in position. No infantry on railway. C&D Coys Pioneers continuing trimming up excavation & collecting rails. Emplacement for heavy trench mortar continued. TOTTENHAM ROAD finished. 180° from ZOUVE VALLEY extnwards. New cut from BROAD ST. to STAFFGATE ST. begun. 2 Secs. +100 Inf on gas boxes. 60 in position. 400 m. trench return. Other works continued. 400 × nails returns	
19/8	115 gas boxes in position; other works continued	Showery
20/8	2½ Secs with 175 Infantry on gas boxes, 156 in position. Other works continued	
21/8	2½ Secs +200 Infantry on gas boxes 220 in position. Other works continued. New Battle H.Q. for 8th Black Watch at junction of GORDON AVENUE & STARGATE ST taken over from 8th B.W. 400 mtrs of trench lead in with 6 light railway track grating 100 × mtrs of CENTRAL AVENUE.	
22/8		
23/8	26th Bde relieved by S.A.Bde. 2/Lt Seer with 135 Inf. on gas boxes. 263 fixed. 27 cars in cut. Barnes party to ammunition chamber at HTM. post'n. Other jobs continued. 12 men attached to 8th B.W. for machine making anti-bombing floors in captured C.T.s	

WAR DIARY
or
INTELLIGENCE SUMMARY.
(Erase heading not required.)

Army Form C. 2118.

Instructions regarding War Diaries and Intelligence Summaries are contained in F. S. Regs., Part II. and the Staff Manual respectively. Title pages will be prepared in manuscript.

Hour, Date, Place	Summary of Events and Information	Remarks and references to Appendices
24/8	2 Secs. 4150 lyds firing gas boxes & improving those already fixed. 284 fixed. Shelter continued. H.T.M. shelters completed. Light railway track laid to within 100' North of CENTRAL AVE.	
25/8	2 Secs. widening front line to gun karage behind gas boxes. H.T.M. Position Ammunition dump begun. Light railway, grading to within 50' of ERSATZ AVE. Track laid to within 300' of ERSATZ AVE. One company of Notts & Staffs (Pioneers) attached to S.A.B.I. Shows O.C. round & allotted him as his work the construction of 4 Stokes & 3 2" Mortar emplacements.	
26/8	2 Secs. widening front line & improvements to gas boxes. Commenced small dugout for visual signallers at Batt. Little H.Q. Stokes emplacements. Rails laid 50' past LIVERPOOL DUMP. 25% complete.	
27/8	2 Secs. widening trench, other works as before. Railway track graded to ERSATZ AVE. Improvements to cutting drainage begun. O.C. & Sec officers & NCOs attended in day for assault of 26.5 Bde for trench arrow. & BROAD ST. 3 min attacks to dug in sight.	
28/8	2 Secs of front line & other works continued. Track laid platoon of 1st S.A.I. within 300' of ERSATZ. Stokes emplacements & OC returned from machine to within 300' of ERSATZ.	
29/8	Work as before. TOTTENHAM road completed. Stokes emplacements. 5. 2 officers & NCOs returned from machine. 20 men & 1 officer & S.A.I. attached for machine ground in morning.	

Army Form C. 2118.

WAR DIARY
or
INTELLIGENCE SUMMARY.
(Erase heading not required.)

Instructions regarding War Diaries and Intelligence Summaries are contained in F.S. Regs., Part II. and the Staff Manual respectively. Title pages will be prepared in manuscript.

Hour, Date, Place	Summary of Events and Information	Remarks and references to Appendices
30/8	Very heavy rain brought about large falls of earth in the trenches. 2 Secs Hallifax Infantry to refrain from railway cutting. Large falls occurred, but the track was kept open, though in very bad condition.	
31/8	Fine day. (See averaged Infantry in BROAD ST.) Overworks on later. Communication trenches are in a bad state and drainage of storm must be taken in hand. Work on point at one point, though works continues.	

1/9/16

N.J. Moorhuy Lt.
O.C. 61st Coy RE

SECRET.

C.R.E. No. B.101/6.

~~O.C. 63rd Field Company, R.E.~~
O.C. 64th Field Company, R.E.
~~O.C. 90th Field Company, R.E.~~
O.C. 153rd Field Company, R.E.
O.C. 154th Field Company, R.E.
O.C. 9th Seaforth Highlanders (Pioneers).
C.R.E. 37th Division.
26th Inf. Bde.
27th Inf. Bde.
1st S.A. Inf. Bde.
~~9th Division.~~

1. The Field Companies 9th Division are allotted areas for the work limited by/boundaries stated below:-

   64th Field Coy.
   Right - CENTRAL AVENUE inclusive.
   Left - INTERNATIONAL AVENUE inclusive, and line S.14.d.5.2 to S.19.b.5.0.
   Rear - BETHUNE - ARRAS road.

   63rd Field Coy.
   Right - Left boundary of 64th Field Company.
   Left - BOYAU TRANCHOT inclusive., and line S.14.b.8.7 to S.13.d.6.4.
   Rear - BETHUNE - ARRAS road.

   90th Field Coy.
   Right - Left boundary of 63rd Field Company.
   Left - BOYAU ROBINEAU, 130th ALLEY inclusive.
   Rear - Present boundary of 153rd Field Company.

2. 154th Field Company will work in its present area.

3. Pioneers (9th Seaforths).

   C and D Companies (with 64th Field Company) ZOUAVE VALLEY railway.

   A and B Companies (with 63rd and 64th Field Companies respectively) making slits for 200 men each in ZOUAVE VALLEY - then on CENTRAL and ERSATZ ALLEYS East of ZOUAVE VALLEY.

G R Hearn
Major, R.E.
Acting, C.R.E. 9th (Scottish) Division.

11/8/16.

16-20· bolts
secured 1/4"
3/4" round
2 + 1/4" strap

SECRET

CRE. B 35/5

OC 63rd Field Coy
64 Field Coy ✓ (63rd to forward map)

The Company under your command will work with 26th Brigade in the right section (with slight modification as notified in order defining areas).

2. A and B Coys 9th Seaforth Pioneers will work in areas allotted to 63 & 64 Field Coys respectively. Their first work will be the deepening & improvement of ERSATZ & CENTRAL AVENUES respectively, east of LOUAVE VALLEY after they have dug slits & shutted them.

3. Subject to instructions of GOC 26th Brigade the most important work is the installation of emplacements for cylinders in the positions indicated on tracing attached (to be passed quickly). The sites should be reported on early and any alterations required on account of difficulties reported.

4. Boxes will be made at CVP. There are frames & sheeting at GOVT DUMP, but I am afraid the sheeting is barely 4'6" long, and too thin to stand pressure over this span. If they can be utilised indent please.

G R Heary
Major RE
a/CRE 9th Division

11/8/16.

64 th. FIELD COMPANY R. E.

9 th. DIVISION

SEPTEMBER 1916

Army Form C. 2118.

64th Field Coy
September '16
vol 17

WAR DIARY
or
INTELLIGENCE SUMMARY.
(Erase heading not required.)

Instructions regarding War Diaries and Intelligence Summaries are contained in F.S. Regs., Part II. and the Staff Manual respectively. Title pages will be prepared in manuscript.

Hour, Date, Place	Summary of Events and Information	Remarks and references to Appendices
VILLERS-AU-BOIS 1/9	3 section in advanced billets at RUGBY working on steam Trench Mortar position. Deep dugouts in front of Coliseum, Battalion Battle H.Q., visual cell, O.P. for R.F.A. on ARRAS ROAD, and infantry in infantry trenches. 1 Section working in shafts at H.Q. (Nieurs.) Div section machine mining (preparatory to a progress of penetration.) (1 Coy of N. Staffords (Pioneers) working on Light railway, (including one drainage) cutting. 1 Coy 9th N. Staffords or C.T.s in the one allotted to this company. 1 Coy 9th N. Staffords (Pioneers) on Stokes gun emplacements and position for 2" Mortar battery.	
2/9	H.T.M. position finished except for main dugout. Visual £ cell completed. Other work as before.	
3/9	Work as before.	
4/9	Work as before.	
5/9	No 4 Section relieved No 3 Section in advanced billets.	
6/9	Stokes work on 2 more dugouts in front line now urgent. Platoons of 9th N. Staffs Battalion in the line. Fixing additional targets in frames of front line. Other works continued. Works as before. 1 Coy of N. Staffords (Pioneers) withdrawn from work. Their work will be completed as labour becomes available.	
7/9		

Army Form C. 2118.

WAR DIARY
or
INTELLIGENCE SUMMARY.
(Erase heading not required.)

Instructions regarding War Diaries and Intelligence Summaries are contained in F.S. Regs., Part II. and the Staff Manual respectively. Title pages will be prepared in manuscript.

Hour, Date, Place	Summary of Events and Information	Remarks and references to Appendices
8/9	Dugout for special apparatus (IT) started in ZOUAVE VALLEY at foot of TOTTENHAM ROAD. Other works as before.	
9/9	Excavation of large chamber of Batt. Battle HQ finished. Shuttering in hand. Works as before.	
10/9	Completion taken in hand of 2" Mortar position left of Q.N. Stafford's (Finnis). Dumbbell's laid all along right railway from CENTRAL AVE. to GORDON AVE. Other works as before.	
11/9	No 3 Section relieve No 2 Section in advanced billets. Large chamber of Batt. Battle HQ. complete. Subsequent enlargement to small chamber began. Other works as before.	
12/9	Chamber of IT dugout completed. Other works as before.	
13/9	Works as before.	
14/9	Started work with part of 8th infantry on opening up new B.O.Y.A.U. west of the ARGYLL'S ROAD. 2" Mortar position completed. Other works as before.	
15/9	Started opening up SOMBARD ST. 1 Cy. Pioneers started work on CAVALIER. Dugout Cy from S.A. Bde consisting of 2 Officers and 80 men was attached to us to get from this morning. They are to live in advanced billets & spend today making shelters for themselves in an old trench off CENTRAL AVE. The other half returns to VILLERS to Cy. HQ.	

WAR DIARY
or
INTELLIGENCE SUMMARY.
(Erase heading not required.)

Army Form C. 2118.

Instructions regarding War Diaries and Intelligence Summaries are contained in F.S. Regs., Part II. and the Staff Manual respectively. Title pages will be prepared in manuscript.

Hour, Date, Place	Summary of Events and Information	Remarks and references to Appendices
15/9 (Continued)	They will be employed on making Bde. H.Q. for 2 Bdes. of 63rd (RN) Divn. in COLISEUM. They will start work tomorrow morning. Other works as before.	
16/9	Work on Bde. H.Q. in COLISEUM cancelled at late hour. Dugout Coy given another day to improve their own shelters. Reconnaissance of Bde. H.Q. for 27th Bde. off MORTLEY AVE made with aid of Bde Staff. Dugout Coy will start on this tomorrow morning. 10th Worcesters (Pioneers) will start work tomorrow 2 Companies on extension to NEW GOTAH & EARLHEM AVE. Dugouts in front line handed over to 63rd Coy R.E. Other works as before.	
17/9	Bde H.Q. began — R.A.M.C. Dugout finished. Other works continued.	
18/9	Began starting CAVE at West end of TOTTENHAM road. Strong rain. 1 Section withdrawn from RUGBY & worked on Divnl. Sch. at MAISON BOUCHE under C.R.E. Bomb Store at GOUY SERVINS for D.A.C. Heavy fall of earth in the trenches owing to the rain.	
19/9	Works continued.	
20-21/9	O.C. 104th Coy R.E. taken round the trenches and work.	
22/9	Ransby over.	
23/9	Dugout Coy of South African Bde returned to their Battalion. Section in advance billets withdrawn to VILLERS. Officer of 1st Dg. Gds. R.E. taken round billets.	Appendix A & B

B/164   A

63. Field Coy.   SECRET

to ✓

7º.

It has been arranged that
104 Field Coy takes over area of
63 + 64 Field Coy.
129 Field Coy takes over area
of 90 Field Coy.

~~Reliefs take place on Septr 25th~~   BM

Representatives will arrive
on 22nd September.

Later reliefs will issue
subsequently. On Sept 25th
104 Field Coy is due to arrive
at CHAUDIÈRE HAIE and
129 Field Coy at PETIT SERAINS

         G R Hearn
21/9/16.   Major R.E.
         a/CRE 9 Divn

SECRET.
===========

B.164/1

O.C. 63rd Coy.
O.C. 64th Coy.
O.C. 90th Coy.
C.R.E. 24th Division. (for information)
================

    The Field Coys. R.E. 9th Division will be relieved by Field Coys. R.E. 24th Division in accordance with the attached table.

2.   Please acknowledge.

W.L.Wood

Lieut. R.E.
Adjutant 9th Divisional Engineers.

22.9.16.

Army Form C. 2118.

WAR DIARY
or
INTELLIGENCE SUMMARY.

(Erase heading not required.)

Instructions regarding War Diaries and Intelligence Summaries are contained in F.S. Regs., Part II. and the Staff Manual respectively. Title pages will be prepared in manuscript.

Hour, Date, Place	Summary of Events and Information	Remarks and references to Appendices
8/9	Dugout for special apparatus (IT) started in ZOUAVE VALLEY at foot of TOTTENHAM ROAD. Other work as before.	
9/9	Excavation of large chamber of Battn. Battle H.Q. finished. Shuttering & flooring etc. in hand. Works as before.	
10/9	Completion taken in hand of 2" Mortar position left by 9th N. Staffords (Finish). Dutchman's Road all along light railway from CENTRAL AVE to GORDON AVE. Other works as before.	
11/9	No. 3 Section relieve No. 2 Section in advanced billets. Large chamber of Battn. Battle H.Q. completely Embankment to small dugouts begun. Other works as before.	
12/9	Chamber of IT dugout completed. Other works as before.	
13/9	Works on Defences	
14/9	Started work with party of Infantry on opening up NEW BOYAU road of the ARDEA'S ROAD. 2" Mortar position completed. Other works as before.	
15/9	Started opening up SOMBARD ST. 1 Coy Pioneers started work on CAVALIER. Dugout Coy from S.A. Bde cominicto of 2 Officers and 80 men was attached to us Coy HQ. from this morning. they are to live in advanced billets & spend today making shelters for themselves in an old trench. Other centre AVE. The other half returned to VILLERS to Coy H.Q.	

Army Form C. 2118.

WAR DIARY
or
INTELLIGENCE SUMMARY.
(Erase heading not required.)

Instructions regarding War Diaries and Intelligence Summaries are contained in F. S. Regs., Part II. and the Staff Manual respectively. Title pages will be prepared in manuscript.

Hour, Date, Place	Summary of Events and Information	Remarks and references to Appendices
15/9 (Gavrelle)	They will be employed on making Bde. H.Q. for 2 Bdes of 63rd (R.N.) Divn. in COLISEUM. They will start work tomorrow morning. Other works as before.	
16/9	Work on Bde. HQ in COLISEUM carried on late hours. Dugout for gun another day to improve their own shelters. Reconnaissance of Bde HQ for 27th Bde. Off MORTLEY AVE made with aid of Bde Staff. Dugout for mile start in stairs tomorrow morning. 2 Companies Lt. Worcesters (Pioneers) will start work tomorrow on extension to NEW GOVAN & CENTRE AVE. Dugouts in front line handed over to 63rd Coy. R.E. Other works as before.	
17/9	Bde H.Q. dugout —R.A.M.C dugout finished. Other works continued.	
18/9	Began shafts. CAVE at West end of TOTTENHAM road. 1 section withdrawn from RUGBY & worked on Divnl. School at MAISNIL BOUCHÉ under C.R.E.	Strong rain.
19/9	Bomb Store at GOVT SERVINS for D.A.C. Many falls of roof in the tunnel owing to the rain.	
20 - 21/9	Works continued.	
22/9	Oct. 164th Coy. R.E. taken round the trenches and works handed over.	
23/9	Dugout Coy of South African Bde returned to their Battalions. Section in advance (with withdrawn to VILLERS. Officers & 129 of oth.r. taken round billets.	Appendix A & B

(73989) W4141—463. 400,000. 9/14. H.&J.Ltd. Forms/C. 2118/10.

RELIEF TABLE.

Date	Unit	From	To	Remarks.
Sept. 23	129 Field Coy.	x	Pt SERVINS	
	104 " "	x	Bois de la HAIE	
	64 " "	....	....	To concentrate at VILLERS AU BOIS
Sept.24	122 Field Coy.	Pt. SERVINS	Villers AU BOIS	
Sept. 25	90th Fd.Coy.	....	....	To concentrate at GOUY SERVINS relieved by 129 Field Coy. 24th Division.
	63rd Fd.Coy.	....	....	To concentrate BOIS de la HAIE relieved by 104th Field Coy. 24th Division.
Sept. 26	103rd Fd.Coy.	Pt.SERVINS	GOUY SERVINS	Into billets vacated by 90th Fd.Coy.

SECRET.

Copy No: 2

9th Divisional Engineers OPERATIONS
ORDERS No. 6............ 22.9.16.

Reference Sheets 36 b 51 c 1/40000.

1. The R.E. 9th Division, will move to the THIRD ARMY TRAINING AREA in accordance with the attached table.

2. H.Q.R.E. will close at CAMBLAIN L'ABBE at 10 a.m on September 26th and open at LE CAUROY at mid-day on same day.

3. The positions of Field Companies will be communicated to H.Q.R.E. on completion of each move.

4. Billets in HOUVIN HOUVINEVL will be allotted by H.Q.R.E.

5. Please acknowledge.

Issued at 12-1 p.

Lieut. R.E.
Adjutant 9th Divisional Engineers.

Copies to -

No 1 to 63rd Field Coy.
   2 ,, 64th ,,   ,,
   3 ,, 90th ,,   ,,
   4 ,, C.R.E. 24th Division.
   5 ,, 9th Division.

MARCH TABLE.

Date	Unit	From	To	Remarks
Sept. 24	64th(Field)Coy.R.E.	VILLERS AU BOIS	MINGOVAL Area	To move and billet under orders issued by 1st S.A.Infantry Brigade. Billets of 64th Field Coy. will be taken over by 155th Field Coy.
Sept. 25	23rd(Field)Coy.R.E.	VILLERS AU BOIS	Bois de la Haie Billets formerly occupied by E Coy. R.E.	Billets of 23rd Field Coy. to be taken over by 104th Field Coy.
Sept. 26	64th(Field)Coy.R.E.	MINGOVAL area	HOUVIN HOUVINEUL	To move under orders to be issued by 1st S.A.Brigade.
Sept. 26	90th(Field)Coy.R.E.	GOUY SERVINS	MINGOVAL AREA	Billets of 90th Field Coy. to be taken over by 103rd Field Coy. To move and billet under orders issued by 127th Infantry Brigade.
Sept. 27	90th(Field)Coy.R.E.	MINGOVAL Area	HOUVIN HOUVINEUL	To move under orders to be issued by 27th Infantry Brigade.
Sept. 27	23rd(Field)Coy.R.E.	Bois de la HAIE	VILLERS BRULIN	Not to enter VILLERS BRULIN till 12 noon.
Sept. 28	23rd(Field)Coy.R.E.	VILLERS BRULIN	HOUVIN HOUVINEUL	

Copy.........

1st South African Infantry Brigade.

23rd September 1916.

SECRET URGENT.
Map Reference
Sheet 36B S.E. + S1c.
1/20,000

1ST SOUTH AFRICAN INFANTRY BRIGADE OPERATION ORDER 59.

1. **MOVE** — The Brigade will move to the 3rd Army training area in accordance with the attached march table.

2. **MOVEMENT.** — Movement will be by companies, with 5 minutes between companies, and usual precautions will be taken regarding enemy aircraft.
   Os.C. Units are responsible that march discipline is strictly maintained on the line of march. Units must march promptly to time in accordance with the attached march table, and the routes laid down must be adhered to.

3. **INSPECTION OF BILLETS.** — Os.C. units will detail an officer (to be accompanied, in the case of infantry units, by the Quarter-Master) to inspect billets and camping sites which have been occupied by their units.
   A written report signed by that officer - in the case of Infantry Units by the two officers - will be forwarded in each instance to Brigade Headquarters, to reach there by 6 pm on the day of the inspection.

4. **TRANSPORT.** — Transport will join up with units on the morning of the 24th.

5. **MARCHING-IN STATES.** — Marching-in states will be rendered in accordance with Brigade Standing Orders. An addition will be made to the state showing the number of men, if any, who fell out on the line of march.

6. **BATTALION HEADQUARTERS.** — Os.C. units will report to Brigade Headquarters each day without delay where they have taken up their Headquarters.

Major.
Brigade Major.

Issued by orderly at 23/9/16.

Copy No	1 to 1st S.A.Infantry	Copy No	11 to 26th Infantry Brigade
2	2nd do.	12	27th do.
3	3rd do.	13	9th Division
4	4th do.	14	Brig General
5	28th M.G.Coy.	15	Brigade Major.
6	S.A., L.T.M.Battery	16	Staff Captain.
7	64th Field Co, R.E.	17	Officer
8	Bde Signal Section.	18	War Diary
9	107th Coy A.S.C.	19	176th Tunnelling Co.
10	S.A.Field Ambulance	20	Brigade Transport Off

MARCH TABLE TO BE SUBSTITUTED FOR ONE SENT OUT WITH
1ST SOUTH AFRICAN INFANTRY BRIGADE OPERATION ORDER NO. 59.

Date	Unit	From	To.	Route	Hour of march	Remarks
Septr.24.	Bde.H.Q.	CHATEAU de la HAIE	VILLERS CHATEL	CAMBLAIN L'ABBE & CAMBLIGNEUL	Noon	
	1st S.A.I.		CAMBLIGNEUL	(BETHONSART CAMBLIGNEUL & VILLERS CHATEL	11.45 am	(Starting point fork rds. (near Rly. Station.
	2nd S.A.I. 3rd S.A.I.	CAMBLAIN L'ABBE GUOY SERVINS ES. CAUCHIE	VILLERS CHATEL CHELERS	ES. CAUCHIE-W.7;c.Central 11.30 am W.7.c.Central-CAUCCURT GUESTREVILLE	11.15 am.	
	4th S.A.I.	CAMBLAIN L'ABBE	VILLERS BRULIN	CAMBLIGNEUL-VILLERS CHATEL-MINGOVAL	11.15 am	(Starting point fork rds. 2 near Rly station.
	28th M.G.Coy	GUOY SERVINS	GUESTREVILLE	Cambligneul & Bethonsart	11.30 am	Starting point X roads W.5.c.Central.
	S.A.L.T.M.By.	PETIT SERVINS	le TIRLET	--do--	11.15 am	Starting point X roads W.4.b.8.8.
	64th Field Co.R.E.	VILLERSauBOIS	VILLERS BRULIN	CAMBLIGNEUL-MINGOVAL	11.45 am	
Septr.25.	Bde.H.Q.	VILLERS CHATEL	AMBRINES	MINGOVAL-SAVY-BERLES- VILLERS SIR SIMON	11. am	
	1st S.A.I.	BETHONSART- MINGOVAL	MAIZIERES	(VILLERS BRULIN-BETHEN: (:COURT - TINQUES.	10 am	Starting point BETHONSART.
	2nd S.A.I.	VILLERS CHATEL	LIGNEREUIL	Mingoval-Savy-Berlette- Tilloy-Izel.	10.30 am	
	3rd S.A.I.	CHELERS	MAGNICOURT sur CANCHE	AVERDOING--GUOYenTERNOIS	10.30 am	
	4th S.A.I.	VILLERS BRULIN	AMBRINES	BERLES	9.30 am	
	28th M.G.Coy	GUESTREVILLE	MAIZIERES	BETHENCOURT-TINQUES-	8.45 am	
	S.A.,L.T.M.By.	le TIRLET	GUOY en TERNOIS	BETHENCOURT-TINQUES- AVERDOING.	9. am	
	64th F.Co. R.E.	VILLERS BRULIN	HOUVIN-HOUVIGNEUL	(BETHENCOURT-TINQUES (MAIZIERES-MAGNICOURT	9.30 am	

Pse acknowledge

64 th. FIELD COMPANY R.E.

9 th. DIVISION

OCTOBER 1916

Army Form C. 2118.

WAR DIARY
or
INTELLIGENCE SUMMARY.
(Erase heading not required.)

Instructions regarding War Diaries and Intelligence Summaries are contained in F.S. Regs., Part II. and the Staff Manual respectively. Title pages will be prepared in manuscript.

Place	Date	Hour	Summary of Events and Information	Remarks and references to Appendices
VILLERS AU BOIS	24/9/16		Company marched at 8.30 am. to VILLERS BRULIN.	Appendices C & D
	25/9		Company marched at 9.30 a.m. to HOUVIN HOUVIGNEUL.	
	26/9 - 30/9		Very little work on parades. The men were given a thorough rest & no parades were ordered for the afternoon which were devoted to football.	

W Woolway Major
O.C. Bat. Coy R.E.

2/10/16

vol 18

WAR DIARY
or
INTELLIGENCE SUMMARY.
(Erase heading not required.)

Army Form C. 2118.

64th Field Army R.
October 1916

Instructions regarding War Diaries and Intelligence Summaries are contained in F. S. Regs., Part II. and the Staff Manual respectively. Title pages will be prepared in manuscript.

Place	Date	Hour	Summary of Events and Information	Remarks and references to Appendices
HOUVIN HOUVIGNEUL	1, 2/10		Company routine. 2 Sappers awarded Battn. to instruct Infantry in digging.	
	2/10	9.30 am	Parade 9.30 am. Wet rain. Inspection by G.O.C.; this was cancelled as Sun. was not got into position.	Wet
	4/10		Parade again ordered & again cancelled after the men appeared on parade. D. & O.C. came round in his car & asked what men could be collected together for him.	Wet
	5/10		Marched to WILLERS at BOFFLES. Transport marched with Sappers.	Appen. A,B,C
BOFFLES	6/10		Rested at BOFFLES (Sappers). Transport marched to TALMAS.	
	7/10	6.0 am	Marched at 6.0 am. Halt at point B and baths arrangement at 8.0 am. Buses arrived & men embarked by 12 noon. Bus broke down but eventually all the company were collected at GENERCOURT by about 7.0 pm. Transport found in from TALMAS.	Appen. D
	8/10		Transport marched to FRICOURT. Sappers marched to DERNANCOURT, entrained at & detrained at BOTTOM WOOD. Then marched back to FRICOURT. H.M. READ joined party.	Appen. E Wet
	9/10		No 1, 2, 3 sections took on advanced Willers in BAZENTIN LE GRAND from	

Army Form C. 2118.

WAR DIARY
or
INTELLIGENCE SUMMARY.
(Erase heading not required.)

Instructions regarding War Diaries and Intelligence Summaries are contained in F. S. Regs., Part II. and the Staff Manual respectively. Title pages will be prepared in manuscript.

Place	Date	Hour	Summary of Events and Information	Remarks and references to Appendices
BAZENTIN-LE-GRAND			3 Sections of 2/3 London Field Coy R.E. at night took SAP holes on the line from Bn. Div. Bde HQ at BAZENTIN-LE-GRAND.	
	10/10		HQ. & No.1 & No.4 Sections took over from 4/3 London Fd Coy in FRICOURT. No.4 Section came up to BAZENTIN & lying itself in. Off. & Pads reconnoitred site for new C.T. up to front line, to be dug tonight. No. 2 Section collecting tools in BAZENTIN LE PETIT; No. 3 Section to HIGH WOOD - MARTINPUICH road. By night 450 Inf. + 2 Coy Pioneers on new C.T. from HIGH WOOD, along RUTHERFORD ALLEY, CRESCENT ALLEY, FLERS LINE to MILL. Infantry in line fairly quiet, joined up posts No.2 & S.R. MILL post, No.3 O.S. No. 2 Sec on alley which is BAZENTIN LE PETIT - No. 3 top of road.	
	11/10		By night 1 Coy Pioneers + 250 Infantry completed trench through from HIGH WOOD to front line. Infantry in line completed joining up posts. Attack ordered for today; zero at 2:15 p.m. No. 2 Sec but in reserve in Appen. E.G. FLERS SWITCH. 2 Lt Bezant took reports at Battalion HQ at 1.0 p.m. Infantry attacked at 2:15pm. Situation obscure till 5.0 p.m. when O.C. went out to clear up situation before dark. Found many men	
	12/10			

T2134. Wt. W708-776. 50C000. 4/15. Sir J. C. & S.

WAR DIARY or INTELLIGENCE SUMMARY

Army Form C. 2118.

Place	Date	Hour	Summary of Events and Information	Remarks and references to Appendices
	13/10		in our trenches + a few about M17c 50 digging in in shell holes. Reports to Battn. B.C. decided to relieve 23 + 94 S.A.I. by 3 S.A.I. left our action (M.9.I) A C.o. on the spot in case it was wanted + returned towards 1.0 P.M. Apparently the casualty infantry were moving down machine gun fire from the left ourselves about WARLENCOURT. The situation cleared slightly during the day. 2 posts were reported, one at M22 b 8.8, one at M17c 4.2. Division ordered them to be connected up, where A Coys went up to do so the front was at the Mill the latter at about M17c 6.1. He therefore dropped the sunken trench. N°2 Sec. and 7 S left dug a new C.T. from M22 b 6.0 to the front line at about ½ M22.b 7.6. During the day N°s 3 and 4 Sections worked on Willow Tramway from about M24 a 9.2 down the line of willows – the valley East of EUCOURT L'ABBAYE It H.S DESART Re. round.	Appen H.I
	14/10		N° 1 Sec worked for 4 hours in the morning on the HIGH WOOD – BAZENTIN LE PETIT road under orders of O.C 50th C.M. At night it strengthened the post at M17c 6.1 The Infantry in this line were ordered to occupy the post at M16d q.3 immediately	

WAR DIARY
or
INTELLIGENCE SUMMARY.
(Erase heading not required.)

Army Form C. 2118.

Place	Date	Hour	Summary of Events and Information	Remarks and references to Appendices
	15/10		after dark, when a trench was to be dug across from M16d7o, through post q.3 to M17c.5.0. They started about 11.30 owing to late arrival of a large working part on the work. The trench was not dug. B Coy. of the Pioneers dug their share of the trench (a C.T.) without waiting for the Infantry. No.3 & 4 Secs. on Willow Tramway.	
	16/10		No.2 Sec. on Willow tramway all day; No.3 Sec. y in the morning & No.1 in the evening formation level to within 120' of CREES SWITCH. At night No.3 Section strengthened the post occupied last night. Dugin at a dugout entrance, making 2 Vickers gun emplacements, & starting a new trench towards our front line. The Infantry dug a C.T. from our front line up to the post. Nos 1 & 2 Sections on Willow Tramway: No.4 Sec. on Willow Tramway in the morning and went out at night to continue work on N.E. PIMPLE post, begun last night by No.3 Section.	
	17/10		Nos 1&2 Sections on Willow Tramway: No.3 on Willow Tramway in the morning and waiting at night to consolidate a strong point at M17c.44 when it had been captured by the Infantry. This they failed to do and the section did	Offizier K.L.

Army Form C. 2118.

WAR DIARY
or
INTELLIGENCE SUMMARY.
(Erase heading not required.)

Instructions regarding War Diaries and Intelligence Summaries are contained in F.S. Regs., Part II. and the Staff Manual respectively. Title pages will be prepared in manuscript.

Place	Date	Hour	Summary of Events and Information	Remarks and references to Appendices
	18/10		not do any work. Orders received from C.R.E. to make a new Bde. H.Q. at SEVEN ELMS at M28d3.5; Urgent platoons from S.A.Bn were obtained for this and attached to the company (1 officer + 60 men)	Appx J
	19/10		No 3 Section was still working to consolidate until relieved about midday by No 2 Section. No 2 Sec. worked until about 10 pm when it was ordered to make two strong points on a new C.T. dug towards the enemy lines by Pioneers. No 1 Section worked on Willow Tramway all day & No 4 Sec in the morning. 2 Lt R.J. WACHER R.E. joined the company for duty. No 1 Sec on Willow Tramway all day. No 4 Sec on RUTHERFORD ALLEY trenching all day. At night No 3 Section again working for the Infantry to take point M17c4.4; again without success. S.A.Bn relieves by 27th Bde.	Appx M
	20/10		No 1 Section on Willow Tramway all day; No 2 & Section on RUTHERFORD ALLEY all day. Howards on work in front line to 90th Coy R.E. from 5.0 p.m.	
	21/10		Nos 1 & 4 Secs on RUTHERFORD ALLEY - reverting trench and working to a template. No 2 Section working in a communication trench from S.9.c.8.0. to S.3.c.9.5. No 3 Section on Willow Tramway.	

Army Form C. 2118.

WAR DIARY
or
INTELLIGENCE SUMMARY.
(Erase heading not required.)

Place	Date	Hour	Summary of Events and Information	Remarks and references to Appendices
	29/10 to 25/10		Nos. 1 & 4 Sections recutting & duckboards; RUTHERFORD ALLEY; No. 2 Section on cross country track; No. 3 Section on Bathhouses at BAZENTIN LE PETIT, excavating site & building wooden framework. Dugout platoon finished two entrances at SEVEN ELMS with 20 cases in each & put 6 cases in the third entrance.	Appdx N, O
	26/10		Marched to BOTTOM WOOD SIDING; entrained train detained at MEAULTE; marching to MILLENCOURT; transport marched from BAZENTIN to MILLENCOURT	Appdx P,Q,R.
MILLENCOURT	27/10 28/10		Resting at MILLENCOURT; kit inspection for refitting. Marched from MILLENCOURT to RUBEMPRÉ	Appdx S
	29/10 30/10		Diamond personnel moved by bus to ARRAS; transport moved to DOULLENS Resting in ARRAS; transport moved from DOULLENS to ARRAS. Coys. att'd to 35th Div. have round the trenches & work attached for work to CRE 35th Div.	Appdx T
	31/10		Officers On subjects taken round the trenches & works explained. Marking out & drainage arrangements. Battle for the men.	

M Moore Captn
O.C. No. 6, N.Z.
1/11/16

64th. FIELD COMPANY R. E.

9 th. DIVISION

NOVEMBER 1916

Confidential

9th Division

Herewith war diary of the 64th Field Coy R.E. for the month of October 1916.

W R Wood
Lt
ADJUTANT 9th DIVISIONAL ENGINEERS

3/11/16

Army Form C. 2118.

WAR DIARY
or
INTELLIGENCE SUMMARY.
(Erase heading not required.)

64th Field Company RE
November 1916

Vol 19

Place	Date	Hour	Summary of Events and Information	Remarks and references to Appendices
ARRAS	1/11		No.1 Sec L night with 1Coy 4th SAI on recutting, firestepping, duckboarding trench. No.2 Sec L day with 1Coy 4th SAI on laying 60cm tramway in MONDAY AVE. from CHTZK FARM to TELUS REDOUBT. No.3 & 4 Sec with 1Coy 4th SAI, also I platoon on making four new deep dugouts in WORKS LINE. 1NCO & 6 men S.P.R. & Section with 1Coy 4th SAI on carrying petrol home from pump house in ST NICHOLAS to the trenches S.T. and K section.	
	2/11 3/11		Works continued	
	4/11 5/11		Works continued. S.P.R. 3rd Divn revert round works on a tour of inspection.	
	6/11		Works continued. 1 Sgt & 6 sappers were asked to be detailed for work on WATERLOO St. tunnel dugout. No.2 Bde Trench Mortar Division has been damaged & cannot be fit for use to-day. Tunnels pushed in to gain 9' cover on doorway. Timber cannot be got to cerit sides entrances, pieces a shortage which means [illeg] as in Army role. 200' of Chalk Mr. tramway (laid today)	Heavy & continuous rain
	7/11		All dugout entrances fell in owing to heavy continuous rain mishaps stopped	
	8/11		Yesterday's work spent in surfing entrances of dugouts with any timber which could be salved from the ruins.	Fine
	9/11		Work started on dugouts again	Fine

WAR DIARY or INTELLIGENCE SUMMARY

Army Form C. 2118.

Place	Date	Hour	Summary of Events and Information	Remarks and references to Appendices
	10/11		Group of Offr. excavators in each Shaft.	
	11/11		TM Bomb carried by enemy relays into WATERLOO St. It has been decided to construct this trench throughout with A frames. Avg. footage on Shafts of dugouts increased to 4 ft.	
	12/11		All TM pipe lines in J sector haven's been buried. Wire connecting Ors Avg footage on Shafts Hqtrs. Lines has been put up between Sunday & Wednesday	
	13/11		Burying of pipe lines carried on in K sector. Run from LILLE Rd to Thursday Ct. started. Very little work done on WATERLOO ST owing to TM & rifle grenade bombardment by enemy. Footage on Shafts H.Q.	
	14/11		Burying of pipe lines completed party onthe tramping to railway (CHIMERIN)	
	15/11		Sou A frames have to be upkeep in WATERLOO ST. On Shaft pressure in dugout St LAWRENCE.	
	16/11		1 Coy 1st South African Infy Regt. arrived in ARRAS, worked on tramping tonying pools on Shaft now up to 150 men. Railway has reached Trench 40	
	17/11		Chambers entered in headquarters at St Laurence THELUS REDOUBT and 7 WORKS.	
	18/11		O Second Company 1st 1st REGT SAI arrived in ARRAS. Party were ridden to army camps away bay of chalk from dugout entrances. A workshop on Trench 40 taken down and widened to take tramway movements.	

Army Form C. 2118.

WAR DIARY
or
INTELLIGENCE SUMMARY.
(Erase heading not required.)

Instructions regarding War Diaries and Intelligence Summaries are contained in F.S. Regs., Part II. and the Staff Manual respectively. Title pages will be prepared in manuscript.

Place	Date	Hour	Summary of Events and Information	Remarks and references to Appendices
	19/11		A/c Regt was given 4 dugouts and scantier hut with 48 shafts onto stopfires the 1st Regt. Was given one depot under his same condition. Orders received at 9.0 p.m to move 20th to WANQUETIN.	
	20/11		Left ANDRES at 5.25 a.m for trenches at LOUEZ. Continued march at 12.30 pm. Arrived at WANQUETIN at 3.30 pm. Copy of report to O/c 35th Divn Survey amount of work completed attached.	
WANQUETIN	21/11		No. 1 and Sec. started putting partition in officers hut + erecting Nissen hut. Nos 2 + 3 Sec. training with Radio Officer.	
	22/11		All sections hutting.	
	23/11		Completed Nissen hut. Completion moved + fitted in gas chamber.	
	24/11		2 NCO. for 2 weeks attached to Divl Gas Officer at BERNEVILLE. Nos 1 + 4 Sec. hutting.	
	25/11		No. 4 Sec. putting down French huts + transported to new site. Nos 2+3 Sec. hutting. Other huts continued.	
	26/11		Capt (Gas Mounted) Lealey marched to SIMENCOURT to work on Trenches with O.C. VI Corps. 1 NCO + 13 men left Andres in WANQUETIN to complete	

Army Form C. 2118.

WAR DIARY
or
INTELLIGENCE SUMMARY.

(Erase heading not required.)

Instructions regarding War Diaries and Intelligence Summaries are contained in F. S. Regs., Part II. and the Staff Manual respectively. Title pages will be prepared in manuscript.

Place	Date	Hour	Summary of Events and Information	Remarks and references to Appendices
SOMEYCOURT	27"		accommodation of Officers & 4th SAI	
	28"		started work on hutments at D Coy 7th Seaforths	
	29"		282 huts	
	30"		378 huts	
	31"		373 hutments	

D.S. Mackenzie Lt. Col.
O.C. 64th Coy R.E.

4/7/16

64 th. FIELD COMPANY R. E.

9 th. DIVISION

DECEMBER 1916

S.21

Adjt M. 9th Divn.

Herewith please find my
War Diary for last month.

1/12/16

N Woolmer Capt RE
O.C. 64th Coy RE

WAR DIARY or INTELLIGENCE SUMMARY

Vol 20 — 64th Field Coy R.E.

Army Form C. 2118

Instructions regarding War Diaries and Intelligence Summaries are contained in F. S. Regs., Part II. and the Staff Manual respectively. Title pages will be prepared in manuscript.

(Erase heading not required.)

Place	Date	Hour	Summary of Events and Information	Remarks and references to Appendices
SIMENCOURT	1/12		Warning orders received for moving into ARRAS; probable on 2nd Dec.	Appendix A
	2/12		O.C. preceded the Coy. to take over from 204th Coy R.E. Orders received to move on 3rd Dec.	Appendix B
	3/12		Coy moved into ARRAS by road arriving about 5.30 pm. Quarters got into in the "Infantry Barracks"	
ARRAS	4/12 5/12		Officers & N.C.O.'s visits the tasks to see the work. Works began according to programme. 2nd in Coy'd. Capt. FOSDYKE Cluny to return from leave.	
	6/12		Capt. Cluny to go to "Divisional School at GIVENCHY LE NOBLE" as instructor for 3 weeks. Works in hand: — APRIL Tramway; Reconstruction of 2" T.M. Emplacement at FEBRUARY AVE.; 2" T.M. Emplacement in A'work; Deep dugout in PADDINGTON St; Two bomb stores, 2" T.M. Position with deep dugout & communication at head of NOVEMBER AVE; OCTOBER Tramway;	
	7/12		Battalion Relief; no working parties. Lt. G.E. FISCHER R.E. rejoins the Company from 41st Divn.	
	8/12 to 11/12		Works continued. Reconstruction of 2" T.M. position of FEBRUARY completed.	

Army Form C. 2118.

WAR DIARY
or
INTELLIGENCE SUMMARY.
(Erase heading not required.)

Instructions regarding War Diaries and Intelligence Summaries are contained in F. S. Regs., Part II. and the Staff Manual respectively. Title pages will be prepared in manuscript.

Place	Date	Hour	Summary of Events and Information	Remarks and references to Appendices
	12/12		A great deal of "patching up" is necessary in NOVEMBER AVE. TM position owing to very inferior work having been put into them. Reconstruction & A-framing of between end of FEBRUARY AVE. Taken in hand with 6 R.E. & 30 Inf. Strips of hurdles for again being installed in all CTs. "Bomb stops" begun in CTs just where they meet the front line. Gates being cut in same of REDOUBT LINE 3' wide and 5'0" apart. Other works continued	
	13/12		Works as before	
	14/12 15/12		Lt. C.T. ALLEN RE rejoined the Company from Hospital (sick.) Works continued. Battalion relief. No working parties. No work for Sappers. 2 Officers and 80 O.R. 9th dugout platoon of Battalion were attached to the Coy for work on New Advanced Bde H.Q. E.D. CANDLE WORKS Billets in X.CRTS.	
	16/12		Dugout platoon & later made in trench by night. Water supply kept carried out. Works continued. B Coy Pioneers started opening up old French trench from JULY Cookhouse to 89 ST.	
	17/12 to 19/12		Works continued. Station started at "C" work.	

WAR DIARY
or
INTELLIGENCE SUMMARY.
(Erase heading not required.)

Army Form C. 2118.

Place	Date	Hour	Summary of Events and Information	Remarks and references to Appendices
	20/12		New Advanced Divisional Dressing Station near Coy Workshops reconnoitred with O.C. 28th F.A. Own lines in July Cockchange Others works continued.	
	21/12		PADDINGTON ST advance saphead sworn to prevent hostile Tm fire.	
	22/12		2nd Lieut Parker ABLE OFF to look into the question of water supply - report any improvements required. Our aim - to deliver water in R Sector, this has not so far been accomplished. New Bde H.Q. in I Sector reconnoitred with G.O.C. Battalion relief. No working parties; Sapping works as usual. One block completed.	
	24/12		No day working parties; night parties as usual.	
	25/12 to 26/12		Works continued	
	27/12		Pioneers began works on branch of OCTOBER TRAMWAY for strong Trench Mortar.	
	28/12		Started work on Advanced Dressing Station with 3 R.E. + 24 R.M.C. Pioneers finished old French tunnel (NEW CUT) to Support line.	
	29/12 to 30/12		Works continued. Very heavy rain has brought in many large falls of ground.	
	31/12		Battalion relief. No parties. Sappers resting.	

RMorton Capt M.S.

11/1/17

O.C. 64th Co. M.S.

63rd Field Coy R.E. ✓
64th   "   "   "
90th   "   "   "

A

SECRET

B 207/1

1. The Infantry Bdes. 9th Div. will relieve the Infantry Bdes 35th Division on Dec 2nd, 3rd, and 4th.

2. 27th Inf Bde will march to ARRAS today & relieve 106th Inf Bde in K sector on Dec 2nd.

3. ~~prepared~~ Field Coys R.E. should be ~~~~ to move on Dec 2n — orders will be issued, it is hoped, later today.

4. Please acknowledge.

W. L. wood
Lt.
R.E.
ADJUTANT 9th DIVISIONAL ENGINEERS

1/12/16
8-30 AM

9th DIVISIONAL ENGINEERS OPERATION ORDERS. No. 11.

Copy No. 2
1/12/1916.

1. The Field Coys. R.E. 9th Division will relieve the Field Coys. R.E. 35th Division in left Division area of the VI Corps in accordance with the attached table. Dismounted men will probably move by bus.

2. An Advanced party from each Field Coy. will proceed to ARRAS on December 2nd to inspect its respective sector and take over billets etc.,

3. A Motor bus will report to O.C. 63rd Field Coy. R.E. at MAGNICOURT-SUR-CANCHE about noon December 2nd. O.C. 64th Field Coy. will make his own arrangements.

4. Guides for advanced parties of 63rd and 90th Coys. will be at C.R.E's office DUISANS (L 8 c 57) on December 2nd.

5. O.C. 63rd Field Coy. will see that all accounts for pickets etc., cut by him in Reserve Area are settled and will send handing over notes of works in hand to this office.

6. O.C. 64th Field Coy. will send handing over notes of works in hand to this office.

7. H.Q., R.E., 9th Division will move from ROELLECOURT to DUISANS on December 5th.

Issued at

7-30 p.m.

Lieut: R.E.,
Adjutant 9th Division.

Copies to.

    No. 1. 63rd Field Coy. R.E.
    No. 2. 64th Field Coy. R.E.
    No. 3. 90th Field Coy. R.E.
    No. 4. C.R.E. 35th Division.
    No. 5. 9th Division.
    No. 6 War Diary.
    No. 7 Office.

MARCH & RELIEF TABLE.

Date.	Unit.	From.	To.	
Dec. 3rd.	64th Field Coy. R.E.	SIMENCOURT.	Inf. Barracks Rue QUATRE CROSSES, ARRAS.	To relieve 204th Field Coy. R.E. in J Sector. Arriving after dark.
	90th Field Coy. R.E.	MANICOURT-SUR-CANCHE.	- ditto -	To relieve 205th Field Coy. R.E. in K Sector. Arriving after dark.
Dec. 4th.	204th Field Coy. R.E.	ARRAS.	"	} Moving before daylight.
	205th Field Coy. R.E.	ARRAS.	"	
	83rd Field Coy. R.E.	MANICOURT-SUR-CANCHE.	Rue de CHANOINES Brewery.	To relieve 203rd Field Coy. R.E. in I Sector. Arriving after dark.
Dec. 5th.	203rd Field Coy. R.E.	ARRAS.	.	Moving before daylight.

TRANSPORT LINES.

Dec. 3rd.	64th Field Coy. R.E.		DUISANS.	
Dec. 3rd.	90th Field Coy. R.E.		PUISANS.	
Dec. 4th.	83rd Field Coy. R.E.		LOUEZ.	

Jan - March 1917

Army Form C. 2118.

WAR DIARY
or
INTELLIGENCE SUMMARY.

(Erase heading not required.)

64th Field Company R.E.

January 1917

Place	Date	Hour	Summary of Events and Information	Remarks and references to Appendices
ARRAS	1		Rest day, no parties	
	2-5		Work continued	
	6		All four entrances of Arrowed Belttra started	
	7		New cut completed	
	9 to 10		Infantry reliefs; no parties	
	11		"C" Work Station completed	
			Work started on Station at head of SPRING TRAMWAY. A Work TMB completed. Repairs to TMB OFF JULY AVENUE taken in hand. A truckload of Stokes bombs exploded on to October Tramway. Mains blown down about 50' of trunk. New rail laid on track.	
	13		cleared by 11.30 am. next morning.	
			Lt SWAIN RE (T) arrived on a "Cook's Tour".	
	15		Work started out Pday Pivoers on spur of MARCH AVENUE and diversion to avoid "Dead Man Corner". Bar shaft of Belttra to left.	
	17		Rest day; no parties	
	19		Capt PD Tolpin clearing to a Kimberley course at Bridge School ARE. Lt SWAIN to Coy. Work started on Gunnar Station.	

Army Form C. 2118.

WAR DIARY
or
INTELLIGENCE SUMMARY.
(Erase heading not required.)

Place	Date	Hour	Summary of Events and Information	Remarks and references to Appendices
	20		2. Staff to AUBIGNY for the Base. D Coy furnish working party MARCH avenue by order of Divn	Snow fallen
	21		Work started on M.G. Emplacement in Railway Embankment in I Sector. This enfilades	4 two feet.
			the German lines in G.12 and G.18.	
	23		Repairs to July T.M.B. completed. Repairs to damaged dugout in Trench 89 completed.	
	25		I.N.C.O. and one man hit by rifle grenade at Spring Station. No parties.	
	29		D Coy furnish men working party on HTM. hand of October Tramway. B Coy onto HTM. emplacement	
			in J 2 sub section. Work started on OP. Archway in Sucre.	
	30		Spring Station completed.	
	31		It return to Bridges School, Aire. Bin chandon of Blattie completed. OP Archway completed.	

The hard prolonged frost has frozen up all the pipe line. When the thaw comes
there will be very large falls of earth in all the trenches.

N. Woolwin Captain.
O.C. 54 ⁂ C, R.E.

2/2/17

SMALL "A" FRAMES

REASONS FOR THEIR ADOPTION.

Owing to the destructive effect of hostile Trench Mortar fire the most suitable form of revetment for the front line is a sandbag wall.

No sandbag wall will stand for long without a proper foundation.

The churned-up state of the ground in the front line makes it impossible to obtain this by digging only. The best way of obtaining such a foundation is by the use of Small "A" Frames and corrugated iron.

In addition the Small "A" Frames and corrugated iron provide a drain for the trench, and support for the duckboards.

NOTES ON PLACING THE FRAMES IN POSITION.

It is essential that all the following rules be rigidly adhered to in revetting with these frames.

1. Each sheet of corrugated iron must overlap the next by six inches.
2. A frame must come opposite the centre of each overlap.
3. Another frame must come in the centre of each sheet.
4. The corrugated iron must come right down to the bottom of the frames.
5. All the earth and mud must be excavated from between the frames: this forms a drain under the duckboards.
6. The earth must be well rammed down behind the corrugated iron — especially at the very bottom.
7. The first course of sandbags must be kept three inches back from the edge of the corrugated iron so that, when the pressure of the other courses comes, they will not bulge over the edge of the corrugated iron.

2.1.1917.

C.G. WOOLNER, Captain.
O.C. 64th Coy., R.E.

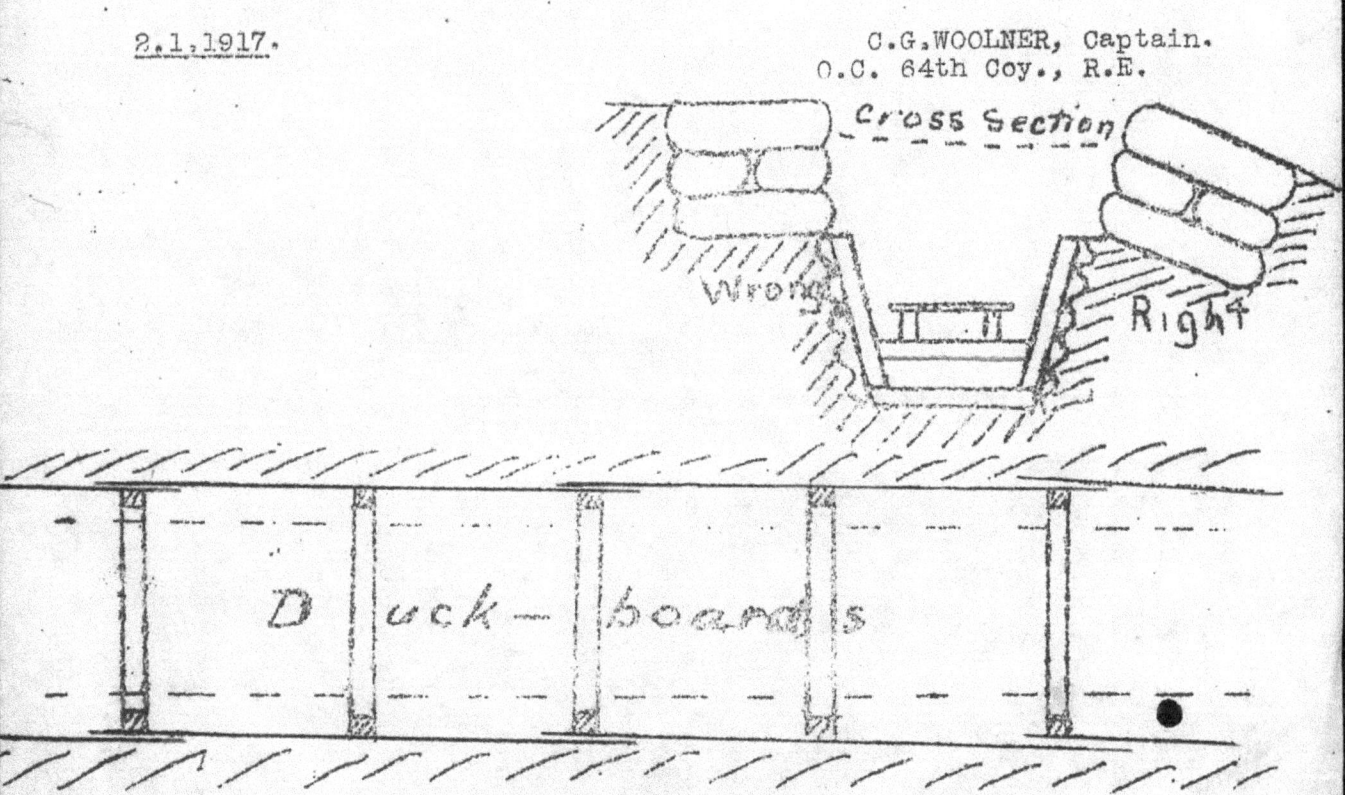

Army Form C. 2118.

WAR DIARY
or
INTELLIGENCE SUMMARY.   64th Field Coy, R.E.
(Erase heading not required.)

February 1917

Vol 2

Place	Date	Hour	Summary of Events and Information	Remarks and references to Appendices
ARRAS	2		Rest day. No work.	
	3		No. 11 M.G. dugout completed. Capt Clarry returned from Arras.	
	4		Started putting from places on Stn. Tramway	
	6		Started work on mess. ST. NICHOLAS GATE habitable for the company.	
	8		Started work on Trench O.P.s for R.F.A. and T.M.Bde. Started new pipe line for R.F.A. in ST. NICHOLAS	
	9		Started work on Lathes O.P.s for R.F.A. in ARRAS & BLANGY	
	10		Rest day. No work.	
	11		Started work on improvements to M.S. dugout behind Bilworks. Trade on position adjacent at No. 7 M.S. (Cofruiti Avenue).	
	12		A Co. Pinsen started reclamation. JULY AVE. work of candleworks. Halahon returning from ARRAS.	
	13		Capt Wootten left for Fd. Co. Commanders Course at GHQ School MEPARCQ.	
	14		McCay Pioneers found it almost impossible to dig from 2/feet into the ground.	
	16		Headline of Company moved from DUISANS to ETRUN. Horses accommodated in the open.	

Army Form C. 2118.

WAR DIARY
or
INTELLIGENCE SUMMARY.
(Erase heading not required.)

Instructions regarding War Diaries and Intelligence Summaries are contained in F. S. Regs., Part II. and the Staff Manual respectively. Title pages will be prepared in manuscript.

Place	Date	Hour	Summary of Events and Information	Remarks and references to Appendices
	17			
	18		Prisoners started on 2nd or 2'TM emps. Sites near TUNEArme a trench to act as assembly trench & subsequently 1st battery position. Company voting.	
	19		20 boys from South African Bn employed attached to Coy for when popular in ST NICHOLAS. Started two coys of A.T. Regn forming labs in Jone Avenue Tat 20/- chalk or 40/- brown permian in S.T homo	
	20		Commenced removing barracades in BLANGY Road & resuming part Mo Rouen bloating trench thro' Candle Factory into food vaults	
	21		Sect 63 "CORE attached/unknown 2 TM emp.	
	23		Only 50 men available from Brigade owing to their having carried the trenches to fall in average 2.18" inches of chalk on duckboards. Trenches in chalk should be attend S/hards apparently to allow of small falls but blocking for duckboards.	
	24		Capt-C/G. Wortner R.E. Works Company & CAULDWELL R.E. attached to coy from SME CHATHAM. Handed on Workshops to 1st Division.	
	25		20 men of dupont platoon marched to their Rgl- A/o Po started attending MIMOCH Ame wounded.	

Army Form C. 2118.

WAR DIARY
or
INTELLIGENCE SUMMARY.
(Erase heading not required.)

Place	Date	Hour	Summary of Events and Information	Remarks and references to Appendices
	26		Post out of ground lath, woodwork and digging moved again Company section. Took on Pioneer workshop.	

Magn Greeve
Capt RE.

O.O. 64th Fd. COY. R.E.

WAR DIARY or INTELLIGENCE SUMMARY

Army Form C. 2118.

MARCH 1917 **64/1/Co 12E** Sheet No 1 Vol 23

Place	Date	Hour	Summary of Events and Information	Remarks and references to Appendices
MARAS	2/3		"C" Coy Pioneers continued to work on SPRING TRAMWAY. Front falls gently down daily.	
	3/3		Underage men of South African Bde left to rejoin their regiments.	
	6/3		The frost appears to have at last gone. 2ft into the ground all unmetalled trenches fall in gradually as the thaw increases. To the depth of the frost 4 Pioneer platoons from 26th Bde attached to company for work on Bde Battle HQ's Blangy Road Battalion HQ's and 2" TM Emplacements. Company scouts returned to the right half of the divisional front is from NEWCUT to the river.	
	8/3		Stairwell to "B" on component part dugouts for 2" TM emplacement. Emplacement himselves completed. (18 on company front.) Artillery trenches & bridges across trenches commenced.	
	12/3		Owing to heavy rain the trenches particularly unrevetted CTs have fallen in to the depth of the frost which now appears to be out of the ground. A + B Coy's Pioneers taken off TM Emplacement of Tramway to dig-out MAY & AUGUST AVENUES. 1 Section started revets FEBRUARY AVENUE with Frames & C.I.	

Army Form C. 2118.

WAR DIARY
or
INTELLIGENCE SUMMARY.
(Erase heading not required.)

Place	Date	Hour	Summary of Events and Information	Remarks and references to Appendices
	15/3		Company Rostens. Two of the four Pioneer platoons returned to their regiments.	
	17/3		M's 24 dugout connected with no 25. Tunnel complete.	
	19/3		Dugouts for hirsh OP's completed with slates on camouflage. OP's themselves. Section 63rd ME started work of No 12 dugout enlargin for Battalion HQ.	
	20/3		Bn OP. in White House complete.	
	23/3		Four Tunnel OP's complete. Russian platoons of J. Seaforth & 10th A+SH attached to Coy. 10R killed.	
	24/3		Workshops & Ammunition recesses for HTM in Julep May. 26th Bde HTM completed.	
	25/3		Pilegie OP. completed.	
	27/3		All Tunnel OP's finished exception at April.	
	29/3		Ammunition recesses Jul & May HTM complete.	
	30/3		Workshop & Ammn recesses for HTM in Spin Tramway. also splinter proofs for 26th Bde Stokes Ambn in April.	
	31/3		Reconstruction of old French pontoon bridge (St Nicholas) for foot transport. No 14 dugout completed.	

D.S. Malcolm Major RE
OC 6th Coy RE

2/4/17

9th Division

64th Field Coy.
Royal Engineers
April 1917

WAR DIARY
or INTELLIGENCE SUMMARY

Army Form C. 2118.

64th Field Company R.E.

April 1917

Vol 2 4

Place	Date	Hour	Summary of Events and Information	Remarks and references to Appendices
ARRAS	1.		Works continued. No. 2 Section constructing shelters for themselves at G.22.b.41.85. Two sections resting. No. 3 & 4 Sections moved into Caen in St NICHOLAS	
	3.		Water point at S.A. Bde. H.Q. completed. Shelters complete for Stokes bombs. H.Q. & No. 1 Sec. moved into Caen.	
St NICHOLAS	4.		Lt Parker wounded (at duty). Attached now to 9th D.A.C. reinforcement unit.	
	5.		No. 1 Section taken to site & preparing site to bridge for assembly work. No. 4 Section working on artillery track was much harassed by persistent shelling. Lt Carter sent made to work in no mans land. Owing to full moon	
	6.		Lt Carter succeeded in completing blowing of assembly hole for first mean of S.A. Bde.	
	7.		Sgt Milne severely wounded by a short from our own guns. He had great hard work of No. 4 Section Bridge on artillery track which has been hit by shells was replaced. Second bridge on S.A. Bde. H.Q. complete.	
	8.		Infantry bridge successfully placed in position after dark by No. 1 Section. Orders issued for attack at 5.30 am tomorrow.	Appen. A & B
	9.		Div. attacked at 5.30 am all objectives captured according to time-table. Little opposition encountered	

Army Form C. 2118.

WAR DIARY
or
INTELLIGENCE SUMMARY.
(Erase heading not required.)

Instructions regarding War Diaries and Intelligence Summaries are contained in F.S. Regs. Part II. and the Staff Manual respectively. Title pages will be prepared in manuscript.

Place	Date	Hour	Summary of Events and Information	Remarks and references to Appendices
ST. NICHOLAS	9 (cont.)		beyond BLUE LINE so that N°2 Section & Pioneer Platoon 5th Cameron had no difficulty in constructing strong point behind BROWN LINE. Work started 3 pm. Section recalled about 10.30 pm. N°3 3rd Section left at 9.15 am. to work on FAMPOUX road through BLANGY. 3 Platoons D Coy 9th Seaforths (Pioneers) started on track from FEBRUARY SAPHEAD to cross roads at western end BLANGY. Lt Cauthon reconnoitred the footpaths as far as BLUE LINE, bridge at BLANGY LOCK, bridge at H.S.C. 0.0.0, or (for change in landmarks) and HERSIN FARM (for water). I. Paton reconnoitred bridge at BLANGY and ATHIES. N°1 Section learn to mention road in BLANGY. Further reconnaissance of road by O.C. at 6.30 pm.	Appendix C Appendix A Appendices E, F, G Appendices H, J. Appendix K
	10	7.15 pm	3rd Section for work on road. Reconnaissance of road to FAMPOUX. Lt Cauthon reconnoitred for materials. 3 pm N°1 Section for work on road. N°2 do. at 4 pm.	Appendix L Appendix M
	11		Work on road. N°s 1 + 2 Sections men to billets in BLANGY. Headline moved to G.16.d.4.3.	Appendix N
BLANGY	12		Work on road. N°s 3 + 4 Sections moved to billets in BLANGY. HQ to chateau G.15.b.9.5.10	Appendix O
	13		Reconnaissance of footpaths by Lt Cauthon. Reconnaissance of Pump Station in ATHIES & footpath by Lt Cauthon. Work on road. 26th Bde taken over tactics.	Appendix P & R Appendix S

Army Form C. 2118.

WAR DIARY
or
INTELLIGENCE SUMMARY.

(Erase heading not required.)

Instructions regarding War Diaries and Intelligence Summaries are contained in F. S. Regs., Part II. and the Staff Manual respectively. Title pages will be prepared in manuscript.

Place	Date	Hour	Summary of Events and Information	Remarks and references to Appendices
BETHUNE	14 + 15		Lt Allen taped out support line for 26th Bde. Tent working parties on the tapes.	Appen. T&U
	16 + 17		Work on road. Lt Walker wounded. 26th Bde relieved by 51st Divn.	Appen. V&W
	18		Work on road. No. 4 Sec moved to shelters on BLUE LINE.	Appen. X
	19		Work on road. No. 1 Sec moved to shelters on BLUE LINE	Appen. Y
	20		Work on road. No. 2 Sec moved to shelters on BLUE LINE	Appen. Z
			Work on roads.	
ARRAS	21		63rd & 64th Coys exchange billets. Coy moved to ARRAS at 9.30 a.m. Horse lines to St Nicholas bridge.	Appen. AA & BB
	22		Rest. Kit inspection etc.	
	23		Attack at Huits an Bj. by 37th Divn. Nos 1+2 Sections paraded at 5.0 a.m. to work on the road through FAMPOUX. Started work after reconnaissance about 10.0 a.m. Withdrawn about 2.30 p.m. Could only do about 3/4 hr. frightful work owing to heavy shelling. 3 & 4 Sections paraded at 11.0 a.m. as second shift but were out route without working as shelling was too heavy. Two long craters cleared and offroad west of FAMPOUX.	Appendix CC
	24 . 25		Rest. Gas respirator drill etc. Lt Allen to Hospital (sick)	
	26		Rest.	

WAR DIARY
or
INTELLIGENCE SUMMARY.

Army Form C. 2118.

Place	Date	Hour	Summary of Events and Information	Remarks and references to Appendices
ARRAS	27		Company carries out the orders of CE XVIIth Corps vice 63rd Coy R.E. Nos 1, 2 were seen on road	Appendix DD + EE, FF
	28 + 29		Work on works under CE XVIIth Corps.	
H.7.b.cent	30		Company relieves 152nd Coy R.E. in railway cutting H.7.b. central. House buis to G.16.6.05.10	Appen GG.

General :-

(1) Instead of digging an assault trench within 200' of the German front line a series of large holes were blown. These were often required within 20 ft. Ammonal charges placed in small holes at. They were blown by 20 lb. Ammonal charges placed in small holes 4'6" deep + tamped. Electric firing failed owing to shells cutting the leads faster than they could be mended. Each charge had to be fired by safety fuze. These holes were blown three nights before the attack +, being inconspicuous, were not registered on by the enemy, as a trench most certainly would have been. It might be better to have the charges 5'6" instead of 4'6".

(2) The great amount of general done on the works were amply repaid by—
The importance of building in a service bottom of large trench, hand packed on counter, from the the start was very evident.

A. M. Poolin Major RE
OC 6th Coy RE

2/5/17

D. 9/2.
SECRET.

Appendix A

9th Divisional Engineers Operation Order No. 1.

Reference 1/10,000 map ARRAS.

1. The attack of which the plan was furnished in Preliminary Instructions No. 3 will take place on April 9th. Zero will be at 5.30 a.m.

2. Battle positions will be occupied by 4 a.m.

3. Reports of occupation of battle positions from Field Coys. (less 63rd Field Coy.) and 9th Seaforths (Pnrs) with a statement of distribution of units will be furnished to ETRUN on completion of forming up.

C R Hearn

Lieut-Colonel, R.E.
C.R.E., 9th Division.

H.Q.
9TH DIVISIONAL
ENGINEERS.
No.
Date 8/4/17.
11 a.m.

O.C. 63rd Field Coy. R.E.
O.C. 64th Field Coy. R.E.
O.C. 90th Field Coy. R.E.
O.C. 9th Seaforths (Pioneers).

Appendix B

ORDERS BY O.C. 64th FIELD COY. R.E.

General.

9th Division will attack on Z day, the 9th of April. Zero will probably be in the early morning.

No. 2 Section is placed at the disposal of G.O.C. 26th Brigade and will construct a supporting point near L'ABBAYETTE. Pioneer Platoon of 5th Camerons Highlanders will assist in this work and will move with No. 2 Section.

The remainder of 64th F'ld Coy will be employed on repairs to the ST NICHOLAS - ATHIES road between the head of FEBRUARY SAP and the BLUE LINE. D Company 9th Seaforth (Pioneers) will assist in this work.

DISPOSITIONS.

Every man in the Sections will parade for work except Section Cooks. At Zero Sections will be in the following positions, ready to move at 10 minutes notice:-

No. 2 Section (with Pioneer Platoon 5th Camerons) in shelters at the RAVELIN.

No. 1, 3 & 4 Sections in the cave

O.C. 64th Company will be at 26th Brigade Headquarters. FORESTIER REDOUBT.

O.C. No. 2 Section will keep in touch with 26th Brigade Headquarters from Zero onwards.

H.Q. of D Company Pioneers will be in dugouts west of OIL WORKS.

H.Q. of 9th and 526th (DURHAM) Field Coys of the 4th Division will be on the BLUE LINE.

EQUIPMENT.

Equipment for men going into action will be:-

Marching Order without packs (haversacks worn on the back - water bottles to be filled)

Box Respirators and Tube helmets.

Articles to be carried in haversack:-

Iron Rations, Waterproof Sheet, mess tin with remainder of days ration.

No 2 Section will carry in addition cap comforter and cardigan.

AMMUNITION.

50 rounds per man, except No 2 Section who will carry 100 rounds.

No 2 Section and Pioneer Platoon of 5th Camerons will carry 2 MILLS Bombs per man in their pockets. These will be collected in the supporting point at L'ABBAYETTE.

PACKS.

All packs (containing surplus kit) will be stacked by sections in their billets by Zero and left in charge of Section Cooks.

WOUNDED

Wounded men are not to discard arms and equipment unless wounds are so severe as to render men incapable of carrying them.

Slightly wounded men are not to leave work except by command of an officer.

Men are forbidden to escort wounded

comrades to the aid post.

Medical AID POST at the junction of SPRING and SUMMER TRAMWAYS.

Advanced Divisional DRESSING STATION at ST. NICHOLAS.

DOCUMENTS

All ranks are forbidden to carry any letters, papers, orders, maps, or sketches, which in the event of capture, would give information to the enemy.

TRANSPORT

Lieut Allen will remain at ETRUN. Three pontoon wagons, each loaded with 2 Artillery Bridges will be parked on Y/Z night at about G.16.d. central.

The teams, (2 Mules and 2 Horses each) with one spare pair and two spare drivers under 2/Cpl Ford will be stationed on the south bank of the River SCARPE near bridge No 3.

Drivers will carry iron rations and rations for Z day. Forage for Z and Z+1 days will be brought up on the wagons.

Pack Animals with Pack Saddlery will remain at ETRUN to bring up anything which may be required. All roads will probably be closed to wheeled transport.

REPORTS

Report to 26th Brigade Headquarters which will be in FORESTIER REDOUBT, until the BLUE LINE is captured when it will move up to PENIS. (G.18.b 25.25).

8/4/17

L.G. Woolven Major RE
O.C. 64th Cy RE

Appendix C

OC.
6th Field Coy RE.

Beg to report that I have started work on SUPPORTING POINT at L'ABBAYETTE, Map Ref. being ARRAS 51B N.W.3. H 14 beer 27.51.

Site approved by L⁺ GILES. M.G.C. 26ᵗʰ Brigade

Situation quiet. 4ᵗʰ Div Troops passing to BROWN LINE. No shelling.

R.J. Wander
Lt RE

3 pm
9/4/17

1755

May 1917
64 Field Co
Royal Engineers

Army Form C. 2118.

WAR DIARY
or
INTELLIGENCE SUMMARY.

64th Field Company

May 1917

(Erase heading not required.)

Place	Date	Hour	Summary of Events and Information	Remarks and references to Appendices
H7b.Central	1		Men making shelters for themselves. Officers & NCOs round the works & equipment to Divisional Shops	
	2		NCOs & 17 men went to Divisional Shops	
	3		No. 2 Sec. on fatigue for C.R.E. Remainder Working material for artillery dugouts	Appendix A
	4		Work started by Nos. 1,3,4th Sections on deep dugouts in battery position. Working in two shifts 4 am — 11:30 am and noon to 8 pm. Strelee superadum infantry parties on wiring & consolidation of EFFIE	
	10		Working moving shaft; 32 shafts now all completed to soft. Of cover. Company relieved by 77th Field Coy marched to Avenue des St NICHOLAS huts till 6:45 pm then marched to Y Huts	Appendix B & C
Y Huts	11		Resting	
Moncheaux	12		Marched to MONCHEAUX starting at 7:15 am & arriving about 1·10 pm	Appendix D
La Thieuloye	13		Marched to LA THIEULOYE starting at 5:00 am arriving about 9:30 am	Appendix E
	14		Resting	
	15 to 30		Training (see Programme)	
	31		Inspection by C.R.E. 11:30 am	Appendix F & G

31/5/17

A.M. Mahoun Major R.E.
O.C. 64th Co. R.E.

"A" Form.
MESSAGES AND SIGNALS.

Army Form C.2121 (in pads of 100).

TO	O.C. 63rd Field Coy. R.E.	O.C. 9th Seaforths
	O.C. 64th Field Coy. R.E.	(Pioneers).
	O.C. 90th Field Coy. R.E.	

Sender's Number.	Day of Month.	In reply to Number.	
D.71	30th		A A A

63rd Field Coy. R.E., and 90th Field Coy. R.E. will be at the disposal of 26th and 27th Brigades respectively for the making of Brigade and Battalion H.Q. as may be required aaa 64th Field Coy. R.E. to work for R.F.A, Tracks etc. aaa Two Companies of 9th Seaforths to stand by for night work aaa Orders for remainder of 9th Seaforths will be issued later aaa

Appendix A

From C.R.E., 9th Division.

Capt. R.E.
(Z) Adjt. 9th Divl. Engrs.

D. 107.

SECRET.

Appendix B

O.C. 63rd Field Coy. R.E.
O.C. 64th Field Coy. R.E.
O.C. 90th Field Coy. R.E.
O.C. 9th Seaforths (Pioneers).

The following Companies and Pioneers will take over from Field Coys. R.E. and Pioneers 9th Division on or about 9/10th inst.

78th Field Coy.	from 63rd Field Coy.
93rd Field Coy.	from 90th Field Coy.
77th Field Coy.	from 64th Field Coy.
7th Yorks & Lancs	from 9th Seaforths (Pnrs).

All these units of the 17th Divn. have been instructed to get into touch with the unit which they are relieving. Each of the relieving units has been instructed to prospect the work.

Acknowledge.

Captain, R.E.
Adjt. 9th Divl. Engrs.

6/5/17.

SECRET.

Appendix C

C.R.E. OPERATION ORDER NO. D. 125.

1. Moves of R.E. Units of 9th Division will be carried out as follows:-

(a) Evening of 10th inst. 63rd Co. R.E. will march to "Y" Huts.

(b) Evening of 10th inst. 64th Co. R.E. will march to "Y" Huts.

(c) Night of 9/10th inst. 90th Co. R.E. will march to ARRAS.

(d) May 11th 63rd Co. R.E. will march from "Y" Huts to MONCHEAUX.

(e) May 11th 64th Co. R.E. will march from "Y" Huts to MONCHEAUX.

(f) May 10th 90th Co. R.E. will proceed by tactical train from ARRAS to MONCHEAUX, under arrangements with 27th Brigade.

NOTE. Tactical train arrangements will be notified by 9th Divn. "Q" to 27th Brigade.

2. Billets in MONCHEAUX for Field Cos. R.E. are being arranged by this office.

3. ACKNOWLEDGE.

E.K. Hearn
Lieut.Col

9/5/17.

~~Captain~~, R.E.
~~Adjt~~. 9th Divl. Engrs.

O.C. 63rd Field Coy. R.E.
O.C. 64th Field Coy. R.E.
O.C. 90th Field Coy. R.E.
C.R.E., XVII Divn. (For information).
War Diary.
File.

SECRET.
Copy No. 12

Appendix D

26TH. BRIGADE OPERATION ORDER NO.113.

Reference/   10-5-17.
LENS sheet 11 - 1/100,000.

1. (a) The 26th. Brigade will move on May 12th. to the BAILLEUL-AUX-CORNAILLES area, in accordance with the attached march table.
   (b) The 4th. Bn. S.A.Infantry, 63rd. & 64th. Field Companies R.E., will move under the orders of the G.O.C., 26th. Brigade.

2. The following distances will be kept on the march:-

   400 yards between battalions.
   200 yards between Companies.
   100 yards between transport of battalions.

3. Normal halts will be observed during the march.

4. Lorries for surplus kits and Stokes mortars will be supplied.
   Their distribution will be notified later.

5. A bus for billeting parties will be at Brigade H.Q., 'Y' Huts, at 7.am. on May 12th.

6. First line transport and baggage wagons will accompany units.

7. Brigade H.Q., will close at 'Y' Huts at 8.am. on May 12th. and will re-open at BAILLEUL-AUX-CORNAILLES on the same date.

8. ACKNOWLEDGE.

                                                                           Captain,
                                                                     Brigade Major,
Issued at 1.pm.   26th. Infantry Brigade.

Copies to 1. 8th. Black Watch.
              2. 7th. Seaforth Highlanders.
              3. 5th. Cameron Highlanders.
              4. 10th. A. & S. Hlrs.
              5. 26th. M.G.Company.
              6. 26th. T.M.Battery.
              7. 26th. Bde. Signals.
              8. 26th. Bde. Tspt. Officer.
              9. 26th. Bde. Supply Officer.
           10. 4th. Bn. S.A. Infantry.
           11. 63rd. Field Coy. R.E.
           12. 64th. Field Coy. R.E.
         x13. 9th. Division G.
           14. 9th. Division Q.
           15. A.D.M.S., 9th. Division.
           16. 105 Coy. A.S.C.
           17. 27th. Brigade.
           18. S.African Brigade.
           19. Town Major, 'Y' Huts.
           20. Staff Captain.
           21. War Diary.
           22. File.

MARCH TABLE FOR March 12th.

ITEM.	UNIT.	FROM.	TO.	ROUTE.	TIME TO PASS STARTING POINT.	REMARKS.
1.	63rd. Fd. Coy. R.E.	'Y' Huts.	MONCHEAUX.	Main ARRAS-ST POL Rd. SAVY-PENIN-MAIZIERES-GOUY-EN-TERNOIS.	7.am.	To march under Officers Commanding after clearing starting point.
2.	64th. Fd. Coy. R.E.	'Y' Huts.	do.	do.	7.15.am.	
3.	4th. S.A. Infy.	'Y' Huts.	MONCHY BRETON.	Main ARRAS-ST POL Rd. TINCQUES-CHELERS.	7.30.am.	
4.	26th Brigade H.Q.	'Y' Huts.	BAILLEUL-AUX-CORNAILLES.	Main ARRAS-ST POL Rd. TINCQUES-X roads 700X N. of U in HAUT BARLET FARM.	8.am.	
5.	26th T.M.Baty.	'Y' Huts.	do.	do.	8.5.am.	
6.	10th. A. & S. Hrs.	'Y' Huts.	do.	do.	8.10.am.	
7.	8th. Black Watch.	'Y' Huts.	AVERDOINGT.	Main ARRAS-ST POL Rd. TINCQUES-X Rds. N. of first E in LE QUESNEL.	8.40.am.	
8.	7th. Seaforth Highrs.	'Y' Huts.	MAIZIERES.	Main ARRAS-ST POL Rd. Savy-PENIN.	9.10.am.	
9.	5th. Cameron Highrs.	'Y' Huts.	PENIN.	Main ARRAS-ST POL Rd. SAVY.	9.40.am.	
10.	26th M.G.Coy.	'Y' Huts.	PENIN.	As for item 9.	10.10.am.	

D. 140/1.

Appendix E

O.C. 63rd Field Coy. R.E.
O.C. 64th Field Coy. R.E.
O.C. 90th Field Coy. R.E.

9th Division R.E. Operation Order.

1. 63rd 64th and 90th Field Cos. will be clear of MONCHEAUX by 11 a.m. tomorrow and will proceed to following destinations:-

(a) 63rd Field Coy. will be informed direct by 26th Inf. Brigade as to their destination and when and where billeting representative should report.

(b) 64th Field Coy. will be informed by S.A. Brigade as to their destination and billeting representative should report to Staff Capt. S.A. Brigade at Bde. H.Q. ORLENCOURT at 10 a.m. tomorrow.

(c) 90th Field Co. R.E. will be informed direct by 27th Inf. Brigade as to their destination and when and where billeting representative should report.

(2) H.Q. R.E. will move to ROLLECOURT.

3. Os.C. Field Cos. R.E. will make their own arrangements as regards time of departure and route taken provided they are clear of MONCHEAUX by 11-0 a.m. on 13/5/17.

4. O.C. 63rd Field Co. R.E. will provide a draught animal to move the Maltese Cart attached to H.Q. R.E. This animal should be at H.Q. R.E. at 9-30 a.m.

5. ACKNOWLEDGE.

Captain, R.E.
Adjt. 9th Divl. Engrs.

12/5/17.

10-5-1917.

Appendix F

PROGRAMME OF TRAINING

64th FIELD COY. R.E.   WEEK ENDING MAY 26th 1917

LA THEULOYE (N.30.d.5. sheet 56c)

Day.	General Nature of Training		Remarks
	7.0 – 7.30 am.	9-30 am – 1-0 pm.	2-0 – 6-0 pm.
SUNDAY.			
MONDAY.			
TUESDAY.			
WEDNESDAY.			
THURSDAY.			
FRIDAY.			
SATURDAY.			

23-5-1917.

Appendix G

PROGRAMME OF TRAINING

64th FIELD COY. R.E. at **LA THIEULOYE.** (n.30 a 6.9 Sheet 36ᴮ ¹⁄₄₀₀₀₀.)   Week Ending June 2nd 1917.

GENERAL NATURE OF TRAINING.

Day.	7·0 – 7·30 a.m.	9·30 a.m. – 1·0 p.m.	5·0 – 6·0 p.m.	Remarks.
SUNDAY.	—	Church Parade		
MONDAY.	Physical Training			
TUESDAY.	do	Route march		
WEDNESDAY.	do			
THURSDAY.	do			
FRIDAY.	do			
SATURDAY.	do	Route march		

1755

June 1917
64 Field Co
Royal Engineers

Army Form C. 2118.

WAR DIARY
or
INTELLIGENCE SUMMARY.

64th Field Company R.E.

JUNE 1917

Vol 26

(Erase heading not required.)

Instructions regarding War Diaries and Intelligence Summaries are contained in F.S. Regs., Part II. and the Staff Manual respectively. Title pages will be prepared in manuscript.

Place	Date	Hour	Summary of Events and Information	Remarks and references to Appendices
	1		Coy. marched at 7.10 a.m. to LIGNY-ST FLOCHEL to entrain for ARRAS. Arrived ST LAURENT BLANGY about 3.0 p.m. Transport arrived about 5.0 p.m.	Appendix A
	2		Work as follows:- 1 Section maintenance of bridges in H.24 & 2 Section running pontoon service on R. SCARPE from ATHIES to "G" Bridge (H.24 central) and CRUMP WHARF (H & 25 B).	
	3		1 Section on repair to footpath & haulage waterway clean. 2/Lt Cauthen temporarily attached to 96th Coy R.E.	
	5		75 Infantry attached for heavy pontoon. 2nd Lt. fixed on section for work on Divisional Swimming Bath (ST. NICHOLAS WORK), Sewer on FAMPOUX road, and watering. R.E. dump at ATHIES.	
	6		Work started on CUTLERY WHARF (H.24 & 25.B.60)	
	9		Capt. Clancey to Y Huts to instruct 110 Infantry in swimming. 2/Lt Cauthen from 96th Coy R.E. 8th new strand complete at ATHIES. New R.E. dump completed.	
	12		Work handed over to 9th Coy R.E. (except pontoon service).	Appendix B
	13		Capt. Clancey from Y Huts. Pontoon service handed over to 9th Coy R.E. at noon.	
	14		Coy. under orders of C.E. XVII Corps. Working party exempt from 4 Section for work	Appendix C
	15		3 subalterns for work.	

23531 Wt.W23H/1454 700,000 5/15 D.D.&L. A.D.S.S./Forms/C. 2118.

Army Form C. 2118.

WAR DIARY
or
INTELLIGENCE SUMMARY.
(Erase heading not required.)

Place	Date	Hour	Summary of Events and Information	Remarks and references to Appendices
	16-30		Work on roads. 3 sorties per day.	

1/7/17

N Mashingham Lt.
O.C. 6th Coy.

Appendix A   SECRET.

9th DIVISIONAL ENGINEERS OPERATION ORDER NO. D.154.

Ref. 1/100,000   LENS.
     1/20,000   Trench Maps
                    51.b.N.W.
                    51.c.N.E.
     1/10,000   PLOUVAIN.

1. The 9th Division (less Artillery) will relieve the 51st Division (less Artillery) in the Right Subsector XVIIth Corps on May 31st/1st June and 1st/2nd June.

   Relief will be completed by 4 a.m. June 2nd.

2. The 26th Infantry Brigade will relieve the 154th Infantry Brigade in the right Subsector on the night May 31st/June 1st., the 27th Infantry Brigade will relieve the 153rd Infantry Brigade in the left Subsector on the night 1st/2nd June. The S. African Brigade will be in Divisional Reserve.

   Headquarters of Brigades will be situated as follows:-

       26th Brigade   Railway Cutting H.14.a.1.9.
       27th Brigade   H.16.d.1.7.
       S.A. Brigade   1 Rue d'Ancre, ARRAS.

3. (a) The Boundary between 9th and 34th Divisions will be:-

   Junction of CROOK and CHAPLIN Trenches (inclusive to 9th Division) - Communication trench from CALABAR to CUTE Trench at I.13.a.80.95. (exclusive to 9th Division) Junction of CAMEL and CADIZ Trenches at H.18.b.45.70 (inclusive to 9th Division) thence CAMEL Trench to 9th Division as far as road junction H.17.a.80.95 - thence SUNKEN ROAD to junction with GAVRELLE switch at H.10.d.75.55. thence to railway bridge H.8.c.0.0 and due West along grid line to old British front line at G.11.d.9.0.

   (b) The Boundary between 26th and 27th Brigades will on first taking over the line be the same as that between the 154th and 153rd Brigades. After completion of the relief on the 2nd June the boundary will be:-

   Junction of CRUSH Trench with the railway (inclusive to 27th Brigade) - Junction of CRETE and COLON Trenches (inclusive to 27th Brigade) - Junction of CUSP and CORFU Trenches I.13.c.7.1 (inclusive to 26th Brigade) - Junction of CORONA Trench and CORONA SUPPORT I.13.d.9.2 (inclusive to 26th Brigade) - and thence a line to the bend of the SUNKEN ROAD at I.14.c.5.4. (SHERIFF POST.)

   (c) Southern Boundary River SCARPE.

4. G.O.C. 9th Division will assume command at 10 a.m. 2nd June at which hour Divisional Headquarters will close at ROELLECOURT and open at G.16.b.7.7. (near CANDLE FACTORY.) H.Q., R.E. will be at 9th Div. H.Q.

(2).

5. Field Companies R.E. will move as follows:-

 63rd Field Coy. (dismounted personnel by bus, transport by road) to ARRAS on May 30th, to relieve 404th Field Coy. R.E. on same day.

 90th Field Coy. (dismounted personnel by bus, transport by road) to ARRAS on May 31st, to relieve 401st Field Coy. R.E. on same day.

 64th Field Coy. on June 1st (dismounted personnel by train - entrain at LIGNY-St.FLOCHEL, detrain at ARRAS; transport by road to ARRAS) to relieve 400th Field Coy. R.E. on same day.

 Each Field Coy. will send up an advance party early on the day before taking over, in order to go round the line. These advance parties will go up on cycles and will be in charge of an officer.

6. Horse Lines of Field Coys. and H.Q., R.E. will be at G.16.a.4.4.

7. Movements of 9th Division from ARRAS will be by road South of River SCARPE to BLANGY, thence across River SCARPE to Cross Roads G.18.c.5.4 and so to ATHIES.

 The road via ST NICHOLAS to ST LAURENT BLANGY has been allotted to the 17th and 34th Divisions.

8. ACKNOWLEDGE.

              Captain, R.E.
            Adjt. 9th Divl. Engrs.

28/5/17.
Issued at 2-30 PM

O.C. 63rd Field Coy. R.E.
O.C. 64th Field Coy. R.E.
O.C. 90th Field Coy. R.E.
C.R.E., 51st Division.
War Diary.
File.

S E C R E T.

APPENDIX.

ISSUED IN CONNECTION WITH 9th DIVL. ENGINEERS OPERATION ORDER NO. D.154.

1. **AMMUNITION.**
   S.A.A., Grenades, etc:-
   Main Divisional Dump.   BRASSERIE ST NICHOLAS.
   Advanced Divisional Dump.   H.13.b.6.5.
   Brigade Dumps.   H.17.c.1.5.
                                   H.18.d.2.5.
                                   H.23.b.5.5.
               Along sunken road through H.24.b.
                                   I.13.a.2.4.

   Note. Limbers can proceed by road as far as H.18.c.9.7. thence to Brigade Dump by hand.
   Pack Mules can proceed to Brigade Dump at H.24.d.6.8.
   Brigade transport will bring the stores required from Main Divisional Dump.
   Captain R.P.PERRIN will be in charge of Divisional Ammunition Dumps.

2. **WATER.**
   Water Head   H.13.b.
   Refilling Points for Carts and Bottles   G.16.b.8.1 and HERVIN FARM.
   Wells in FAMPOUX and ATHIES
   Water troughs for Horses:-
                                                   (G.13.d.2.6.
                                                   (G.13.d. & G.14.c.
                                                   (G.15.b.8.6.
                                                   (G.16.d.4.5.
                                                   (H.13.b.2.8.

3. **R.E. DUMPS.**
   Main Dump.   G.23.b.4.2 and February Circus
                                   ST NICHOLAS.
   Advanced Dump.   H.13.d.3.3.
   Barbed wire and screw Pickets. H.17.c.1.6.

4. **MEDICAL.**
   Main Dressing Station.   ~~HAUTE AVESNES~~ Deaf & Dumb Institute ARRAS
   Advanced Dressing Station.   ~~ST NICHOLAS.~~ L'ABBAYETTE
   Walking Wounded   ST NICHOLAS. G.16.b.1.1.

5. **BATHS.**   HOSPICE DES VIEILLARDS, ARRAS.
                                   CANDLE FACTORY.
                                   HERVIN FARM.

6. **SALVAGE DUMPS.**
   Main Dump.   ST NICHOLAS. G.16.d.3.7.
   Forward Dumps.   (OIL FACTORY.
                                   (L'ABBAYETTE.

7. **CEMETERIES.**
   ARRAS.   FAUBOURG D'AMIENS.
   ST NICHOLAS.   G.15.b.0.2.
   L'ABBAYETTE.   H.14.b.8.2.
   FAMPOUX.   H.23.b.7.4.

8. **21st MOBILE VET. SECTION.**   CANDLE FACTORY.

D.180/4.

S E C R E T.

Appendix B

O.C. 63rd Field Coy. R.E.
O.C. 64th Field Coy. R.E.
O.C. 90th Field Coy. R.E.
O.C. 9th Seaforths (Pioneers).
C.E. XVII Corps. (For information.)
9th Division (G) (" ")
9th Division (Q) (" ")
C.R.E. 4th Division (For information.)
A.D.M.S., 9th Division. (For infromation.)
War Diary.
File.

With Reference to 9TH DIVISIONAL ENGINEERS OPERATION ORDER D. 180 of 9/6/17.

Section 2. para. (e) should read as follows:-

63rd Field Coy. with transport will take over the Camp at present occupied by 21st West Yorks Regt. G.17.c.9.7., and 64th Field Coy. will remain in their present billets at G.18.c.5.8.

J. Cutley
Captain, R.E.
for C.R.E., 9th Division.

12/6/17.

D. 180/1.
S E C R E T.

O.C. 63rd Field Coy. R.E.
O.C. 64th Field Coy. R.E.
O.C. 90th Field Coy. R.E.
C.E., XVII Corps.
War Diary.
File.

ADDENDUM to 9TH DIVISIONAL ENGINEERS OPERATION
ORDER D.180 of 9/6/17.

63rd and 64th Field Coys. R.E. will come under the orders of C.E. XVII Corps from 5 a.m. on June 14th.

(signature)
Captain, R.E.
for C.R.E., 9th Division.

10/6/17.

D. 180.

S E C R E T.

O.C. 63rd Field Coy. R.E.
O.C. 64th Field Coy. R.E.
O.C. 90th Field Coy. R.E.
O.C. 9th Seaforths (Pioneers).
C.E. XVII Corps (For information.)
9th Division G. (For information.)
9th Division Q. (For information.)
C.R.E. 4th Division (For information.)
A.D.M.S., 9th Division. (For information.)
War Diary.
File.

9TH DIVISIONAL ENGINEERS OPERATION ORDER.

Ref. Map: ARRAS, Edition 6A.
           1/10,000.

1.   9th Division (less Artillery and two Field Coys. R.E.) will be relieved by 4th Division (less Artillery) in the Right Sector of XVII Corps front on the nights June 11/12th and 12/13th.

    Reliefs in Front Line to be completed by 4 a.m. on June 13th.

2.   Relief of Field Coys. R.E. and Pioneers will be as follows:-

(a)   406th Field Coy. R.E. will take over work from 90th Fld. Coy. R.E. in Left Sector on night 11/12th June. 406th Field Coy. will take over the billets at present occupied by 63rd Field Coy. R.E. in Railway Embankment H.13.b.95.15 on night June 12/13th.

(b)   526th (Durham) Field Coy. R.E. will take over work from the 63rd Field Coy. R.E. in the Right Sector on the night 12/13th June. 526th Field Coy. will take over the billets in Railway Triangle H.19.central occupied by 56th Field Coy. R.E.

(c)   9th Field Coy. R.E. will take over work from 64th Field Coy. R.E. on the 12th June. 9th Field Coy. will take over the billets at present occupied by 90th Field Coy. at G.24.a.8.6. on night June 12th. Infantry of 9th Division engaged in towing will be relieved at same time as 64th Coy. hand over work.

(d)   63rd, 64th and 90th Field Coys. will vacate their present Horse Lines at G.16.a.4.4. as these will be taken over by Field Coys. of 4th Division.

(e)   63rd and 64th Field Coys. with transport will take over the Camp at present occupied by 21st West Yorks Regt. G.17.c.9.7.

(f)   Dismounted personnel of 90th Field Coy. will proceed by

busses........

busses which leave ROUND POINT, ARRAS at 10 p.m. on the night of 11th June for MONCHY BRETON.

Transport will proceed by road under arrangements made by O.C. 90th Field Coy.

A representative of 90th Field Coy. will get into touch with 26th Infy. Brigade regarding arrangements for billeting at MONCHY BRETON.

(g) PIONEERS.

21st West Yorks (Pioneers) will take over from the 9th Seaforths (Pioneers) on June 12th.

Billets of 9th Seaforths (Pioneers) are at G.18.c.4.8. and Horse Lines at G.16.b.4.7.

Dismounted personnel of 9th Seaforths (Pioneers) will proceed by busses, which leave ROUND POINT, ARRAS at 6 p.m. on June 12th for AVERDOINGT.

Transport will proceed by road under arrangements made by O.C. 9th Seaforths (Pioneers).

(h) Parties at 9th Divn. R.E. Dumps will be relieved on 12th June by parties from 4th Divn.

3. Completion of relief will be reported to H.Q. R.E.

4. A.D.M.S., 9th Division will arrange with A.D.M.S. 4th Division regarding medical attention of Field Coys. R.E. (9th Divn.) left in the Line.

5. 63rd and 64th Field Coys. R.E. will be rationed by the Company of 9th Divl. Train which will be left behind for the purpose of supplying R.A. units.

6. ACKNOWLEDGE.

Captain, R.E.
for C.R.E., 9th Division.

9/6/17.

Appendix C

C.E. 17th Corps.
No. CE.25/C/4
Date 13.6.17

O.C. 64th Field Coy. R.E.

From morning of the 14th instant, when you come under the Corps for work on roads, you will take over the maintenance and repair of the main road South of the SCARPE Canal, from the East of the railway arches at H.19.b.4.6. through FEUCHY Village up to the level crossing at H.23.b.7.3. South of FAMPOUX Village. Also the cross roads up to the South bank of the Canal at FEUCHY and FAMPOUX.

The work up to and including the roadway through FEUCHY Village will consist in widening the existing road formation and spreading metalling for a full width of 18 feet; also in completing the drainage, filling in any doubtful trenches or dug-outs, and preparing a level marching berm along one side.

It should be possible to work throughout this length in scattered parties during the day. Beyond FEUCHY, however, where the road comes under direct observation of the enemy, work can only be carried out during day time on dull days when visibility is bad, and in small parties.

Stone will be sent out by lorry and horse wagon as required, and for this arrangements should be made direct with 2nd Lieut. BANCROFT, R.E., Field Engineer. Surplus stone may be dumped at a site to be selected in the neighbourhood of FEUCHY.

Colonel,
for C.E., XVII Corps.

13/6/17.

Copy to:-

2nd Lieut. BANCROFT, R.E., for information and guidance.

1755

July 1917

Vol 27
Army Form C. 2118.

WAR DIARY
or
INTELLIGENCE SUMMARY

64th Field Coy. R.E.   JULY 1917

Place	Date	Hour	Summary of Events and Information	Remarks and references to Appendices
ST LAURENT - BLANGY	1		Lt A.E. Rankin MC posted to 63rd Coy R.E. 3 sections on roads.	Appendix A
	2		3 Sections on cleaning canal. 1 Section with Inf. on roads.	Appendix B, C
	4		Lt Plaskitt to 63rd Coy R.E.	
	12		Lt Caithness returned from leave. Work on canal finished except for 1/2 Section work.	Appendix D
	16		gnrs. Sections on roads.	
			Lt Prid on leave to England.	
	19		Company marches to FOSSEUX	Appendix E
FOSSEUX	20		Resting.	
	21		No 2 Section Lt Ince to EQUANCOURT for work on new Divl. HQ. Coy inoculated.	
	24		Transport left at 3.15 am for ABLAINZEVELLE. Company marched 11.15 pm to entrain at SAULTY STATION.	Appendix F, G
	25		Detrained BAPAUME 6.15 am. Marched to RUYAULCOURT. Transport arrived at —	
			YPRES from ABLAINZEVELLE.	
RUYAULCOURT	26		Relieved 503rd Coy R.E. 3 Sections moved to forward billets in HAVRINCOURT WOOD	
	27		Sections make reconnaissance advanced billets. Officer NCO.s round the trenches.	
	29		Arthur from leave. 2 Sections to TUFNELL AVE.	

R. Moslin Major RE
OC 64 R.E.

692

Appendix A

O.C. 63rd Field Coy. R.E.
O.C. 64th Field Coy. R.E.

    Capt. A.E. COLLIER, M.C., R.E. (S.R.) having been ordered to report to the War Office, Lieut. A.C. RANKIN, M.C., R.E. (S.R.) will be transferred to the 63rd Field Coy. R.E. as second-in-command, and will take over temporary command of the Company forthwith.

    Date of relief to be reported by O.C. 63rd Field Coy.

                                    Lieut-Colonel, R.E.
                                    C.R.E., 9th Division.

1/7/17.

Appendix B

Handed in at RCO Office 11-0 Received 11-17

TO OC 64th Fld Co RE

Sender's Number: CRE25/A/5 Day of Month: 30/6

Arrange to take over with effect from morning of 2nd July work on roads north of SCARPE at present being carried out by 63rd Field Coy. RE also working of job in canal at broken railway bridge aaa One company of Middlesex Regt will be detailed later to assist you with road work aaa You should see work in hand in clearing canal before taking over and get into touch with officer i/c Canals aaa Addsd OC 64th Fld Coy RE Repld OC 63rd Field Coy RE and 2/Lt BANCROFT RE

FROM PLACE & TIME
CRE 17th Corps Troops

"C" Form
MESSAGES AND SIGNALS.
Army Form C.2123

TO: OC 6th Fd Co RE

Sender's Number: CRE 25/A/8
Day of Month: 1

Reference my wire CRE 25/A/7 of date aaa You should employ most if not all 3/10 Middlesex Coy on south road railway arch to FEUCHY with a few sapper ncos to supervise aaa a few sappers will suffice to maintain the north road from Railway arch to ATHIES and onwards for the present aaa I want the larger number of your company engaged in clearing debris of railway bridge from canal and removing large masonry blocks which at present obstruct channel aaa for this latter work

"C" Form
MESSAGES AND SIGNALS.

Army Form C. 2123.
(In books of 100.)

Prefix	Code	Words	Received	Sent, or sent out	Office Stamp
	£ s. d.		From	At ... m	
Charges to collect			By	To	
Service Instructions				By	

Handed in at .... Office .... m. Received .... m.

TO ②

*Sender's Number	Day of Month	In reply to Number	A A A

You can have ten to twenty hant's labour from store depot as Provided to oc 63rd Field Coy RE aaa aadsd oc 6oth field Coy RE aaa Repto oc 63rd field Coy RE

FROM: CRE 17 Corps Troops

PLACE & TIME:

* This line should be erased if not required.

Appendix D

O.C. 90th Field Coy. R.E.,
Chateau Grounds,
ST. LAURENT BLANGY.

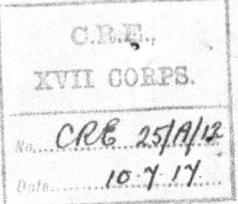
C.R.E., XVII CORPS.
No. CRE 25/19/12
Date. 10.7.17

From Thursday, the 12th instant, you will take over from the O.C. 64th Field Coy. R.E., all road repair, maintenance and improvement work on the North side of the SCARPE Canal, which is at present under his charge. That is to say, along the GAVRELLE Road from the railway bridge up to the POINT DU JOUR, and along the FAMPOUX Road from the railway bridge to the road junction at the East end of FAMPOUX, H.18.a.1.1. The cross roads at ATHIES and FAMPOUX leading from the main road to the lock bridges over the canal should also be cleared, repaired, and drainage attended to.

Colonel,
C.R.E., XVII Corps Troops.

10/7/17.

Copy to:-
O.C. 64th Field Coy. R.E., for information and guidance.

"O" Form.
MESSAGES AND SIGNALS.

Army Form C. 2123.
(In books of 100.)

No. of Message _____

| Prefix | Code | Words 39 | Received From R.o. By Tan | Sent, or sent out. At ___ m. To ___ By ___ | Office Stamp. 10-18 TELEGRAPH |

Charges to Collect _____
Service Instructions Appendix E

Handed in at ___ Office 10.a m. Received 10.18 m.

TO R.E. OC 64 Field Coy

*Sender's Number	Day of Month	In reply to Number	A A A
1842	19		

64th Field Coy will move to FOSSEUX forthwith aaa advanced party should report here to take over billets allotted they 9th Divn G aaa acknowledge aaa

Have started packing up DWC

FROM PLACE & TIME CRE 9th Divn 10. am

*–This line should be erased if not required.

SECRET.   D218/1

9th DIVISIONAL ENGINEERS.

Appendix F

WARNING ORDER.

1. 9th Division (less Artillery) with Divisional Supply Column will be transferred to 4th Corps on 31st inst, and will relieve 58th Division (less Artillery) with Divisional Supply Column.

2. Moves will take place as follows:-

   (a) Personnel will move by rail from 17th Corps area to BAPAUME and thence by route march:-

   26th Inf. Brigade   )
   27th Field Ambulance   )   on 25th July.
   64th Field Coy., R.E.   )

   S.African Inf. Brigade   )
   S.African Field Amb.   )   on 27th July.
   63rd Field Coy. R.E.   )
   197th M.G. Company.   )

   27th Inf. Brigade   )
   28th Field Amb.   )   on 29th July.
   90th Field Coy., R.E.   )

   Orders for entrainment will be issued later by Q 9th Division. (attached)

   (b) Transport will move by road in accordance with attached march table.

   (c) Divisional Supply Column will move by road under orders which will be issued later.

3. On arrival in 58th Division area each Brigade group will come temporarily under the orders of the 58th Division until the 9th Division takes over from the 58th Division on the 31st July.

4. Brigades will relieve Brigades of the 58th Division in the line as follows under orders of the 58th Division.

   26th Inf. Brigade will relieve 175th Inf. Brigade in left Sector on the night 26/27th.

   S. African Inf. Brigade will relieve 174th Inf. Brigade in centre Sector on night 28/29th.

   27th Inf. Brigade will relieve 173rd Inf. Brigade in right Sector on night 30/31st.

5. Acknowledge.

ADJUTANT 9th DIVISIONAL ENGINEERS
for Lieut-Colonel. R.E.
C.R.E. 9th Div. Engrs.

21/7/17.

MARCH TABLE.

1.	2.	3.	4.	5.	6.	7.	8.
Serial No.	Date.	Unit.	From.	To.	Route.	Billets from.	Remarks.
1.	July 24th.	Marching portion of 26th Inf. Bde. 27th Field Amb. 64th Fd. Coy. R.E. 105th Coy. A.S.C.	WARLUS DAINVILLE BERNEVILLE WANQUETIN	ABLAINZEVELLE	Any.	Town Major.	Marching portions of Bde groups will move in 5 columns as follows:- (i) Transport of 2 Bns & M.G.Co. (ii) Transport of 2 Battns. (iii) Field Ambulance. (iv) Field Coy. R.E. (v) Train Coy. Each column will be in charge of an Officer, and an interval of 500 yards will be maintained between columns.
2.	July 25th.	------do------	ABLAINZE-VELLE.	YTRES.	-	-	
3.	July 25th.	Transport 197th M.G. Coy.	BERNEVILLE	ABLAINZEVELLE	Any.	Town Major.	
4.	July 26th.	Transport 197th M.G. Coy.	ABLAINZEVE-LLE	YTRES	-	-	
5.	July 26th.	Marching portion of S.A. Inf. Bde. 63rd Fd. Amb. 107th Coy. A.S.C.	BERNEVILLE SIMENCOURT AVESNES LE COMTE	ABLAINZEVELLE	Any.	Town Major.	
6.	July 27th.	------do------	ABLAINZE-VELLE.	YTRES.	-	-	
7.	July 28th.	Marching portion of 27th Inf. Bde. 28th Field Amb. 90th Fd. Coy. R.E. 106th Coy. A.S.C.	MANIN IZEL-LEZ HAMEAU	ABLAINZEVELLE	Any.	Town Major.	
8.	July 29th.	do.	ABLAINZEVELLE	YTRES.			

SECRET.

Ref map
LENS 11
VALENCIENNES 1/100,000

Appendix G

Copy No...... 22.

26th. Infantry Brigade Operation Order No. 127.

22/7/17.

1. The 26th. Infantry Brigade will move into the 4th. Corps area on the 25th. inst.

2. Marching transport will proceed by road on the 24th inst. in accordance with attached table A.

3. The remaining personnel will move by train to BAPAUME in accordance with attached tables B.1 and B.2.
The personnel detailed in table B.2 will bivouac on the night of 24/25th. in field opposite SAULTY Station.

4. The Staff Captain will carry out the duties of entraining Officer.
Captain Hunter, 5th Cameron Highlanders will proceed on first Omnibus train to assist in detraining.

5. An entraining state, shewing numbers of Officers, Men, Horses, 2 wheeled vehicles and Bicycles etc., will be sent to this Office by 6.pm tomorrow, 23rd. by each Unit. A copy of this state will be taken by the Officer in charge of each billeting party, which will proceed by first Omnibus train, and report to Captain Hunter at detraining station. These parties should be provided with bicycles.

6. One lorry will report at each Unit's Headquarters at 6.pm on 24th. to convey surplus stores and Q.M's party to SAULTY Station. These stores will proceed by Omnibus train and will be met by lorries at Station of detrainment.

7. The Brigade will move from BAPAUME to billets on the 25th. in accordance with attached table C.

8. Units will arrange to carry dixies so that Tea can be made before entraining. Dinners will be eaten at BAPAUME.

9. Representatives of each unit entraining will report to Staff Captain 1 hour before departure of their train.

ACKNOWLEDGE.

Captain,
a/Brigade Major.
26th Infantry Brigade.

Issued at 11.pm.

```
Copy No.1   to  8th Black Watch.         22.  64th. Fd. Coy. R.E.
     2          7th Seaforth Hrs.
     3          5th Cameron Hrs.
     4          10th A. & S. Hrs.
     5          26th M.G. Company.
     6          26th T.M. Battery.
     7          26th Brigade Signals.
     8           "     "   Transport Officer.
     9           "     "   Supply Officer.
    10          105 Company A.S.C.
    11          175th Brigade. (58th Division).
    12           9th Division 'G'.
    13 & 14      9th Division 'Q'.
    15          27th Brigade.
    16          S. African Brigade.
    17          C.R.E., 9th Division.
    18          27th Field Ambulance.
    19          Staff Captain.
    20          War Diary.
    21          File.
```

Transport March Table 'A'.

Date.	Column.	Units.	From.	Starting point.	Time.	To.	Route.	Remarks.
24th July.	1.	105 Coy. A.S.C.	AGNEZ.		3.25am.	ABLAINZ. VILL.	WARLUS-DAINVILL-ACHICOURT-AGNY-AYETTE.	Head of column to pass junction of AGNY & ARRAS-AYETTE Roads at 6.am.
do.	2.	7th Seaforth Hs. 10th A. & S. Hrs. 26th M.G.Company.	DAINVILL. do. BERNEVILL.	Rd. Junction 100 yds S. of Q in CITADELL.	5.10am.	do.	ACHICOURT-AGNY.	To pass above junction 6.10am.
do.	3.	8th Black Watch. 5th Cameron Hs. Brigade H.Q.	DAINVILL. WARLUS. do.	do.	5.20am.	do.	do.	To pass above junction 6.30am.
do.	4.	64th Fd. Coy. R.E.	FOSSEUX. Simencourt	Cross roads BEAUMETZ.	7.am. 5.30 start	do.	GOUY-BEAUMETZ-RIVIERE-RANSART-ADINFER-AYETTE-SIMENCOURT-BEAUMETZ.	
do.	5.	27th Fd. Amb.	WANQUETIN.	MON FR.	7.15am.	do.	and as in No.4.	
25th July.	1.	105 Coy. A.S.C.	ABLAINZ VILL.	Cross roads.	6.am.	ACHIET L. GRAND-BAPAUM-YTRES- LE TRANSLOY-ROCQUIGNY Bus.		
do.	2.	7th Seaforth Hs. 10th A. & S. Hrs. 26th M.G.Company. 8th Black Watch.	do.	do.	6.10am	do.	do.	
do.	3.	5th Cameron Hrs. 26th Brigade H.Q.	do.	do.	6.20am	do.	do.	
do.	4.	64th Fd. Coy. R.E.	do.	do.	6.30am	do.	do.	
do.	5.	27th Fd. Ambulance.	do.	do.	6.40am	do.	do.	

NOTE: Each unit will send forward 1 representative to report at Town Major's Office ABLAINZVILL. at 8.am. Each Column will be under an Officer. 500 yards distance will be maintained between columns. Officers chargers to be left at BAPAUME Station. From VILLES, Transport will join its Units at places laid down in Table 'C'.

Entraining Station— Table 'B'(1). Railway Moves for July 25th. Detraining Station—
SAULTY.   BAPAUM..

No. of train.	Type.	Units & Order of entraining.	HOUR. Dep.	HOUR. Arr.	R E M A R K S.
1.	Omnibus train. 1 Coach. 30 Covered wagons. 17 Flats.	Brigade H.Q. & 1 L.G.S. Wagon. Signal section. 4 limbered G.S.Wagons per Bn. (L.G.transport). 2 Cookers, 1 Mess cart per Bn. Pack animals (Officers chargers to go by road). Medical personnel of Battalions with Maltese cart. * Field Coy. R.E.: . .	2.am.	6.am.	Transport of 64th Fd.Coy. R.E. will be at SAULTY Station by 11.pm on 24th. & personnel by 12.30am on 25th. To be at SAULTY at 12.30am.
		Billeting parties of Units.			

* Finds loading and unloading party of 100 men.

2.	do.	Brigade M.G.Company (less * marching transport & 3 L.G.S. wagons). 2 limbered wagons per Battalion. (tools). 2 Cookers & 2 Water carts per Bn.	5.am.	9.am.	Leave BERNAVILLE. at 6.pm & march to SAULTY via B.AUMETZ, thence main ARRAS - DOULLENS Road. Head of all entraining transport etc., of (1) 8th B.Watch, (2) 10th A.& S.Hrs. & (5) 7th Seaforth Hrs., under an Officer of 7th Seaforth Hrs. & arranged in 2 echelons as shewn in column 3 will pass DAINVILLE Station in above order at 6.pm. Entraining transport etc. of 5th. Cameron Hrs. will march from WARLUS at 6.pm via BERNAVILLE-BEAUMETZ.
		* Finds loading and unloading party of 100 men.			

Table B (1) contd.

No. of train.	Type.	Units & Order of entraining.	Hour.	R E M A R K S.
		26th. T.M.Battery.		The 26th. T.M.Battery will march in rear of transport of the M.G. Company.
		27th. Fd. Ambulance.	personnel	Will arrive at SAULTY at 3.50.a.m. any transport going by rail will arrive at 2 am.

Table "E" (2). Railway Moves for July 25th.

Entraining Station—
BAPAUME.

Detraining Station—
BAPAUME.

No. of train.	Type.	Unit & Order of entraining.	HOUR. Dep.	HOUR. Arr.	REMARKS.
1.	Coaching Stock. 2 Brake vans. 44 Third class coaches. 2 First class coaches. 2 Covered Goods vans.	5th Cameron Highrs. 8th Black Watch. 26th Brigade H.Q.	8.am.	12 noon.	5th Cameron Hrs. & Brigade H.Q. march via BERNEVILLE-BAPAUME, arr. Station 6.30am. 8th B.Watch march via main ARRAS-DOULLENS Road, arr. Station 6.30.am.
2.	do.	7th Seaforth Highrs. 10th A. & S. Highrs.	9.am.	1.pm.	7th Seaforth Hrs. march via ARRAS-DOULLENS Road, to arrive Station 7.30.am. 10th A. & S. Hrs. as above, to arrive Station 7.30.am.

March Table 'G'.

T.M. Unit.	Starting point.	Time.	From.	To.	Route.	REMARKS.
1. 64th Fd.Cy.R.	Junction of BANCOURT & BAPAUME-L.TRANSLOY Roads.	9.am.	BAPAUME.	Camp near NEUVILLE BORJONVAL.	L.TRANSLOY - RCCQUIGNY - YTRES.	All Units arriving BAPAUME by first & second Omnibus trains to arrange for breakfasts at BAPAUME.
2. 27th Fd.Amb.	do.	10.30am.	do.	do.	do.	All train transport to march with its unit from BAPAUME.
3. 26th T.M.Bty.	do.	10.45am.	do.	do.	do.	
4. 26th M.G.Coy.	do.	11.am.	NEUVILL-BOURJONVAL.	do.	do.	
5. 26th Bde. H.Q.	do.	2.15.pm.	do.	do.	do.	
6. 5th Camerons.	do.	2.30.pm.	do.	do.	BANCOURT-BAPTINCOURT-RUYAULCOURT.	
7. 8th B.Watch.	do.	3.pm.	RUYAULCOURT.	do.	do.	
8. 7th Seaforths.	do.	3.30pm.	do.	BARTINCOURT.	do.	
9. 10th A.& S.H.	do.	3.50pm	do.	do.	do.	

1755

August 1917

WAR DIARY or INTELLIGENCE SUMMARY

Army Form C. 2118.

64th Field Company R.E.

Vol 28

Month: August 1917

Place	Date	Hour	Summary of Events and Information	Remarks and references to Appendices
RUYAULCOURT	2		No. 2 Section rejoins Coy from EQUANCOURT. 8mm relieved at YPRES for work at Divl. HQ. 1 Sec. cutting trace + risers in TUFNELL AVE. 1 Section trenching + dubbing. HENLEY AVE: 1 Section cutting trace in Outpost line. Screen in OXFORD ROAD, excavating + dubbing. TUFNELL AVE.	
	3		8mm rejoin from YPRES. YORKSHIRE ALLEY starts.	
	4		No. 2 Section relieves No. 4 in advanced billets. Reinft'g drains with brushwood.	
	6		2nd Allen on leave to England.	
	8		1 Section in works: remainder resting.	
	9		Dubbing HUBERT AVE:	
	10		Bridge over TUFNELL AVE: by right battalion HQ.	
	11		2/Lt EPMEDLAND RE (T.F.) join from the Base. No. 4 Section relieves No. 3. Shelter in brushlie started.	
	12		Demolition of concrete pillars + prominent objects at BUTLER'S CROSS. Hutting started. 1 Section on works: remainder resting.	
	14		2/Lt Allen from leave. Afranks started in YORKSHIRE ALLEY.	
	17		Enshg Adrian Hut at Divl. HQ. New Bde HQ. in NEUVILLE started. 1 large + 1 Sapper accompany raid by 10th A & SH art. middle charges. No dugouts found. one	

2353 Wt W3544/1451 709,000 5/15 D.D. & L. A.D.S.S./Forms/C.2118.

Army Form C. 2118.

WAR DIARY
or
INTELLIGENCE SUMMARY.
(Erase heading not required.)

Place	Date	Hour	Summary of Events and Information	Remarks and references to Appendices
	19		Change Unknown into enemy strong point, one lost remainder brought back.	
	20		No 3 Section relieves No 1 Section in advanced billets. Coy HQ. Stacks off HUBERT AVE.	
	21		Rest day	
	25		2 Lt Fischer (at XVII hrs school) on leave to England. No 1 Section relieves No 2 Section in advanced billets.	
	26		Scene to HUBERT ROAD. Capt. 2.i.c. Dunn Ashton round the line.	
	27		Oc. 122nd Coy R. Fahnen round the line	
	29		Relieved by 122nd Coy R.E. Marched to GOMIECOURT at 11:30pm.	Appendix A.
	30		Arrived at GOMIECOURT at 5:30 am. Redistributing day.	
	31		Making Bivouacs all section. Gas drill at 2.0 pm. OC Coy. to address team.	
			Attached - Sketch of types of dugouts under construction by Infantry Pioneer Platoons. 16 were taken in hand by 130 infantry and advancing gallows completed in twenty weeks.	Appendix B.

W. Preston Jenkins
Capt. RE

D.N.C
Capt. RE

Appendix A

SECRET.

Copy No. 2...

Ref. map 57C.

9th Divisional Engineers Operation Order No. D.289.
By Major S.W.S. HAMILTON, D.S.O., R.E.
a/C.R.E., 9th (Scottish) Division.

1. Field Companies of 9th Division will be relieved by Field Companies of 36th Division on 28th, 29th and 30th inst.

2. 63rd Field Coy. R.E. will be relieved by 121st Field Coy. R.E. in TRESCAULT section on the 28th inst.
   90th Field Coy. R.E. will be relieved by 150th Field Coy. R.E. in HERMIES section on the 29th inst.
   64th Field Coy. R.E. will be relieved by 122nd Field Coy. R.E. in HAVRINCOURT section on 30th inst.

3. On day of relief each Field Coy. of 9th Division will march to destination as follows:-

   63rd Field Coy. R.E. to ACHIET-Le-PETIT.
   90th Field Coy. R.E. to COURCELLES-Le-COMTE.
   64th Field Coy. R.E. to GOMIECOURT.

4. Transport of 64th Field Coy. R.E. to be clear of line RUYAULCOURT-BERTINCOURT during hours of darkness on night of 29th inst.

5. Billeting will be carried out under Brigade arrangements.

6. H.Q. R.E. 9th Division will close at YTRES at 10 a.m. on 31st August, and re-open at the same hour at ACHIET-Le-PETIT.

7. ACKNOWLEDGE.

H.Q.
9TH DIVISIONAL
ENGINEERS.
No.......

Lieut. R.E.
Adjt. 9th Divl. Engrs.

25/8/17.
Issued at 7 p.m.
Copies to:
1. O.C. 63rd Field Coy. R.E.
2. O.C. 64th Field Coy. R.E.
3. O.C. 90th Field Coy. R.E.
4. O.C. 9th Divl. Sig. Coy. R.E.
5. 9th Division G.
6. 9th Divl. Train.
7. A.D.M.S. 9th Divn.
8. C.R.E. 36th Division.
9. C.E. IV Corps.
10. C.E. VI Corps.
11. War Diary.
12. Office copy.
13. Spare.

Dugout in Platoon Locality.

Appendix B

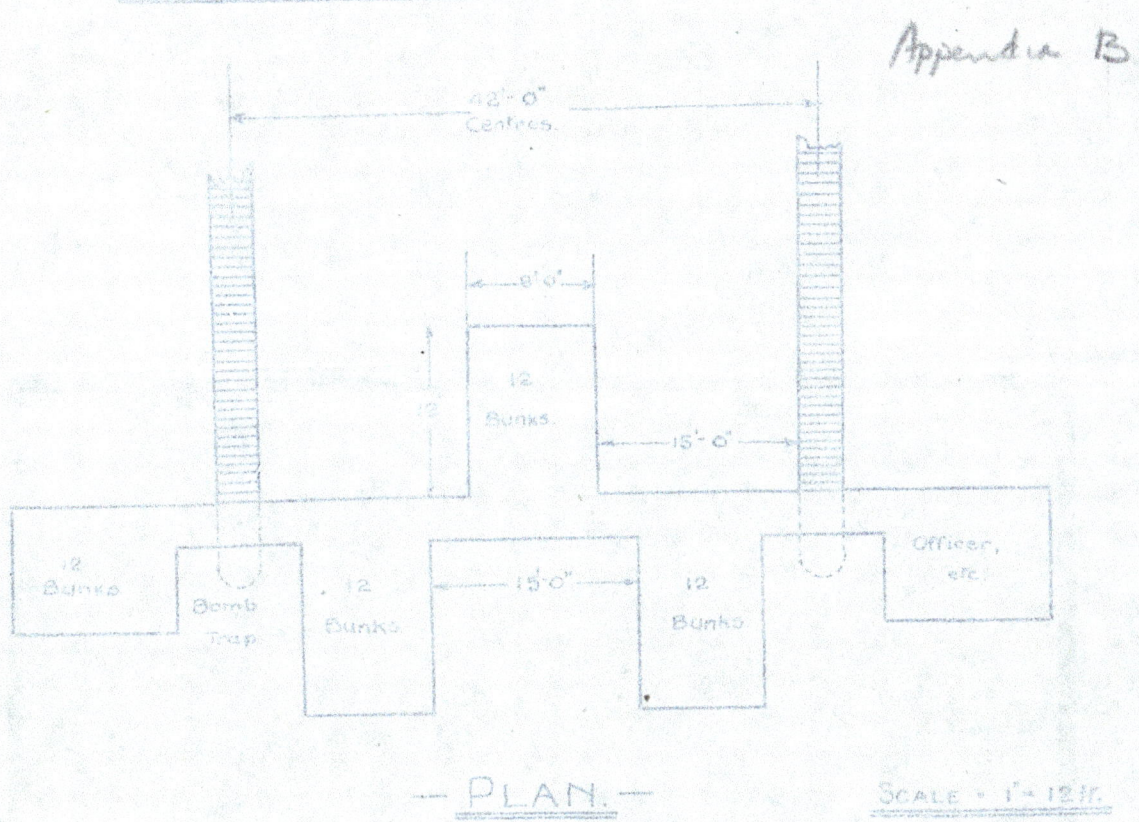

Plan.

Scale 1" = 12 ft.

Dugout Entrance.

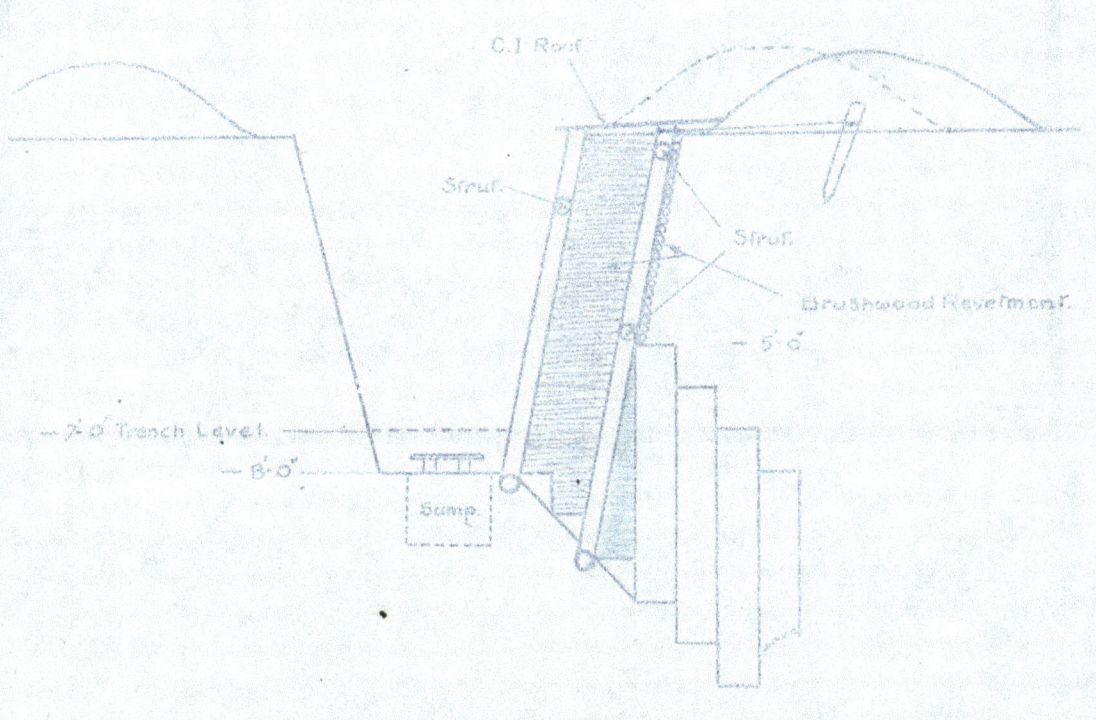

Side Elevation.

1755

Sept 1917

Army Form C. 2118.

WAR DIARY
or
INTELLIGENCE SUMMARY. 64th Field Co. R.E.

(Erase heading not required.)

September

Instructions regarding War Diaries and Intelligence Summaries are contained in F. S. Regs., Part II. and the Staff Manual respectively. Title pages will be prepared in manuscript.

Vol 29

Place	Date	Hour	Summary of Events and Information	Remarks and references to Appendices
GOMIECOURT	1		Inspection of gas appliances, gas drill for whole company	
	2		Section Drill 10.am. Mounted Section map drill & troop drill	
	3		Coy. drill 9 a.m. Church parade. 9.30pm practice march with geophones	
	4		Coy. Section drill. Intercoy. pontoon trestle drill. afternoon football	
	5		Coy drill 9 a.m. Marched demonstration to ACHIET LE PETIT. CRE's Inspection & presentation of parchment for good service to 2 Cpl Cameron No. 42094 at 3.30pm	
	6		Parton & trestle drill. Demolitions sparse looking. Branch instruction. Football	
	7		Marched to BAPAUME at 12.15pm. Entrained for Poperinghe lg.t BAPAUME at 5.30pm	
	8		Arrived POPERINGHE at 5.0 am & Marched to No 3 area HATOU	
	9		Coy Standing by to move forward to YPRES.	
	11		No. 3 Section remain Nissen huts at HATOU. Parties working out trenches	
	12		Rest.	
	13		Move to rest camp to make room for 26th Bde H.Q.	
	14		Move to billets in the Ramparts at YPRES.	Appendix A
	15		Move to other billets in YPRES	
	16		Move to other billets in YPRES taking over from 429th Cy.R.E. & parades for	Appendix B

Army Form C. 2118.

WAR DIARY
or
INTELLIGENCE SUMMARY.
(Erase heading not required.)

Place	Date	Hour	Summary of Events and Information	Remarks and references to Appendices
	18		Work at 5.0 a.m. 2 Section on trench tramway from OXFORD ROAD towards BAVARIA HOUSE. 2 Sections on Geo-blankets in RAILWAY WOOD. Lt. Col. FISCHER urgent & repairs to FREZENBERG road. Lt. Col. FISCHER rejoins from XVII Corps School.	Appen. C, D, & E.
	20		Attack by V Corps. Whole Company on mule track from RAILWAY WOOD to KIT & KAT. Lt. Col. Fischer wounded.	Append. F, G & H
	21		Whole Company on track running SSE from BAVARIA HOUSE.	Appendix I
	22		General improvements to tracks. Bivouac.	
	23		Handed over to 56th Coy. R.E. Stayed in same billets. Work on tracks. Killed from shrapnel.	Appendix J
	24		1 & 2 Sections at 3.30 a.m. reported to 183 Coy R.E. for work on tank route near STEENBECK. Some gas encountered. Considerable shelling. Remainder of Coy. in shelters.	Appen. K, L
			in YPRES with 2nd C.E. V Corps.	
	25		3rd Section on tank route with 183 Coy R.E. Hqrs. in shelters.	Appen. M
	26		M.G. & on shelters. Lt. REINHOLD joins from Base.	
	27		1, 3, 4 Secs. on shelters. No. 2 Sec. reports to 568 Coy R.E.	
	29		Relieved by R. Coy of 6th Div. Marched to POPERINGHE area starting at 10 a.m. & arriving at 8 p.m.	Appen. N, O
	30		Marched to LEDRINGHEM.	Appendix P

A.M.Moorhem Major R.E.
O.C. Coy L.6, R.E.

2/10/17

Army Form C. 2121

URGENT

(Appendix A.)

TO: 64 Field Co RE
9th Divn G

Sender's Number: D322/2
Day of Month: 13

In continuation of this office D322 dated 12/9/17 AAA following received from 9th Div AAA 64th Field Coy RE will move tomorrow from WATOU to SHELTERS in YPRES now occupied by 467 Field Coy AAA 64th Field Co to clear road junction L.11.b.2.6. by 11-30 a.m AAA. Transport in Camp at H.16.a.5.7 AAA acknowledge AAA addressed 64th Field Co RE rpt 9th Div G

From: CRE
Place: 9th Div.

Adjt 9th Divn Engrs.

SECRET.   Appendix B.   Copy No. 2

9th Divisional Engineers Operation Order D.331
by Lieut-Colonel G.R. HEARN, D.S.O. R.E.
C.R.E., 9th Division.

14th Septbr. 1917.

Reference Map: Sheet 28, 1/40,000.

1. The 9th Division is relieving the 42nd Division in the line on the nights 16/17th and 17/18th September.

2. The 27th Infy. Brigade will relieve the 126th Infy. Brigade in the right sub-sector on the night 16/17th. Headquarters in RAILWAY WOOD I.11.b.

   The S.A. Infy. Brigade will relieve the 125th Infy. Brigade in the left sub-sector on the night 17/18th. Headquarters at MILL COT, I.5.a.

   The 26th Infy. Brigade will take over the accomodation occupied by the 127th Infy. Brigade, with Headquarters at H.7.c.2.6.

3. The relief by the Field Coys. R.E. 9th Division of the Field Coys. R.E. 42nd Division will take place as follows:-

   64th Field Coy. R.E. will relieve the 429th Field Coy. R.E. on the 16th Septbr.

   90th Field Coy. R.E. will relieve the 428th Field Coy. R.E. on the 16th Septbr.

   63rd Field Coy. R.E. will relieve the 427th Field Coy. R.E. on the 17th Septbr.

4. O's.C. Field Coys. concerned will arrange details of relief.

5. 9th Divisional R.E. will take over the dump of 42nd Divisional R.E. at H.7.a.6.9. on the 17th instant.

6. 64th Field Coy. R.E. will detail one N.C.O. and 2 sappers to control the transit dump at I.7.b.8.7. on the 17th instant. I.7.c.9.5

7. Small R.E. dumps in Brigade areas will be taken over by Field Coys. concerned, on relief.

8. H.Q., R.E. 9th Division close at POPERINGHE at 10 a.m. on the 18th inst. and open at H.7.d.9.5. at the same hour, when G.O.C. 9th Division assumes command of the sector from G.O.C. 42nd Division.

9. ACKNOWLEDGE.

(signature)
Capt. R.E.
Adjt. 9th Divl. Engrs.

Issued at 12 noon.

Copies to:-
No. 1. O.C. 63rd Fld Coy. R.E.
2. O.C. 64th Fld Coy. R.E.
3. O.C. 90th Fld Coy. R.E.
4. O.C. 9th Seaforth Hrs.(Pnrs).
5. 9th Division G.
6. 26th Infy. Brigade.
7. 27th Infy. Brigade.
8. S.A. Infy. Brigade.
No. 9. C.E. V Corps.
10. O.C. 9th Div. Sigs.
11. 9th Divl. Train.
12. A.D.M.S. 9th Divn.
13. D.A.D.V.S. 9th Divn.
14. C.R.E. 42nd Divn.
15. War Diary.
16. File.
17. Spare.

Appendix C

H.Q.
9TH DIVISIONAL
ENGINEERS.
No. 3/21
Date

O.C. 64th Field Coy. R.E.

As explained to you verbally, the works allotted to you for the present are :-

(a) Maintenance and clearance of debris from the POTISJE - FREZENBERG Road.

(b) Reconnaissance and construction of a tramway more or less parallel to the above road either North or South, and possibly using an existing boarded track, as boarding of the tramway will be necessary.

(c) Work for artillery as detailed for D/295, and other work will be required.

(d) Reconnaissance of drainage channels.

G R Hearn

Lieut-Colonel, R.E.
C.R.E. 9th Division.

14/9/17.

Appendix D

S.654

C.R.E. 9th Divn.

I have reconnoitred routes for tramway as detailed in your 3/2. There are two possible routes:—

(1) Starting from dump on OXFORD ROAD C.29.c.45.00. along ditch as far as old German front line. Thence along H track to CAMEROON RESERVE at about C.29.d.8.5. Thence to C.30.c.2.6. Thence along H track to the HANEBEEK at C.30.c.40.55. Thence to the road about 100° East of BAVARIA HOUSE.

(2) Starting from CAMBRIDGE ROAD at I.5.a.35.50. along ditch to CRUMP FARM. Thence across No Man's Land to German front line at about I.5.b.5.7. Thence alongside German tramway to IBERIA RESERVE. Thence along existing track to the HANEBEEK at about C.30.c.7.2. Thence to road about 100° East of BAVARIA HOUSE.

Of these routes I prefer the former for the following reasons:—
(1) It starts from an existing dump while
(2) starts from a battery position.

(b) The ground in the German front system is far worse in (2) being a mass of wire & trenches.

(c) The ground North of the road appears to be less shelled.

(d) (1) follows existing features & will be therefore less conspicuous.

(e) German tramway formation on southern route is completely waterlogged & useless.

(f) Where (2) crosses HANEBEEK the stream is very wide & swampy while North of the road it is much more clearly defined.

Unless I hear to the contrary by this evening I shall employ my carrying party tonight on laying out the rails along Route (1).

C.H. Woolm
Major R.E.
O.C. 1x¹ Coy R.E.

CRE. 9th Divn.   Appendix E

I am starting work tomorrow morning on the FREZENBURG road.

Beyond C30d2.5 it has never been reclaimed & is in a very bad state; as the heavy barrage starts at about this point & the road is beyond the crest about 100" further on, I do not see any use in taking it in hand.

Will you please let me know what width of roadway I am to work to? The existing road is a strip of pavé about 9' wide with mud on each side. The ditches are about 20 ft apart on an average.

Much of the road is mended with timber slabs. Are these to be left or is soling & metal likely to be available? I am afraid the wooden road will go to pieces in the winter.

C. Woodhan
Major RE
OC. 64th Coy RE

15/9/17

SECRET.
D.350/1.

Appendix F

INSTRUCTIONS FOR THE OFFENSIVE FOR 9TH DIVISIONAL ENGINEERS AND 9TH SEAFORTH HIGHRS. (PIONEERS)

By Lieut-Colonel G.R. HEARN, D.S.O., R.E.
C.R.E., 9th Division.

1. The following will be the distribution of R.E. and Pioneers during the attack :-

   (a) 4 parties each consisting of a N.C.O. and 2 sappers, and each equipped with 3 heavy mobile charges, will be attached to each of the attacking Infantry Brigades, for the purpose of blowing in concrete shelters.
   Brigades will detail 6 men to accompany each of these parties as carriers.
   These parties will assist in the consolidation of the shelters when captured.

   (b) 1 section from the 90th and 63rd Field Coys. respectively will be attached to 27th and S.A. Brigades to construct crossings over the HANEBEEK.

   (c) 63rd, 64th and 90th Field Coys. (less the parties referred to in (a) and (c)) will be employed under the orders of the C.R.E.

   (d) Half a Company of Pioneers will be attached to each attacking Infantry Brigade to assist in the consolidation of captured concrete shelters.

   (e) The Pioneer Battalion (less 1 Company) will be in reserve for the purpose of extending and improving communications, under orders of the C.R.E.

   (f) The officers commanding the sections referred to in para. (b) will be the liaison officers at the Brigade Battle H.Q.

2. ACKNOWLEDGE.

Capt. R.E.
Adjt. 9th Divl. Engrs.

17/9/17.

Copies to:-
O.C. 63rd Field Coy. R.E.
O.C. 64th Field Coy. R.E.
O.C. 90th Field Coy. R.E.

SECRET.

9th Divisional Engineers Operation Order No. D.372.

by Lieut-Colonel G.R. HEARN, D.S.O., R.E.

Reference 1/10,000 trench map,
FREZENBERG and GRAVENSTAFEL sheets.

Appendix G

Copy No. 2....   19/9/17.

1. **ATTACK.**

(a) 5th Corps will take the offensive on September 20th. Zero hour will be at 5-40 a.m.

(b) The attack will be carried out by 9th and 55th Divisions with 3rd and 59th Divisions in Corps reserve.

(c) Dispositions of Corps and Divisions on right and left of 9th Division will be as notified in Preliminary Instructions D.338.

II. **DISPOSITIONS IN 9TH DIVISION.**

9th Division will attack with 27th Brigade on right and S.A. Brigade on left. One battalion 26th Brigade will be attached to each of these two Brigades.

26th Brigade, less 2 battalions and 26th M.G. Coy. will be in reserve. Two battalions of 3rd Division will also be at disposal of G.O.C. 9th Division as a reserve.

III. **OBJECTIVES AND BOUNDARIES.**

These have been notified in D.349/1 on the maps issued therewith.

IV. **CONSOLIDATION.**

The capture and retention of ZONNEBEKE redoubt and BREMEN redoubt are of special importance. Hostile concrete shelters will be occupied by garrisons and the positions will be consolidated. Special precautions will be taken to ensure that mopping up is thoroughly carried out.

V. **ASSEMBLY.**

27th Brigade East of WESTHOEK ridge.

S.A. Brigade East of FREZENBERG ridge.

26th Brigade (less one battalion and one Coy.) in old British and German systems C.29., C.30., I.5., and I.6.
One battalion 26th Brigade in YPRES South area.
One Coy. 26th Brigade in S.A. Brigade assembly positions.

VI. **ROUTES FOR ASSEMBLY.**

27th Brigade by Track 'F' and tracks South of it in Divisional area.

S.A. Brigade by Tracks 'K' 'G' 'H'.

26th Brigade to bivouac in YPRES South area. Head not to pass MENIN gate before 7 p.m.

- 2 -

3rd Division. One battalion will be accomodated in BRANDHOEK No. 2 area.

VII. DISTRIBUTION OF R.E. AND PIONEERS.

90th Field Coy.   5 parties each of 1 N.C.O. and 2 sappers for demolitions of concrete shelter doors.
One section to bridge HANEBEEK in two or more places.
2½ sections in reserve for night work.

63rd Field Coy.   4 parties each of 1 N.C.O. and 2 sappers for demolitions of concrete shelter doors.
One section to bridge HANEBEEK in two or more places.
2½ sections in reserve for day work if necessary.

64th Field Coy.   Party on gas tight doors Divisional H.Q.
One section repairing shell holes FREZENBERG road.
Remainder on No. 3 mule track, working by sections by day.

Pioneers.   ½ Coy. with 27th Infantry Brigade to consolidate captured shelters.
½ Coy. with S.A. Infantry Brigade to consolidate captured shelters.
Three Coys. in reserve for night work under orders of C.R.E.

Instructions for Battle kit are contained in SS.135, Sectn.31.

VIII. LIAISON AND H.Q.

The section officers 90th and 63rd Field Coys. with their sections attached for bridging the HANEBEEK will be at 27th and S.A. Brigade Battle H.Q. respectively to act as liaison officers until ordered forward.

Field Coy. Commanders will be at their billets and will send an orderly to advanced Divn. H.Q. in RAMPARTS South of the MENIN GATE.

Reports to advanced Divn. H.Q. MENIN GATE after 6 p.m. 19th September.

Brigade H.Q. will be as follows :-

27th.   KIT & KAT dugout.
S.A.   C.30.d.2.8. dugout.
26th.   RAILWAY WOOD.

IX. ACKNOWLEDGE.

                                                              Capt. R.E.
Issued at 6-15 p.m.   Adjt. 9th Divl. Engrs.

Copies to :-
No. 1. O.C. 63rd Fld Coy. R.E.   No. 5. 9th Divn. G. (For information.)
    2. O.C. 64th Fld Coy. R.E.
    3. O.C. 90th Fld Coy. R.E.   6. C.E. V Corps (For information.
    4. O.C. 9th Seaforth Hrs.(Pnrs).   7. C.R.E. 3rd Divn. (For information.
                                            8. War Diary.
                                            9. File.

"A" Form.   Army Form C. 2121.

MESSAGES AND SIGNALS.   No. of Message

TO { O C 64 Field Coy   Appendix H

Sender's Number: H 20/1   Day of Month: 20   In reply to Number: AAA

64th Field Coy will be employed exclusively on Southern mule track which must be through to 100* from KIT & KAT by 10 p.m. aaa position of end of track to be reported to GOC 27th Brigade aaa following points require special attention aaa notice at junction with plank track aaa beaconing at frequent intervals aaa stakes at twists & turns aaa improvement of ramps aaa report early of Pioneer assistance required to complete in time

From: CRE 9th Division
Place:
Time: 9.23 a.m.

Censor: GR Hearn

"A" Form.
MESSAGES AND SIGNALS.

TO: OC 63
    Bde
    90

Appendix I

Sender's Number: H 21/4
Day of Month: 9 Sept

Distribution of work 90 Field Coy
with 2 Coys Pioneers advanced tracks
27 Bgde aaa 63rd with 2 half
Coys Pioneers on forward tracks
S. Bgde aaa 9th Field Coy
with two half coys Pioneers and
Artillery shuttle tracks aaa
Pioneer Officers to get in touch
with Field Coy Commanders before
5 pm.

From: CRE 9th Division
Place:
Time: 11.30 am

G.E. Hearn
Lt Col CRE

S E C R E T.

Appendix J

Copy No. 2

9th Divisional Engineers Operation Order No. D.380.
By Lieut-Colonel G.R. HEARN, D.S.O., R.E.
C.R.E., 9th Division.

21-9-17.

Reference Map, Sheet 28 N.W. 1/20,000.

1. 9th Division (less Artillery) will be relieved by the 3rd Division (less Artillery) on the nights 22nd/23rd and 23rd/24th Septbr.

2. 9th Division on relief will be accomodated in the WINNEZEELE area.

3. The relief will be carried out as follows :-

(a) 90th Field Coy. R.E. will be relieved by 529th (East Riding) Field Coy. R.E. on the afternoon of 22nd Septbr.

(b) 63rd Field Coy. R.E. will be relieved by 438th (Cheshire) Field Coy. R.E. on the afternoon of 23rd Septbr.

(c) 64th Field Coy. R.E. will be relieved by 56th Field Coy. R.E. on the afternoon of 23rd inst.

4. 64th Field Coy. R.E. and 9th Seaforth Hrs. (Pioneers) will remain in the forward area for work under C.E. V Corps.
63rd and 90th Field Coys. R.E. will come under the orders of C.E. V Corps for work on huts.
On relief
5. 90th Field Coy. R.E. will take over billets of 529th (East Riding) Field Coy. R.E. at H.16.a.5.5., with transport lines at H.16.a.9.9.

On relief 63rd Field Coy. R.E. will take over billets of 56th Field Coy. R.E. H.Q. at H.8.d.6.4., transport lines at H.8.d.8.5.

On relief 64th Field Coy. R.E. will remain in their present billets at YPRES, and transport lines will be taken over from 438th (Cheshire) Field Coy. R.E. at H.8.b.9.8.

6. 9th Seaforth Hrs. (Pioneers) will hand over work to 20th K.R.R.C. (Pioneers) by 5 p.m. on 23rd Septbr.

7. On day of relief billots will be clear by Field Coys. concerned at 3 p.m.

8. ACKNOWLEDGE.

Capt. R.E.
Adjt. 9th Divl. Engrs.

Issued at 11 p.m.

Copies to :-
No. 1. O.C. 63rd Fld Coy. R.E.
2. O.C. 64th Fld Coy. R.E.
3. O.C. 90th Fld Coy. R.E.
4. O.C. 9th Seaforth Hrs. (Pnrs).
5. 9th Division G.
6. 9th Division Q.
7. 9th Div. Train.
No. 8. A.D.M.S. 9th Div.
9. A.D.V.S. 9th Div.
10. O.C. 9th Sig. Coy.
11. C.R.E. 3rd Div.
12. C.E. V Corps.
13. War Diary.
14. File.

O.C. 64th (Fd) Co. RE   Appendix K   R/212

Ref. C.R.E. 9th Div's Op. Order No. D.380 dated 21.9.17 —

On relief by 56th (Fd) Co. RE, you will carry on ~~to do~~ the work, hitherto performed by 467th (Fd) Co. RE (28/H.12.a.0.6) of improving billets in YPRES.

Please get into touch with Town Major YPRES and with O.C. 467th (Fd) Co. R.E. When you have acquired an idea of the work to be done, ring up this office on the telephone and arrange an appointment to come & see the Chief Engineer.

22.9.17

J.W. Richard
Capt. RE
for CE V Corps

O.C. 64th Fd. Co. R.E.   Appendix L

2 Sections to report to Capt. BUCHANAN
183 Tun. Co. R.E. at 5.30 a.m. on 24th Sept at
C.24.a.4.8, at crossing of
STEENBEKE.

Tools.
    Shovels   (1 per Sapper)
    Cross-cut saw   1
    Maul   1
    Hammer   1
    6" Nails   5 lb.

Loading party of 1 N.C.O. & 8 men to be at 9th Divn Transit Dump at 10 p.m. 23rd inst. To load stones as follows on pontoon wagons which will be sent by No. 7 Pontoon Park

Stores now in Transit Dump.

    100   Fascines
    500   Sandbags

Stores which will arrive by lorry.

    36   Pickets
    20   Slabs.

23/9/17

JW Richard
Capt RE
for OC ve[n]ps

"C" Form (Duplicate).
MESSAGES AND SIGNALS.

Army Form C. 2123.
(In books of 50's in duplicate)
No. of Message 55

Service Instructions. *Appendix M*

Handed in at .... Eco .... Office .... m. Received .... m.

TO 64th Coy RE 17.9.9

Sender's Number	Day of Month	In reply to Number		A A A
Detail	two	Officers	with	though
to	next	Capt	BUCHANAN	at
be	Tues	Coy	RE	
look	ready	by	WIELTJE	G28B5.70
at	1.30	am	25"	meet
	complete	work	later	
		Detail		
	loading	duty	to	meet
at	loaded	button	wagons	at
CONVENT DUMP		YPRES	at	Spoil
night	to	accompany	wagons	&
		works	and	offload
	also	Ack.		

FROM PLACE & TIME CE 5th Corps

"C" FORM.
MESSAGES AND SIGNALS.

Army Form C. 2123.
(In books of 100.)

Prefix	Code	Words	Received.	Sent, or sent out.	Office Stamp.
AA 115		81	From Bud Rub	At	N
Charges to Collect			By	To	
Service Instructions				By	
Handed in at Bill			Office ... m.	Received ... m.	

TO 64th Field Coy RE

*Sender's Number.	Day of Month.	In reply to Number.	
S 849	28/9/17		AAA

Move tomorrow 29th to rejoin your Division in ZEGERSCAPPEL area aaa area commdt WINNEZEELE will arrange staging billets in WINNEZEELE area for tomorrow aaa Route from POPERINGHE via ST JANSTER BIEZEN AND WATOU aaa Billets to be handed over to incoming companies details as to which will follow aaa added 63rd 64th and 90th Field Companies reptd Division 2nd Anzac "G" and "Q" and area Comdt WINNEZEELE with reference to 2nd Anzac GA 881.

(ZEGERSCAPPEL)

FROM
PLACE & TIME CE 2nd Anzac

* This line should be erased if not required.

Knight
Hindle } Nº 4
Owen
Thomas } Nº 4

"C" FORM.
MESSAGES AND SIGNALS.

Army Form C. 2123.
(In books of 100.)

No. of Message... 35

Prefix... AAA Code...... Words... 53

Received. From... BUO By... 20 at

Sent, or sent out. At... To... By...

Office Stamp.

Handed in at... BUO ... Office ... m. Received... 1.40 ...m.

TO Appendix O 64th Field Coy RE

Sender's Number	Day of Month	In reply to Number	AAA
S/850	29-9-17		

Arrange to take over tomorrow at 8 am 64th
2gst Billets of for
Field Coy RE at 1/R&S Cignpam aaa
your incoming 66th Divn
added CRE 66th Field Coy
RE and Anzac "Q"
and "Q" with reference
to my S/849 and
GA-881 also from Major
YPRES

FROM CRE 2nd Anzac
PLACE & TIME

25
64 Fed cop RC

SECRET.

Appendix P

9th Divisional Engineers Operation Order D.397
by Lieut-Colonel G.R. HEARN, D.S.O., R.E.
C.R.E., 9th Division.

9TH DIVISIONAL ENGINEERS.
Copy No. 2.
29th Septbr. 1917

Reference Maps: Sheets 19 and 27.

1. Field Companies R.E. 9th Division will proceed by march route to billets as under on Septbr. 30th 1917.

    63rd Field Coy. R.E. to 26th Bde. area. ZEGGERS CAPPEL area at T.29.
    90th Field Coy. R.E. to 27th Bde. area near RUBROUCK.

    64th Field Coy. R.E. to S.A. Bde. area near LEDRINGHAM.

2. Billeting parties are to report respectively to Area Commandants :-

    63rd Field Coy. R.E.   ZEGGARS CAPPEL.
    90th Field Coy. R.E.   RUBROUCK.
    64th Field Coy. R.E.   ARNEKE.

3. ACKNOWLEDGE.

Issued at 6 p.m.

2nd Lieut. R.E.
a/Adjt., 9th Divl. Engrs. R.E.
ADJUTANT 9th DIVISIONAL ENGINEERS

Copies to :-
No. 1. O.C. 63rd Field Coy. R.E.
 "   2. O.C. 64th Field Coy. R.E.
 "   3. O.C. 90th Field Coy. R.E.
 "   4. 9th Division G.
 "   5. 9th Division Q.
 "   6. C.E. II Anzac Corps.
 "   7. A.D.M.S. 9th Divn.
 "   8. 9th Div. Train.
 "   9. D.A.D.V.S. 9th Divn.
 " 10. Area Commandant, RUBROUCK.
 " 11.   "   "   ZEGGARS CAPPEL.
 " 12.   "   "   ARNEKE.
 " 13. War Diary.
 " 14. File.
 " 15. Spare.

1755

October 1917

64 Field Co

Royal Engineers

Army Form C. 2118.

WAR DIARY
or
INTELLIGENCE SUMMARY. 64th Field Company RE.
(Erase heading not required.)

Vol 30

Instructions regarding War Diaries and Intelligence Summaries are contained in F. S. Regs. Part II. and the Staff Manual respectively. Title pages will be prepared in manuscript.

Month and year: October 1917

Place	Date	Hour	Summary of Events and Information	Remarks and references to Appendices
LEDRINGHEM	1		Attended transferred to 90th Co, RE. All Officers attend staff(?) contents of Co, mess, Coy routine.	Appendix A
	3		Training started according to programme	Appendix B
	4		Lecture to all Officers & Cpls. Subject: Military law.	Appendix C
	6		Lt. Cauthon with 4 N.C.O.s to 48th Div. in CANAL BANK to take over.	
	7		Transport marches at 11.15am to ST. JANS TER BIEZEN.	Appendix E.
	8		Sappers march to train at ESQUELBECQ at 7.15am. Detrained at BRIELEN. March to dugouts at C22.b.7. Transport marches to BRIELEN.	Appendix D. E, G, H.
			At CULFORD form from 90th Co, RE.	
	9		Improvements to dugouts. Officers & N.C.O.s on reconnaissance	
	10		HQ. & No.1 take over billets from 475 G, RE in CANAL BANK. Nos 2, 3, 4 Sections on tracks.	
	11		Nos 2, 3, 4 Secs. on tracks. No.1 Sec. on preparing guide tape for assembly + places came to assembly routes.	
	12		Major G. WOOLMER Commanding Coy transferred to command 5th H Squadron RE Capt D. NAPIER - CLOVERING becomes commander of Coy.	

Army Form C. 2118.

WAR DIARY
or
INTELLIGENCE SUMMARY.

(Erase heading not required.)

Instructions regarding War Diaries and Intelligence Summaries are contained in F. S. Regs., Part II. and the Staff Manual respectively. Title pages will be prepared in manuscript.

Place	Date	Hour	Summary of Events and Information	Remarks and references to Appendices
	12		Attacks by Enemy 2 hrs 2.15 hrs in two equal parties attached to leading battalion of 2ft IBde to-day. LEKKER BOTERBEER and PRODEROM Canyons p'l light infantry bridge and buckhorn. hot such as attack drawn seemed remainder of Coy. with 2 platoons of 20 KRR Pioneers and 1Coy Hood Bn. to R.A.D. certain, duckboard tracks 1000 yards river town.	Map of power POELCAPPELLE. Edition/10,000
	13		MOSRATA & MOUSETRAPS Tracks continued. Tapes laid out to BURNS-FINCH HOUSE and lamps at 200 intervals on tracks seen down nights 13/14 to guide infantry relief.	
	14		Tracks continued work been done today help infantry reliefs of enemy who taken no action.	
	15			
	16		Reconnaissance for R.pl.Balk HQ near ALBATROSS 5m station into enemy shelter	
	17		Excavate for 24ft English Shelter behind HORTER (Manchester house)	
	18		ALBERTA track now at BURNS HQ. hrs track from MONTROSS 5m to WELLINGTON WORCESTER.	
			Italia	
	20		2Lt MACKAY RE. joins Coy from Base.	
	22		MOUSETRAP track now reaches ADLER 2m. at D 3a 50,15. Paced track from ALBATROSS to WELLINGTON reaches D 2 b. 15.20.	

Army Form C. 2118.

WAR DIARY
or
INTELLIGENCE SUMMARY.
(Erase heading not required.)

Place	Date	Hour	Summary of Events and Information	Remarks and references to Appendices
	22		Staff at HUBNER completed. 8 RAP. made at D.1.2.59 who tuned English Shepko.	
			Recaptured by enemy "Pluder" near HUBNER & erecting 2 more Infanterien Ruhens hutten	
	23		Company Stand to 24.9 h to RE moved to HOOMHOODT. Supper by bus. Transport by road.	
	24		Marched to JEFFRINCKOVEK.	
	25		Marched to COUDEKEQUE BRANCH S of DUNKIRK.	
	26		" " "	
	27		Coy. marched & Billets in TETEGHEM.	
	28		Church parade. Washing wagons in afternoon.	
	29		Marched to BRAYDUNES.	Appendix J
	30		Marched to SURREY CAMP Division took over NEWPORT BAINS Section.	
	31		1 line with left flank on horses 2nd Medland on L'day. Plan to Plans to Pans Inf. Jonale affairs 1 section loading up lorry stores of 12th Pontoon park from canal near BRAYdunes one section loading lorries to coy dump Bellenhoek at MANCHESTER Dam. Dump. McCullogh on leave to U.K.	

Major Maurice
Major RE
O/C 67/6 Fd RE

URGENT.

Appendix A

H.Q., DIVISIONAL ENGINEERS.
11/6 8

O.C. 63rd Field Coy. R.E.
O.C. 64th Field Coy. R.E. ✓
O.C. 90th Field Coy. R.E.

    All officers will meet C.R.E. at 2-30 p.m. on 1/10/17 at road junction near VIOLON d'OR, H.11.c.8.8. - Horses or bicycles.

    Officers will bring :-

Maps (Sheet 27 or HAZEBROUCK 5A)
F.S. Pocket Books.
Message Books.

and subaltern officers will bring Prismatic Compasses.

    Acknowledge.

D H Jones 2 Lt R.E.
for Lieut-Colonel, R.E.
C.R.E., 9th Division.

30/9/17.

Harkinson
Decker
Cardin Aweke 3-4

Appendix B

	Wednesday 3rd	Thursday 4th	Friday 5th	Saturday 6th	Sunday 7th	Monday 8th	Tuesday 9th
8.0 – 8.30 a.m.	Physical Training	P.T.	P.T.	P.T.	–	P.T.	P.T.
9.15 – 10.15 a.m.	Company drill	Company drill		Company drill	Church Parade	Company drill	Gas drill
10.30 – 11.30 a.m.	Squad drill & Handling of arms	Weldon Trestle & Gas drill	Route march	Handling of arms Saluting		Bayonet fighting Bombing	Pontoon drill Weldon Trestle
Hour – 12.30 p.m.	Bayonet fighting Saluting	Weldon Trestle Gas drill		Bayonet fighting Bombing (if possible)		Bayonet fighting Bombing	Pontoon drill Weldon Trestle
Afternoon	Lecture	Lecture on Military Law & C.B.'s	–	Knotting and Lashing	–	Lecture	Fire control

NB. Organised football as possible will be arranged in the evening.

3/10/17

A. Woolacott
Major O.C.
O.C. 64th G.Res.

Appendix C

O.C. 9th Div. Sig. Coy. R.E.
O.C. 63rd Field Coy. R.E.
O.C. 64th Field Coy. R.E.
O.C. 90th Field Coy. R.E.

9th Divisional Engineers.
Officers Training Course.

All officers of the above unit will attend a lecture on Military Law by the C.R.E. at H.Q. R.E. ARNEKE (Map ref. Sheet 27 H.18.c.1.9) at 3 p.m. on 4th October 1917.

For the convenience of officers located in ZEGGARS CAPPEL area, a lorry will leave Area Commandant's office, ZEGGARS CAPPEL, at 1-45 p.m.

9TH DIVISIONAL ENGINEERS.
No. 11/74
Date 3/10/17.

D.H. Jones
2/Lieut. R.E.
a/Adjt. 9th Divl. Engrs.

SECRET.

Appendix C.

9th Divisional Engineers Operation Order D.411
by Lieut-Colonel G.R. HEARN, D.S.O., R.E.
C.R.E. 9th Division.

Copy No. 2

6th Octbr. 1917.

Reference 1/100,000 Map 5A.

1. Field Companies with cook's cart (not exceeding 2 axles from each Company), will proceed to new area XVIII Corps by tactical train on October 8th 1917.

2. Transport not proceeding by train will march on 7th inst. in two groups to ST. JAN TER RIEZEN between WATOU and POPERINGHE, starting point cross roads WORMHOUDT.

3. First group will comprise :-

    26th Brigade,   64th Field Coy.
    63rd Field Coy.,   28th Field Amb.
    105th Company, A.S.C.,

    Head of column to pass starting point at 11 a.m.

4. Second group will comprise :-

    D.H.Q.,
    27th Infy. Brigade,   S.A. Field Amb.,
    90th Field Coy.,   106th Company, A.S.C.
    27th Field Amb.,

    Head of column to pass starting point at 12 noon.

5. Each group will be under command of O.C. Train Coy., who will report to Brigade H.Q. concerned to arrange details.

6. Transport of Field Companies R.E. will move by road on Octbr. 8th from ST. JAN TER RIEZEN to FRASCATI (Sheet 28, C.26.c.8.6.) under orders of senior R.E. officer with transport.

7. ACKNOWLEDGE.

2/Lieut. R.E.
a/Adjt. 9th Divl. Engrs.

Issued at 10-30 p.m.

Copies to :-
No. 1. O.C. 63rd Field Coy. R.E.   No. 9. 9th Division G.
"   2. O.C. 64th Field Coy. R.E.   " 10. 9th Division Q.
"   3. O.C. 90th Field Coy. R.E.   " 11. A.D.M.S. 9th Divn.
"   4. C.E. V Corps.   " 12. D.A.D.V.S. 9th Div.
"   5. C.E. XVIII Corps.   " 13. 9th Div. Train.
"   6. 26th Infy. Brigade.   " 14. 9th Div. Sig. Coy.
"   7. 27th Infy. Brigade.   " 15. War Diary.
"   8. S.A. Infy. Brigade.   " 16. File.
                                          " 17. Spare.

SECRET.

9th Divisional Engineers Warning Order D.410.
by Lieut-Colonel G.R. HEARN, D.S.O., R.E.
C.R.E., 9th Division.

Copy No. 2
5-10-17.

Reference 1/100,000 Map 5A.

1. The 9th Division will concentrate in the XVIII Corps forward area with a view to relieving the 48th Division in the line.

2. 27th Brigade moves on morning of the 8th by tactical train to BRAKE Camp, 1½ miles North-west of VLAMERTINGHE.

   26th Brigade moves on afternoon of the 8th by tactical train to DRIELEN.

   S.A. Brigade moves on afternoon of 10th by tactical train to BRAKE Camp.

3. For the purpose of these moves, Field Coys. will be attached as follows :-

   64th Field Coy.   --   26th Brigade.
   90th Field Coy.   --   27th Brigade.
   63rd Field Coy.   --   S.A. Brigade.

   It is possible, however, that Field Coys. will be accomodated in camps to be arranged by C.E. XVIII Corps.

4. Divisional Headquarters close at ARNEKE and open at BRAKE Camp at 4 p.m. October 8th.

5. ACKNOWLEDGE.

                                        2/Lieut. R.E.
Issued at 8 p.m.   a/Adjt. 9th Divl. Engrs.

Copies to :-
   No. 1.   O.C. 63rd Field Coy. R.E.
    "   2.   O.C. 64th Field Coy. R.E.
    "   3.   O.C. 90th Field Coy. R.E.
    "   4.   26th Infy. Brigade.
    "   5.   27th Infy. Brigade.
    "   6.   S.A. Infy. Brigade.
    "   7.   9th Division G.
    "   8.   9th Division Q.
    "   9.   A.D.M.S. 9th Division.
    " 10.   D.A.D.V.S. 9th Division.
    " 11.   9th Div. Train.
    " 12.   9th Div. Signal Coy.
    " 13.   War Diary.
    " 14.   File.
    " 15.   Spare.

"A" Form
MESSAGES AND SIGNALS.

Army Form C. 2121
(In pads of 100.)

TO {
O.C. 63rd Field Co RE
O.C. 64th Field Co RE
O.C. 90th Field Co RE
}

Sender's Number: 431
Day of Month: 7th

Warning order AAA Personnel and Transport of 63rd and 64th Field Cos must be at ESQUELBECQ at 8.25 am AAA 90th Fd Co personnel at ARNEKE at 11.30 am AAA Transport at ESQUELBECQ at 3.30 pm AAA this will be confirmed when definite orders received from Corps AAA

From: CRE
Place: 9th Divn
Time: 6 pm

Byrne
Lieut RE
Adjt 9 Divl Engrs

"A" Form
MESSAGES AND SIGNALS.

Army Form C. 2121
(In pads of 100.)

Appendix E

TO:
- O.C. 63rd Field Coy. R.E.
- O.C. 64th Field Coy. R.E.
- O.C. 90th Field Coy. R.E.

Sender's Number.	Day of Month.	In reply to Number.	AAA
D 415	7/10		

Warning Order No. 431 confirmed aaa Personnel report at stations at times mentioned with the exception of 90th Coy. transport aaa Train times are Serial No. B entrain 8-45 a.m. depart 9-25 a.m. arrive 12-30 aaa Serial No. C omnibus type entrain 9-30 a.m. depart 12-25 arrive 3-35 p.m. aaa Serial No. E entrain 2-45 p.m. depart 3-40 p.m. arrive 6-30 p.m. aaa Serial No. F omnibus type entrain 1-30 p.m. depart 4-25 p.m. arrive 7-35 p.m. aaa Any personnel for which above trains cannot find accomodation will travel by No. G reinforcement train departing ARNEKE about 4 p.m. via ESQUELBECQ aaa 90th Coy. transport will entrain in Serial No. F at 1-30 p.m. not at 3-30 p.m. as stated in this office 431 aaa 1 officer and and 10 O.R. of each Coy. accompany transport aaa Acknowledge aaa

From: C.R.E. 9th Divn.
Place:
Time: 10.50 p

2/Lieut. R.E.
AdAdjt. 9th Div. Engrs.

"A" Form.
MESSAGES AND SIGNALS.
Army Form C.2121 (in pads of 100).

Appendix G

TO: 63 Field Coy
64
90

Sender's Number: H 8/1
Day of Month: 8

Coys will take over work other Field Coys 48 Division as detailed in warning order with effect from 6am 10/10/17 aaa in view of long distance march to work from FRASCATI at least 2 sections each 64 & 90 must be billeted in forward area aaa CRE 48 will see forward area Commandant about this aaa OCs 64 & 90 to see him this evening aaa remaining 2 sections each Coy will take over billets 475 & 476 respectively & hold till further orders aaa 63rd Field Coy will similarly hold billets 474 aaa 48 Field Coys march out afternoon 16th

From: CRE 9 Division
Time: 4.15 pm

G R Hearn
Lieut CRE

SECRET.

Appendix H

O.C. 63rd Field Coy. R.E.
O.C. 64th Field Coy. R.E.
O.C. 90th Field Coy. R.E.

Herewith Administrative Instructions
No. QS/14.

      63rd and 64th Companies proceed)
with 26th Brigade;   ) See tables
      90th Company proceeds with   ) A & B.
27th Brigade.   )

      Coys. will detail 1 officer and 10 other ranks to accompany transport proceeding by omnibus train (see table B).

Please acknowledge

D.H. Jones
2/Lieut. R.E.
a/Adjt. 9th Div. Engrs.

9TH DIVISIONAL ENGINEERS.
No. D412/1
Date 7/10/17.

D412.

SECRET.

9th. Division No. QS/14.

ADMINISTRATIVE INSTRUCTIONS

issued in connection with 9th. Division Operation
Order No.154 of 5th. October 1917.

1. Two Coaching Stock Trains and one Omnibus Type Train will be available for each Brigade for the move to the forward area.

2. Details of Entraining and Detraining Stations are shewn in Table "A" attached. Train timings will be wired later.

3. Each Coaching Stock Train will accommodate two battalions of Infantry and a portion of Brigade Headquarters. The composition of the Omnibus Type Train is shewn in Table "B" attached.

4. Personnel of Divisional Headquarters and the personnel of Field Companies and Field Ambulances who cannot be accommodated in the Coaching Stock Trains, will travel by Reinforcement Train.

5. Each Brigade will send a representative beforehand to confer with the R.T.O. at the Entraining Station and to arrange details of entrainment. A respresentative will also be sent to Superintend entrainment and will hand over to the R.T.O. a complete marching out state showing the number of officers, men, horses, four-wheeled vehicles and two-wheeled vehicles proceeding by each train.

6. Each Brigade Machine Gun Company will provide a loading and unloading party for the horses, vehicles and stores carried by the Omnibus Train on which it travels.

7. All loading parties, horses, vehicles and baggage will be at the entraining station three hours before the departure of the train by which they are proceeding. The remainder of the troops will report 1½ hours before departure.

8. All Transport not allowed for in Omnibus Type Trains on 8th. instant will march on the 7th. instant in two groups to a Staging Camp at ST. JANTER BIEZEN, starting point Cross Roads WORMHOUDT.

    First Group :- 26th. Inf. Brigade, 63rd. Field Coy. R.E., 64th. Field Coy R.E., and 105th. Coy. A.S.C., under the Command of the O.C., 105th. Coy. A.S.C.

    Second Group :- Divisional Headquarters, 27th. Inf. Brigade, 90th. Field Coy. R.E., 27th. Field Ambulance, S.A. Field Ambulance, 21st. Mobile Veterinary Section and 106th. Coy. A.S.C., under the Command of the O.C., 106th. Coy. A.S.C.

Commanders of Groups will report to their Brigade Headquarters to arrange details for the march on 7th. to Staging Camp and for march on 8th. to Transport Lines in New Area.

9./

(2)

9. Advance parties of each Group will ride on ahead of their Columns and report to the Area Commandant, ST. JANTER BIEZEN.

They will take over from him 6 tents and 55 bivouac shelters for each of the Brigade Groups.

This tentage will then come on charge of the Brigades concerned, and will be carried with them for the accommodation of their Transport wherever they go.

Such of this Tentage as may be occupied by Field Companies and Field Ambulances on the night 7/8th. will be handed over on morning of the 8th. to the B.T.Os. of the Brigades concerned, and will not be retained by the former Units.

10. 28th. Field Ambulance will march with Transport direct to NOUVEAU MONDE, D.24.b.9.7., on 8th. instant.

Transports of 27th. and S.A. Field Ambulances will move independently from staging area at ST. JANTER BIEZEN on 8th. instant to GWENT FARM, A.28.a.3.7., (Sheet 28), and L'ABBE FARM, F.29.d.5.9., (Sheet 27), respectively.

Marching portions of 27th. and S.A. Field Ambulances will proceed by Reinforcement Train from ARNEKE to POPERINGHE on 8th., marching, on detrainment, to GWENT FARM, and L'ABBE FARM respectively.

11. The Transport of the three Field Companies will march on 8th. instant under orders to be issued by their Group Commanders to FRASCATIS, C.26.c.8.6. (Sheet 28), where they will be joined, on evening of 8th., by the remainder of their Field Companies.

12. Demands for Lorries to convey stores on the 8th. and 10th. instants should be forwarded to this office at once. Lorries can do one trip only.

13. Orders for the move of Transport of the S.A. Brigade will be issued later.

Lieut.-Colonel,
A.A. & Q.M.G.,
9th. Division.

6th. October 1917.

Copies to :-

26th. Inf. Brigade.
27th. Inf. Brigade.
S.A. Inf. Brigade.
C.R.E.
9th. Train.
A.D.M.S.
D.A.D.V.S.
D.A.D.O.S.
Camp Commandant.
A.P.M.

212th. Employment Coy.
Salvage Coy.
"G".
V Corps "Q".
XVIII Corps "Q".
R.T.O., ARNEKE.
R.T.O., ESQUELBECQ.
R.T.O., VLAMERTINGHE.
R.T.O., POPERINGHE.
Area Commandant, ST. JANTER BIEZEN.

TABLE "A".

TABLE OF TRAIN ARRANGEMENTS FOR MOVE OF 9th. DIVISION.

Serial No.	Date.	Nature of Train.	Formation.	Entraining Station.	Time of Departure.	Detraining Station.	Time of Arrival.
A.	8th. Oct.	Coaching Stock.	26th. Brigade.	ESQUELBECQ.		BRIELEN.	
B.	"	Coaching Stock.	26th. Brigade.	ESQUELBECQ.		VLAMERTINGHE.	
C.	"	Omnibus Type.	26th. Brigade Group (see Table "B (1)")	ESQUELBECQ.		BRIELEN.	
D.	"	Coaching Stock.	27th. Brigade.	ARNEKE.		VLAMERTINGHE.	
E.	"	Coaching Stock.	27th. Brigade.	ARNEKE.		DIRTY BUCKET CORNER.	
F.	"	Omnibus Type.	27th. Brigade Group (see Table "B(2)")	ESQUELBECQ.		DIRTY BUCKET CORNER.	
G.	"	Reinforcement.	Divisional Hd-Qrs. and Details.	ARNEKE.		VLAMERTINGHE.	
H.	10th. Oct.	Coaching Stock.	S.A. Brigade.	ESQUELBECQ.		POPERINGHE.	
I.	"	Coaching Stock.	S.A. Brigade.	WATTEN.		DIRTY BUCKET CORNER.	
J.	"	Omnibus Type.	S.A. Brigade.	ST. OMER.		VLAMERTINGHE.	

TABLE "B (1)".

26th. Infantry Brigade.   OMNIBUS TRAIN.   ESQUELBECQ - VLAMERTINGHE.   R E M A R K S.

	Personnel.		Horses.	L.G.S.	Two-Wheeled Carts.	REMARKS
	Off.	O.R.				
Brigade H.Q. & 1 L.G.S. for Cooks.	1	14	9	1	-	Extra Officers and men by Coaching Stock Trains.
Signal Section.	1	27	9	1	1	
4 Cookers, 2 Water Carts, 1 Maltese Cart, 1 Mess Cart per Battalion.	-	32	56	16	16	
Chargers & Pack Animals. 18 per Battn.	1	72	72	-	-	
26th. L.T.M.B. including 6 Hand Carts and 8 Mortars.	4	50	-	-	-	Extra .on by Coaching Stock Trains.
*26th. M.G. Coy. 1 Cooks' Cart, 1 Water Cart.	10	130	6	-	2	
64th. Fd. Coy. R.E. 1 Cooks' Cart. 1 Water Cart.	1	10	23	-	2	Remainder of personnel which cannot be fitted into Coaching Stock Trains will proceed by Reinforcement Train from ESQUELBECQ.
63rd. Fd. Coy. R.E. 1 Cooks' Cart. 1 Water Cart.	1	10	23	-	2	
	18	345	158	18	23	

59 axles.

* Finds Loading and Unloading Party of 100 men.

TABLE "E (2)".

27th. Infantry Brigade.   OMNIBUS TRAIN. – ESQUELBECQ to VLAMERTINGHE.

	Personnel. Off.	Personnel. O.R.	Horses.	L.G.S.	Two-Wheeled Carts.	REMARKS.
Brigade H.Q. & 1 L.G.S. for Cooks.	1	14	9	1	1	Extra Officers and Men by Coaching Stock Trains.
Signal Section.	1	27	9	1	1	
4 Cookers, 2 Water Carts, 1 Maltese Cart, 1 Mess Cart per Battalion.	–	33	56	16	16	
Chargers & Pack Animals. 18 per Battn.	–	–	72	–	–	
27th. L.M.T.B. including 8 Hand Carts and 8 Mortars.	4	50	–	–	–	Extra Men by Coaching Stock Trains.
*27th. L.G. Coy. 1 Cooks' Cart. 1 Water Cart.	10	130	6	1	2	Remainder of personnel which cannot be fitted into the Coaching Stock Trains will proceed by Reinforcement Train from ARNEKE.
90th. Fd. Coy., R.E. 1 Cooks' Cart. 1 Water Cart.	1	10	3	–	2	
27th. Fd. Ambulance. 2 L.G.S.	1	10	4	2	1	
S.A. Fd. Ambulance. 2 L.G.S.	1	10	4	2	1	
	18	345	159	20	21	

61 axles.

* Includes Loading and Unloading Party of 100 men.

SECRET. D489　　　　　　　　　　　　COPY NO. 2

C.R.E.'s OPERATION ORDER No.1.

  Reliefs between R.E. and Pioneers of the 9th Division and 41st Division will take place in accordance with attached table.

2. ACKNOWLEDGE.

              G R Hearn

              Lieut. Colonel R.E.
28.10.1917.   C.R.E. 9th Division.

Copy No. 1 ~~63rd Field Coy.~~
" " 2 64th Field Coy.
" " 3 ~~90th Field Coy.~~
" " 4 9th Seaforth Hldrs.(P)
" " 5 9th Div. "G"
" " 6 9th Div. "Q".
" " 7 26th Inf. Bde.
" " 8 27th Inf. Bde.
" " 9 South African Bde.
" " 10. C.E. XVth Corps.
" " 11 C.R.E. 41st Div.
" " 12 A.D.M.S. 9th Div.
" " 13 War Diary.
" " 14 File.

Appendix I

Date.	Unit.	From.	To.	Move by.	Transport to.	Relieve.
28th	237th Field Coy.	Sheet 19.D.10.a.1.9. BRAY DUNES.	TETEGHEM.	Road	–	–
28th	63rd Field Coy.	SYNTHE	R.32.a.5.0. SURREY CAMP.	Dismounted by bus. Mounted by road	SURREY CAMP.	237th Field Coy.
28th	90th Field Coy.	TETEGHEM	SYNTHE	Road	–	–
29th	228th Field Coy.	WELLINGTON CAMP	SYNTHE	Dismounted by bus. Transport by road.	–	–
29th	90th Field Coy.	SYNTHE	SURREY CAMP.	–	SURREY CAMP.	228th Field Coy.
29th	63rd Field Coy.	SURREY CAMP	WELLINGTON CAMP R.35.d.1.5.	Road	X.3.c.3.7.	–
29th	64th Field Coy.	COUDEKERKE BRANCHE.	BRAY DUNES	Road	BRAY DUNES.	–
30th	233rd Field Coy.	Line.	BRAY DUNES	Road	Bray Dunes.	–
30th	64th Field Coy.	BRAY DUNES.	SURREY CAMP.	Road.	SURREY CAMP.	Orders will follow.
30th	90th Field Coy.	SURREY CAMP.	LINE	Road.	COXYDE BAINS R.31.c.0.2.	233rd Field Coy.
29th	9th Div. Pion. less 1 Coy. to LA PANNE, via ADINKERKE.	COUDEKERKE BRANCHE	KENT CAMP R.33.b.2.6.	Dismounted by barge. Transport by road.	KENT CAMP.	19th Middlesex.(F)

1755

November
1917

Army Form C. 2118.

WAR DIARY
or
INTELLIGENCE SUMMARY

64th U Coy R.E.   **November 1917**

(Erase heading not required.)

Instructions regarding War Diaries and Intelligence Summaries are contained in F.S. Regs., Part II. and the Staff Manual respectively. Title pages will be prepared in manuscript.

Place	Date	Hour	Summary of Events and Information	Remarks and references to Appendices
SURREY CAMP	1st-9th		2 Sections Rendering Pontoons of 12th & 71st Pontoon Parks fwc. Canal at Bray-Dunes. Work on Cellars at OOST-DUNKIRK Bains. (68th Field Coy.)	DUNKIRK 1A HAZEBROUCK 5F Maps
	10th		Capt. A.C. RANKIN. R.E. ^ took over temporary command of Coy — pending MAJOR. F.D. NAHER. CLAVERING's leave — Major CLAVERING leave to ENGLAND —	
	10th–11th–12th 13th		Work as usual on Cellars at OOST-DUNKIRK-BAINS —	
	14th		Section packing up preparatory to move on 15th —	
SURREY CAMP	15th		Coy. left SURREY CAMP 8.30 am reached via ADINKERKE, GHYVELDE to FERME DU NORT (1 mile S.E. of UXEM) arriving 3.30 pm — Distance 16½ miles	
UXEM –	16th		Coy left UXEM 8.30 am arrived WORMHOUDT "A" area 2.30 pm marched via ~~Furnes~~ BERGUES & WORMHOUDT (Billets in farm 1½ mile S.W. of WORMHOUDT) Distance — 14½ miles — Lt. CULLIFORD returned from leave —	
UXEM – WORMHOUDT				
WORMHOUDT ZERMEZEELE	17th		Coy left billet 9.30 am reached a ZERMEZEELE, Billeted in town ½ mile South of F in ZERMEZEELE, arrived 12.0 noon — distance 5 miles	
ZERMEZEELE BANDRINGHEM	18th		Lt. CAWTHRA leave to ENGLAND — Coy left ZERMEZEELE 8.0 am — marched via ZUYTPEENE, EBBLINGHEM to BANDRINGHEM arriving 1.30 pm Distance 12½ miles	
BANDRINGHEM RECQUEBRECK	19th		Coy. left BANDRINGHEM 8.30 am marched via QUIESTEDE, CLARQUES, MONTLEMAITRE, to RECQUEBRECK arriving 1.15 pm — 11 Distance miles —	

2353 Wt W2544/1454 700,000 5/15 D.D.&L. A.D.S.S./Forms/C. 2118.

Army Form C. 2118.

WAR DIARY
or
INTELLIGENCE SUMMARY.
(Erase heading not required.)

Place	Date	Hour	Summary of Events and Information	Remarks and references to Appendices
RECQUEMBRUCK	20th		Left RECQUEBRUCK 8.30 am – marched via MERCK to FAUQUEMBERGUES. there received information that billets in ASSONVAL (on details in Brigade orders) not available, marched to RENTY arriving 12.0 noon – CAPT. RANKIN went to Brigade at VERCHOCQ to obtain billets – Capt. RENTY 2.30 pm & marched to ROLLEZ via VERCHOCQ arriving 4.10 pm – Distance 13 miles –	Major HAZEBROUCK.S.A. LENS. 11.–
ROLLEZ			Coy. resting –	
ROLLEZ	21st			
ROLLEZ	22nd		Coy. left ROLLEZ 8.30 am marched via COUPELLE-VIELLE, FRUGES, RUISSEAUVILLE to PLANQUES arriving 1.30 pm – Distance 9¼ miles –	
PLANQUES (LENS 11.)	23rd		Coy. Resting –	
PLANQUES				
PLANQUES	24th		At 7.30 am received orders to proceed CLAIRMARAIS (2 days march) – Coy left PLANQUES 11.0 am – marched via FRUGES: FAUQUEMBERGUES: THIEMBRONNE: BRIONVILLE to WISMES arriving 6.0 pm – Distance 17 miles – LT.ALLEN and 2 cyclists left for CLAIRMARAIS to take over billets & work from 59th & 50th Field Coys (5th Div.)	
WISMES (HAZEBROUCK.S.A)				
WISMES	25th		Coy left WISMES 8.0 am – marched via LUMBRES. TATINGHEM. ST OMER. CLAIRMARAIS to COIN PERDU arriving 3.30 pm. distance 18 miles –	
COIN PERDU				

Army Form C. 2118.

WAR DIARY
or
INTELLIGENCE SUMMARY.
(Erase heading not required.)

Place	Date	Hour	Summary of Events and Information	Remarks and references to Appendices
COIN PERDU	25th		LALLEN reports he arrived CLAIRMARAIS 4.0 p.m. on 24/11/17 but cd find no trace of field Coys of 5th Div — No 527 Coy has marched out early on 24th without leaving anyone to hand over work etc. This Coy had occupied billets 1 mile NE of "S" in CLAIRMARAIS (MONASTERY CAMP) Were now occupied on 24th by 121 Siege Battery RGA. the cars fnd	Map. HAZEBROUCK 5H
			no trace of 59th Coy — Coy resting —	
COIN PERDU	26th		Capt McRankin returned to 63 DCo on return of Major Sharp / Maycum from leave.	
	27/k		Reconnoiting jobs etc wagonlum.	
	28		Owing to Lt 59 Coy having left — great delay in finding out the work — not started at HA Road station. Conf. Recon on Balk horse evaded government hanging	
			doors & bunking, material lacking	
	29		Work continued. Material still not to hand. Saw CE X Corps re drinks & hutting arranged.	
	30		Material arrived last night which now going on well & put progress made.	
			Intimation received that Lt. CANTLINA wc was appointed 2/Capt as 2nd/Command of company	

Sharpe/Maycum
Major RE
OC 69th Coy RE

WAR DIARY
or
INTELLIGENCE SUMMARY.
(Erase heading not required.)

Army Form C. 2118.

64th A Coy R.E.
Vol 32

Place	Date	Hour	Summary of Events and Information	Remarks and references to Appendices
HEUDICOURT	13th		Shelling started in front line here & reported hits from *16.32 started to support line behind QUENTIN MILL	
	14th		Repair of pumping station in GOUZEAUCOURT started	
	16th		Balce have for water tanks completed	
	18th		Unwilland reports from 4th Army School	
	20th		20 shells have been used in hour	
	22nd		Orders orders to OK	
	23rd		70 men of 2nd & 3rd Regt SMI attached for work within GOUZEAUCOURT village	
	24th		Dugout started at HQ Coy HQ & Regt Bn HQ	
	27th		Pump at Gouzeaucourt now in working order. Started making forward redoubt 1st & 2nd section at Q.35.c.17. 5th Div No 1st & 4th Coy S.M attached for work in defence of GOUZEAUCOURT	
	28th		Coy HQ moved to FINS.	
	30th		Work parties for Gouzeaucourt from 301 Bde relieved by 20 officers & 120 OR from 2nd & Bde.	
	31st		One section moved forward billets at Q.35.c.12 Wednesday reports from hospital	

MAJOR R.E.,
O.C. 64th FD. CO. R.E.

1755

Dec 1917

Army Form C. 2118.

WAR DIARY
or
INTELLIGENCE SUMMARY.

DECEMBER 1917   64th Bn COY

Place	Date	Hour	Summary of Events and Information	Remarks and references to Appendices
COINPEROU	1st		Acting on orders received late last night Coy. moved at 9.0 am this morning to SENLIS to join the S.A. Bde GROUP. Personnel by bus, transport by road (82 miles)	'A'
SENLIS	2nd			'B'
	3rd		Left at 10.10 pm for ANVIN. Entrained with S.A. Bde Group & arr at 8.0 am & detrained at PERONNE	
	4th		CHIPPILETTE, about 2 pm marched to MOISLAINS arriving about 8.0 pm. Left MOISLAINS at 2 pm marched to HEUDECOURT attached for work to CRE GUARDS Divn.	'C'
HEUDECOURT	5th		Worked on Reserve line wiring & preparing firesteps Infantry & GOUZEAUCOURT-WOOD	
	6th		Intl section ordered to return to METZCOURT HEADQPS ie as yesterday	
	7th		2 Section makin strong point at REVELON Fm. 1 section owners Bde HQ	
	8th		1 Section wire wrenching Work under CRE Gds Divn. worth S.A. Bde. Capt Carstens returned from leave.	
	9th			
	10th		Warm up GOUZEAUCOURT Valley started. 1 NCO & 2 Sappers destroyed 6 German TMs at X.16.9.5.95 in No mans land. Capt Carstens leaves for R.E. School BLENDECQUES	Strength 57
	12th		Lt MCKAY to hospital	
	13th		B Coy officers left the Pioneers attached to Bde Started improving Support line	

"A" Form.
MESSAGES AND SIGNALS.

Prefix... Code... m	Words.	Charge.	This message is on a/c of:	Recd. at ...m.
Office of Origin and Service Instructions.	Sent		...Service.	Date...
	At...m.			From...
	To...			
	By...		(Signature of "Franking Officer.")	By...

TO { 4 Units

| Sender's Number. | Day of Month. | In reply to Number. | AAA |

(H) Entraining states will be handed to Staff Captain by advance officers.

(J) Units will move under their own arrangements to reach ANVIN at times stated

(K) Order of Entraining of 1.20 AM Train 3rd inst as stated
Order of Entraining of 4.20 AM Train 3rd inst as stated

(L) Staff Captain will remain at ANVIN and leave by last Train

(M) Bde HQrs will close at HEUCHIN at 10.30 AM on 2nd and open at PERONNE on same day. Location to be notified later aaa
acknowledge aaa.

From: South African Bde.
Place:
Time: 2.40 AM.

The above may be forwarded as now corrected. (Z) Utshaw Major

Censor. Signature of Addressor or person authorised to telegraph in his name.

"A" Form.
MESSAGES AND SIGNALS.

Army Form C. 2121.

TO: 3rd Sect

AAA

(c) Personnel will report at ANVIN 1½ hours before departure of Train
(d) An officer from each Unit entraining will report to Staff Captain at RTO's office ANVIN ½ hour before arrival of Transport for instructions
(e) One Company of 4th SAI has been detailed to load all Trains of SA Bde Group
(f) One Company of 1st SAI has been detailed to ~~load~~ off load all Trains of SA Bde Group at PERONNE
(g) Supply waggons loaded will accompany units on their respective Trains 107 Coy. will ensure this being done

(continued)

Prefix....Code....m Office of Origin and Service Instructions.	Words. Charge. Sent At........m. To By	This message is on a/c of: ....Service. (Signature of "Franking Officer.")	Recd. at .... m. Date........ From........ By........

TO: 2nd Sheet

Sender's Number.	Day of Month.	In reply to Number.	A A A
cooker	and	team	by
Train	leaving	at	10.20 pm
2nd inst	aaa	28th F.Ambulance	
one Coy	2nd SAI	one Company	
32nd SAD	with	cookers and teams	
by	Train	leaving	at
1.20 AM	3rd Inst aaa	64th	
Field	Coy R.E	107 Company	
A.S.C.	one Company	4th SA Inf	
with	cooker and team	by Train	
leaving	at 4.20 AM	on 3rd inst	
aaa.			

(a). Transport will accompany units except where otherwise specified
(b) Transport and horses will report at ANVIN 3 hours before Time of departure of Train
(Continued)

From
Place
Time

"A" Form.
MESSAGES AND SIGNALS.

Prefix	Code	Words	Charge	This message is on a/c of:	Rec'd at m.
Office of Origin and Service Instructions		Sent At m. To By		Service	Date From By

Secret

TO: ~~(struck through addressees)~~

Sender's Number	Day of Month	In reply to Number	AAA
*BM.331	2nd		

In	addition	to	trains
detailed	in	my	BM 326
the	following	trains	are
allotted	to	SA Bde	Group
and	Units	will	leave
at	hours	stated	aaa
1st SAI	less one Coy	and Cookers and	
train	by	train	leaving
at	1.20pm	2nd inst	aaa
2nd SAI	less	one Company and	
Cookers	and train	by	train
leaving	at	4.20pm	2nd inst
aaa.	3rd SAI	less	one
Company	and	Cookers	and train
by	train	leaving	at
7.20pm	2nd inst	aaa.	4th SAI
less	one	Company	and

From
Place ..... Ⓑ ..... Authorised
Time

(Z)
Censor.   Signature of Addressor or person authorised to telegraph in his name.

* This line should be erased if not required.

"A" Form.
MESSAGES AND SIGNALS.

Army Form C. 2121.

Prefix: FHW Priority

Recd. at 8 PM
Date 30.11.17
From KO
By Burden S.

TO 64TH Field Coy RE.

Sender's Number	Day of Month	In reply to Number	AAA
G 784	30.11.17		

The Coy will move tomorrow to SENLIS aaa transport by road personnel by bus aaa busses will be at road junction half mile South West of COIN PERDU at 9.40 AM aaa Route Arques Wizernes Fruges aaa Acknowledge aaa

From 9TH DIVISION

"A" Form.
MESSAGES AND SIGNALS.

Army Form C. 2121.
(In pads of 100.)

TO:
- 64th Field Coy. R.E.
- S.A. Bgde.
- 9th Divn. G.
- 9th Divn. Q.
- 9th Divn. Sigs.
- C.E. III Corps.
- C.R.E. Guards Divn.

Sender's Number: D532
Day of Month: 3/12
In reply to Number: AAA

S.A. Bgde with 64th Field Coy. R.E. S.A. Field Ambulance 107th Coy. A.S.C. will move tomorrow morning to HEUDICOURT to relieve Right Bde. Guards Division on night 4/5th AAA One car and two lorries will be at Brigade H.Q. 8 a.m. to convey Brigade representatives Battalion I.O's and representatives from each Infantry Company M.G. Coy. T.M.B. Guards D.H.Q. NEUVILLE 57C. P.22. Right Brigade H.Q. to be notified later AAA Orders to move to HEUDICOURT following AAA Acknowledge AAA Addsd. 64th Fld Coy. R.E. rptd. S.A. Bde. 9th Divn. G. 9th Divn. Q. 9th Div. Signals C.E. III Corps C.R.E. Guards Divn. AAA

From: C.R.E. 9th Division.
Place:
Time: 10-22 p.m.

Capt. R.E.
Adjt. 9th Div. Engrs.

SECRET

9th Divisional Engineers Operation Order No.D.529
by Lieut-Colonel G.R. HEARN, D.S.O., R.E.
C.R.E., 9th Division.

Copy No. 2
30/11/17.

1. 9th Division will move by railway to new area commencing Dec. 1st.

2. 26th Infy. Bde. move to BLANGY, HUMIERES, WAVRANS area, and entrain at last named place.

   27th Infy. Bde. move to HESDIN area, and entrain at HESDIN.

   S.A. Infy. Bde. move to BERGUENEUSE area to entrain at ANVIN.

   9th Div. Artillery entrain first at all these stations mentioned above.

3. 63rd Field Coy. to move under orders of 26th Inf. Bde.

   64th Field Coy. to move dismounted by bus, and transport by road to SENLIS, and come under orders of S.A. Inf. Bde.

   90th Field Coy. to leave present billets at 2 p.m. 1st Dec. and move to PLANQUES, and there to come under orders of 27th Inf. Bde.

4. 90th Field Coy. on march must not interfere with movements of 26th and S.A. Inf. Bdes., and move by route MAISONCELLE and CREQUY.

5. ACKNOWLEDGE.

Issued at 11 p.m.

Capt. R.E.
Adjt. 9th Divl. Engrs.

Copies to :-
No. 1. O.C. 63rd Field Coy. R.E.
 " 2. O.C. 64th Field Coy. R.E.
 " 3. O.C. 90th Field Coy. R.E.
 " 4. 26th Infy. Bde.
 " 5. 27th Infy. Bde.
 " 6. S.A. Inf. Bde.
 " 7. 9th Div. G.
 " 8. 9th Div. Q.
 " 9. 9th Div. Train.
 " 10. A.D.M.S. 9th Div.
 " 11. War Diary.
 " 12. File.
 " 13. Spare.

"A" Form.
MESSAGES AND SIGNALS.

Army Form C. 2121.
(In pads of 100.)

TO	64th Field Coy. R.E.	9th Div. Sigs.
	~~S.A. Bde.~~	9th Div. Train.
	~~9th Divn. G.~~	C.E. III Corps.
	~~9th Divn. Q.~~	CRE Guards Div

Sender's Number.	Day of Month.	In reply to Number.	
D 536	4/12		A A A

64th Field Coy. march with S.A. Brigade
to HEUDICOURT and will be billeted
there AAA To report to C.R.E. Guards
Division and work under his orders
on 5/6th until relieved AAA Old billets
Guards Field Coys. not available AAA
acknowledge AAA Addressed all concerned

From C.R.E. 9th Divn.

Time 3-45 p.m.

Capt. R.E.
(Z) Adjt. 9th Div. Engrs.

SECRET.

9th Divisional Engineers Warning Order D.537.
by Lieut-Colonel G.R. HEARN, D.S.O., R.E.
C.R.E. 9th Division.

Copy No. 2
4-12-17.

1. 9th Division will relieve the Guards Division on front E. of GOUZEAUCOURT.

2. The C.R.E. will arrange relief of Field Coys. and Pioneer Battalion.

3. 64th Field Coy. has been ordered to move to HEUDECOURT.

4. 63rd Field Coy. R.E. and 90th Field Coy. R.E. to be prepared to move at 9 a.m. 5th inst.

5. 9th Seaforth Hrs. (Pioneers) arrive MOISLAINS night 4/5th.

6. Field Coys. R.E. and Pioneer Battn. of Guards Division will work on night 5/6th.

7. Accomodation of Field Coys. R.E. Guards Division will probably not be taken over by R.E. 9th Divn.

8. G.O.C. 9th Division will take over command of the Division front at 10 a.m. Dec. 6th.

9. ACKNOWLEDGE.

Capt. R.E.
Adjt. 9th Divl. Engrs.

Copies to:-
No. 1. O.C. 63rd Field Coy. R.E.
 " 2. O.C. 64th Field Coy. R.E.
 " 3. O.C. 90th Field Coy. R.E.
 " 4. O.C. 9th Seaforth Hrs. (Pioneers).
 " 5. 26th Infy. Bde.
 " 6. 27th Infy. Bde.
 " 7. S.A. Infy. Bde.
 " 8. 9th Division G.
 " 9. 9th Division Q.
 " 10. C.R.E. Guards Divn.
 " 11. C.E. III Corps.
 " 12. War Diary.
 " 13. File.

1755

Jan 1918

Army Form C. 2118.

WAR DIARY
or
INTELLIGENCE SUMMARY

64th 2d Corps

Jany. 1918

Vol 33

Place	Date	Hour	Summary of Events and Information	Remarks and references to Appendices
FINS.	1st		Distribution 1 Coy. 1 section defence of GOUZEAUCOURT. 1 section making forward billets at Q.33.c.22. 1 section front line shelters + dugouts. 1 section accommodation in back area (shelters). Area was blown down by explosion in tramway land with complete success, no after-m - Diam 3'-0". A canvas tube 3" diam was filled with 20lbs Ammonal carried out by the patrol & lashed into the tree 2ft from the ground and fired by electricity.	Sketch 57c
	2nd		Two sections moved into found billets.	Had
	3rd to 7th		Work as usual	
	8th		Mess returns from leave.	
	9th		Fired 20lb 60cm hydraulic mines laid from X.10.a.24 to X.10.c.19 to W.6.b.55	
	10th		Wells etc. visited W.6.6.3.9.	
	11th		Further progress on line to OK	
	12th		Line finished head at Q.86.d.12.	
	13th		Three sects in 15 bungalows in forward support lines. Forward park to 120 men from 26th Bde relieved to Base, from which line in GOUZEAUCOURT	
	14th		Coy reheved of front area work, now with 2 sections in GOUZEAUCOURT & 2 sections in Shelters & Grave work.	Appendix A.

2353. Wt.W2344/T454. 700,000. 5/15. D.D.& L. A.D.S.S./Forms/C.2118.

Army Form C. 2118.

WAR DIARY
or
INTELLIGENCE SUMMARY.
(Erase heading not required)

64th Fd Co R.E.   JAN Contd

Place	Date	Hour	Summary of Events and Information	Remarks and references to Appendices
FINS	14th		Bunks for 1 batln at FINS Nissen H.Q. at NURLU	
	15th		Bunks for 1 Bde at FINS MOISLAINS + HEUDECOURT	
			Shafts of dugout in posn in GOUZEAUCOURT started. Wire finished. 30 infantry from 26th Bde attached	
	18th		All Bunks pritn at FINS pulled up again. Co camp is to be dismantled	
	19th		Erection of 2 brick fireplaces in each Adrian Hut started at MOISLAINS. improvements to Bde & 7H.Q. huts	
	20th		New Camp of NISSEN HUTS at SOREL started	
	23rd		Dis-H.Q. complete	
	24th		26th Bde pack withdrawn SATURE pack arrived tomorrow	
	25th		Lt CULLIFORD to 5th Army H.Q. to act as O.C. Theatrical Troupe	
	26th		Wharf – MOISLAINS completed	
	29th		Coy moves to BRAY. leaving FINS 8.0am reaching train BRAY at 3.0pm Hudson's 234 Co RE	Appendix B
BRAY	30th		Lt NIVEN reports from leave. Coy resting	
	31st		Lt NEEDHAM. leave to U.K. 2 Section pontoons in SOMME. 2 section work on billets & laying for 26th Bde	

Major Morin
MAJOR R.E.,
O.O. 64th FD. CO. R.E.

SECRET.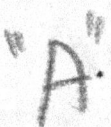

9th Divisional Engineers Operation Order No.E.20.
By Major A.E. DRUCE FIELDING, R.E.
a/C.R.E., 9th Division.

12th Jany. 1918.
Copy No.4......

Ref map 57 C.
Reference 9th Div. Order No.177.

1. From 14th inst. inclusive the Division front will be held by two Brigades.

2. Brigades in the following order will be withdrawn into rest in the MCISLAINS area and FINS, for about 10 days each:-

   S.A. Bgde.   26th Bgde.   27th Bgde.

3. The dividing line between Brigades holding the front will be R.31.d.50.35. - R.31.d.15.35. - W.6.b.60.95.

4. Command of the two Bgde. areas as above will be assumed by the G.O.C. 26th Bgde. on the left, and the G.O.C. 27th Bgde. on the right, at 9 a.m. 13th Jan. 1918.

5. The 63rd Fld Coy. R.E. will work in the left Bgde. area.
   The 90th Fld Coy. R.E. "   "   "   " right "   "
   The 64th Fld Coy. R.E. will be employed on definite works as ordered by this office.

6. The 63rd and 90th Fld Coys. R.E. will concentrate their efforts on drainage of the trenches, the provision of shelters and of raised duckboarding in the posts, wiring QUENTIN ridge, dugouts in the forward system of trenches, maintenance of tramways &c. The erection of screens must be considered, and put in hand forthwith. Close liaison must be maintained with G.O.Cs. Brigades, and every possible assistance given them.
   The 64th Fld Coy. R.E. will continue work on the GOUZEAUCOURT defences, hutting, &c. The O.C. 64th Fld Coy. R.E. will also see the G.O.C. 9th Divl. R.A., and organise and supervise the work of the batteries on wiring, deep dugouts, and shelters. He will also relieve the eprs. of the other fd. coys. on this work.
   The 90th Fld Coy. R.E. will continue work on the HEUDICOURT defences.

7. Acknowledge.

Capt. R.E.
Adjt. 9th Divl. Engrs.

Copies to:-
9th Division G.
G.R.A.
63rd Fld Coy. R.E.
64th Fld Coy. R.E.
90th Fld Coy. R.E.
War Diary.
File.

SECRET   Copy No. 11

26th (Highland) Brigade Operation Order No. 180.

Reference maps -   29/1/18.
    Sheets 57.c. and 67.c. 1/40,000.
    AMIENS 1/100000.

1.   The 26th (Highland) Brigade Group will move tomorrow January 29th to the BRAY-SUR-SOMME Area, in accordance with the attached tables.

2.   All dismounted personnel will be conveyed by two coaching stock trains from PERONNE (FLAMICOURT Station) to LE PLATEAU (immediately S.W. of CARNOY).

3.   Each train will consist of 44 Third Class coaches (capable of holding 1,760 Other Ranks), two First Class coaches for officers, and two covered vans for Lewis Guns. No baggage will be placed in the Brake Vans at the ends of the trains.

4.   (a) The first train will leave at 11 a.m. and will be made up as follows -
            28th Field Ambulance
            26th M.G. Company
            8th Black Watch
            5th Cameron Hrs.

     (b) The second train will leave at 1 p.m. and will be made up as follows :-
            64th Field Coy. R.E.
            7th Seaforth Hrs.
            26th T.M. Battery
            10th A. & S. Hrs.
            26th Bde. H.Q. Group.

     (c) Units will entrain in the above order.

5.   Lieut. Dickson, 5th Cameron Hrs. will assist in the entraining, and Captain Cavendish, 10th A. & S. Hrs. in the detraining of units.

6. (a) The first train will be under the orders of O.C., 8th Black
                                                                    Watch
        The second "   "   "   "   "   "   " O.C., 7th Seaforth
                                                                    Hrs.
    (b) These officers will be responsible for the carrying out of entrainment and detrainment assisted by the above mentioned officers of the Brigade Staff.

    (c) No officer or man will leave the train at LE PLATEAU until orders to do so are issued by the Os.C., Trains.
        The correct order of detrainment must be strictly adhered to.

7. (a) All personnel will carry rations for the day on the train.
    (b) Refilling point for Jan.29th will be at PERONNE.
        Time 9 a.m. approx.

8.   All transport will move by road in accordance with attached Table "C". The necessary cookers for breakfasts will be detailed by units, and will march independently.

9.   Clock hour halts at ten minutes to every hour will be observed by all units on the line of march.
        Synchronisation of watches with the Brigade Major, at 7 p.m. tonight 28th instant.
        Units at SOREL, FINS, and HEUDICOURT will synchronise by telephone.

- 2 -

10. Distances of 200x between coys., and a minimum of 100x between transport of all units, will be kept while on the march.

11. Lorries on the following scale for surplus kits, packs and blankets will report at the H.Q. of units as follows.
2 Lorries per Battalion, 1 per M.G.Company and T.M.Battery and 1 for Brigade H.Q..

    8th Black Watch   )
    5th Cameron Hrs.) 6 a.m. on 29th.
    26th M.G.Company)

    7th Seaforth Hrs.)
    10th A. & S. Hrs.) 8 a.m. on 29th.
    26th Bde. H.Q.   )

26th T.M.Battery will send a representative to 26th M.G.Company H.Q. by 6 a.m. on 29th to guide lorry to 26th T.M.Batty H.Q., SOREL LE GRAND.

12. Arrival of units, new locations of H.Q., and marching in states, will be forwarded to Brigade H.Q. on 29th Jan..

13. 26th Brigade H.Q. will close at MOISLAINS at 10 a.m. on Jan. 29th and will open at the HOSPICE, BRAY SUR SOMME at the same hour.

Acknowledge by wire.

                                            Captain,
                                       Brigade Major,
                                 26th (Highland)Brigade.

Issued at 2.35 pm

Copies to :-
1 8th Black Watch
2 7th Seaforth Hrs.
3 5th Cameron Hrs.
4 10th A. & S. Hrs.
5 26th M.G.Company
6 26th T.M.Battery
7 26th Bde. Transpt. Off.
8 " " Supply Off.
9 " " Sig. Off.
10 105th Coy. A.S.C.
11 64th Field Coy. R.E.
12 28th Field Ambnce.
13 9th Division "G"
14/16 9th Division "Q"
17 Area Commdt., MOISLAINS
18 " " BRAY-SUR-SOMME
19 R.T.O., MARENNE, PLAMICOURT Stn.
20 R.T.O., LE PLATEAU Station.
21 Staff Captain
22 War Diary
23 File

Movement Table "A" to accompany Operation Order No.130.

Item	Date	Unit	From	To	By	Siding & time of entraining.	Siding & time of detraining.	Route	Remarks.
1.	29th Jan.	105th Coy.A.S.C.	NURLU	BRAY-SUR-SOMME	Route March	-	-	MERCURT - HERBE-COURT - CAPPY.	To start from NURLU at 6 a.m. under own arrangements.
2.	"	28th Fd. Ambnce.	HEUDECOURT (FLAMICOURT Stn.)	P RONNE	Decauville & march route.	A.X.112.FINS 7 a.m.	A.X.2.ST DENIS 8.45 am approx.	-	By march route from detraining siding to FLAMICURT Stn.
3.	"	25th M.G. Company	FINS	B	"	"	As for item 2.	-	As for item 2.
4.	"	8th Black Watch	B. de LECHELLE	"	March route	-	-	AIZECOURT and ST DENIS.	To pass S.P. B.20 .d.0.4. at 8 am.
5.	"	5th Cameron Hrs.	MOISLAINS	"	"	-	-	As for item 4.	As for item 4. To pass 6.10 am.
6.	"	84th Fd. Coy. R.E.	FINS	"	DECAUVILLE & match route.	A.X.13. W.18.a.1.1. 8.30 a.m.	A.X.2. ST DENIS 10.15 am approx.	-	As for item 2.
7.	"	7th Seaforth Hrs.	SORL-LE-GRAND	"	"	As for item 6.	As for item 6.	-	As for item 2.
8.	"	36th T.M. Battery	"	"	"	"	"	-	As for item 2.
9.	"	10th A. & S. Hrs.	B. de GURLU	"	March route	-	-	As for item 4.	To pass S.P. D.20.d.0.4. at 10 a.m.
10.	"	26th Bde H.Q. Group.	MOISLAINS	"	"	-	-	"	As for item 9. To pass at 10.10 a.m.

Movement Table "B" to accompany Operation Order No.180.

Item	Date	Unit and order of detraining.	From	To.	Approx. time of detraining	Remarks.
1.	29th Jan.	8th Black Watch	LE PLATEAU Detraining Station.	CHIPILLY	12 noon	Via BRAY and ETINEHEM.
2.	"	5th Cameron Hrs.		BRAY SUR SOMME	"	To move off in rear of 8th Black Watch.
3.	"	26th M.G.Company		"	"	
4.	"	28th Field Ambnce.		"	"	
5.	"	7th Seaforth Hrs.		MCRCOURT	2 p.m.	Via BRAY – ETINEHEM – CHIPILLY.
6.	"	64th Field Coy. R.E.		BRAY SUR SOMME	"	To move off in rear of 7th Seaforth Hrs.
7.	"	26th T.A.Battery		"	"	
8.	"	10th A. & S. Hrs.		"	"	
9.	"	26th Bde. H.Q. Group.		"	"	

Transport Movement Table "C" to accompany
Operation Order No.180.

Item	Date	Transport of.	From	To	Route	Starting point	Time at which head of column will pass S.P.
1.	29th Jan.	8th Black Watch	MOISLAINS	CHIPILLY	ALLAINES - Mt.St.QUEN-TIN - PERONNE - LA CHAPELLETTE - BIACHES - HERBECOURT - DOMPIERRE - CHUIGNES - CHUIGNOLLES - MERICOURT.	MOISLAINS Church (C.18.c.4.8) (sheet 57.c.)	7 a.m.
2.	"	7th Seaforth Hrs.	do.	MERICOURT	As for item 1.	do.	7.5 a.m.
3.	"	5th Cameron Hrs.	do.	FRAY - SUR - SOMME	As for item 1. as far as HERBECOURT thence via CAPPY.	do.	7.10 a.m.
4.	"	10th A. & S. Hrs.	do.	do.	As for item 3.	do.	7.15 a.m.
5.	"	26th Bde. H.Q.Group	do.	do.	As for item 3.	do.	7.20 a.m.
6.	"	26th M.G.Company	FINS	do.	FINS - NURLU - PERONNE thence as for item 3.	Cross Roads V.29.a.3.2. (sheet 57.c.)	7 a.m.
7.	"	64th Field Coy. R.E.	do.	do.	As for item 6.	do.	7.5 a.m.
8.	"	23th Field Ambnce.	HEUDECOURT	do.	NURLU - PERONNE thence as for item 6.	do.	7.10 a.m.

SECRET.

9th Divisional Engineers
Operation Order No. E.65
by Lieut-Colonel G.F. HEARN, D.S.O., R.E.
C.R.E., 9th. Division.

Copy No. 2......
27-1-18.

1. Brigades will move as follows :-

   26th Bde. group on January 29th to BRAY area.
   S.A. Bde. group on January 31st from line to SOREL, GURLU WOOD &c.
   27th Bde. group on February 1st from line to HAUT ALLAINES.

   Command of sector passes at 10 a.m. February 2nd.

2. 64th Field Coy. will accompany 26th Brigade.
   63rd   "   "   "   "   S.A.   "
   90th   "   "   "   "   27th   "

   9th Seaforth Hrs.(Pioneers) will move on February 1st.

3. Work and billets will be handed over as follows :-

   63rd Field Coy. to 234th Field Coy.
   90th Field Coy. to 225th Field Coy.
   9th Seaforth Hrs.(Pioneers) to 13th Gloucesters(Pioneers).

4. 64th Field Coy. billets will not be taken over. The work will be taken over by Field Coys. working in Brigade areas, i.e.

   GOUZEAUCOURT defences by 234th Field Coy.
   R.F.A. mined dugouts by 234th and 225th Coys.
   Hutting at SOREL by a hutting party to be formed.
   Personnel of 64th Cdy. working on R.F.A. dugouts will be attached to 63rd Field Coy. or 90th Field Coy. for accomodation and rations until relieved. Lieut. Fox STRANGEWAYS, R.E. will arrange this with the Fld Coy. Comdrs. direct, and he will remain at Div. H.Q., moving with H.Q. R.E. to rejoin his unit on February 2nd.

5. Advance parties from 39th Division will arrive as follows :-

   234th Field Coy. on January 28th.
   225th Field Coy. on January 29th.
   13th Gloucesters (2nd in command and 2 officers) on January 28th.

6. Major FURNEAUX and Capt. KEATINGE will hand over all plans and work on Main line of Resistance and Corps Line to 2nd in command of 13th Gloucesters.

7. R.S.M. SELF, R.E. will hand over TYKE dump to representative C.R.E. 39th Division on 30th inst.
   Corpl. WAUGH, 9th Seaforths(Pnrs), will hand over interest in Corps R.E. dump, FINS, to representative C.R.E. 39th Div. on 30th inst.

/8.

2.

8. Loading parties at FINS and TYKE dumps will not be required after 29th inst., C.R.E. 39th Div. providing reliefs on 30th inst.

9. ACKNOWLEDGE.

[signature]
Capt. R.E.
Adjt. 9th Div. Engrs.

Copies to :-
No.1 O.C. 63rd Field Coy. R.E.
2 O.C. 64th Field Coy. R.E.
3 O.C. 90th Field Coy. R.E.
4 O.C. 9th Seaforth Hrs.(Pioneers).
5 9th Division G.(for information).
6 9th Division Q.("   "   )
7 C.R.A.
8 A.D.M.S.
9 9th Div. Train.
10 Lt. Fox STRANGEWAYS, R.E.
11 C.R.E. 39th Division(for information).
12 War Diary.
13 File.

1755

FEB 1918

Army Form C. 2118.

WAR DIARY
or
INTELLIGENCE SUMMARY.
(Erase heading not required.)

64th Field Co. R.E.

FEBRUARY 1918

Vol 34

Place	Date	Hour	Summary of Events and Information	Remarks and references to Appendices
BRAY.	1st	—	½ Coy Pontoon (Pontoon) 8.30 am to 1 pm. ½ Coy Brushwork obstacles experimental type.	
	2nd		½ Coy Bridging ½ Coy works & Squad drill. Baths afternoon.	
	3rd		Church Parade. Rifle range 6 tgts per battn. of 226 & 130 stations. 100 prone a greener football.	
	4th		a.a on 2nd. Football	
	5th		Bridging Scheme at CHIPPY. Hot section. Prevention Hut for Pool in Bray started. Football	
	6th		as yesterday (no 2 section bridging)	
	7th		Bridging Schemes No 3 section. ½ Coy Rowing drill + Lewis machine	
	8-9th		Works. Rowing + range. No.4 section Bridging Scheme. Company drill	
	10th		Church parade. Football. A cross was erected at Deville Wood in memory of the men who fell in last battle of the Somme.	
	11th		Pontoon races. Competition on range. Packing up wagons.	
	12th		Coy returned 63rd Co R.E. at FINS for work under 9th. Divn.	Appendix A

Note on Training. Pontoon drill at the double was substituted for Infantry drill and appeared to achieve the object of making the men more supple, alert & mentally alert. Squad drill was slow. Competitions were held in Trestle drill, Bridge bn Saunders (75ft) boat races rifle range football

Army Form C. 2118.

WAR DIARY
or
INTELLIGENCE SUMMARY.
(Erase heading not required.)

Place	Date	Hour	Summary of Events and Information	Remarks and references to Appendices
FINS.	13/5/20		Coy working on potsin Corpoline behind GOUZEAUCOURT. & also Gplowshire (main line of resistance) for 39/t Division.	Appendix B
	14/5		L/CPL ALLEN left to be attached to HA. at VILLERS FAUCON	
	19/5		2/Lt MCKAY been to U.K. 2/Lt MEDLAND returned from leave	
	21st		Road to SAILLY le SEC. transport & road dismantled by light railway from FINS	
SAILLY LE SEC.	22nd		to BRAY sthence by march route	
	23rd		L/ALLEN returned from attachment to HA. Coy resting. road to Div HQ. to act as CRE.	
	24+25		Major Kapur(Sappers)	Training
	26		moved to BRAY	
	27		Winn & stores sent	
	28.		Pushing up preparation for move to MOISLAINS	

Whaples/Laveny
Major N.Z.
O.C. 6th Field Coy N.Z.

O.C. 63rd Field Coy. R.E.
O.C. 64th Field Coy. R.E.

App. A

63rd Field Coy. R.E. will be relieved by 64th Field Coy. R.E. on February 12th next under the following arrangements :-

Train for 120 men 64th Field Coy. will be in position at BRAY at 6-30 a.m. and will leave at 7 a.m. arriving at FINS about 11-30 a.m.
Train will return with 120 men 63rd Field Coy. from AX 119(FINS) at 1 p.m. arriving at BRAY about 6 p.m.

Transport will move by road on same date.

2. O.C. 64th Field Coy. R.E. will leave a handing over party of 1 N.C.O. and 4 men(cyclists), with rations for 12th and 13th, who will hand over billets to 63rd Field Coy., proceeding by road to rejoin 64th Coy. on Feb. 13th.

3. O.C. 63rd Field Coy. will detail 1 N.C.O. and 4 men(cyclists), with rations for 12th and 13th, who will report to O.C. 64th Coy. on arrival at FINS to act as guides to works taken over by relieving Company. This party will proceed by road to rejoin their Company when no longer required for this purpose.

4. ACKNOWLEDGE.

> H.Q.
> 9TH ROYAL
> ENGINEERS.
> 19/6
> 10/2/18.

B H Jones.
2/Lieut. R.E.
for C.R.E. 9th Division.

Copy to 9th Division G.
 "   " 9th Division Q.
 "   " C.R.E. 39th Division.

S E C R E T.

39th Divisional Order No. 218.

Appendix B.

Ref. Map Sheets
VALENCIENNES 12 & AMIENS 17.

20/2/18.

1. The 64th Field Company, R.E., 9th Division, attached to the 39th Division will rejoin the 9th Division in the BRAY Area on February 21st 1918.

2. Personnel will proceed by Light Railway, entraining at A.X. 13 on 21st instant and detraining at BRAY.
The A.A. and Q.M.G. will notify train arrangements.
Transport will proceed by road, staging the night 21st/22nd February at PERONNE - Accommodation from Town Major PERONNE. The O.C. 64th Field Company, R.E., will issue the necessary orders.
The move from PERONNE will be under the orders of the 9th Division.

3. Rations for consumption on 22nd instant will be carried.

4. ACKNOWLEDGE.

Lieut.-Colonel,
General Staff,
39th Division.

Copies issued at 1.30 p.m. to :-

1 G.O.C.
2 G.
3&4 A.Q.
5 A.D.M.S.
6 D.A.D.V.S.
7 D.A.D.O.S.
8 A.P.M.
9 Signals.
10&11 War Diary
12 39th Div. R.A.
13 39th Div. R.E.
14 116th Inf. Bde.
15 117th Inf. Bde.
16 118th Inf. Bde.
17 13/Glouc.R.
18 228th M.Gun Co.
19 197th M.Gun Co.
20 Div. Train.
21 S.S.O.
22 Supply Column
23 Ammn. Sub-Park.
24 Div. Gas Officer
25 Div. Wing VII Corps Reinforcement Camp.
26&27 VII Corps.
28 2nd Division.
29 9th Division.
30 16th Division.
31 21st Division.
32 Town Major PERONNE
33 64th Field Co. R.E.

SECRET.

C.R.E.
64th Field Coy. R.E. (through 39th Division)
Transport Officer, 64th Field Coy. R.E. (C/O Town Maj. PERONNE).
"Q".
9th Div. Train.

No. X.8/2892/38.   20th February, 1918.
----

1. The 64th Field Coy. R.E. will rejoin the 9th Division on the 21st instant as follows:-

   Personnel On arrival at BRAY by Light Railway on 21st inst. the company will march to billets in SAILLY LE SEC.
   Route: BRAY - Cross Roads J.18.c.8.2. (Sheet 62.D 1/40,000).

   Transport. On 22nd inst. will march from PERONNE to billets in SAILLY LE SEC.
   Route: BIACHES - HER-ECOURT - CAPPY - BRAY - Cross Roads J.18.c.8.2. (Sheet 62.D. 1/40000

2. Rations for consumption of the 22nd inst. will be carried.
   Rations for consumption on the 23rd inst. and onwards will be arranged by 9th Division Train.

3. "Q" will arrange billets.
   "Q" will arrange for transport to convey kit, blankets &c., from BRAY to SAILLY LE SEC.

4. The C.R.E. will report arrival of 64th Field Coy. RE. in billets, to D.H.Q.

                                        A.H. Dolton
                                            Capt
                                        fr. Major,
                                        General Staff
                                        9th (Scottish) Division.

Copies to:
    26th Inf. Bde.
    27th Inf. Bde.
    VII Corps.
    39th Division.

13/6 20 Fine walk in Corypha

21. Moved to Sally le See.

22. Rest

23. Ride to Ypres

25. Transp. Joulich

26. March to Brake

27. Wiring + drill

28. Standing week preparing to Mont. Mord

1. Moved to Yser

9th Div.

64th FIELD COMPANY, R.E.

M A R C H

1 9 1 8

Army Form C. 2118.

WAR DIARY
or
INTELLIGENCE SUMMARY.

(Erase heading not required.)

WAR DIARY

MARCH 1918.

of the

64 FIELD Coy Royal Engineers

JYoung
Capt RE
o/c O.C. 64 Field Coy RE.

WAR DIARY
or
INTELLIGENCE SUMMARY.

Army Form C. 2118.

MARCH. 1918.

Place	Date	Hour	Summary of Events and Information	Remarks and references to Appendices
BRAY	1.	11am	Company proceeded by rout march to MOISLAINS, 7 arriving arrival arriving 7.30 pm. Major F.D. Napier-Clavering MC. RE. reported to Coy from of R.E.	
MOISLAINS	2.		Coy moved into mud huts, mess resting and bathing	
"	3.		Coy paraded 1.15 pm and proceeded by rout march to FALVY arriving 6.30 pm	
FLAVY	4.		Orders under orders from C.R.E., attached to H.Q. R.E. Coy in Billets. B. Ward R.E. attached from 256 T Coy R.E. for work with Labour on Stong Point Braux line.	
"	11		Coy paraded at 12 noon and proceeded by rout march to HAUT ALLAINS arriving 4.30 pm B Ward R.E. rejoined coy	
"	12		Coy proceeded by rout march to FINS, paraded 10 am arriving 1.00 pm Coy batted in afternoon	
"	13.		Coy in billets in FINS, Lt. McKay returned from leave UK. Lt Stangroom R.E. attached for work from 90 Field Coy R.E. Nos 1 + 3 Sections moved into Forward Field in Yellow Support Line Q.35.c.1.2. under Lt Allan , work Enoch Redowt, Strong Points, + handed Yellow System	Shut 57c.SE
	14.		2 Lt. Mackay and Lt Stangroom proceeded to forward field brains through coy HQs.	

INTELLIGENCE SUMMARY.

(Erase heading not required.)

Instructions regarding War Diaries and Intelligence Summaries are contained in F.S. Regs., Part II. and the Staff Manual respectively. Title pages will be prepared in manuscript.

Place	Date	Hour	Summary of Events and Information	Remarks and references to Appendices
FINS.	14.		11th Middlesex attacked 90 Yard Copse & took.	
	16.		Major F.D. Nofin. Canning proceeded on 14days leave to U.K. Capt A. Gwatkin M.C. took over command of the Coy.	
	17.		Ex Gas R.E. against Coy from Army Gas School Instruction.	
	18.		Coy rested & training at present lines.	
GOUZECOURT AU	19.20.21.		Coy employed on Red, Blue, Yellow systems of defence around GOUZECOURT. Pumping plant at GOUZECOURT destroyed by German offensive commenced. 4 O.R. wounded.	
"	22.		Coy employed sending details to Brigade H.Q. in Lurche Rd. near HEUDECOURT. Transport proceeded by road to VAUX WOOD N.W. of MOISLAINS. Sappers destroyed TYNE DUMP and FINS R.E. Dump also Coy huts at FINS. fired and placed charge for blowing up cement. FINS GOUZECOURT road. Thereafter this FINS heavily shelled. 3 O.R. killed. 8 O.R. wounded.	
	23.		Transport moved 8a.m. to MARICOURT. Sappers employed consolidating MOISLAINS MANANCOURT Line. Manning line along all infantry at night who returned took place.	

2353 Wt. W2514/1454 700,000 5/15 D.D.&L. A.D.S.S./Forms/C. 2118.

INTELLIGENCE SUMMARY.

Instructions regarding War Diaries and Intelligence Summaries are contained in F.S. Regs., Part II and the Staff Manual respectively. Title pages will be prepared in manuscript.

(Erase heading not required.)

Place	Date	Hour	Summary of Events and Information	Remarks and references to Appendices
MARICOURT	24	12.30 p.m.	Transport proceeded by road to BRAY. No 1 Section undertakes withdrawal from line and proceeded to BRAY rejoining transport and going into bivouac near there. Sections 2.3.4 under command of 2/Lt Stangways RE and CSM. went into the line on the Right flank of the 27 Inf Bde	
BRAY.	25.		Transport and No 1 Section remained in bivouac at BRAY. resting. No.2.3.4. sections stood fighting on the Rt. flank of 27 Inf Bde to RANCOURT. where they were ordered to withdraw to line held by 5th Camerons 26 Inf Bde and consolidate that position. When the Bosches 26" Inf Bde was attacked. Sappers stood fighting with 5th Camerons through BOEUFS to FLERS. where they were withdrawn from the line, reformed and marched to CORBIE. Capt # Carritte of OC borrowed also 5 OR. 10 R killed. Lt Stangways RE. 90 Field Coy RE. 9.30 p.m. Capt. J.F. Young RE. 90 Field Coy RE. took over Command of Coy. I am a joint unit of sappers from the three Field Coys RE. under the Command of Capt. J.F. Young. 51 Allen RE. +5 OR. 64 Field Coy. 2 off. 80. OR. from 63 Field Coy + 90 Field Coy. Proceed by route march to DERNANCOURT and go into camp to the 27 Inf Bde there.	
BRAY.	26.		Transport moved to MERICOURT arriving 5.3am.	

INTELLIGENCE SUMMARY.

(Erase heading not required.)

Place	Date	Hour	Summary of Events and Information	Remarks and references to Appendices
CORBIE	26th	3am	Nos 2.3.4 Coys Cameron Highlanders marched from CORBIE to MERICOURT L'ABBE and 9o. into reserve to the 5 Cameron 26 Inf Bde. and remain in support on the E. bank of the ANCRE river opposite HEILLY until the 26 Inf Bde was relieved at 2 am 27th inst. when they proceeded to billets at PONT NOYELLES.	
	27" 26	3pm	Transport moved to HENECOURT. At 2pm Capt. M⸵Young received orders from O.C. 27 Inf Bde. to reconnoitre the village of MEAULT. Instructions and ammunition dumps for bringing up to this would later that afternoon from the ALBERT. MEAULT line to the ALBERT. DERNANCOURT line.	
		3pm	Orders were received to form Camps & Hutts. MEAULT village to form a screen & cover the retirement of the rest of the 27 Inf Bde. This was accordingly done. Orders to destroy the Pontoon Bark in MEAULT was also carried out when completed the Batton retired and took up a position on the East ridge of BERNANCOURT along with the S.A. Brigade to complete the Inghilard line after the retirement. This position was held until 7am 27".	
	27	7am	At 7am orders were received from G.O.C. South African Bde. for the Batton	

INTELLIGENCE SUMMARY

Place	Date	Hour	Summary of Events and Information	Remarks and references to Appendices
BERNANCOURT	27th		to take up a position on the ALBERT - BUIRE Railway to cover the retirement of the S.A. Bde who were withdrawing to the line of the ALBERT. BUIRE Railway to conform with the 35 Division on their right. After the position had been taken with the Infantry echeloned from BERNANCOURT and reformed on line of Railway. About Noon the G.O.C. South African Bde. informed Capt. of Wyming that his Division on the right having had their flank turned were withdrawing owing to his Division on the right having had their flank turned were withdrawing to the men to the high ground behind the Railway and instructed the Sappers to form rear guard & Covering party. O.C. Sappers unit sent the 64 Sied Coy party under Draw R.E. to reinforce Capt. Hank 35 Div. 90 Field Coy R.E. party under Lt. Strangways 600 yds to its rear to take up position in the open and cover the retirement of the 63 Field Coy party who were detailed under command of Enfield to do rear guard to the line of railway until forced to withdraw. The positions having been taken up OC Sappers unit, having satisfied himself that his flanks were left intact, reported by runner at 1 am to G.O.C. South African Bde. that he was holding in and that he had could be told of reinforcements were sent. At 1.15 am two men	

INTELLIGENCE SUMMARY.

(Erase heading not required.)

Instructions regarding War Diaries and Intelligence Summaries are contained in F.S. Regs., Part II. and the Staff Manual respectively. Title pages will be prepared in manuscript.

Place	Date	Hour	Summary of Events and Information	Remarks and references to Appendices
DERNANCOURT			Artillery put down a heavy shrapnel barrage on the line of the railway. OC Sappers unit ordered O.Budd & his party to withdraw from WEST side of Railway bank to the EAST side (evenings) and Coy to man in. This was done without casualties. Runners were sent back to O.C. South Africans to have the barrage lifted as there appeared to be no enemy on the West bank after even this position was held until the barrage lifted. the Sappers were surprised by details of the South African Rob. under G.O.C. South African Bde. when the line was restored and handed over intact at 11pm to the 2 N.F. Pionrs. The division being relieved by the 4 Australian Division. Lieutn. R.E. and 64 Coy. Party under orders from G.O.C. 104 Bde. with drew his men at 7pm. Transport proceeded to CONTAY. Sappers marched to WARLOY to billets, arriving to am.	
	28	10am	marched to CONTAY and rejoined Transport	
	28		Coy moved to ALLONVILLE	
	29		Coy moved to CORDONNETTE, when No. 2.3.4 Sections rejoined	
			FLESSELLES.	
	31	8am	Transport left billets by road to ABEELE. Sappers moved 9am. to FIEFFES. Sappers moved 4pm to	

O/C OC. 64 Field Coy RE

J.W.Young Capt. RE
O/C OC. 64 Field Coy RE

9th Divisional Engineers

64th FIELD COMPANY R. E.

APRIL 1918.

WA 36

WAR DIARY

APRIL 1918.

3/64th F Coy. R.E.

Army Form C. 2118.

WAR DIARY
or
INTELLIGENCE SUMMARY.
(Erase heading not required.)

Re APRIL 1918   64" Field Co. R.E.

Place	Date	Hour	Summary of Events and Information	Remarks and references to Appendices
FIEFFES CANDAS	1st		Coy (Divisional Coy) marched to CANDAS. Entrained at 3.30pm o/c Body received transport.	LENS 11.
ABEELE LA CLYTTE	2nd		Coy transport moved to HERLIN-LE-SEC from BURRE-AU-BOIS	
	3rd		Coy detrained at ABEELE 7.0 a.m. All loaded transport and proceeded by buses to BERMUDA CAMP, HAZEBROUCK. Transport moved to NORRENT-FONTES.	SA
			Lt ALLEN and No 3 section left our billets at ST POL BANK from 3rd Australian Field Co. 3 sections with Divisional Troops inspected by Army Commander. Transport moved to BORRE.	
	4th		No 1 + 2 sections proceeded to forward billets at SOUL BANK No 4 section to PIONEER CAMP, KEMMEL. Transport arrived at PIONEER CAMP in afternoon.	
	5th		Took over work on 26" Inf Bde front.	
	6th		Lt CULLIFORD rejoined for duty from St Omer, Convent Party. Work in hand - wells & Oak Support, reserve support line, extension of tramway from LONE TREE DUMP to LOCK 6. BIS.	
			2Lt MUSGRAVE joined Coy from base.	
	7th		2Lt WHINCOP joined Coy from base.	
	9th		Warning orders received 10.15pm to move to FORT VICTORIA, east of LINDENHOEK, to take on work on Bluff, cut south of present front. 27 Inf Bde relieved 26" Inf Bde.	
	10th		Orders were cancelled. Sections standing to in billets. Demolition parties ready. Later orders received from Div to report to O.C. 27" Inf Bde with all available sappers.	

WAR DIARY
INTELLIGENCE SUMMARY (cont'd)

Army Form C. 2118.

APRIL 1918 (CONT'D)   64th Field Co. R.E.

Place	Date	Hour	Summary of Events and Information	Remarks and references to Appendices
	11th		Received orders from 9 Inf Bde to extend right flank of Bde to extent right flank of Bde to extend right (?). Forward defensive flank on right of 11th R.S. with 3 sections 64 to join section 63 to 9 I.C. posts. Handed STABLES over to E end of DAMMSTRASSE. No 1 & 2 Coys with their support 6.27 Inf Bde Transport were to incorporate camp survey... Wilt.... to be picked up at section or struggles... Waterman to be..... Coken reserve at 30 accommodate camp no 10 T12.6.... ... E.... Coy...........	FORTHERHOUSE 11000
	12th		3 sections working on VERSTRAT - KEMMEL line defence. 1 section standing by. 2 sections to move off at 7.30am to line south flank WYTSCHAETE M24 d.1.1.6 N.19 B. 95.20	
	13th		Work as for 12th	
	14th		1 section standing by as for 12th. 2 sections right wing... had 1 VERSTRAT to SUFFER HO. Demolition party organized	
	15th		Section with demolition parties stand by all day long hour. On standard holiday to work south from E.W. end DAMMSTRASSE to ST. ELI.... section & retn to RONALD CAMP to billets.	
	16th		Coy stand by in camp except demolition party - in READY pres to prevent billets N.10 b. central. 1... and I for sent off inspection of Cosp.	

WAR DIARY or INTELLIGENCE SUMMARY

Army Form C. 2118.

APRIL 1918 (contd) 64 Field Coy R.E.

Place	Date	Hour	Summary of Events and Information	Remarks and references to Appendices
	17th		2 sections work on B.H.Q. 3 "hm" astride HALLEBAST - VIERSTRAAT road. Transport moved to ACHIET	(Contribute to Sheet 27)
			2LT. WHINCOP attached to 76"Co.	L.17.central
	18th		2 sections working on fr.17". 1 section wire belt (part completion) carrying party Demolition party standing by. 1 man wounded with No 3. section wiring. MAJOR MATHER-CLAVERING relieved/mobilised	
			U.K. RONALD CAMP shelled. Coy moved to LEICESTER CAMP, N.6.d.	
	19th		2 section working on fr. 19th	Sheet 38.
	20th		Coy moved to MIDDLESEX CAMP. 2 sections night work, digging and wiring strong points near St Eloi craters. Indent on Armor line at RIDGEWOOD	
	21st		3 section working as for 20"	
	22nd		2 sections night work as for 20" 1 section digging/pile trenches camp	
	23rd		No 3 section moved to transport lines for rest. 2 section work as for 20" demolition party stood by.	
	24th		1 section stand by, 1 section night work as for 20"	
	25th		MIDDLESEX CAMP evacuated. 2 sections repair bridge for dismantles	Hurshoot W.O.E
	26th		2 sections stand by to blow bridges. Coy relieved moved to transport lines in lorries	for 6.T.104 W.D.R.E.
	27th		by road.	
	28th		Kit inspection at 9.00—	
	29th		Transport moved to L.9.b.9.5. at 8.0— followed by 64 at 11.0— move G.E.27.c.6.d at 2.0 p— Sheet 27.	
	30th		3 sections moved to forward area to relieve 60th Co. 1 section staying at transport lines	

A.5834 Wt W4973/M687 750,000 8/16 D.D.& L.Ltd. Forms/C.2118/13

Army Form C. 2118.

WAR DIARY
or
INTELLIGENCE SUMMARY.
(Erase heading not required.)

64th Fd. G. R.E.

APRIL 1918.

Place	Date	Hour	Summary of Events and Information	Remarks and references to Appendices
			Demolitions (1) Carried out. Light railway sidings and broad gauge track at PROMA DUMP N.12.c.42 destroyed. It was impossible to blow the culvert at N.12.c.3.1. or VIERSTRAAT cross roads owing to the passage. Water point at N.12.b.27. destroyed.	Sheet 26.
			(2) prepared. Culvert at N.4.c.5.1. prepared but not blown. This was reported destroyed by shell fire. Bridges at H.35.c.3.1, G.30.c.0.9 and G.34.d.5.6. prepared and handed over.	Sheet 28.
			Casualties. 12th 1 O.R. wounded. 13th 1 O.R. wounded. 19th 2 O.R's killed. 25th 3 O.R: killed, 1 O.R died of wounds, 3 O.R's wounded. 26th 3 O.R's wounded. 28th 1 O.R died of wounds.	
			Reinforcements. 6th 1 OFF. 7th 1 OFF. 8th 29 O.R. 28th 27 O.R.	

H.M. Read Jr. R.E.
 O.C. 64th Fd. G.R.E.

1755

MAY 1915

Army Form C. 2118.

64 3rd Coy RE
Bak Holt CoRE
Maj

WAR DIARY
or
INTELLIGENCE SUMMARY.
(Erase heading not required.)

Place	Date	Hour	Summary of Events and Information	Remarks and references to Appendices
RENINGHELST	1st		Work on hutting 30ft huts	
	2nd		Night work on about 20 infantry carrying parts	
	3rd		Night work on about 20 infantry carrying parts	
	Capt April 1 2/Lt RD MACKAY sick to hospital. Subsequently to hospital. Coy relieved by 202nd Field Coy RE. Withdrew to transport lines W of WATOU			App F
	3rd		2/Lt W.G.WINCOT rejoins from OTC BRE. Coy marched to ZEGERS CAPPELLE Division work 28 Hdqtrs Coys	
	4th			
	5th		Marched to ZEGG field	
	6th		Marched to billets near LEDERZEELE	
	7th		handed to RAQUINGHEM 16 miles arrived 4.30pm	
	8th		Company training recreational exercises	
	9th		&c. speed drill & paced ranges in 2 & 1/3 sec area/Lane	Rain
	10th		P.T. Section training Ichnography	
	11th		Coy inspected at 11 am by Major General Turner comdg 9th Division	
	12th		Chief Sappers Pour 75th intoxicancy for 9th Pontoon Park	
	13th		Coy march ended at Fort ASQUIN near WARDRECQUES.	
	14th			
	15th			
	16th		Bridge Competition between the 3 Coys 9th Divn RE. 75th finishing with two trestles at	
	17th		near bank. No steam near bank effective walt lead. This unit won the first prize by 11 mins. Steam beam across the canal a/c 162 mm from start rest. In time. Loaded from rear	

A5834. Wt.W4973/M687. 750,000 8/16 D.D.&L.Ltd. Forms/C.2118/13.

WAR DIARY
or
INTELLIGENCE SUMMARY.
(Erase heading not required.)

Army Form C. 2118.

Place	Date	Hour	Summary of Events and Information	Remarks and references to Appendices
	18th		Distribution Mural returns on Box group parade. Sgt Rummer D.C.M by GOC IInd Army (Genl Plumer) Sapper Sinton MM	
	19th		Musketry recruits 200x Aldersan fires 25 rds Ouseelian urkers on new Rifle range S.22. Church parade – Inoculation 3& OR	
	20th		Ponloons returnrhies Parl. Tredorl drill Rifle range	
	21st		Sports at 3 Coy HQ	
	22nd		Alliance parties to take over and issue infront of METEREN from Brit Divn	
	23rd		Coy moved up to take our 3 sections to forward billet head THIEUSOUKE	App A&B
	24th		1 sect & transport at HONDEGHEM Relieved 223rd Fd Coy R.E. Billeted in village of CHESTRE own to billets B 223 Coy beni shelled heavily. 3 section woken on strong point at PHINCBOOM LA BESACE Jnr & FONTAINEHOUCK N	Appendix D
	25th	a.m 24th	Billets are resumed.	
	26th		New Bn HQ started at STORE FM head support line started. Be sacs sin contr	
	27th	Ro/N 26th	No 4 sectn relieved no 3 at trenches.	
	28th	"	Lt WHINCOP proceeded on special leave	
	29th		Coy relieved by 90th Coy RE on fwd trench work Too% on real woks &	
	30th		billets – find W.J. CHESTRE woks on 1/3 Zone Lurk 2 coys infarlin. Celears in Flour mill Nq CHESTRE, CHESTRE Alprews Inward Roads	App E
	31st			

Major Farmer

MAJOR R.E.,
O.O. 64th FD. CO. R.E.

"A" Form
MESSAGES AND SIGNALS.
Army Form C. 2121 (in pads of 100).

TO: 64th CORE Warning Order

Sender's Number: 19/13
Day of Month: 20

64th Co will move on night 23/24th (unmounted by [lys?]) under orders of 21st Bde & will relieve the 223rd CRE at V8d 3.4 at Transport at V8d 1.7 Work will be front line whilst 26th Bde are holding the line. Shut 24

Taking over party will move 24 hours before main body of Coy.

Wardian

From: CRE

Appendix B

SECRET.

9th DIVISION ORDER NO. 225.   Copy No. 9

1. 9th Division will relieve the 31st Division (less Artillery) and 30th Divisional Artillery in the Left Sector XV Corps between the 22nd and 27th May, in accordance with the attached March Table.

2. The line will be taken over on night 24/25th by 26th Brigade, less 5th Cameron Highrs and with 2nd R. Scots Fus. (S. African Brigade) attached, 2nd R. Scots Fus. being on the right.

   S. African Brigade less 2nd R. Scots Fus. and with 5th Cameron Highrs attached will relieve support Brigade 31st Division on night 24th/25th, 5th Cameron Highrs being in the Reserve Line between X.7.b. and X.3.d.

3. It is intended that at a later date S.A. Bde. will take over command of the right Battn. from 26th Bde. Command of 5th Cameron Highrs. will then pass to G.O.C. 26th Bde. Orders will be issued when this is to take effect.

4. Details of relief will be arranged between Bde. Commanders, C.R.E., A.D.M.S. and M.G. Bn. Commanders of the 9th and 31st Divisions.

5. Details of ombussing are issued herewith.

6. The following intervals will be strictly maintained between Units on the march.-

   500 yards between Battalions.
   100 yards   "   Coys. or their equivalent.
   100 yards   "   Units and their transport or between transports of Units.

7. Relief of 30th Divisional Artillery by 9th Divisional Artillery will be arranged by C.R.As 9th and 30th Division, Relief to be completed by 9 am 27th at which hour arty. command will pass.

8. Relief of Pioneer Battns. will be carried out on 23rd inst. and will be completed, as far as 9th Seaforth Highrs. are concerned, by 11 p.m.

9. Liaison with 168th French Division which will be on the left of 9th Division will be made as follows :-

   26th Bde. will detail one Officer to remain at H.Qrs of Right French Battn. in line (X.5.a.5.2.) and one at H.Qrs. of Right French Battn. in support. (R.34.c.4.0.)

   S.A. Bde. will detail one Officer to remain with H.Qrs. French Divisional Infantry Commander at PIEBROUCK (R.27.a.) to make liaison between his H.Qrs. and H.Qrs. of 9th Division.

   These Officers will take over their duties on the night 24th/25th relieving Liaison Officers of 31st Divn. who will be withdrawn on evening 25th.

10. Completion of moves in 9th Division Area will be reported by wire to 9th Division, and in 31st Division Area to 31st Divn.

2.

11. Command of the Sector will pass to G.O.C. 9th Division at 9 a.m. 25th, at which hour 9th Div. H.Qrs. will close at BLARINGHEM and open at HONDEGHEM.

12. On arrival at HONDEGHEM, 27th Bde. will come into Corps Reserve.
26th Bde. will hand over to 27th Bde. all instructions for Brigade in Corps Reserve.
G.O.C. 27th Bde. will arrange for the necessary reconnaissances to be made on 24th inst., for which purpose a car will be placed at his disposal. He will inform 9th Division "G" when and where this car should report.

13. ACKNOWLEDGE.

T.C. Mudie,
Lt. Colonel
General Staff
9th (Scottish) Division.

21.5.18.

Issued through Signals
at 8.30 p.m.

Copies to:-
No. 1 - 26th Inf. Bde.
2 - 27th Inf. Bde.
3 - S.A. Inf. Bde.
4 - C.R.A.
5 - 8 - C.R.E.
9 - 9th Seaforth Hrs. (Pnrs.)
10 - 9th Bn. M.G.C.
11 - 15 - 9th Train
16 - 9th Signals
17 - 18 - "Q".
19-24 - A.D.M.S.
25 - D.A.D.V.S.
26 - D.A.D.O.S.
27 - A.P.M.
28 - Camp Commandant
29 - XV Corps.
30 - XV Corps H.A.
31 - 29th Division.
32 - 31st Division.
33 - 1st Aust. Division.
34 - 168th French Division.
35 - I.D., 168th French Division.

MARCH TABLE issued with 9th Division Order No. 225.

1. Serial No.	2. Date. May.	3. Unit or Formation.	4. From.	5. To.	6. March or bus	7. Route.	8. Under orders to be issued by.	9. In relief of.	10. Remarks.
1.	22nd	9th Bn. M.G.C. (less 2 Coys.)	BLARINGHEM.	HONDEGHEM.	March		9th Bn. M.G.C.		March to be completed by 9 a.m.
2.	23rd	H.Q. S.A. Bde. 2nd R.S.F. S.A.(O) Bn. 5 Cam.Hrs. SALT.M.B.	HEURINGHEM. HEURINGHEM. ISLINGHEM. RACQUINGHEM. LE RONS.	HONDEGHEM.	March	PONT ASQUIN (B.8.b.2.8)- EBBLINGHEM - STAPLE.	S.A. Bde.		March to be completed by 9 a.m.
3.	23rd	28th Field Ambulance.	RACQUINGHEM.	STAPLE.	March.	PONT ASQUIN (B.8.b.2.8)- EBBLINGHEM.	S.A. Bde.	93rd. Field Amb.	March to be completed by 9 a.m.
4.	23rd.	27th Bde. Det.90th. F.Coy. RE Det. 27th Field Amb.	LUMBRES LUMBRES LUMBRES.	Billets vacated by units in Serial No. 2. 12th R.S. to RACQUINGHEM	March.	Any route.	27th. Bde.		March to be completed by 9 a.m. Det.90th F.Coy.R.E. to join the Coy. at BLARINGHEM
5.	23/24	H.Q.26th.Bde. 8.B.Watch 7 Seaforths. 9 Sco.Rif. 26 L.T.M.B. 64th F.CoyRE	RACQUINGHEM. RACQUINGHEM. RACQUINGHEM. BANDRINGHEM & CAMPAGNE. RACQUINGHEM. RACQUINGHEM.	Support. V.8.d.3.4.	Bus. Dismtd. by bus.	—	26th. Bde.	72nd 1.Bde. 223rd F.Coy	Comes under orders of 31st Div. at debussing point. Details of bus move are issued south. Bn. to go to Advd. support position to be in front buses. Transport by road PONT ASQUIN (B.8.b.2.8) EBBLINGHEM - STAPLE on 23rd. Time to be fixed by G.O.C.26Bde. so as to

Serial No.	Date	Unit or Formation	From	To	March or bus	Route	Under orders to be issued by	In relief of	Remarks
6.	23/24	9th Bn. M.G.C. (less 2 Coys.)	HONDEGHEM	Line	March		51st Divl.	51st Bn. M.G.C.	Comes under orders of 51st Div. at Gemss-ing point. Details of bus move are issued herewith. Transport to be clear of CAESTRE by 7.30 p.m.
7.	23/24	2 Coys. 9th Bn. M.G.C.	BLARINGHEM	Line	Bus		9th Bn.M.G.C.	-do-	
8.	24.	27th Bde.	See Serial No. 4.	HONDEGHEM	Bus		27th Bde.	See Serial No. 2.	Comes under orders of 51st Div. at debus-sing point.
		63rd Fd. Coy.	E of HEURINGHEM A.15.a.7.0. QUIESTEDE	W.1.c.5.6.	Dismtd. by bus		-do-	211th Fd.Coy.	Transport to march via PONT ASQUIN - EBBLINGHEM and STAPLE - tail to reach HONDE-GHEM by 7 pm. Details of bus move are issued herewith.
		S.A. Fd. Amb.		Main Dress-ing Station V.4.	-do-		-do-	95th Field Amb.	
		Det. 27th Field Amb.	See Serial No. 4.	HONDEGHEM thence to LAKREULE	Bus		-do-	94th Field Amb.	
9.	24	90th Fd. Coy.	BLARINGHEM	V.c.12.b.5.9.	march	LYNDE - W of WALLON CAPPEL - LONGUE CROIX	C.R.E.	210th Field Coy.	
10.	24	27th Fd. Amb.	EBBLINGHEM	Line	march		A.D.M.S.	94th Field Amb.	To be clear of Cross Roads NW of WALLON CAP-PEL by 4 pm.

Serial No.	Date.	Unit or Formation.	From.	To.	March or bus.	Route.	Under orders to be issued by	In relief of	Remarks.
11.	May 24/25	H.Q. 26th Bde. 8th B.Watch 7th Sea. Hrs. 9th Sco. Rifs. 26th L.T.M.B.	Support	Line	march		51st Div.	93rd Inf. Bde.	
12.	24/25	H.Q. S.A. Bde. 2nd R.S.F. SA (C) Bn. 5th Cam. Hrs. SALTMB.	HONDEGHEM	Support	march		51st Div.	See Serial No. 11.	

DETAILS OF MOVES BY BUS OR LORRY.

(Issued with 9th Div. Order 225 d/21.5.18.)

Serial No.	Date May.	Unit.	Time.	Embus at	Debus at	Remarks.
1.	23rd.	6th F. Coy.	10 a.m.	RACQUINGHEM, head of column towards ARQUES.	LA BREARDE.	Commanders will ensure that troops are prepared to commence embussing punctually at the hours stated.
2.	23rd.	26th Bde. less 5th Cam. Hlrs. and with 9th Sco. Rif. attached.	6 p.m.	RACQUINGHEM - ARQUES Road, head of column at A.6.c.0.0.	West of CAESTRE Station.	
3.	23rd.	2 Coys. 9th Bn. M. Gun Corps.	4 p.m.	BLARINGHEM, tail of column at Canal.	Q.53.d.	
4.	24th.	27th Bde. less 12th R.S.	1 p.m.	HEURINGHEM - ARQUES Rd, tail of column ¼ mile N of HEURINGHEM	LES CINQ RUES (V.19.c.)	
		Dismtd portions of 53rd Fd. Coy.	"	"	LA BREARDE	
		S.A. Field Amb.	"	"	LA BREARDE.	
		Det. 27th Fd. Amb.	"	"	LA KREULE	
5.	24th.	12th R. Scots	2.30 pm	RACQUINGHEM - ARQUES Rd. N of RACQUINGHEM	LES CINQ RUES	

Appendix C.

SECRET.

Copy No.- 6

9th DIVISION ORDER No. 226
※※※※※※※※※※※※※※※※※※※※※※

1. From 26th inst. 9th Division Sector will be held on a two Brigade front.

2. The Inter-Brigade boundary will run as follows :-

   X.15.a.5.0. (METEREN - FLETRE road to Left Brigade) - X.8.b.7.2 - X.8.a.8.8. (trench junction to Left Brigade) - W.6.d.central.

   The exact boundary points in each trench line will be arranged between G.Os.C. 26th and S.A. Brigades.

3. At 10 a.m. 26th G.O.C. S.A. Brigade will assume command of the Right Brigade Sector and of the 9th Battn. Scottish Rifles. Command of 5th Cameron Highrs. will revert to G.O.C. 26th Bde.

4. (a) The two Companies of the Reserve Battalion at present in the Reserve Line West of X.8.a.8.8. will occupy the ROUKLOSHILLE Switch in the Left Brigade Sector, but will be available for counter attack at the discretion of G.O.C. Left Bde. Sector.

   (b) Two Companies of the Right Battn. of the present Support Bde. will occupy the Reserve Line West of X.8.a.8.8., but will be available for counter attack at the discretion of G.O.C. Right Bde. Sector.

   These moves will be carried out during the night 25th/26th May by arrangement by G.Os.C. 26th and S.A. Brigades.

5. C.R.A. will arrange for liaison between S.A. Brigade H.Q. and the Artillery Group covering the present Right Battn. front.

6. Orders with regard to machine guns will be issued later.

7. Advanced H.Q. of S.A. Brigade will be established at the present H.Q. of the Right Battn. of the Support Brigade, W.9.a.5.5., and will open there at 10 a.m. 26th inst.

8. From 10 a.m. 26th inst., the present Left Battn. of the Support Brigade will be in Divisional Reserve.
   This Battn. will be prepared -

   (a) To take the place of the Battn. in Brigade Reserve in the Left Sector in the event of the latter being ordered to carry out a counter attack.

   (b) To counter attack on any part of the Divisional Sector.

   (c) To man B line.

   (d) To assist Divisions on either flank.

   It will not be called upon without previous reference to Div. H.Q. unless communications between Brigade and Divisional H.Q. are severed, in which case Brigade Commanders will use their discretion

9. C.R.E. will arrange for the accommodation in the neighbourhood of THIEUSHOUK of the Field Coy. and Pioneer Coy. at present occupying the ROUKLOSHILLE Switch.

10. After 10 a.m. 26th inst. Brigades holding the line will be responsible for the defence of, and work on, all lines and defended

2.

localities in the First Zone.
C.R.E. will be responsible for work on the Second Zone and on the ROUKLOSHILLE Switch, working parties being found by the Battalion in Divisional Reserve.

11. All instructions contained in 31st Division Defence Notes will for the present hold good, where not amended by the above.

12. ACKNOWLEDGE.

T.C. Mudie
Lt. Colonel
General Staff
9th (Scottish) Division.

25.5.18.

Issued through Signals
at   a.m.

Copies to:-

```
No.  1 - 26th Brigade
     2 - 27th Brigade
     3 - S.A. Brigade
     4 - C.R.A.
   5-8 - C.R.E.
     9 - 9th Seaforth Hrs. (Pnrs.)
    10 - 9th Bn. M.G.C.
 11-15 - 9th Train
    16 - 9th Signals
 17-18 - "Q"
 19-24 - A.D.M.S.
    25 - D.A.D.V.S.
    26 - D.A.D.O.S.
    27 - A.P.M.
    28 - Camp Commandant
    29 - XV Corps.
    30 - XV Corps H.A.
    31 - 1st Aust. Division.
    32 - 168th French Division.
    33 - I.D., 168th French Division.
```

9th DIVISIONAL ENGINEERS ORDER NO. 102.   SECRET.
REFERENCE D.O. NO. 226.

1. 64th Coy will be responsible for Lt. Bde Area, and 63rd Coy for Rt. Bde Area.

2. 64th Coy will hand over forthwith all work in progress, demolitions &c., in Rt. Bde Area, to 63rd Coy.

3. O.C. 63rd Coy will move his forward billets to any suitable location.

4. 63rd and 64th Coys will each employ approximately 3 sections, less demolition party, on work in or forward of reserve line, and 1 section in rear of reserve line under orders of C.R.E.

5. 90th Coy will hand over demolitions in THIEUSHOUK to 64th Coy and will take over from 63rd Coy the demolitions in, and in rear of, CAESTRE.

6. O.C. 9th Seaforths will move the Coy now bivouaced in ROUKLOSHILLE Switch to COMMANDERIE FM. This Coy will come under technical direction of O.C. 64th Coy R.E.

Lieut.-Colonel, R.E.,
C.R.E. 9th (Scottish) Division.

Appendix "D"

May 25th 1918.

Copies to:-
9th Div. G.
26th Bde.
S.A. Bde.
63rd Coy R.E.
64th Coy R.E.
90th Coy R.E.
9th Seaforths.(Pioneers)
1 Office Copy.

Wardrum(?)

O.C. 64th Field Coy. R.E.
O.C. 90th Field Coy. R.E.
9th Division G.
9th Division Q.

Appendix E

Reference 9th Division Order No. 227.

1. 90th Fld Coy. R.E. will relieve 64th Coy. during night of 30th-31st.
   Company Commanders will arrange details and report completion.

2. 64th Coy. will take over work in 2nd Zone from 90th Coy.

3. Forward billets only will be exchanged.

4. All Defence scheme programmes &c. will be handed over and receipts taken.

9TH DIVISIONAL ENGINEERS.
No. 28/27
29/5/18.

Lieut-Colonel, R.E.
C.R.E. 9th Division.

SECRET   Copy No...1...

Appendix

C.R.E., 49th (W.R.) DIVISION ORDER No. 64
----

1.   On completion of relief by 202nd Field Company R.E., on 5th/6th May, 1918, the 64th Field Company R.E. will concentrate at the Rear Transport lines (1 mile W. of WATOU on the WINNEZEELE ROAD) and get in touch with C.R.E., 9th Division for further orders.

2.   There are no restrictions as to Route but Dismounted men will march in file and Distances on march as laid down in Fourth Army Standing Orders (Page 27), will be strictly adhered to.

3.   Headquarters 9th Division is at K.9.a.3.8.

4.   ACKNOWLEDGE.

                                        Captain R.E. & Adjutant,
                                for C.R.E., 49th (W.R.) Division.

Issued at 1.0 p.m.
3rd May, 1918.

Copy No. 1 to 64th Field Coy., R.E.
"   2 " C.R.E., 9th Division.
"   3 " Hdqrts. S.A. Brigade.
"   4 " 49th Division "G"
"   5 " C.E., XXII Corps.
"   6 " 49th Divisional Signals.
"   7 War Diary.
"   8 File.

O.C. 64th Field Coy R.E.

APPENDIX F/1
3/5/18

Extracts from 9th Div order No 220

Ref Sheet 1/100000 HAZEBROUCK 5a

2   63rd & 90th Fd Coy R.E. will march under orders of CRE.

3   Usual distances will be strictly maintained
    viz
    500 yds between battalions
    100 yds   "   companies
    100 yds   "   Units & their transport or between transport of units of Brigades

5   64th F Coy R.E. will rejoin the Division on a date to be notified later.

7   Clock hour halts will be observed

8   Locations of all Units Headquarters will be reported to D.H.Q.

9   Div H.Q. will close at K.9.a at 2 pm & reopen at the Area Commandants office at ZEGGERS CAPPEL at the same hour

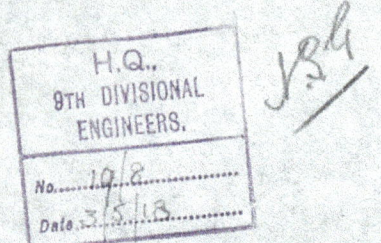

1755

June – ~~October~~ Dec
1918

SECRET

Army Form C. 2118.

Instructions regarding War Diaries and Intelligence Summaries are contained in F.S. Regs., Part II. and the Staff Manual respectively. Title pages will be prepared in manuscript.

WAR DIARY
or
INTELLIGENCE SUMMARY.
(Erase heading not required.)

64th Field Co. R.E.

JUNE 1918

Place	Date	Hour	Summary of Events and Information	Remarks and references to Appendices
HONDEGHEM	1st		Work on defences in divisional area. Formed billet at W26 SD (Sheet 27 BE)	
P35a22 Sheet 27 SE	4/C 5/C	-	Relieved 63rd Coy in right Sector by Divisional H.Q. in 26th Highland Bde taking on Transport. H.Q. Coy moved to camping field at P35a22. Found billets for 3rd admin at W3b77	
	6/C to 14/C 11/C		Work in right sector on 2 C.T.'s dugout for Batt H.Q. wiring support line from FLETRE. hair Bde H.Q. Shellin	
			Handed over right sector to 63rd C of RE. Took over left sector from 90th Co RE. Found billet for 3 section moved to P39 c 37	
	12/C		Work in left sector. Deep dugout for left front H.Q. Shelter for infantry m. Track repts forward and laid out - prep for observation by Balloon. Improving wooden road repairs	
	10/C		New issue trench started from x7 b central to x13 a central	
	13/C 14/C		L/Cull 70203 on leave to UK (14 days). L/Cpl Ainsworth returns from leave	
			Work continued	
	15 16/C 16/C		Holes to own with removed in front line at X16 a 27 to help pairing up posts. Handed over right + left sector to 90th Co RE. took on rear Co RE. Work Anti-balloon Track. Rear line. Artillery tram hole. Formed billet moved to W26 SD	
	19/C 20/C 21/C		Water - Improvements to accommodation in forward area. Work in support + reserve lines. Epidemic influenza causing men to be ineffective for many 5 days. Weekly ration Strength 157 men in field. Moved forward billet to Enomere at Q23 d 30	
	26/C 27/C 12/30/C		Work continued. Stores supply for 50th Bn CT Ash to be stored for pipe + locking two to erect dam	

Major Murray
MAJOR R.E.
64th FD CO R.E.

Army Form C. 2118.

WAR DIARY
or
INTELLIGENCE SUMMARY.

64th Field Co. R.E.

JULY 1918.

Place	Date	Hour	Summary of Events and Information	Remarks and references to Appendices
HONDEGHEM P.36.a.2.2. Sheet 27 S.E.	1st to		Works continued. Pill box at X.1.a. 95.35. commenced, improving cellar accommodation, forward area, work on support lines.	
	3rd		(1) Major COLLIFORD to H.Q. R.E. as a/Adjt. Lt. ALLEN to XV Corps Rest Camp.	
	3rd to 10th		Works continued. Observation-posts back to FONTAINE-HOUCK completed, cellar accommodation finished, bridge posts placed by range line at all road crossings, demolitions at COMMANDERIE FARM completed, work on support started shelters and wire. Pill box at CHOLIC COTTAGE started.	
	4th		Lt. MUSGRAVE admitted to hospital.	
	5th		Major COLLIER attached to Coy.	
	6th		LUNAR HOUSE strong points started.	
	10th		Works continued. Improving accommodation at Batt. H.Q. at X.1.c. 9.0 and at Bde. H.Q. X.1.a. 2.8.	
	11th to 18th		Work on WOOD SWITCH defences, pits, shelters, duckboards, trench, wire, fire positions and wiring.	
	18th		Concrete shelter at CHOLIC COTTAGE started.	
			Concrete work to pill box finished.	
	11th		Lt. ALLEN returned from XVth Corps Rest Camp.	
	14th		Lt. READ on leave (14 days) to U.K. Major COLLIER to 90th Coy.	
	19th		Works continued.	
	20th		3 sections wiring new line of resistance in X.16.c. Relieved 90th Coy. in left section.	
	21st to 26th		Works continued, repair of forward roads, inspection of mining, work on WORPLE pill box continued, erection of shelter in left sector H.Q., preparation for bridge over at X.9.c.3.7. was completed on 3.4", bridge over crater finished on 25"	
	25th		Wire at X.10.b. 9.a. and L X.16.a. and X.16.c. Duckboard Track E.T., drainage of Z line, bridge, Hamland wire at X.9.d.2.1., work on pill box continued, headroad topdout from X.18.a.0.0 to X.16.c. 6.9.	
	31st		Lt. LOW joined Coy from France.	
	28th to 29th		Mr. DEAR returned from leave.	

Army Form C. 2118.

WAR DIARY
or
INTELLIGENCE SUMMARY.
(Erase heading not required.)

64th Fd Coy R.E.   **August 1918**

Place	Date	Hour	Summary of Events and Information	Remarks and references to Appendices
HONDEGHEM P36 a 2.2. Sheet 27 SE	1 to 3		Work continued on drainage of "Z" Line & French C.T. Bridges & Craters at X 9d 20.79	
	4		Repairs of forward roads. Forming & shelters on GREEN LINE. "Z" WAY admitted to Hospital (tonsilitis)	
	4 to 14		Works continued. Commenced work on Shelters at New Forward R.A.P. Q 36 c 2.4. Taped charges & bridges over Craters. Commenced trench from SCOTS ALLEY to join trench of Divn left. Commenced work on New R.A.P. at X 10 c 2.6.	
	14		Lt W.E.T WAY returned from Hospital	
	14 to 16		Works continued. Jumping off trench at X 22 a 05.25 taped during	
	16		Capt T.F.YOUNG M.C. took over as O.C. Coy vice Major F.D.NAPIER-CLAVERING M.C.	
	16		Lt CULLIFORD N.E. to HQRE as Adj.	
	16 to 18		Works continued.	
	18		Forward Belts occupied.	
	18 to 24		Works continued. Camouflage to WORPLE Pill box completed.	
	24		Coy moved to LYNDE area for rest & training	
	24 to 31		Rest & training.	
	26		Lt WHINCOP to Hospital	
	29		Lt ALLEN leave to U.K.	

J.V.S. Livermore Lt R.E.
for O.C. 64th Fd Coy R.E.

WAR DIARY
or
INTELLIGENCE SUMMARY.

64th Fd. Co. R.E.

SEPTEMBER 1918

Place	Date	Hour	Summary of Events and Information	Remarks and references to Appendices
LYNDE	1st to 4th		Coy. in rest & training	
	5th		Section moved by lorry to CAESTRE for work under CRE. 31st Div.	
	6th		H.Q. and transport moved by route march to CAESTRE.	
	7th		Coy. moved to S.16.c.8.7. (Sheet 28) for work on RAVELSBERG road.	
	8th to 11th		Sundry RAVELSBERG and WATERLOO woods.	
	12th		Coy. march by route march to WORMHOUDT. Training.	
	13th to 14th			
	15th		Capt. H.S. GREENWOOD on leave to U.K. Lt. C.J. ALLEN returned from leave to U.K.	
	17th		"Lt. BREDIN transferred from 90th Co. R.E.	
	19th		Transport march by route march to SCOUT CAMP. "Lt. W.E.T. WAY to hospital.	
	20th		Section moved by light railway to SCOUT CAMP (entraining ESQUELBECQ, detrain 9 JAN. to BIEZEN).	
			Coy. moved to Camp at VLAMERTINGHE.	
	26th		Preparations for attack. Tracks from SALVATION CORNER to WELLS X RDS, gas-proof dugouts in ramparts.	
	27th		2 sections moved to LILLO at POTIJZE @, 1 section dem CAVALRY RD. at night.	
	28th		Battle starts. 2 sections with Pioneer near CAMBRIDGE RD. and main road as far as ZONNEBEKE. 1 section on plank road F track through to ZONNEBEKE from MENIN RD.	
	29th		2 sections on main road, 2 on plank road (SMITH RD)	
	30th		All sections on BROODSEINDE- BECELAERE RD. Forward billets at D.29 a.5.3. (Sheet 28)

(BECELAERE, BROODSEINDE, MOLENAARELSTHOEK and MOORSLEDE- WATERDAMHOEK ROADS.
Transport moved to Coy billets on POTIJZE RD.

Army Form C. 2118.

WAR DIARY
or
INTELLIGENCE SUMMARY.
(Erase heading not required.)

6th 1st Company R.E.   October 1918

Place	Date	Hour	Summary of Events and Information	Remarks and references to Appendices
BROODSEINDE	1st		Company in work on BROODSEINDE - BECELAERE Road	
	6			
	10th		Transport moved to billets on BROODSEINDE - BECELAERE Road	
	11"		Company on work on KEIBERG Road	
	16/13		Bn attached Coy in Reserve moved behind attack to vicinity of ROLLEGHEMCAPPELLE	
	14		CAPT GREENWOOD rejoins Company from leave UK.	
	3		"Lieut WAY rejoins Company from Hospital	
	13		Company move to vicinity of WINKLE - S! ELOI	
	15		Lieut WAY to Hospital. CUERNE	
	15		Sections & Pontoon equipment move to LE CHAT. Company ordered to bridge LYS at LYS pulped	
	16		on night 16/17 with others of Cdn Div. Tayler taste with 4 Pontoon bridge	
	17 S		Sections & Pontoon wagons moved to vicinity of GEMEENHOF - remainder of Transport moved	
	17		from WINKLE S! ELOI, to same billets as Sections.	
	18 S		Sections securing landed & making barrel pier bridges.	
	19 S		Company bridged LYS for 36 Bde Kpano over. Pton bridged with barrel pier bridge also cpld	
	19 S		Pontoon used as fanys.	
	20		Company moved to vicinity of BAVICHOVE Sheet 29 H a & 19.	
	20.		Company on work of building bridges beth on LYS	
	24		CAPT. WEBB joins Company to take Command vice MAJOR YOUNG M.C.	
	28		Company at rest for training refitting.	
	31		MAJOR YOUNG M.C. leaves Company to report W.O.	
	24			

W.S. Greenwood
Capt R.E. for O.C.
6th 1st Coy R.E.

Army Form C. 2118.

64th Army R.E.
Nov. 1918.
Sheet 1.

WAR DIARY
or
INTELLIGENCE SUMMARY.
(Erase heading not required.)

Instructions regarding War Diaries and Intelligence Summaries are contained in F. S. Regs., Part II. and the Staff Manual respectively. Title pages will be prepared in manuscript.

Place	Date	Hour	Summary of Events and Information	Remarks and references to Appendices
29/H.4.6.7.9.	1-2		Company Training & refitting	
HEULE.	3.		Company moved to HEULE. G.7.d.7.1.	
	5.		Division inspected by King of Belgium.	
	6.		Lt. O.R. LYSTER attached in duty from 90th Div.Cy.	
NEERHOF.	8.		Company moved to NEERHOF.	
	9.		Company engaged on salvage.	
	10.		Company moved to HARLEBEKE.	
HARLEBEKE.	12.		Company engaged on salvage.	
	13.		Company moved to TENHOVE 29/Q.14.c.3.2.	
TENHOVE	15.		Company moved to QUATRE VENTS 30/S.11.a.99.60.	
QUATRE VENTS	18.		Company moved to TRIPPEN 30/P.13.c.5.5.	
TRIPPEN	20.		Company moved to 30/Q.24.c.6.1.	
30/Q.24.c.6.1.	21.		Company moved to LENNICK ST. QUENTIN.	
LENNICK	23.		Company moved to VLIERBEEK 21/x.2.c.5.4.	
VLIERBEEK	25.		Company moved to COCROUX BIEZ	
COCROUX BIEZ	27.		Company moved to GENVILLE	
GENVILLE	28.		Company moved to BAS VINOVE.	
BAS VINOVE	29.		Company moved to FLEMALLE HAUTE.	

L.J. [illegible]
Major R.E.
O.C. 64 Army Tp. R.E.

WAR DIARY
or
INTELLIGENCE SUMMARY.

(Erase heading not required.)

Army Form C. 2118.

6 4 JD Coy
DEC. 1918.

Place	Date	Hour	Summary of Events and Information	Remarks and references to Appendices
FLEMALLE HAUTE.	1.		Company moved to PEPINSTER.	
PEPINSTER	4.		Company moved to VERVIERS.	
VERVIERS	5.		Company moved to HAHN (GERMANY)	
HAHN	6.		Company moved to MAUSBACH	
MAUSBACH.	7.		Company moved to DÜREN	
DÜREN	8.		Company moved to GREFRATH.	
GREFRATH.	9.		Company moved to NIPPES, N.E. of COLOGNE.	
NIPPES	13.		Company moved to QUETTINGHAM, marching past the Corps Commander in MULHEIM.	
QUETTINGHAM	15.		Company moved to ODEN-WIDDERT.	
	16.		O.R.E. called & instructed Company to to move to KRAHENHÖHE area.	
	18.		Company moved to KRAHENHÖHE.	
KRAHENHÖHE	23.		Lt. Col. D.R. LYSTER handed over to 64 Coy from 90" Coy (Auth. 9 Div. A. 202.2 dated 22/2/18). Two columns & one Coy Armies were demobilized.	
	26.			
	17-31.		Billet improvements carried out.	

O.C. 64" Field Coy R.E.

Army Form C. 2118.

64th Coy R.E
Jan 1918
SHEET 1.

WAR DIARY
or
INTELLIGENCE SUMMARY.
(Erase heading not required.)

Place	Date	Hour	Summary of Events and Information	Remarks and references to Appendices
KRAHENHÖHE	1-14		Training & improvements to huts continued	
	15		Work carried out on roads in Coy Lines	
	16		Work commenced on Rifle Range at STÖCKERERS	
	31		Work & training continued	

W.S. Greenwood
Capt.
MAJOR R.E.,
O.C. 64th FD. CO. R.E.

Army Form C. 2118.

WAR DIARY
or
INTELLIGENCE SUMMARY.
(Erase heading not required.)

FEB. 1919.

416 46

Place	Date	Hour	Summary of Events and Information	Remarks and references to Appendices
KRAHEN-HOHE.	1 to 28		Training, education and work in 26" Bn area continued.	
	15.		Major W.J. Love returned from leave.	
	16.		Lt. C.J. Adam returned from leave.	
	17.		Lt. O.R. Hyatt left unit to leave.	
	24.		Capt H.S. Townsend left unit to leave.	

W.J. Love
Major R.E.
O.C. 64 Field Co. R.E.

Army Form C. 2118.

WAR DIARY
or
INTELLIGENCE SUMMARY.
(Erase heading not required.)

MARCH 1919

Vol 47

Place	Date	Hour	Summary of Events and Information	Remarks and references to Appendices
KRANENHOHE	1st		Training, education and work on 263th and continued	
	5		Lt H.M. Read left unit to join 510 Fld Coy. (29th Div)	
	21		Capt. H.S. Greenwood returned from leave	
	29		2Lt O.R. Eyton returned from leave	

J.S. Greenwood.
CAPT. R.E.
O.C. 64th FD. CO. R.E.

Army Form C. 2118.

WAR DIARY
or
INTELLIGENCE SUMMARY.

(Erase heading not required.)

APRIL 1919. 48

Instructions regarding War Diaries and Intelligence Summaries are contained in F.S. Regs., Part II. and the Staff Manual respectively. Title pages will be prepared in manuscript.

Place	Date	Hour	Summary of Events and Information	Remarks and references to Appendices
HOHENHONE GERMANY	1 to 31.			
	1.		Training, Education, & work in 26th Brigade Area continued.	
	1		Major A. Glen joined Unit for Duty.	
			Lt. Clayton G. etc. " " "	
	2		Lt. Slack J. " " "	
	3		Major D. Webb Demobilized.	
	4		Sgt. Bradley F.B. James Unit for avg.	
	4		Capt. Gremsmore H.S. Demobilized.	
	29		Major A. Glen Leave to U.K.	

G.R.F. Britton
for O.C. 64th FD. CO. R.E.

CONFIDENTIAL.
****

WAR DIARY
OF

64th. FIELD COMPANY, R.E.

From.........1st May 1919   To........31st May 1919.

(Volume......)

Army Form C. 2118.

WAR DIARY
or
INTELLIGENCE SUMMARY.
(Erase heading not required.)

64th FIELD Co. R.E.   MAY 1919

Place	Date	Hour	Summary of Events and Information	Remarks and references to Appendices
KRAHENHOHE	1st to		1st Lowland	
GERMANY	31st		TRAINING, EDUCATION & WORK in 2nd BRIGADE continued.	
	9th		Lt. Gordon G.M. Special leave to U.K. for one month.	
	13		Major A. Glen returned from leave to U.K.	
	14		186678 L/Cpl. Guillemard E. through GAS COURSE at Divisional Gas School O.H.M.G.S. Passed & recommended as GAS N.C.O.	
	27		Lt. Bredin G.R.F. leave to U.K. for 14 days.	
	28		145796 L/Cpl. Osborne H.R. through GAS COURSE at Divisional Gas School O.H.M.G.S. Passed & recommended as GAS N.C.O.	
	31.		First Cricket Match for COLOGNE POST Cup played against 83rd DUBLIN GENERAL HOSPITAL at LANGENFELD resulting in win for this Company.	
	20		Lt. Belcher C.J. attached to C.R.E. as Stores Officer. OFFENCE & DEFENCES SCHEME: Arrangements made prior to 22nd for sub-division of Company to form Independent & Composite sections in view of the possibility of further advance into enemy territory.	

A. Glen
MAJOR, R.E.,
O.C. 64th FD. CO. R.E.

CONFIDENTIAL.

WAR   DIARY

of

64th. Field Company R.E.
LOWLAND DIVISION.

from 1st. June 1919.   to 30th. June 1919.

(Volume No.   )

Army Form C. 2118.

WAR DIARY
or
INTELLIGENCE SUMMARY.
(Erase heading not required.)

No 4 FIELD Co. R.E. JUNE 1919

Place	Date	Hour	Summary of Events and Information	Remarks and references to Appendices
Kampinchurst Cologne	3		King's Official Birthday. Ceremonial Parade & Feude de Joie at 10-10 am. The day was then observed as a holiday.	
	4		Eager Match for Cologne Test Cup against 53rd Hants Southern Division. Result - Won for this Company.	
	15		Whitsun Monday. No Parades. Day observed as Holiday.	
	16		Cricket Match Cologne Test Cup against 15th East Yorks. Result - Won for this Cy.	
	19		Officers "Defenses Scheme" Wiggers Mobile Scheme left Kampinchurst by Buses & proceeded to Leichlud Byre to be disposed of as required. No 2 Mobile Section & H.Q. Details moved off at 14:10 hrs & proceeded to join 170th Field Coy R.E. at Agur.	
	20 to 28		Standing by for orders in the event of an advance into enemy territory. All troops confined to Buers.	
	25		Received intimation by wire from GHQ that Peace had been signed at 16:00 hrs.	
	30		Company & no Brigade Mobile Section returned to Kampinchurst.	

A. Flew.

WAR DIARY

of

64th. FIELD COMPANY R.E. LOWLAND DIVISION.

FROM 1st. JULY 1919.   to   31st. JULY 1919.

(V O L U M E 5)

Army Form C.2118.

WAR DIARY
or
INTELLIGENCE SUMMARY.
(Erase heading not required.)

64 FIELD COY. R.E.   JULY 1919

Place	Date	Hour	Summary of Events and Information	Remarks and references to Appendices
Horren Germany	2nd		The Brigade Mobile Section rejoined the Coy from Nimor.	
	4th		Observed as a General Holiday. Cricket Match and Sports versus 90th Field Coy at Krakenhohe.	
	7th		Major A. Tyler D.S.O M.C. and C.S.M. Rimmer D.C.M. proceeded to Paris to represent the Lowland Div. R.E. in the Paris Victory March	
	9th		Advance Party proceeded to Horren to take over billets and workshops	
	10th		Advance Party of the 226 Fd Coy R.E. Light Division arrived at Krakenhohe to take over from the 226 Fd Coy R.E. billets	
	11th		The Company proceeded to Horren by train.	
	17th		Cricket Match (Cologne Pool Cup) against Lowland Div. R.E. Coy at Dormagen could not by two joints.	
	18th		Major A. Tyler D.S.O M.C and C.S.M. Rimmer D.C.M. returned from Paris.	
	19th		Observed as a General Holiday for Peace celebrations	
	23rd		Capt. C.J. Allen and 20 men proceeded to Nideggen for work in connection with IV Coy Searchlight Tattoo.	
	27th		Lt. Gordon left the Coy to join the 207th Fd Coy R.E. as Second in command.	
	28th		A/t. Bradley left the Coy to be attached to the De Gorie French Army	
	30th		Lt. Brodin left the Coy for demobilization	

N. Allen
MAJOR R.E.,
O.C. 64th FD. CO. R.E.

CONFIDENTIAL

WAR DIARY

of

64th. Field Company R.E.

From:- 1st. August 1919   to:- 31st. August 1919.

VOLUME

Army Form C. 2118.

WAR DIARY
or
INTELLIGENCE SUMMARY.
(Erase heading not required.)

64th FIELD CO. R.E.

AUGUST 1919.

Place	Date	Hour	Summary of Events and Information	Remarks and references to Appendices
HORREM GERMANY	1st to 31st		Training & work in 1st Lowland Brigade Area continues.	
	6th		Mounted NCO took first prize for best turned out NCO at Division Horse Show.	
	7th		Pontoon Wagon + 6 Horse Team took 1st prize at IV Corps Horse Show.	
	17th		Pontoon Wagon + 6 horse Team took 2nd Prize at Rhine Army Horse Show.	
	17th		Toolcart + 4 horse Team took 3rd prize at Rhine Army Horse Show.	
	21st		2 Lt G Bradley R.E. Proceeded to U.K. to report to War Office.	
	22nd		Capt C.J Allen R.E. Proceeded to Division as acting Adjutant.	

J. Allen
MAJOR R.E.,
O.C. 64th FD. CO. R.E.

CONFIDENTIAL.

War Diary of

64th Field Company R.E.

From 1st Sept. to 30th Sept. 1919.

Vol......

Army Form C. 2118.

WAR DIARY
or
INTELLIGENCE SUMMARY.
(Erase heading not required.)

SEPTEMBER 1919

Instructions regarding War Diaries and Intelligence Summaries are contained in F. S. Regs., Part II. and the Staff Manual respectively. Title pages will be prepared in manuscript.

Place	Date	Hour	Summary of Events and Information	Remarks and references to Appendices
	2nd		Training in the 1st Lowland Brigade Area continues	
	4th		Lt J Fluck and Lt O R Lysater left the Company to report to the War Office London for service in Egypt.	
	6th		Educational Exam for 3rd Class Army Certificates. Company Dance to which members of the W.R.A.F. were invited.	
	10th		Football match with 1/5 K.O.S.B at Zons.	
	15th		Capt C J Allen rejoined by from H.Q. Lowland Div. R.E.	
	16th		Company Dance to which members of the W.R.A.F. were invited.	
	18th		All stores and requisitions handed over to the Burgomeister Dormagen in accordance with instructions received from C.R.E. Lowland Division.	
	23rd		Major A Glen 250 mc RE assumed the duties of C.R.E. Lowland Division vice Lt Col Giles transferred to U.K.	
	24th		Divisional Cinema visited by H.Q.	

Army Form C. 2118.

WAR DIARY
or
INTELLIGENCE SUMMARY.
(Erase heading not required.)

SEPTEMBER 1919 (CONTD)

Place	Date	Hour	Summary of Events and Information	Remarks and references to Appendices
	26th		Transport two pontoons proceeded to Düren halting for one night at Bedburg. Pontoons loaded at Dormagen Station and sent by rail to Düren.	
	27th			
	29th		Boy proceeded by lorries to the Cavalry Barracks, Düren. Pontoons unloaded at Düren Station and brought to Cavalry Barracks.	
	30th		Training and work in 2nd Lowland Brigade Area	

MAJOR R.E,
O.C. 64th FD. CO. R. E.

64TH
FIELD COMPANY,
R.E.
Date 1-10-19